THE GREAT DIFFERENCE

Hong Kong University Press thanks Xu Bing for writing the Press's name in his Square Word Calligraphy for the covers of its books. For further information, see p. iv.

香港新界百年史

賴恬昌題

THE **GREAT DIFFERENCE**

Hong Kong's New Territories and Its People 1898–2004

James Hayes

香港大學出版社

HONG KONG UNIVERSITY PRESS

Hong Kong University Press
14/F Hing Wai Centre
7 Tin Wan Praya Road
Aberdeen
Hong Kong

© Hong Kong University Press 2006

ISBN-13: 978-962-209-794-0
ISBN-10: 962-209-794-4

Secure On-line Ordering
http://www.hkupress.org

British Library Cataloguing-in-Publication Data
A catalogue record for this book is available from the British Library.

Cover design by Inspiration Design House
Printed and bound by Kings Time Printing Press Ltd., in Hong Kong, China

Hong Kong University Press is honoured that Xu Bing, whose art explores the complex themes of language across cultures, has written the Press's name in his Square Word Calligraphy. This signals our commitment to cross-cultural thinking and the distinctive nature of our English-language books published in China.

"At first glance, Square Word Calligraphy appears to be nothing more unusual than Chinese characters, but in fact it is a new way of rendering English words in the format of a square so they resemble Chinese characters. Chinese viewers expect to be able to read Square Word Calligraphy but cannot. Western viewers, however are surprised to find they can read it. Delight erupts when meaning is unexpectedly revealed."

— *Britta Erickson, The Art of Xu Bing*

Dedicated to my friends and colleagues in the Land Executive,
Land Inspector, and Liaison Officer Grades of the
New Territories Administration, whose loyalty, knowledge,
and experience were such precious assets for the Department,
and for the former Hong Kong Government

Contents

Preface

A returned native-born centenarian could not possibly recognize today's highly urbanized New Territories as the place in which he or she grew up. Yet despite being swamped many times over by the present population, the descendants of those rural dwellers who passed under British rule in 1898 have somehow managed to retain their homes, their traditions, and their character. Given the pace and intensity of Hong Kong's modernization in the postwar period, just how did this come about; especially when a very different fate awaited those whose forbears happened to live in the New Kowloon portion of the leased territory, not to mention those descended from its then numerous indigenous boat people?[1] Told within the wider panorama of Hong Kong's history over the period of the Lease, this book is largely their story during the Century of Change.

I first started to write about the New Territories over forty years ago, when comparatively little work had been published and there was a job to be done by historians and social scientists. Nowadays, a great deal more information is available, based on original research in the villages, locally available documentation, and oral history. However, since most of this writing — my own included — has been narrowly focused, my aim here is to present something broader and rather different.

As in my earlier writings, but especially here, I am Janus-faced, utilizing my experience to look at events through my government spectacles, but using my other, historian's, set to contrive a more balanced view. In this regard, I have been mindful of the observation made by a reviewer of the memoir of my government service,[2] that I had not stepped outside my own perspective. While not entirely in agreement, given its particular focus, I have taken this remark to heart here, in what is properly a history.

My partiality for old-fashioned country people, and the living culture of bygone days will be evident. Yet this book was never intended as a partisan boost for the indigenous community. Contradictions and inconsistencies abound in its members' record. They are well-disposed, they are hostile, they are cooperative, they are obstructive, they are courteous, they are rude and boorish, they prize money and private gain above all things but can be generous with time and money in the public interest, and so on. They are, after all, human beings like the rest of us: albeit writ large. Yet the positive side of their character is enduring and for real, and their achievements have not been inconsiderable. It has been my good fortune to have worked among, and with, many fine people, and I am privileged to count a few among my oldest and closest friends.

The book could not have been written without the help provided by the many elderly persons of both sexes who were kind enough to give details of their lives, especially their early years, and answer my questions. I remain deeply grateful to them all, as to the friends who made the introductions and assisted with visits and interviews. In Hong Kong, Wan On (溫安) and Yeung Pak-shing (楊百勝) have all along been of particular assistance.

I must also pay tribute to fellow authors and researchers. Over many years, Hong Kong (the New Territories especially) has been extraordinarily fortunate in capturing their attention. No doubt, like me, they have found something particularly compelling about the rural society of Old China and its transition to modern times. Whatever the reason, there has been a wealth of detailed studies to draw upon for this book. Where many have helped, selection is invidious, but I have always found the work of Göran Aijmer, Hugh Baker, Chan Wing-hoi, David Faure, Patrick Hase, Graham and Betsy Johnson, Michael Palmer, Anthony Siu (蕭國建) , James and Rubie Watson of great assistance.[3] More recently, my friend Tim Ko Tim-keung (高添強) has been an inspiration, especially in regard to his home village, the former settlement of Hakka stone-cutters at Ngau Tau Kok in East Kowloon, part of the territory leased in 1898, which it was my appointed task to clear for development in 1966.[4] To all these friends, and many others, grateful recognition is recorded here.[5]

Once more, I must express my deep appreciation for the forbearance which my dear wife, Mabel Chiu-woon Wong (黃超媛) has always shown to my laboured attempts to write history. She knows only too well what to expect when I start on another book, and yet always provides the support which is indispensable to completion. Once more, too, my kind friends Mariann Ford in Sydney and Peter and Irene Williams in England have assisted with reading drafts and providing invaluable suggestions. Along with R. Ian

Dunn, my ever obliging friend and worker of magic in all matters photographic, they have helped to reassure me along the usual rocky and lengthy journey to completion. I am especially in Mariann's debt, in this and earlier books, for the interest she has always taken in my writing and the acute and incisive comments she has so willingly and thoughtfully provided at all stages.

I also acknowledge the great help given by Bernard Hui of the Hong Kong Public Records Office, who has ever responded to requests for documents or information; and by Dr. Colin Day, Publisher of the Hong Kong University Press, for his constructive encouragement and ready hand on the tiller! I am also grateful to my very capable editor, Phoebe Chan, and production team at the Press for their great assistance throughout.

The captions to the images used here indicate their source, with many thanks to all concerned. Those at Plates 2, 12 and 18 are from Edward Stokes's *Hedda Morrison's Hong Kong: Photographs and Impressions 1946–47* (Hong Kong University Press, 2005). The original negatives are held by the Harvard-Yenching Library, Harvard University. Ed's help is gratefully recorded here. I also thank Mr. T. C. Lai (賴恬昌先生) for providing the Chinese calligraphy which graces the title page.

After completing the first draft of this book I looked into Chan Wai Kwan's study, *The Making of Hong Kong Society: Three Studies of Class Formation in Early Hong Kong* (Oxford, Clarendon Press, 1991) to find that he, too, had emphasized the difference between the older Colony and its new Extension in 1898: the one with, as he writes, the social structure of a traditional Chinese agricultural society, the other with a commercial economy, a colonial administration, and a racially mixed society — already firmly established (p. 16). He had then added that "Whilst it is true that after several decades of development, today's Hong Kong Island and New Territories have become a single, inseparable entity, and that it will be interesting to investigate this process of assimilation, quite a different study will be required on this worthy subject" (p. 17). Though stemming entirely from Lockhart's memorable phrase, I hope that this book will go some way towards realizing Dr. Chan's goal.

To be regarded as an insider's account, it is based on information and materials obtained through my government service and during ongoing historical research over a long period. Intended to provide an overview, it is meant to be useful to other researchers, and for this reason is provided with plentiful references and sometimes lengthy notes: for there is still much work to do on the topics and wider questions raised in the Introduction and here and there in the text (for convenience, indexed on p. 288).

Another such query relates to the financial benefits accruing to the village populations through cash compensation for land resumed for development, the sale of letters of exchange, village resitings, and the Small House Policy, which I have not attempted to estimate here; my only advice to would-be researchers being the reminder that they did not extend to places where private land was not required for a public purpose, nor to everyone.

While the chapters were always intended to be free-standing, the notes were originally provided as footnotes, for greater accessibility, but as their length has created a problem, they now appear in the rear of the volume. The book is, otherwise, intended for the general reader, especially those with a connection with Hong Kong, or an interest in the place and its people. Like my other books, it has been a labour of love, a partial recompense for all that Hong Kong has given to me.

James Hayes
Sydney 2006

Abbreviations and Romanization

ABBREVIATIONS USED IN THE NOTES

ADR	Annual Departmental Report (published)
CNTA	City and NT Administration (from 1981)
CS	Colonial Secretary (from 1974 Chief Secretary)
CSO	Colonial Secretary's Office
CSO/CSO Ext	Titling of prewar land files in CSO, now in HKPRO
DAB	District Advisory Board (1977–81)
DAFF	Department of Agriculture, Forestry and Fisheries
DANT	District Administration, New Territories
DB	District Board (from 1981), retitled District Council (2000)
DC & I	Department of Commerce and Industry
DCNT	District Commissioner, New Territories (1948–1974)
DO	District Officer
DONT	District Officer, New Territories (up to 1948)
DOS	District Office (or Officer) South
DOTW	District Office (or Officer) Tsuen Wan
DPW	Director of Public Works
Exco	Hong Kong Executive Council
GIS	Government Information Services Department
GN	Government Notification (in HKGG)
GR	General Regulations (earlier Gen. Orders)
GS	Government Secretariat (up to 1974, Colonial Secretariat)
HAD	Home Affairs Department (1973–1981)
HK	Hong Kong Annual Report (followed by year; but beginning with HK 1973 the reports are stated to be a review of the previous year)

HKAR	HK Administrative Reports (published in BB and SP)
HKGG	Hong Kong (earlier "Hongkong") Government Gazette
HKPRO	The Public Records Office of Hong Kong
HKS/HKTS	*Hong Kong Standard/Hong Kong Tiger Standard*
HKSAR	Hong Kong Special Administrative Region
HYK	Heung Yee Kuk
ICAC	Independent Commission Against Corruption
JHKBRAS	*Journal, Hong Kong Branch, Royal Asiatic Society*
KCR	Kowloon Canton Railway
LN	Legal Notification
LPW	Local Public Works (an annual vote)
Legco	Hong Kong Legislative Council
NCNA-HK	Xinhua News Agency — Hong Kong
NT	New Territories
NTA	New Territories Administration (to 1981)
NTDD	New Territories Development Department (1973)
NTSD	New Territories Services Department (1979: from 1985, retitled Regional Services Department)
OMELCO	the Private Office of the Unofficial [= non-official] Members of the Executive and Legislative Councillors. Later styled UMELCO, the Office of the Unofficial Members of Exco and Legco
PRO	Public Record Office, London
PWD	Public Works Department
RAS	Royal Asiatic Society of Great Britain and Ireland
RC	Rural Committee
RD	Resettlement Department (1954–73)
RG	Registrar General (after 1913 retitled SCA)[*]
RHKP	Royal Hong Kong Police
RSD	Regional Services Department (see NTSD)
RSNT	Regional Secretary, New Territories (1981–94)
SCA	Secretary for Chinese Affairs (1913–1973)
SHA	Secretary for Home Affairs (from 1973)
SCMP/SMP	*South China Morning Post / Sunday Morning Post*, Hong Kong
SNT	Secretary for the New Territories (1974–81)

---

[*] The Registrar General of the 20th century was the government's professional Land Officer and Official Receiver.

SP   Sessional Papers (printed Papers Laid before the Legislative
            Council of Hong Kong)
TWDO   Tsuen Wan Development Office, NTDD
UMELCO   Office of Unofficial Members of the Executive and
            Legislative Councils: see also OMELCO
VR   Village Representative

G. C. Hamilton's *Government Departments in Hong Kong 1841–1969* (Government Printer, 1969) is a useful guide to names and personnel up to the time of publication. He was Deputy Colonial Secretary.

See also Ho Pui Yin, *A Guide to Government Agencies in Hong Kong 1842–2002* (Hong Kong University Press, 2002), a comprehensive guide to the much enlarged and frequently reorganized modern Hong Kong Civil Service.

NOTE ON ROMANIZATION

In writing about Guangdong or any other south-eastern province of China, it is necessary to use a combination of the predominant local language (in this case Cantonese), and pinyin in the text, as appropriate to place and subject. Place names in the former British Crown Colony of Hong Kong are in Cantonese Romanization, and follow the official publication, *A Gazetteer of Place Names in Hong Kong, Kowloon and the New Territories* (Hong Kong, Government Printer, 1960). Those in China are either in long-used English renderings, or else in pinyin, in line with Chinese national practice. Chinese characters are provided in the glossary.

My revered boss, the late K. M. A. Barnett, a noted linguist and scholar, had this to say on the subject: "Nothing," he wrote, "will ever persuade me that Cantonese, Hakka and Hokkien place names should be written in letters indicating a pronunciation which no local would understand. Just you try getting a boat to 'Shayuyung'! [The place is Shayuchung.]"

NOTE ON MAPS

The maps at Plate 1 and 4 are historical. Modern maps of Hong Kong and the Canton Delta are provided in the endpapers of all postwar Hong Kong annual reports to date. Plate 2 shows Kowloon and the NT as viewed from Hong Island in 1946.

Introduction

James Stewart Lockhart called it "the great difference". Returned from a twelve-day inspection tour of the newly leased extension to Hong Kong territory in August 1898, Lockhart, a senior Hong Kong colonial official, had used this phrase to emphasize the gulf between "the Chinese inhabitants of Hongkong [sic] and of the new territory". But as I shall show in chapter 2, it could be applied equally well to the two places, the old and the new parts of the now expanded British Crown Colony. It is my purpose herein to follow through "the great difference", over the ninety-nine years of the Lease.[1]

Appointed a Cadet Officer in the Hong Kong Civil Service in 1879, Lockhart's career in Hong Kong would take him to the influential senior posts of Registrar General (1887) responsible for management of the Chinese population of the Colony, and later to Colonial Secretary (1895), responsible to the Governor for the smooth running of the administration. As Registrar General, he had developed a closer, more formalized liaison with Chinese elites, and his known abilities and reputation as an official who understood the Chinese people would lead the Foreign Office to entrust him with inspecting the newly leased extension to the Colony and reporting on it, to them and to its Governor.[2]

The New Territories, as they became known (though at first in the singular[3]) were quite unlike the Hong Kong of Lockhart's day. The older parts of the Colony, which up to this point had comprised only Hong Kong Island and Kowloon, had been ceded to Britain during the series of hostilities beginning with the Opium War (1840–1842). They had now been under British rule for almost sixty years in the case of the Island, and for forty in the case of Kowloon. Each passing day took them further from the content and sentiment of traditional China, as represented by the new accession. The New Territory was also much larger than the existing Colony, being twelve times its size. Moreover, its population of some 80,000 was long-settled, in comparison with the overwhelmingly migrant, largely male community of the 250,000 other Chinese living, working, or passing through British Hong Kong in 1898.

The period of the Lease was hardly uneventful. British Hong Kong had ever been affected by international as well as national events. Internally, making its history the more intriguing, the presence after 1898 of two disparate sections of the community within a greatly enlarged Colony, each of them dynamic in its own fashion, created a fascinating, almost *yin-yang*-like interaction between them.[4] Present throughout the ninety-nine years of the Lease, it became especially active when, as land provider, the NT became essential to the further development of Hong Kong in the early postwar years. It became so again, and for quite different reasons, in the last decade of British rule, when a rift developed between the indigenous community and the by now far more numerous remainder of the population. These discords stemmed largely from the legal and administrative arrangements made for the indigenous inhabitants at the beginning of the century, but were also due to their very different histories and attitudes.

Given the complexity of the subject, I have thought it helpful in this introduction to provide an overview of the book's topics and themes, also mentioning some of the questions which have occurred to me during its preparation, and now referenced in the index.

Chapter 1 describes the New Territory and its community in 1898, bringing out its continuous and long settlement, colourful history, tight social organization, and largely self-sufficient economy. Chapter 2 then explores "the great difference", contrasting the newly leased extension with the Colony to which it was about to be joined. Mention is also made of the armed opposition to the British take-over; and of New Kowloon, that part of the leased territory below the Kowloon hills, which would be administered as part of the metropolitan area. Chapter 3 describes the all-important land survey and settlement of titles conducted in 1900–1905, which through retaining ownership of landed property in accordance with Chinese custom, preserved the fundamentals of the pre-1898 system.[5] However, this was after stripping it of features "incompatible with the principles of British administration",[6] notably in regard to the organization and incidence of the Chinese land tax and its collection through intermediaries.

The new system for administering the New Territory, put in place by the Hong Kong authorities with guidance from London, together with events in the NT up to the Japanese capture of the Colony in 1941, are described in chapter 4. Next, the War and Occupation 1941–45 — for various reasons a watershed in the history of both the NT and Hong Kong at large — are dealt with as a separate topic in chapter 5. A traumatic and difficult time, the Occupation was yet seminal for later political developments, such as the elected village representative and rural committee systems (1948 on) and the curious involvement of some indigenous communities and their leaders in the Communist Disturbances of 1967.

Chapter 6 describes the New Territories in the opening decades of the postwar period, when radical and fundamental change would overtake the rural life and economy. Within less than twenty years beginning in the late 1950s (and not only by reason of Hong Kong's switch to industrial manufacturing and the onset of large-scale development) rice farming went into a sharp decline, ending the characteristic subsistence economy of the rural NT. Development and modernization were greatly aided thereby; so, too, was the conversion of much of its upland area for use as fully managed country parks, in order to provide recreational space for the ever-growing urbanized population of the Colony. A different, but equally essential, aid to development was the systemization of rural representation mentioned above, along with the reordering of the Heung Yee Kuk (Rural Consultative Council) by statute in 1959. Thereby, it was possible to negotiate development, with mutual flexibility and compromise, avoiding potential strife.[7] Meantime, as described in chapter 7, the removals and resitings for successive water schemes, begun in the 1920s to supply the urban population, had quickened pace with the construction of four major reservoirs after 1945. The effects of uprooting and a changed environment on all these former rural dwellers are deserving of a fuller account than is possible here.

Chapter 8 deals with land recovery and village removals and resitings for the planned "New Towns" which are such a prominent feature of today's New Territories; and for related infrastructural projects such as highways and cross-border links, and the extension of the Mass Transit Railway system. The evolution of compensation policies and how they affected and were received by village landowners are also covered. During this period of village removals, which were always negotiated, but within an approved but flexible policy, their leaders' pragmatic approach was instrumental to achieving planning targets. In the process, the native population survived, to provide identity and leadership for the very large urban communities being established in their home areas. As already indicated, the remaining villagers of New Kowloon would be differently treated, and something of their much less fortunate history is provided in closing this chapter.

Chapter 9 describes the rural community in its heyday, and how its leaders led the way, through the new District Advisory Boards,[8] in building the desired new-style dialogue with the authorities and in developing the recreational and sporting programmes needed in the "New Town" districts. Through continuing to mount the traditional festivals, the rural groupings also kept the spirit of Chinese popular culture alive among their huge populations. These contributions were yet another manifestation of the "great difference"; for British Hong Kong possessed little that was comparable in scope, historical depth, and intensity of feeling, to the living cultural heritage of the indigenous communities.[9] Meanwhile, in rural areas not subject to development, the social and economic effects of Hong Kong's speedy industrialization and modernization were quietly but inexorably taking effect, as examined variously in chapter 10.

Chapter 11 focuses on a different dimension: namely, the drama inside the indigenous community during the 1967 Disturbances when, unprompted from Beijing, a sizeable proportion of both leaders and led had taken a pronounced anti-government stance. Latent resentments left over from Anglo-Chinese history underlay this situation, not omitting more recent influences traceable to events during the Japanese Occupation 1941–45. Something of an enigma, and warranting fuller enquiry, the events of 1967 are another reminder that "the great difference" was still operating. So, too, was the NT leaders' strenuous lobbying for the protection of accumulated native interests during the Sino-British negotiations for the return of Hong Kong to Chinese rule in 1982–84, and again in the late 1980s during the preparation of the Basic Law for the future Hong Kong Special Administrative Region.

Chapter 12 considers convergence and, paradoxically, a new divergence, between the old and new segments of Hong Kong's population in the last decades of British rule. By then virtually indistinguishable in externals and life-style, the indigenous community's reactions to various public issues would help to put it "off-side" with the general public. A disregard for the environment and the public weal had been noted and deplored, whilst poor behaviour during the debate to allow female succession to village property was viewed with disapproval. Dissatisfaction over its members' special privileges, not infrequently abused, and the Heung Yee Kuk's strident anti-government campaigning for them, served to intensify the increasingly evident public distaste for the older population. These, together with other, still unfolding issues,[10] which carry the story beyond 1997, are also covered in chapter 12 and its concluding epilogue, with some pertinent questions.

1

The Leased Territory in 1898[1]

In default of modern mapping, no accurate figures for the geographical composition of the New Territory in 1898 are available, but in 1960, before development overtook the area, they were reported to comprise 365.5 square miles, and to include 235 islands and islets.[2]

There was a similar lack of precision in regard to population. In an appendix to his Report to the Hong Kong Government, James Stewart Lockhart gave some tentative estimates, but they were no more than that, and, in retrospect, not very accurate: "There are," he wrote, "no reliable statistics possessed by the Chinese Government of the present population of the San On district. No census appears to have been taken for many years." His estimates were "based on inquiries of inhabitants of villages, and on personal inspection".[3] It was not until the 1911 Colony census that comprehensive figures were secured for the territory, with all villages and even the smallest hamlets included in the printed report. The total land population was then given as 94,246.[4]

PART ONE: RURAL SOCIETY

David Faure defines the bases of local society in the opening statement of his book on village and lineage in the eastern parts of the New Territories, overall the most detailed account of settlement patterns in the Hong Kong region:

> Until urbanization came to the New Territories of Hong Kong, the area consisted of settlements made up of either a single group or several groups of people all of whom within the group traced their descent from a common ancestor. In the English literature, these settlements have usually been referred to as "villages" and groups tracing common descent as "lineages".

He follows on with a detailed review of the complexities of these terms, as seen by himself and other scholars in the field.[5] In this less specialized history, I shall be using them in their more general applications.

There were a great many of both in the territory in 1898. The *lineages* ranged in size from those with several tens of members to some with several thousands. The *villages* were equally varied, but the greatest number of the New Territory's seven hundred or more old villages (necessarily an approximation) had small populations of between fifty to one hundred persons.[6] Many were single lineage settlements, large, medium and small, while others comprised a number of lineages living together; but in the extensive plains of the northwest, the largest lineages lived either in single *village complexes*, or their segments occupied similar complexes in a number of localities.[7] Whatever their age, local settlements were tightly clustered, their houses packed inside walled villages or enclosed rectangles without walls; or else nestling in one or more rows against a rise or hillside, like "a flock of sheep huddled for safety against a hedge" as viewed by one visitor to China in the 1930s.[8] Much of the rural architecture was defensive in nature. See Plates 3 and 6.[9]

Length of settlement was again varied. By 1899, the largest of the local lineages had been resident in the territory for almost nine hundred years, and many of the smaller ones for at least several hundred.[10] Judging from family genealogies, they had been moving into the area all through this long time span, save during the early years of the Qing (Manchu) dynasty in the mid-17th century, when as in many other parts of the Chinese coastline, the inhabitants had been ordered to move inland to deny assistance to a persistent opponent of China's new rulers.[11] Until then, incoming migrants had been largely Cantonese or, like the local tribespeople, had assimilated over time to this dominant group. Thereafter, with official encouragement intended to offset population loss during the rigorously enforced evacuation, there had been an influx of Hakka speakers, with another big incursion between 1840 and 1860 from the East River district of Guangdong. By the time of the Lease, Hakkas would account for almost half the land population.[12]

Where land was vacant and unsettled, founding ancestors had been able to establish themselves without difficulty. By the custom of the county, they might find themselves having to pay rent to a resident or absentee owner of the sub-soil (or make such payments to a rising lineage extending its authority with or without some supporting title) but this was not, in itself, a major obstacle to occupation.[13] Several families might come together, or men of different lineages would bind themselves as sworn brothers, the better to face the unknown. Once settled, it was not unusual to bring the bones of fathers and grandfathers and their wives to the new home for re-burial.

There was more of a problem when newcomers came into an established village. It was usual for them to have to live outside it until they became acceptable, which could take a long span of years. They would also have to face up to the fact that rights of cutting grass and firewood, grazing animals, and the like on adjoining hillsides had already been apportioned between villages, and among village families.[14]

Over the centuries following their initial settlement, some lineages had become numerous and powerful. Others had languished, barely keeping up numbers from one generation to another, while some had simply died out.[15] There was, inevitably, a good deal of jockeying for position, with fluctuating fortunes among the more prolific and ambitious lineages over centuries of local settlement.[16] At all levels, the lineage and family (rather than their individual male members) were the important elements in social organization.[17]

The history of the area had been turbulent.[18] External threats were common, either from robber bands or pirates. The latter were especially menacing in the twenty years before 1810, when large pirate fleets descended on the coastal regions of the Canton Delta, and again in the 1840s and 1850s.[19] At the same time, some local villages were notorious for their piratical activities.[20] Internally, inter-village feuds were common. Indeed, they amounted to mini-wars, often lasting for years and marked by deaths in armed struggles and the destruction of houses and crops. The causes of strife were as varied as might be imagined, but in these agricultural communities were often rooted in access to, or protection of, precious water for irrigation, and other economic assets, such as the control of ferries and markets.[21] Disputes over the *fung-shui* of settlements or ancestral graves were not uncommon, because everyone believed that sitings were directly linked with prosperity or adversity. Superior geomantic skills were in demand, since they could be used to injure the *fung-shui* of another village, lineage, branch lineage or family, or even to drive out earlier settlers.[22] In major disputes, fighting would be resumed periodically, sometimes when petty incidents sparked off simmering antagonisms.[23] Villages in the area of large, powerful lineages chafed at the lack of independence under their domination.[24] Fighting even took place between segments of major lineages settled in different parts of the territory.[25] Some lineages simply had a bad reputation for being pugnacious.[26] The cast-iron bells in the village temples all carried the inscription *guotai minan* (The Country Prosperous, The People at Peace) but this was seemingly ever more an aspiration than the reality: and as Patrick Hase has observed, "a peaceful and bucolic existence was a traditional blessing, but one only achieved intermittently".[27] This was despite occasional attempts by the authorities to curb local excesses.[28]

A rich fund of stories underlays the ebb and flow of individual and village fortunes. Some of them survive to this day, embroidered over generations of telling. The prosperity of the Lam Tsuen valley (for instance) was said to have been affected by the Guanyin (Goddess of Mercy) Mountain, which despite its benevolent name was actually a cock which fed on the villagers' rice from two stones on the hillside at its foot. Being set one atop the other, they were regarded as being a set of grind-stones for processing the grain. Local tradition had said that Lam Tsuen would have prosperity for three generations, after which the cock would have eaten it all up.[29] In another story, from Yuen Kong, a large village in the adjacent Pat Heung, at the site of a ruined Pak Tai temple I was told that it had been erected by the powerful Tang lineage to harm the villagers' *fung-shui*. When viewed from the surrounding hills, Yuen Kong was shaped like a turtle, a creature notable for its longevity, and the Tangs' idea had been to site the temple on its head: thereby putting an end to the settlement's otherwise long life. In 1922, after almost two centuries, someone (probably a geomancer) explained what had happened, whereupon the villagers rebuilt the temple on the site where it still stands today, receiving a renovation in 1972.[30]

Some stories go back a very long way indeed. One such was the extent of land to be given under imperial grant in the Hong Kong region as far back as the 13th century, credited to have been determined by floating a wooden goose on the sea, and allowing its movements to fix the boundaries. Another centred on the extinction of a powerful local lineage by the first Ming emperor in the late 14th century.[31]

Above the village was the *heung* (xiang) or sub-district, a traditional grouping of villages for mutual aid and ritual protection against adverse elements, both human and supernatural. A map prepared at the time of the Lease purports to show the names and boundaries of the various sub-divisions of the "New Territory" as they then existed (Plate 4).[32] There were around twenty-seven of these, under individual names and described by different terms.[33] However, they amounted to much the same thing, and in their late nineteenth century form were certainly local, self-managing organizations, ready to be activated for the common weal (or just as likely, aggressive private interest) whenever the need arose. The larger lineages (by now all Cantonese speakers) had the same capability to mobilize their own members, their tenants, or men from client settlements. This would be demonstrated in the armed uprising against the British occupation of the NT in 1899, when, as noted by Hugh Baker, "all the planning was done by and communications established at the level of the literati of the five [great] clans", resident in the "Un Long District" shown on the map just mentioned.[34]

Besides the *heung*, there were the market towns, with their own circles of participating villages.[35] The rights to establish markets at Taipo and Yuen Long, the two largest in the leased territory, had been granted centuries earlier to members of the Tang lineage, settled in nearby village complexes.[36] Smaller markets also existed. All such inland markets operated to a fixed schedule of business days, with "cold" or inactive days in between: but there was also a special type of market in the territory's several busy fishing ports, the largest at Cheung Chau, an island south of Lantau. These are best described as coastal market centres, operated every day, to meet the varied needs of their land and sea populations.[37] The market towns provided services for the farmers, for both buying and selling (at that time, mostly done by men), while brides were mostly sought and exchanged within the marketing area through a network of "middlemen", mainly women from the villages.

Markets are of interest for a less obvious reason. Thirty years ago, an elderly chairman of a rural committee, with whom I had an interesting discussion during an otherwise unremarkable Heung Yee Kuk dinner, told me how in his youth (he was born in 1914) it was possible to pin-point a person's origins from his speech, because of the variations still commonly detectable between marketing areas.[38] Such linguistic particularism, said Mr. Tang Hop-wan, was due to the limitations imposed by poor communications (most travel was done on foot) and to local solidarities.[39] Even during my own service in the 1950s, variations from standard Cantonese were still obvious in different parts of the NT, and also within the experience of two leading overseas anthropologists who first began work in the San Tin and Ha Tsuen sub-districts in the late 1960s.[40]

PART TWO: MANAGING THE COUNTRYSIDE

Prior to 1898, a major feature of the territory was the hold which the rich and powerful had over the cultivators of the soil, partly through their ownership of land registered with the County magistracy for tax purposes, and also through local custom whereby the land was regarded as being divided into surface and sub-soil, with rent usually payable by the cultivators of the surface to the owner of the subsoil. The rent charge was (notionally) supposed to cover the latter's tax liability for the land in question.[41] A marked feature of this practice was that, over centuries, commensurate with their tenants' labours and growing numbers, the areas over which the sub-soil owners claimed and levied rent charges had been ever increasing, bringing wealth to them but — since the recorded areas and tax levels in county land records seldom changed — denying it to the government.[42]

Between them, the Tangs of Kam Tin and Lung Yeuk Tau had levied rent charges in many parts of Hong Kong, Kowloon and the present New Territories.[43] On the mainland, the Liu (Liao) of Sheung Shui also held sub-soil rights and levied annual charges.[44] In most parts of Lantau Island, cultivators paid rent charges to the Li Kau Yuen Tong, whose sub-soil (tax) rights there dated back to the 13th century, while on the neighbouring islands of Peng Chau and Cheung Chau, other absentee lineages claimed to own the sub-soil.[45]

By 1898 there appears, also, to have been the bald assumption of rights over land and cultivators by dominant lineages which, by *force majeure*, had simply extended their control over villages in their adjoining areas and maintained it through village guard forces which enforced obedience. This was reportedly the situation in at least part of the northern NT, where James L. Watson found one such lineage which appeared to have had no legal rights of ownership to even part of the land over which it collected rents.[46]

Viewed overall, one or other was the situation in which Hakka newcomers were liable to find themselves after being encouraged to enter what would become the New Territory in the decades after the "Evacuation of the Coast". Although Barnett mentions that, by 1898, the Punti clans were only able to hold their own in the great valleys of the north-west, and were experiencing difficulties in collecting rent from their Hakka perpetual tenants in upstream areas,[47] it seems that the latter were still, in part, an oppressed minority. Even decades after the Land Settlement, the memory of their subordinate or client status was part of the lore acquired by Walter Schofield when a District Officer.[48] And as late as the mid-1950s, elderly Tangs of Kam Tin would be telling an enthralled young female university student that they, as Punti, were "insiders", whereas the Hakka were still seen as "intruders" and despised as being poorer than themselves.[49] This was truly a mirror held up to history, providing a telling insight into Hakka-Punti relations before the Lease of 1898.

In the Tangs' case, in aggregate the most powerful of all NT lineages, the scholar-gentry status of many of its educated members, whether by examination or purchase, was due to wealth acquired from rents and market fees.[50] It was men of this sort who constituted the higher-level leadership in the countryside, with free access to the county magistrate and other officials, creating a two-way intercourse which was mutually advantageous. Such was mostly denied to smaller lineages, few of which could produce graduates by either means.[51] The connection can also be glimpsed in the intriguing surviving regulations of the "Governors' Temple" at Shek Wu Hui, which detail the ceremonial and feasting required when higher graduates and officials passing through the area stopped to pay respects to their memory.[52]

Nonetheless, it would be misleading to infer from the above that a tight control was everywhere applied, and at all times. The reverse was often the case, especially where rent-charge owners were absentee, while even in areas where resident lineages were dominant, small lineages would join together to oppose unjust or oppressive actions.[53] Moreover, in all settlements, tenant and satellite alike, there was the need for self-management in many aspects of daily life.

With few exceptions, the village headmen (or *Heung Cheung*) together with lineage and branch lineage elders, assisted by helpers who would become leaders in their turn, must have carried out the management duties so essential to an orderly life, including organization of the regular, periodic or occasional rituals protecting their members. In the larger villages, they had watchmen under their control, who helped maintain peace and could deal with petty offenders.[54] Above the villages, at the *heung* or sub-district level, higher leaders provided assistance at need. In the market towns and coastal market centres, local shopkeepers sitting together in the kaifong or neighbourhood committees, managed the varied business of their communities. Non-cooperative persons and outright offenders were mostly dealt with in accordance with the customs of the village, the *heung*, or the market town, but at need had been taken to an official.[55] Alliances (*yeuk*) were often based on an important local temple, as at the Governors' Temple in Shek Wu Hui, mentioned above.

As the American historian Hosea Ballou Morse, a member of China's foreign-led Imperial Maritime Customs service from 1874, summed up the position: "Eighty percent or more of the Chinese population live their daily lives under their customs, the common law of the land, interpreted and executed by themselves."[56] This would continue for as long as the old, closed, ways of life prevailed, as they would do in the NT for long after the Lease, despite exchanging rulers and the changes they brought with them. Even as late as 1958, it was reported from the Tang lineage villages of Kam Tin that the people "live according to their traditions and old rules, with public opinion as a powerful social control".[57]

Up to this point in the narrative, given the great emphasis on local management, the reader might well have been wondering at what point the imperial government would enter stage. Country-wide, the plain fact is that provincial government in late imperial times was more supervisory than executive, in that *it did not manage the countryside*. At the county level, with scanty resources and few personnel,[58] a magistrate's principal duties were to collect the taxes, maintain public order, and punish criminals.[59] He could not carry out these duties unaided, far less manage the villages and market towns.[60]

Another, quite intriguing, aspect to the average magistrate's position, was that he would always have to take account of powerful backers in his bailiwick. Right under our noses, in a most unlikely location that was far from the seats of powerful lineages, we have the example of a Taoist religious house established on Lantau Island in 1883. Its backers were two senior officials, both Guangdong natives, one a Viceroy no less, the other a provincial Literary Chancellor, whose names and titles to this day remain carved on the door frames of this otherwise very ordinary institution. Nowhere in the New Territory is there another such circumstance. It is hardly surprising that the district magistrate of the day felt obliged to issue a public notice, carved onto a memorial tablet, which extended official protection to the abbot and his disciples.[61] Truly a unique example in the New Territory, but surely to be found elsewhere.

PART THREE: A SUBSISTENCE ECONOMY[62]

In 1898, and for many years after, the villagers' basic means of livelihood and the single most important economic activity of the territory, was the biannual rice crop. Farming took place on the broad plains and river valleys, and also on slopes and in the hills, wherever a water supply was or could be made available. As a British District Officer would comment early in the Lease, "Broadly speaking, every possible acre of ground is planted with rice."[63]

Water was essential. A system of dams and channels aided the natural flow from higher streams, and the fields themselves were carefully graduated in height, one from another, so as to permit a smooth flow of water to assist the growing crops. Walking on a warm day in the summer months of the year, the sound of water dropping quietly from one field into another had been one of the commonest, and most delightful, sounds of the countryside. Irrigated fields at altitudes over 1,000 feet were not uncommon. Producing two crops during the year, farming had been carried on in this way for many centuries (Plates 5–6, 29–30, with the survey sheet at Plate 13).[64]

Fishing by various means was another major economic activity for coastal villagers and local boat people alike. Where the terrain allowed, fishing from small boats, by seine or stake-net, was carried out in season, and continued for half a century after 1898, until most local waters had been fished out or polluted. The shore, too, provided food for man and livestock. Examples of how the sea had shaped the local village lifestyle could be found in many outlying places. This was a pattern to be found everywhere in coastal areas of the Hong Kong Region: for a late example see Plate 27.[65]

These basic items in a subsistence economy were supplemented by items like grass and firewood which brought in cash or could be bartered, or by specialist activities that had to be paid for, like building and carpentry. Itinerant artisans were once very common, and provided the main income of some villages.[66] From well before 1898, a feature of some family budgets was the remittances sent home by members working in the city or overseas, or as seamen on ocean-going ships.[67]

Expressed in terms of household economy, rural housing, and social practices, the situation of the average New Territories farming family in 1898 appears to have been surprisingly little different from the Chinese norm, as established by John Lossing Buck and other agricultural scientists in the 1920s and 1930s, and despite regional differences fitted into the general pattern with an amazing facility. The small sum needed to maintain existence, the high percentage of food provided by the family farm, the poor standard of housing and sanitation with minimal furnishings, the combination of enjoined thrift in contrast to the high expenditure on major ceremonial and social occasions, with the tendency to indulge in good years instead of making improvements to material welfare, were common characteristics across the country.[68]

Buck's assessment is supported by the impressions I gained thirty years later, during my early years in the District Administration, when the village economy had changed little in essentials from prewar days, and indeed from much earlier. I also endorse his conclusion that, despite his low standard of living and often straitened circumstances, the Chinese farmer was "able to preserve on the whole a cheerful and not unkindly nature, highly to his credit".[69]

It was, too, one usually sustained by an independent spirit.[70] This, then, was the likely situation of the average farming family in the leased territory in 1898, then and for decades to come, within the social and political background stated in the body of this chapter.

PART FOUR: THE VILLAGE CULTURE

It is not possible to pass over this topic, since it was part of rural life, a living commentary on the beliefs and practices of the people. It derived from the major corpus of the national culture, of which the Confucian ethic was the dominant part. Upbringing (training) and education featured strongly in it, moulding succeeding generations in a more or less uniform pattern across China.[71]

Until comparatively recently, little attempt had been made to investigate village culture in Hong Kong. Yet it held many surprises.[72] In 1981, speaking on the progress of his ongoing Oral History Project at the Chinese University of Hong Kong, David Faure said that it was only after he, his colleagues and student helpers had got to know the villagers better through their search for inscriptions and land documents, that they "realize[d] that up to the War (1941–45) there was a very rich local literature in the New Territories".

> This consisted of songs, poetry, and legal as well as ritual documents, that were primarily written by villagers themselves. Second, there were many songs that were sung, passed on from generation to generation by word of mouth that had never been recorded. Some of these songs were sung by the bride and her family at the time of the wedding. Another group was sung at funerals. Yet another group consisted of "mountain songs", sung as a social activity between young men and young women from different villages. These songs, like the written literature, give us very vivid pictures of village life.[73]

Judging by the sheer volume of material recovered from the countryside, this was a tradition to be found everywhere.[74] It also featured in the literary competitions organized by the Governors' Temple at Shek Wu Hui mentioned above, as evidenced by its surviving regulations, which from their content derive from imperial times.[75]

Translations of stories from the Tang lineage of Kam Tin made by the Hong Kong scholar Sung Hok-pang for *The Hong Kong Naturalist* as far back as the 1930s, indicate the contributions to be made in this important cultural field among the large lineages, with their long history of local settlement.[76] In the 1960s, two tales from the Tangs' Ping Shan branch appeared in the short-lived Chinese language *New Territories Weekly*. As befitted a scholar-lineage, they were linked to local successes in the imperial examinations. Unpublished translations of other Ping Shan stories have also come to light.[77]

Similarly pleasant surprises awaited anyone who took an interest in the architecture of the New Territories. Again, it was not until the 1970s that more interest was shown in this important area of local culture. A survey was funded by the Hong Kong Tourist Association and carried out by students from the School of Architecture at the University of Hong Kong.[78] The outcome was a most attractive publication prepared by the Information Services Department of the Hong Kong Government, subsequently reprinted a decade later.[79] This book concentrated on the large buildings of the major lineages, featuring their walled villages, ancestral halls, study halls, temples, pagodas and residential buildings, and photographing the wealth of decoration in stone, pottery, wood, and stucco which characterized the vernacular architecture. Despite loss through neglect and demolition, there are still lesser examples of the kind to be found in other old villages in the territory which provide us with a good impression of what was to be seen in 1898.

We cannot doubt the spirit permeating the rural community of those times. In a paper on the literary legacy, Patrick Hase has reviewed the poems of Hui Wing-hing (1839–1921) a village schoolmaster of the day, commenting on how they "breathe that aura of complete self-confidence, community spirit, and easy independence that seem to have characterized local villages in the last century". Working independently, and from other sources, I have long come to precisely the same conclusion.[80]

For better or worse, *fung-shui*, too, was part of the village culture: not only because (as we have seen) it features prominently in history and legend, but because it was so embedded in the minds of the people. As a Lantau village elder told me in the 1960s, "To we men of Tang, *fung-shui* is *the* important thing". Of equal importance to the individual were the Eight Cyclical Characters (*bazi*) for every person's date and time of birth (by year, month, day, and time) needed to cast the horoscopes used to establish astrological compatibility for betrothals and weddings, and to determine the outcome of all manner of human enterprises.[81]

CONCLUSION

It remains to be stated that Lockhart argued eloquently in his report for the inclusion of the market town of Shenzhen and the surrounding plain on both sides of the agreed frontier within a new boundary alignment for the leased territory. Not least, as he wrote, because it "obviates any interference with the present system of local self-government, on the support of which the success of British administration in the new territory must to a great extent depend".[82] It was not to be, but had Shenzhen been incorporated into British territory in 1898, one may well doubt whether the Chinese Government would have bothered to create a Special Economic Zone there in 1979, with its great impact upon the continuing development of Hong Kong thereafter.

2

The Existing British Crown Colony and "the Great Difference"

BRITISH HONG KONG

Let us now look at the other side of "the great difference", the British Colony of Hong Kong, the place to which the New Territory would now be joined.

For its 19th-century Western visitors, "Hong Kong" meant the Island, and more specifically, what they called the City of Victoria, though this name was more in official than everyday usage. In 1881, walking into the town after landing at the naval dockyard during their world voyage on board HMS *Bacchante*, two young British royal princes noted that the streets were "wide and clean, full of chairs with green canopies and wickerwork sides, on long bamboo carrying poles, and of jin-ricki-shas. On either side of the street are lofty white arcaded houses in the Italian style; and groves of trees, wooded drives, and walks lead away up the slopes of the hills".[1] It was always this, the European section of the city, which so impressed visitors. In 1878, the celebrated Victorian lady traveller, Mrs. Bishop, had styled it, "the most imposing city of the East", going on to say that, "The magnificent city of Victoria extends for four miles along its southern shore, with its six thousand houses of stone and brick and the princely mansions and roomy bungalows of its merchants and officials scrambling up the steep sides of the Peak. It is hardly too much to say that it is the naval and commercial terminus of the Suez Canal."[2] A decade or so later, a visiting member of the British parliament, had written how "it would always remain a marvel how from a scorching rock had been evolved the Elysian graces of Hong Kong".[3]

Victorian lady travellers were especially taken with the place. Mrs. Gordon-Cumming, an artist with an artist's eye, as her ship entered the Harbour at Christmas 1878 was equally impressed: "I had not the remotest conception that I was coming to anything so beautiful ... its beauty, so suddenly revealed, left me mute with delight"[4]: while Mrs. Howard Vincent styled it "the prettiest of Eastern cities" and provided attractive descriptions of its variegated life on land and sea.[5] Taking a rather different approach, the globe-trotting Baron de Hübner, who had visited Hong Kong in 1871 and left a vivid account of the place, likened Hong Kong "to Ventnor or Shanklin [Isle of Wight] seen through a magnifying glass and under a jet of electric light".[6]

After waves of rebuilding, little remains of Curzon's "Elysian graces" today, but thanks to the camera and the work of contemporary photographers and present-day publishers, we are able to see what attracted such enthusiastic praise of the port-city from so many travellers of the times.[7]

Extending mainly to the west, the Chinese section of the city presented a great, but equally compelling, contrast. Its dwellings were described by Governor Sir George Des Voeux in 1888 as being "constructed after a pattern peculiar to China, of almost equally solid materials, but packed so closely together and thronged so densely as to be in this respect probably without parallel in the world". Continuing, he remarked, "It is believed that over 100,000 people live within a certain district of the city of Victoria not exceeding a half square mile in area. It is known that 1,600 people live in the space of a single acre".[8] A decade after, an Acting Governor, in his farewell address to the Legislative Council, referring to his own efforts to provide recreational space in the Chinese quarter of the city, to help combat plague, noted that such houses contained a "reeking mass of humanity", inhabiting rooms "into which the sun never enters, and where the fetid air has no motion".[9] A Chinese house "is very much like a rabbit warren", opined an Acting Attorney General in 1902.[10]

As for the Chinese inhabitants themselves, they were overwhelmingly migrant in 1898, and still largely male, as had been the case for most of the period since Hong Kong had come under British rule.[11] People came and went without restriction, their decisions determined by the employment market, the advice of friends and relatives, or the situation at home in China. In addition, there was a large movement of Chinese through the port, in both directions. For the most part, they lived in the crowded tenements described above, as well as in makeshift dwellings in which basic amenities were equally lacking, to an extent which encouraged epidemics and even plague. They were artisans, shop-men, coolies (waterfront especially) and hawkers in the main. This was essentially a male society, with recreational amusements to suit. Life there was feverish and exciting, and very different from the settled humdrum existence of rural life, which was something that most had probably left their homes to avoid. In many respects, though still on Chinese soil and close to their homes, their social existence was not unlike that of their fellows who had gone much further afield to live and work among non-Chinese.[12]

However, besides this dense mass, there was, by 1898, a small but prosperous – and in a few cases, very rich — Chinese elite. Mostly merchants and entrepreneurs, some had British nationality, available since Governor Pope-Hennessy's time (1877–82), and many were already well disposed to make the British Colony their home.[13] Two were serving on the Legislative Council and others on influential boards and committees. It was on behalf of this group that the two Councillors lobbied Lord Charles Beresford when he visited Hong Kong in the course of his commercial mission to China in that year (see below).[14]

There was another component of the Colony, nowhere expressed so strikingly as by Professor King, as his ship left Hong Kong for Canton on the cloudy evening of 8 March [1909]:

> ... the view was wonderfully beautiful. We were drawing away from three cities, one, electrically-lighted Hongkong rising up the steep slopes ...; another, old and new Kowloon on the opposite side of the harbor; and between these two, separated from either shore by wide reaches of wholly unoccupied water, lay the third, a mid-strait city of sampans, junks and coastwise craft of many kinds segregated, in obedience to police regulation, into blocks and streets with each setting sun, but only to scatter again with the coming morn.[15]

This "mid-strait" city was populated by boat people of various geographical origins. These mainly comprised the Cantonese speaking Tanka, indigenous to the province, who provided the lightering and ferrying services for the port, but also included Hoklo speakers originating from the adjoining province of Fujian, some locally based and similarly engaged. Others were simply passing through Hong Kong at intervals on their regular trading and cargo-carrying coastal voyages, as they have done almost to this day. There were also, even at turn of century, locally based or visiting fishing craft, less routinely engaged, turning smuggler and even pirate as opportunity offered.[16]

This urbanized agglomerate, on sea as on land, was managed by a body of colonial officials, underpinned by a police force that consisted of British, Indian, Malay and Chinese rank and file, with assistance at need from a large military garrison of British and Indian units. The Colony had been placed under Western law and administration from the start, and Chinese law and custom was, in general, not applied by the Courts though observed to a degree outside them.[17]

More specifically, government was in the usual pattern of a British Crown Colony, with a Governor assisted by appointed Executive and Legislative Councils, the majority of whose members were officials. Policy and finance were determined by the Governor in Council, and his decisions were conveyed to departments by a Colonial Secretariat headed by the Colonial Secretary who supervised general administration. A number of specialist departments managed land and building, the port and harbour, public works, police and prisons, public education, among others. The Registrar-General's department was responsible for liaison with the Chinese population, and with the assistance of Chinese elites, for advising on its management.[18] The law courts administered English common law.[19] It was a tight organization that suited a geographically small but crowded territory very well.

It was also, on occasion, a fairly arbitrary one. One example from 1900 may serve, among the many that could be cited. As a precaution against plague, a By-law of the Sanitary Board, requiring houses in the villages [as already with urban tenements] to be lime-washed throughout by their owners "not less than twice every year during May–June and November–December", was passed by the Legislative Council [whose approval was required to bring it into law]. It was only through the efforts of Hon. Dr. Ho Kai, aided by one other Member of Council, that the initial unanimous vote was overturned. One can imagine what a furore this would have created in the New Territory.[20]

Educational Opportunity in the Colony

From early days there had been an effort to widen the outlook of children at school by incorporating changes into the traditional Chinese curriculum, based on the classical books, with their historical and moral emphases. Albert Smith, visiting Hong Kong Island in 1857, wrote of

> coming to a little Chinese school [at Happy Valley] supported by the English [subsidy], with the pupils at small desks, and the old schoolmaster in the corner. It was a very pleasant sight. There were English maps and alphabets round the wall, and the boys had little double-paper books, with Indian ink tablets and pencils.[21]

The work of improving "village schools" (this term was also used for subsidized primary schools within the growing city and its environs) proceeded apace under the assiduous sure guidance of a Scottish scholar, Frederick Stewart, who extended the introduction of Western subjects and Western methods into Queen's College, the foremost Anglo-Chinese secondary institution, after he became headmaster there in 1872.[22]

Stewart was a major figure in the educational field until his early death in 1889, although by then Colonial Secretary. It would appear that the boys who attended his schools, especially a handful of bright lads from the villages of Hong Kong Island, found ready employment in Western business firms, law offices, and government departments. It was these educational opportunities and attainments, and their wider outlook, which further distanced the inhabitants of Hong Kong from their country cousins across the way.[23] The value of an Anglo-Chinese education in Hong Kong was not lost on discerning Chinese in adjoining San On and other Chinese counties in the Canton Delta either.[24] Many boys from this and other schools in the Colony also found employment in the treaty ports and in China, especially in the yamens of progressive senior mandarins, and with the foreign-led Chinese Imperial Maritime Customs.[25]

The annual Educational Reports for the few years before 1898 show some of these trends at work. In 1895, the government "had announced its determination henceforth to promote English rather than Chinese education among the native population"; stating that "the demand, on the part of the Chinese, for an English education is increasing", and that "the need for a Training School for native teachers of English, for the benefit of local schools in general, is gradually becoming more pressing".[26] The managers of Grant-in-Aid schools were being seen to conform to this increasing emphasis on western education, and their higher rate of efficiency and payment by results, was an aspect which, it was affirmed, "outweighs with Chinese parents all other considerations".[27] The Colony's prospective usefulness to China in the modernizations yet to come was already becoming evident.[28]

Hong Kong's Trade and Shipping

If we wish to look more broadly at what Hong Kong had become by 1898, there are no better subjects than trade and shipping. Hong Kong's central position between India and Japan, and its convenience for the China trade, featured prominently in the resolutions transmitted by the Hong Kong General Chamber of Commerce to Lord Charles Beresford during his commercial mission to China on behalf of the [British] Associated Chambers of Commerce in 1898. These considerations, they advised, together with "the unique advantages" they conferred, made the port "of supreme importance to British trade".[29]

By this time, Hong Kong had become of major importance in the foreign trade of China. In 1897, the total tonnage of shipping entering and clearing the port was stated at 15,565,843, of which 8,268,770 was British, some 64% of the whole. The comparable figures for Shanghai were roughly half in each category, while the value of the Hong Kong share of the foreign trade with China was estimated at GBP 50 millions, far more than Shanghai's at the time.[30]

The much longer address sent to His Lordship on behalf of the Chinese mercantile community of Hong Kong, spoke of "the distinguished privilege of becoming subjects of the mightiest and most glorious Empire the world has ever seen", and contrasted it with the backward condition of the Chinese empire, listing for him the major features of its polity which, in their view, grievously inhibited its efficiency and progress in all things, and especially trade and commerce.[31]

The contents of Lord Beresford's book made China's parlous — almost perilous — condition at this time only too clear.[32]

A Contrast Indeed

In these and other ways, the contrast between the old and newly added parts of the Colony and their people could hardly have been greater. The one was bustling, innovative and outwardly, even internationally, oriented. With an ever-growing trade and population, it must already have acquired that characteristic Hong Kong "buzz" which for so long has typified the place and its people. The other, seldom visited, was a place where, "Under Chinese rule", as Stewart Lockhart felt bound to report in 1898, "enterprise has been at a discount, and progress has been at a standstill for centuries", adding that, "The San On district of today must be much the same as it was four or five hundred years ago".[33] It was an exaggeration that nonetheless made its point, and one justified to a degree by the state of the countryside, which was characterized by the almost total lack of roads and wheeled transportation.[34] In default, men and women were the principal burden-bearers.

THE NEW TERRITORY

Small wonder, then, that as one of Hong Kong's principal officials, with direct links to the leaders of the Chinese urban community as well as to the Western elite, but with a strong sense of the worth of the ordinary Chinese,

Stewart Lockhart should have been struck by the great difference existing between the two sets of inhabitants, Southern Chinese though both were, and the two places.[35] Acutely aware of the problems that this could create for the colonial authorities, he thought it necessary to remind the incoming Governor, Blake, that the Chinese of Hong Kong had been accustomed to British rule for a period of more than fifty years, whereas the people of the new territory had hitherto had no experience of it. "At first everything will be strange to them, and it will require much tact and discretion to administer their affairs in such a manner as to allay that suspicion and alarm for which the Chinese race are so notorious".[36]

No doubt influenced by Lockhart, the Acting Governor, Major-General Wilsone Black, had written to the Secretary of State in London in much the same vein. "We should govern somewhat in the present Chinese system, i.e. the Village elders to rule the villages, which, grouped in tepo limits,[37] form a Tung having a council composed of representatives from the village elders. Each Tung will send a representative to the Council of the Resident".[38] The latter, to be styled a Commissioner or Resident, should be someone "possessing intelligence, common sense, and a knowledge of the Chinese character. Casting about in my own mind for the local man, I early pitched upon the Colonial Secretary, Mr. J. Stewart Lockhart, as the man I would appoint if the decision lay with me".[39]

How best to administer the New Territory had thus been an issue from the start. The differences of which Lockhart spoke ranged from the physical features of the New Territory to the character and accustomed mind-set of its people. While the Extension was not really very large, its mountainous terrain, many islands, and poor communications would have made administration of the New Territory from the centre both an expensive and impractical proposition. In regard to the others, these had been shaped in large measure by the form and traditions of that hoary leviathan, the Chinese imperial government, briefly touched upon in its local *personum*, the county magistrate, in chapter 1. Such were essential parts of "the great difference".

The Confucian tradition upon which government was based has been described by a leading American historian as being "authoritarian, ideological, bureaucratic, and humanistic in a peculiarly Chinese way".[40] There was ever a heavy official emphasis on its subjects being *liangmin* or "good people":[41] and the populace at large was well-advised to be so, since this particular brand of humanism did not extend to wrongdoers or offenders. The imperial officials, civil and military, might be thin on the ground at the county level, but they had retained the capability to overawe the people.[42] It was decidedly not advisable to become entangled with them or their minions.[43] Their actions could be arbitrary, and even despotic.[44] Judicial processes were severe, and deliberately so, intended to reduce crime and deter litigation.[45] The treatment of those awaiting trial was likewise callous,[46] while the outcome was often to be determined by bribes. Fear had engendered caution, and this persisted unless the people were provoked unjustly and beyond reason.[47]

Therefore most people steered clear of officials if they could. Soon after the take-over, Lockhart, seeking to explain to the Governor and Members of the Legislative Council why Chinese in the NT were paying scant attention to calls to come forward to assist in the land work begun by the colonial government, would suggest reasons other than the facile presumption of non-cooperation and off-handedness on their part.[48] And even thirty years after the territory came under British rule, W. H. Peplow, a Land Bailiff in the District Office South, whose duties took him everywhere, wrote of the frustrations caused in his work by the people's dislike of official querying:

> Sometimes I have had to find a certain man in connection with Govt. business. Seeing four or five villagers together I have asked for him by name. Immediately they want to know what he is wanted for. After about a quarter of an hour's talk explaining, one of them will step forward and say he is the man. It is useless asking why he did not say so before, everything should be explained beforehand to them, and, should it be a serious matter, one will simply be told that the man is not there; he has gone to the country or some such excuse, and in nine cases out of ten, the person so informing you is the one you want.[49]

Thus besides whatever their reservations about that unknown quantity, the British colonial government, the NT people were encumbered with a good many notions about their own, sometimes dearly bought. It is hardly to be wondered at that some of these created problems for the Hong Kong authorities, while others (especially the general respect for authority, albeit with the people's own reservations) would prove beneficial in the longer term once the good intentions and comparative mildness of British rule had been established.[50] But first, Hong Kong and London had to confront and face down a robust and determined opposition to the transfer of power in the territory.

A Timely Reminder of the Difference

There was considerable delay in taking over the New Territory. A full ten months elapsed before the British flag was hoisted there on 16 April 1899.

Before and long after Lockhart had presented his Report, the British authorities in London, Peking and Hong Kong were threshing out various contentious issues with the Chinese government.[51] To these delays were added the desire for Lockhart to be present at the take-over ceremony (after his inspection of the leased territory, he had resumed his overseas leave and did not return to the Colony until late February 1899) and for him to agree and demarcate its northern boundary with a Chinese official (Plate 7). Time would also be required to make basic administrative and logistical arrangements for administering the territory immediately after the take-over.

Once the British government had finally decided not to permit Chinese jurisdiction of any kind within the New Territory, and to allow Blake to go ahead (late March 1899) further delay was occasioned by unrest at Tai Po where the matsheds needed for the take-over ceremony were under construction. The likelihood of more serious opposition led Governor Blake to go in person to Canton to see the Viceroy, and the take-over eventually took place on 16 April 1899, a day earlier than scheduled, owing to further acts of violence and the large number of armed Chinese in the area.

By then, organized by several segments of the Tang lineage with grudging assistance from other major lineages, and with the participation (it was thought) of men from Sham Chun (Shenzhen) and elsewhere in Chinese territory, an armed uprising was in progress in the northern NT. After two sharp engagements at Tai Po the day before the flag-raising ceremony on 16 April 1899, and another on 17 April at the pass connecting the Lam Tsuen valley with the Pat Heung plain, the remaining Chinese insurgents were dispersed the following day after making a determined but unsuccessful attack on the British force which had pursued them there.[52] The troops had then marched to all adjoining parts, blowing up the gates of some walled villages in the process. Owing to prompt action, discipline, and superior fire-power, the resistance was overcome within only six days.[53]

But a lesson had been learned. Viewed in retrospect, these events involving the local population had been an indication of the power of combination, with the ever-present likelihood of support from agnates and others from across the border. Nothing of the kind would have been possible in Old British Hong Kong where none of the preconditions for a similar movement had existed. The uprising had also demonstrated the power of rumour among a people traditionally prone to alarms and excursions.[54]

In his important Proclamation, prepared for and read out during the take-over ceremony, Blake had assured the people that "your commercial and landed interests will be safe-guarded, and that your usages and good customs will not in any way be interfered with".[55] Shortly after the uprising, he had also been quick to make it clear to them (through Lockhart) that, even if without title, the rights of persons in long occupation of land would be confirmed at the land settlement.[56] Blake certainly showed his sensitivity and common sense over that period, to the point of disapproving of some of Lockhart's punitive measures and overruling his desire to punish the ringleaders of the resistance movement.[57] A few months later, accompanied by Lockhart, he made two visits to the New Territory (2 and 4 August 1899) to meet the gentry and elders of the affected areas, to explain his policies and enlist their support (Plates 9–11).[58]

A Simpler Form of Administration

With consent from London, the Hong Kong authorities opted for controlling the New Territory through District Officers charged with general duties and land administration, and exercising both police and civil jurisdiction. Complementing Ordinances made land ownership conform to Chinese law and custom, enforceable at law, while the villages and sub-districts were left in the charge of their own leaders, under the watchful eyes of the district officers and the police.[59] By 1910, the administrative, judicial and policing arrangements had settled into a mould which would last until the 1950s.[60]

In providing for separate administrative and legal systems in the urban and rural parts of the Colony, "the great difference" noted by Lockhart and endorsed in London was consolidated thereby. For both good and ill, it would be perpetuated for many decades to come.

New Kowloon

It is appropriate, at this point, to consider New Kowloon. This comprised the seven and a half square miles of territory north of the boundary fence erected to mark the northern boundary of Old British Kowloon, ceded to Britain in 1860.[61] Lying beneath the protective barrier of the Kowloon Hills, which cut it off from the rest of the New Territory, this area was immediately recognized as possessing "a growing importance as an outlet for the expansion of the Colony", and to have a "far greater superficial value relative to the rest of the New Territory".[62] Moreover, its proximity to Old British Kowloon and Hong Kong Island would, as Stewart Lockhart suggested in 1899, render the people more amenable to Western methods and better able to understand the meaning of what they were required to do than might have been the case with villagers in more remote districts.[63]

It was therefore absorbed into the older part of the Colony and its inhabitants made subject to the rules and regulations governing the rest of the population of Hong Kong.[64]

In 1906, in "the first detailed Census taken of this portion of the Colony", New Kowloon was described as "comprising the Police Districts of Sham Shui Po and Kowloon City", with a population count of 15,319.[65] Most, but not all, of its old villages and hamlets were listed at the more extensive Colony Census of 1911.[66] The omission was one of several indications of a less than fatherly approach to the old residents of the area.[67] And so it proved. Over the ninety-nine years of the Lease, they were treated very differently, and with much less consideration, from the population north of the Kowloon Hills. Their contrasting fates will be described in chapter 8.

3

Survey, Land Court, Registration, and Customary Law

Land would always be an important element in the NT. Up to the time traditional farming began its decline in the 1960s, it would provide a livelihood for the majority of the indigenous inhabitants, and also for the tens of thousands of immigrant vegetable and livestock farmers who, from the late 1940s on, supplied an ever-growing percentage of the Colony's food supplies. But from a "whole Colony" point of view, and almost from the start of the Lease, possession of the New Territory would enable the Hong Kong government to secure land there for various purposes at all times.

In the first forty years of the Lease, roads, railways, reservoirs and other public services were needed to improve communications and provide for better control, help bring in modernization, and cater for an expanding urban population. In the final thirty years, as part of a far greater requirement, the NT would provide land for the "New Towns" programme, the container ports, and both the internal and connecting infrastructures needed to link up with and service a reinvigorated China, now embarked upon its "Four Modernizations". The end result would fuel Hong Kong's long continuing economic and social growth, and cement its "world city" status.

For all these requirements an accurate survey of the New Territory was a necessary adjunct. But this is to look far ahead.[1] In the first instance, we must ask how and why, in 1898–1899, the colonial authorities decided that a survey of holdings, and the settlement of titles by a specially constituted Land Court, would (among other measures) be essential for the proper absorption of the leased territory and its people into the Colony of Hong Kong.[2]

REASONS FOR THE SURVEY

As Special Commissioner, Lockhart (as directed from London) had given his close attention to the land situation, especially in regard to registration of ownership, the tax revenue produced from landed properties, the parties from whom tax was collected, and how its collection was managed.[3]

It was soon evident to him that the Chinese system of land administration was subject to major objections, and could not be taken over as it was. One problem was stated in the following terms:

> All documents relating to land in the New Territory were registered in the San On District registry, but that registry is only a deed registry and not a registry of titles to land ...
>
> The great difficulties to be got over arise from the circumstances that most valuable lands have more than one title, yet if each title is taken alone it appears to be in order.

Land in dispute at Cheung Sha Wan, on the shores of north-west Kowloon, looking directly onto Hong Kong Island and its already famous harbour, exemplified this predicament. By virtue of its situation, it was indeed "most valuable" land:

> ... the land of Ch'eung Sha Wan including the foreshore and the sea in front is claimed under four distinct titles vested in four different families. Two of the titles to the same land are derived direct from the Viceroy and Governor of Canton under recited Imperial Order. The two other titles, before the Convention, conclude by Vesting Orders made at trials before the San On Magistrates, one Magistrate deciding that the same land belonged to the Tang Clan, and another Magistrate deciding that the same land belonged to the Chiu Clan.[4]

But the problems embraced more than a system of deed registration which could produce such confusion. Besides the fact that there were no accurate survey records and that the district land registers were out of date, it was of even greater concern that much of the tax revenue was in the hands of intermediaries, who collected their rents from those farming the land and forwarded what was due to the authorities.

These "rent charge owners" (also styled "taxlords" by the Hong Kong authorities)[5] were the persons or families who had acquired rights over surface and sub-soil as a consequence of imperial grants or purchases of land from the authorities in times past.[6] Their holdings were registered in the district land registry, but more often than not, were in the names of owners long since dead by hundreds of years. Their descendants were not themselves cultivating the land, but were collecting rents in silver or grain from persons holding surface rights (in effect, the right to cultivate) on renewable perpetual leases. They also received payments from other persons, to whom the surface rights had been sold by the lessees in unregistered customary deeds (commonly called "white" as opposed to "red" or registered deeds) Such sales were permissible under local customary law, but under condition of paying the same amounts to the sub-soil (i.e. registered) owners, as usually stipulated in the deeds of sale.[7] Generally speaking, the latter were often lineage trusts with managers, but not always.[8]

Despite many generations of occupancy, none of the persons holding surface rights under customary law had registered titles to the land they occupied. They relied only on the "perpetual leases" re-issued periodically by the sub-soil owners, or on the customary "white" deeds in their keeping. In short, such persons were invisible in bureaucratic terms, since none of them appeared in the district registers. A dismissive remark recalled by a Hong Kong official at the handover of Old British Kowloon in 1860 was very likely characteristic of the mandarins' approach to this very numerous, if subordinate, group of persons.[9] It seemed, too, that they were often unknown to the sub-soil owners, since it became clear to Members of the Land Court that many of the latter had no idea who their tenants were, being content so long as rent was being received.[10]

Another anomaly was soon to be revealed, amounting to a further and unauthorized extension of the local rights being assumed by those holding land by registered title. In such cases, the tax amounts shown in the deed registry would prove to be for areas far less than those currently under cultivation by the tenants. One instance of the kind reported by a Member of the Land Court, revealed the true position on the ground: not only in regard to the small amount of land in the original grant, but also the confused situation in regard to its location, and to its ownership within the lineage concerned.[11] In this wise, sub-soil families prospered exceedingly, but the imperial revenues from land stagnated.[12]

Even on the limited basis of the initial enquiries, this situation was unacceptable to the colonial authorities. It became necessary to regularize occupation, and apportion land tax (after 1899, Crown Rent) obligations accordingly. This was best achieved by embarking upon a land survey, demarcation, and settlement of titles in the New Territory at an early date. In terms of cost and effort, this work would be a major undertaking, of a kind seldom attempted in China.[13] Indeed, the situation revealed by Lockhart and others would continue on the Mainland into the 1930s and beyond, and the few cases in which similar reforms were effected proved how right the Hong Kong authorities had been to proceed.[14]

THE SURVEY

In 1898 the land under occupation was a veritable patchwork of irrigated fields. Seen from high ground, they stretched across the plains, reaching up between the spurs of hills and mountains to isolated pockets or high plateaux. Village families usually held not one field but parcels of small cultivated plots, distributed here and there within each village locality. Overall, their number was very great, but as the survey and demarcation would show, many fields were tiny, and family holdings were mostly small (Plate 13).[15]

The survey, begun in late November 1899, was carried out by European and Indian staff on loan from the Survey of India.[16] Every plot and field, house and structure, even agricultural matsheds standing in the fields, had to be included. There had been no incivility or hindrance to the survey work. In fact, the cultivators were reported to have taken little notice of the operations going on among their fields.[17] Save in the broad plains of the Northern NT, the work was very demanding. At the close of the field season 1901–1902, the Officer-in-charge had written: "The nature of the country is broken and mountainous, and the greater part is some of the most difficult country to survey that I have ever seen" (Plate 12).[18] At the close of the work — it was apparently finished in May 1903, although the General Report covers the period November 1899 to April 1904 — a total of 328,639 holdings, covering 40,737.95 acres had been surveyed and demarcated.[19]

SLOWNESS IN SUBMITTING CLAIMS

The early period of the survey seems to have been characterized by a marked disinclination on the part of the inhabitants to make claims to the land they owned or occupied. Made known by official Notifications in the Government Gazette, this requirement was backed up by notices posted locally in the areas to be surveyed, followed up with reminders by visiting police.[20] However, as H. H. J. Gompertz, President of the Land Court, would report, on Tsing Yi Island, although ample notice had been given that claims had to be received by 1 October 1900, the first claim was not received until nine days after, with the rest, 77 in all, following gradually up to 2 May 1901.[21]

On nearby Ma Wan, where the Notification and notices had been issued at the same time, Gompertz found that, just four days before the expiry date, only one claim had been submitted. Deciding to visit in person on 28 September with a Hakka interpreter, he was met in no accommodating spirit by the inhabitants:

> They informed me that they had all reported their claims either at Tai Po or Ping Shan and that some of them had registered their deeds in the Land Office [in Hong Kong] and did not see why they should report again.[22]
>
> I explained to them the meaning of the notice and the importance of reporting before it should be too late. On Monday Oct. 1st I received two more claims. During the rest of October 24 more claims were brought in and in November 19 claims. In all I have received 92 claims for the Island of which however only three were "duly presented" the rest being "Late claims".[23]

By June 1901, he had concluded that "Judging from the experience of the past twelve months [July 1900–June 1901], it seems that nothing but demarcation will really stir up more than a very small fraction of the population to report their claims".[24]

DEMARCATION

Demarcation was fundamental to the work of the Land Court in settling titles, and to the preparation of an accurate Rent Roll which would enable the collection of all Crown Rents. It entailed matching each of the individual plots shown on the cadastral survey sheets (which gave the position and area of individual holdings) with a claimant (or claimants) who, when called upon to do so, would have to substantiate the claim in person before a member of the Land Court.[25] Given that practically all families in the villages owned (or as good as owned) some land, demarcation would require the active cooperation of the people almost everywhere.[26]

The demarcation work began in June 1900 and was finished in June 1903.[27] It became a large-scale operation. By March 1902, the Chinese demarcation staff had risen to 190 men, divided into field parties of four: three coolies and one Demarcator to each party.[28] After a plot had been identified, a number was allocated to it and marked on the appropriate survey sheet, and a "chit" bearing the same number was given to the person or persons claiming ownership or occupation (Plate 15).[29] Full particulars of the claims were to be entered in the demarcation registers.

The proceedings were nothing if not thorough, and certainly picturesque. We can envisage the teams "sweeping over a district, taking village by village consecutively", as the report has it. Notices were to be posted at least a week in advance in adjoining areas, and the demarcator and his coolies were "to go about and inform people that they must come forward and point out their land". The evening before an area was to be covered, it was to be marked out with tall bamboos surmounted with a red flag, to be left standing while the work proceeded. One of the coolies accompanying the demarcator was to carry the bamboos, one a pickaxe, and the third was to help the demarcator with his enquiries into the ownership of the lots. The coolie with the pickaxe was to carry the slips of paper to be marked and distributed to claimants; presumably on the premise that if he could be entrusted with the pickaxe, he must be a reliable man.

The work had gone on slowly at first. This was due, in the main, to the various practical difficulties enumerated in Gompertz's report for 1901, although these included the fact that information had been "less readily forthcoming on Chinese holidays and festivals and during seed-time and harvest", and that there had been reluctance to claim "poor pieces of hill cultivation" on which no Chinese taxes had been paid. However, he was still able to report that the operations had been met in a friendly spirit by the inhabitants.[30]

REFLECTIONS ON INITIAL NON-COMPLIANCE IN MAKING CLAIMS

Looking through the published documents today, I would say that the people of Tsing Yi and Ma Wan were hardly to blame for their failure to submit claims to land on time. There had been a real confusion about notices and requirements, caused largely by the government itself. Measures adopted soon after taking over the New Territory had later to be modified in the light of experience and during ongoing debate within official circles.

Eager to begin collecting revenue from the territory, there had been the intention to compile a provisional Rent Roll. To this end, landowners and occupiers of land had been required to register their holdings under specified arrangements indicated as early as July 1898.[31] Before long, these had been changed, whereby registration could be made to the new Land Offices at Tai Po and Ping Shan. The response can only be described as good, with 21,736 submissions made at Tai Po and 5,613 at Ping Shan by 20 January 1900.[32] Concurrently, the government intended that owners of Chinese (official) deeds should register them at the Land Office in Hong Kong, with a view to granting them Crown leases in lieu of existing Chinese titles or else providing certificates of title acknowledging existing Chinese title. The first deed was registered on 3 June 1899, and by the end of the year 134 had been translated and registered, with some 200 left over for investigation and decision.[33] Upward of 1,000 petitions relating to land questions and disputes had also been received.[34]

These facts help to explain the poor responses made by the people of Tsing Yi and Ma Wan. As Gompertz himself was later to admit, the deed registrations under a long-existing Hong Kong Ordinance, had left many persons "happy in the belief that they have thereby done everything that is necessary", and that making claims at the Tai Po and Ping Shan Rent Roll Offices, as directed, had left others "not understand[ing] that they had to come in again".[35] The authorities had themselves created the confusion in people's minds.[36]

It was only after they realized there were major obstacles to issuing Crown Leases on the basis of Chinese deeds, and to constructing a Crown Rent Roll from claims submitted under the original arrangements, that there had been a change of approach.[37] There were, in truth, no shortcuts to getting what the authorities required. Chastened by experience, by late 1900, they had recognized the need to press on with the survey, combine it with the demarcation, and chase in and scrutinize all claims to land. Considerably later, they would assign three younger Cadets to finalize the settlement of titles across the New Territory. This, by dint of hard work, the three men managed to achieve, over a period of nine months in 1904.[38]

Eight years later, Orme (the District Officer of the day) was able to describe the various stages of the Survey and Land Settlement in a clear and succinct fashion. However, as we have seen, they were not as clear in practice, owing in part to the complexity of the land situation, the various changes in execution made along the way, and what may be styled the false start noted above. Also, the printed papers and reports covering the work are occasionally contradictory and perplexing, and sometimes inadequate for providing answers to questions of detail.[39]

OTHER REASONS FOR POOR COOPERATION

The initial confusions apart, there were other reasons for the hesitation in cooperating with the work of the Land Court. Many occupiers of land must have been quite satisfied with their perpetual leases or customary deeds (the long-established norm in the region) with their built-in protective safeguards.[40]

And, within many lineages, it seems likely that a form of self-regulation and registration would have been long in place.[41] Thus, many occupiers might have regarded the Survey and Land Settlement as being (for them at least) quite superfluous.[42] Also, since, from the outset, it had been clear that they had much to do with paying Crown Rent for everything they held, the villagers were suspicious, and generally wary of the new government's proceedings.[43] Perhaps, too, they had thought that, as sometimes happened under Chinese rule, they could safely ignore the whole thing: the fuss would be temporary, and soon die down.[44] Finally, and quite apart from specific issues, there was (as Lockhart said) the legacy of the Chinese past to take into account.[45]

In short, and as usual, the causes were many and varied.

THE LAND COURT

The Court was constituted under the Land Court (New Territories) Ordinance No. 18 of 1900.[46] Its Members' work lasted for rather longer than expected, and there had been two enquiries in Legislative Council. In late 1901, the Colonial Secretary had replied to a request for information on Claims sent in up to 30 June 1901, and on Claims "finally disposed of by the Land Court up to that date".[47] In April 1903, he had to face a more serious probe after one of the "Unofficial" Members of Council had asked for "an explanation of the delay in settling this matter, almost four years having elapsed since the date of the concession".[48] After years of preparation, the work of the Court was finalized in 1904, as described.[49]

Among the batch of progress reports on settling titles, Clementi's[50] is especially interesting, as much for its travel details as for the impressive amount of work done. Finally moored in the Yuen Long creek, his houseboat (presumably serving also as his office) had been towed along the western coast from New Kowloon to the Sham Chun River, and also to the islands of Peng Chau, Cheung Chau, Tsing Yi and Ma Wan. Between the first week in June 1904 until signing the final schedules at the end of September, he had dealt with titles in no fewer than 67 survey districts, recording with obvious satisfaction "that no appeal to the Supreme Court has been lodged against any judgement delivered by me".[51] This proud claim must be seen in the context of his criticisms of earlier decisions of the Land Court, in which he is supposed to have had the support of H.M.'s Consul-General at Canton.[52]

Their labours completed, the findings were recorded in a set of large volumes, one for each of the 355 Survey Districts. Each volume would comprise a Block Crown Lease, one or more survey sheets, and the accompanying Schedules of Crown Lessees. Most importantly, these noted the Crown rent due on each lot and the names and addresses of the persons responsible for making the annual payments.[53] Together with the various supporting office records needed to operate the new system for registering all subsequent transactions in land, they would ensure, as far as possible, the efficient and comprehensive collection of Crown Rent. In short, the hitherto invisible (p. 31) occupiers of land had been transformed into highly visible Crown Lessees.

FEATURES OF LAND ADMINISTRATION AFTER THE LAND SETTLEMENT

The Continued Importance of Customary Documents

From this point on, the contents of the Block Crown Leases and the new registration system introduced with the New Territories Land Ordinance of 1905 would underpin land administration there. The new records would be kept in separate District Land Registries established in the Northern and Southern Districts, to hold, maintain, and update them. And in the course of the daily round, practice and precedent in all matters relating to land would be established through the instructions received from the Colonial Secretary's Office, soon to be enshrined in the "Notes for Use in the New Territories District Land Offices, 1908".[54]

However, the new registration did not develop quite as smoothly as hoped. While the New Territories Land Ordinance of 1905 had provided six new forms for use in recording all sales, mortgages and leases,[55] the introduction of these forms cut right across the much older Chinese formats for recording transactions in land, in particular the "white" (or unregistered) deeds mentioned above. Products of the customary law, in universal use, their longevity and overall utility had been due in the past to the support provided by the managers of lineage, village and sub-district bodies, with recourse to the district magistrate at need.[56] They had been the time-honoured means for transferring land between ordinary folk, and local people were not about to relinquish their use.[57] The safeguards provided in the text of the customary formats were still needed and would guarantee their continuance for another half century, for almost as long as villagers were living traditional lives.[58]

For decades longer, then, the customary formats remained in use, written on the rough-textured sheets of the past or, as now often happened, on officially issued "stamped papers".[59] In the new district land registries, it became the practice to accept both as proof of transactions in land. The essential details would be entered onto a printed "Memorial" by District Land Office staff, the parties would sign or add their mark, witnesses likewise, and if approved and signed by the District Officers as Assistant Land Officers would be placed on the registers, after which the originals were returned to the purchasers.[60] As for the six new formats stipulated in the Ordinance, these were only used where it suited the intending purchasers.[61]

Custom Perpetuated in Registering Title

All claims to ownership during the Survey and Land Settlement had been made in accordance with prevailing practice under Chinese customary law.[62] Where undisputed in hearings before the Land Court (as we have seen, all but a very few judgements were appealed against[63]) they were accepted, and entered into the Schedules of Crown Lessees. Thereafter, provision for custom to continue when registering successions, trusteeships, and managerships of lineage trust properties was made in the New Territories Land Ordinance of 1905 and subsequent legislation.[64] Summarized, it may be stated generally as follows.

In the case of land held by individuals, only males could inherit, and if there was more than one recognized inheritor (as in the case of brothers) succession would be registered in all their names. No female could inherit, because she would marry and take the land out of her family. Where there was no son to inherit, even male cousins would take precedence over a daughter. A woman could become a trustee for a minor, but only until he or they came of age. In the case of land held in common under various forms of customary trust — mostly connected with the lineage and some or all of its members — registered managers would administer the property, and both members and managers would again be male only.[65] No significant change was made in these provisions until an amending Ordinance to permit female succession to family property was passed in 1994.[66]

Prewar and early postwar, the great majority of applications for succession, and for the appointment of trustees and managers, were initiated by those involved and scrutinized by their fellows. The District Administration would only press for action to enable updating of the registers if it required land for public works, since it could not pay compensation until this had been done.[67] Either way, the procedures were the same, and no change in the registers would be approved by the District Officers until they had been carried out.[68]

Gradual Acceptance of the New Registration System

Nonetheless, the British practice of registering all land transactions as Memorials, tied accurately to the other records held in the registries, would eventually find public acceptance. Initially, there would have been considerable anxiety at the lack of proof for ownership under the new arrangements. The Block Crown Leases were official records, locked away in the land registries, and the only documents issued to owners were the receipts given for annual payment of the Crown rent on their properties.[69] However, this important omission was remedied by the issue of certificates listing each owner's holdings (known as *chap chiu*) in the first decade of the new century and upon request thereafter (Plate 14).[70] Other aspects of the new arrangements also promoted acceptance. The mapping and lot numbering carried out during the survey and settlement of titles made identification of properties for sale or mortgage far easier for both parties than the vague statements of boundaries usually to be found in customary deeds.[71] Thus, before long, Lot and Demarcation District numbers might be included in the still customary documentation. Also, the road, rail and ferry services introduced into parts of the NT by 1941 would make it easier for some of those wishing to register transactions to get to the District Land Registries.[72]

But whatever the benefits of the new systems, there was a downside too. Besides mistakes made by government clerks during the massive recording and copying exercise (and there were stated to be many such[73]) some of these errors were due to the owners themselves. The titles entered into the registers could only be as good as reported by the people. Contemporary accounts, and disputes over ownership that surfaced much later, make it clear that reporting during demarcation and before members of the Land Court was not always accurate or comprehensive.[74] Inside families and lineages, it was often being assumed that, since all concerned knew what was what, and would act in accordance with the canons of brotherly conduct, there was no need to correct errors or omissions made when reporting ownership or discovered thereafter.[75] And however caused, errors and discrepancies would continue to surface in the course of land work far into the future, especially when land was being resumed for development.[76]

CUSTOMARY LAW DURING THE LEASE

Although its subject matter takes us to the end as well as the beginning of the Lease, and out of turn in this largely chronological account, some notice must be taken of a recent book by Allen Chun.[77] Examining the field from a different viewpoint, and based on both anthropological fieldwork and archival research, he suggests that what the government and most historians and anthropologists of Hong Kong consider to have been "traditional society" had in fact been altered by the land settlement. Also, that it had continued to be altered by colonial land policies and the new land-related registration system applied during the Lease, to an extent that he believed warranted his including "The "Fictions of Colonial Practice" in the subtitling of his book. The titling also takes in what he calls "the Changing Realities" of Land.

The land settlement had certainly made major changes to the fabric of traditional society, furthered by the greater degree of public security which followed marine and land policing after the Take-over. Also, the Government's land policies (albeit to meet changing circumstances) would assuredly give rise, before and after the War and Occupation, to the rural lobby's pet theme: that it had denied them rights enjoyed under Chinese rule.[78] Chun is also right to notice what is styled "the disciplinary reordering of routine life" represented by the colonial government's evolving rules and regulations;[79] an observation supported by Howard Nelson, who concluded from his village field work in 1967–68 that the Hong Kong authorities' greater efficiency and proximity to the lives of the people "in themselves constituted a major intervention into Chinese social organization".[80] As for the "changing realities of land" itself, this too cannot be gainsaid, albeit it was driven by the need for flexibility in determining new (and acceptable) forms of compensation.[81]

But in regard to the colonial administration's "unnaturally stifling meaningful possibilities for change" in the customary law,[82] I do not see how this can be. I have already provided the context in which these statements should be viewed: that customary forms of documentation had continued in use for at least five decades after the land settlement; how updating of the registers in regard to successions, trusteeship and managership had been initiated *in the villages* and scrutinized there; and how there was considerable neglect in doing so over decades, because, within the customary arrangements which still dominated rural life into the 1950s, such action was considered unnecessary, since all knew who was entitled to what, and to exercise which rights (pp. 37–39, with notes).

While acknowledging that Allen Chun's various propositions deserve more detailed consideration than is possible here, I must stress that by then, many, even most, NT villages had hardly changed in externals and lifestyle from the start of the Lease, and that the mindset of their inhabitants reflected the still rather primitive conditions of the day. I must also pass on my impressions of the vigorous customary law and practice which operated in the countryside.

In the rapidly changing village world of the 1960s and 1970s, adherence to them became gradually less possible, while the District Administration itself became increasingly taken up with other duties during the fast-track development of the territory. Yet, even so, the customary law retained some of its old vigour. My experience in Tsuen Wan District between 1975 and 1982 showed that it was still a living process, within the local tradition of self-management.[83] It was also capable, at need, of innovation: as exemplified by the expedients resorted to by managers of lineage trusts when, following resumptions of property, they were obliged to consult and decide on the distribution of compensation in cash or Letters of Exchange among the membership: by this time, to be construed as including minors, even babies, and females.[84] Into the 1980s, village representatives and lineage elders would find it increasingly difficult to deal with problems arising;[85] but the continued relevance of the land-related customary law for the maintenance and identity of the indigenous communities — not excluding those now living in the large number of resited villages[86] — was clearly understood by all concerned, even at the end of the Lease.[87] It is for all the above reasons that I take a different line from Allen Chun and others on these subjects.[88]

CONCLUSION

Some further words on the survey itself are warranted. Far from perfect, the survey sheets produced from 1900 to 1904 were considered, postwar, to be "inadequate for efficient land administration". Pressured by the needs of development, a new survey was begun in 1957.[89] However, a complete re-survey was determined upon, to include the contouring essential to the new development and engineering schemes, and in 1963 a contract for an air survey of the Colony was awarded.[90] Nonetheless, problems ascribable to the original Survey and Land Settlement continued to cause difficulties for all concerned,[91] albeit the survey's shortcomings had been made known by the chief surveyor from the outset.[92]

4

"Give and Take" in the New Territory up to 1941

THE DISTRICT ADMINISTRATION[1]

By the time the Land Court had finished its work and the new District Land Registries had been set up, a pattern of administration had been evolved that met British requirements, but it was not until 1910 that a new department was created under the title of "District Office".[2] Each of its two principal officials exercised the combined duties of several posts: namely, District Officer (for general administration and limited civil jurisdiction), Assistant Land Officer (for registry and land matters), Assistant Superintendent of Police (for police and criminal cases), and Collector of general revenue and Crown Rent, and each was gazetted in these appointments.[3] The two were empowered under various Ordinances and Regulations, of which the most important, and lasting, was the New Territories Ordinance of 1910, described by the Attorney-General in Legislative Council as "a consolidation Bill [whose] object is to consolidate the entire laws governing the New Territories". This had replaced the New Territories Land Ordinance 1905, more narrowly focused on land, being intended to "facilitate the transfer of land in the New Territories and for settling disputes in respect thereof, and for other purposes".[4]

The authorities were pleased with their new creation. "Simplicity always means economy", Governor Lugard told members of his Legislative Council in 1910, "and the New Territory is one of those parts of our administration which a conscientious official can look at complacently, knowing it is run economically if nothing else".[5]

However, the District Officers did not constitute an autonomous unit, but like the other departments of government were under the control of the Colonial Secretary and the Governor and his Councils, and financed from the centre.

CO-OPTION AND COOPERATION

As we have already seen, it was intended from the start to utilize the local leadership, and this resolve had not been blunted by the armed opposition encountered when the Hong Kong authorities went to take over the territory, even though this had been organized by some of the leading men of the northern NT.[6] The credit for this step must rest with Governor Blake who made special mention of his decision in a farewell address to the Legislative Council in late 1903:

> Two courses presented themselves — repression or co-operation. The leaders of the people had almost to a man actively engaged against us, but if these leaders were put aside and degraded from the position of local consideration and authority hitherto enjoyed by them, we should have been face to face with a hostile population, without the means of communicating with them through trusted local intermediaries whose assistance is so essential to good government.

Blake was, as Frank Welsh observes, "a large, cordial Irishman" who had at one time been a police officer and resident magistrate in Ireland.[7] With, as he told his Councillors, "some experience of coercion" there, he had explained to them why he advised against it. Thinking also that the leaders' opposition had been misguided, and occasioned by their having believed "the scandalous statements of our intentions that were so freely circulated" before the take-over of the territory, he had chosen cooperation.[8] More, in a manner that was typical of the man, he had gone out in person (as we have seen) to conciliate the assembled gentry and elders at Tai Po and Ping Shan a few months after the insurrection had been quelled.[9]

Those assembled to meet the Governor in each place were then styled "committee-men". This was because they had been appointed as such under the provisions of the Local Communities Ordinance passed in April 1899.[10] The Ordinance had also provided for district and sub-district courts comprising local leaders, and these were to exercise a limited civil and criminal jurisdiction, under supervision. However, there had been second thoughts, and all legal jurisdiction had been left in the hands of the officials charged with administering the territory.[11] Notwithstanding, it is plain from all the evidence available that the District Officers worked very closely with the old-style leadership during the forty years leading up to the Japanese attack on Hong Kong in 1941.

LOCAL LEADERS AND THEIR PLACE

Despite the loss of sub-soil rights and the income received from their perpetual lessees and other tillers of the soil, the major lineages of the New Territory were still a force to be reckoned with. A glimpse of the Tang lineage of Kam Tin in the early decades of British rule is afforded by W. H. Peplow, a Land Bailiff in the District Office, whose book published in 1930 provides many illuminating passages on the New Territories of his day. In the 1920s, he was given a silk scroll by a member of the lineage, which was still, he wrote, "probably one of the first and wealthiest families in the Territories". The scroll set out the history of the Tangs' principal ancestral grave in Tsuen Wan and the positions held by their ancestor's various descendants from the Song dynasty onwards, ending with some late Qing appointments to office. "Up to the present," it was proudly (if rather erroneously) announced, "the Tang family is still as prosperous, rich and noble as ever."[12]

The respect accorded to such men and their influence with the people led the authorities to make greater use of their talents. In 1926, they had invested several with the title of Tsz Yi, or "Head-boroughs" as they were styled in the District Officer, North's annual report:

> The appointment, which is honorary, lasts a year, and confers a valued recognition on the long and faithful service rendered by men without whose help the thirty years' successful administration of the District would have been, if not impossible, at least a much more difficult and onerous task.[13]

They included at least one Tang. These appointments would have been welcomed by the recipients and by the New Territories' community at large, and as the DO's frank acknowledgements make clear, these men's assistance was needed and greatly valued.[14]

The help given by other leaders in various parts of the Territory had long been acknowledged too.[15] Township heads (known as *Kaifongs*), village headmen (*Heung Cheung*) and lineage heads had all played a most important supporting role under Chinese rule and would continue to do so under the British. Generally speaking, they had not aspired to higher education or official posts, but they were often men of some calibre, with a great deal of authority in local business so long as they carried the community with them.

As under the Chinese arrangements, their posts were not accorded official recognition.[16] Nonetheless, one need only read Peplow's account of his District Officer's visit to Tai O on Lantau Island, to try cases in the local police station (like other outlying stations gazetted as a Court for this purpose) and to attend to local land and other business, to realize that these men were a necessary adjunct to the work of the District Administration. "The head Kai-fong is generally the first man to greet us, and he is by virtue of his position asked to accept a seat near the D.O.". He would also accompany the DO's party when it toured around the place to deal with local matters needing his attention (see Plate 16).[17] They would, of course, walk, as unlike the Chinese officials before 1898, the British District Officers did not use chairs — another point of difference, albeit a minor one.[18] Underpinning the police and the District Officers, such men were an indispensable factor in the maintenance of harmony and good order in normal times. Relying on elites had been the name of the game for a very long time, and not only in Hong Kong.[19] Plate 17 shows a typical gentry member of the day.

Nor should it be overlooked that the routine management of their townships, villages and sub-districts continued to rest with such men and their helpers. In the case of the Kaifong bodies in the townships, this remained the case until, in the late 1950s, the government began to provide more direct services to these well-populated communities. I am not aware of any prewar descriptions of their duties, but some early postwar accounts give a good idea of what these were.[20]

A NEW STYLE OF GOVERNMENT

From the outset, the colonial authorities had promised better government than had obtained under Chinese rule. Their good intentions were soon made clear. In the spring of 1902, one of the periodic "water famines" (as they were called at the time) had led to water being brought in lighters from Tsuen Wan to Hong Kong.[21] The *Blue Book* mentions a payment of $333, "Compensation for stoppage of sandal-wood mill near Tsun Wan and for use of Mill Race during water famine, 1902". A novel experience for those concerned, even more remarkable than the payment of compensation were the attempts to find the rightful payee, it being recorded that "The delay in settling this matter arose from the death of the owner of the mill and the difficulty of ascertaining to whom the money should be paid, his relatives residing in the interior of China".[22]

This care and concern in regard to compensation must have been gratifying. However, it had also showed that the authorities would not hesitate to take back leased land for development projects whenever the need arose.

TAKING BACK

The constant search for water sufficient to meet the needs of the ever-growing urban population meant that Waterworks schemes would be high on the list of projects for which there was a "land-take". The provision of extra water storage at the Kowloon Reservoir in 1910, with a further extension to it in 1923 which required the removal of an entire village, was followed in 1928 by the clearance of the eight settlements of the Shing Mun valley with their 855 inhabitants for the Shing Mun, or Jubilee, Reservoir, to be completed in 1935.[23]

Roads and railways were other major takers of private land. The construction of the road to Taipo in the early years took cultivated land at many places along the route. This was followed by the border road connecting Yuen Long with Castle Peak in 1910, and later by the western route through Tsuen Wan and on to Castle Peak between 1917–20.[24] The Kowloon-Canton Railway (British Section) also took its share of village land, including a maintenance strip, and likewise the light railway between Castle Peak and Sha Tau Kok, built in 1921. Year by year, minor improvements to roads were also being put in hand.[25]

A more unusual resumption was for an aerodrome, as it was styled at the time.[26] In 1936, in the centre of the large Pat Heung plain, 277 acres were purchased and leveled for this purpose, though never used as such. This land was taken over by the government's Agricultural Department in 1947 to be developed as an experimental and demonstration station, but as only a small portion was being used, the rest was let to local farmers on annual tenancy.[27] The former owners of this land could hardly have been pleased.

In all cases, compensation was paid for resumed land, as this was now the norm under colonial rule, and where villages were required to be removed, alternative sites would be provided by the government, on which the displaced villagers could build new houses with the cash compensation paid for properties owned in their old homes.

POLICING THE NEW TERRITORY

The work of the colonial police in the NT was as important for its law-abiding inhabitants as that of the District Administration. Its task was exacting. Besides policing the land, including the frontier, a marine force was needed to maintain law and order in the waters of the Colony. A later Commissioner of Police (D. W. MacIntosh) estimated these to take in 500 miles of coastline and 600 square miles of sea.[28] Many villages could only be reached by sea, and these were constituted as two "launch districts" for policing and emergency purposes.[29]

The land frontier was a special problem, owing to its geographical nature and the fact that it was crossed daily by many people.[30] It was described in the Commissioner's booklet as being:

> a river, which starts on the west from a bay called Deep Bay. The river narrows quickly to a stream but over two bridges and by boat ferries comes and goes the movement [of people] from China. Some eight miles almost due east, the stream becomes a mere trickle and then a ravine through the hills where the frontier emerges at the eastern landward end at another bay called Mirs Bay. Both bays are widely used for both fishing and boat traffic.

To assist in maintaining law and order, a network of police stations was built across the territory, connected by telephone to each other and to police headquarters.[31] Other stations made use of existing accommodation, as at Tung Chung on Lantau Island where it was located inside an old Chinese walled fort. Liaison and goodwill between the Police and the District Administration was necessary and mutually advantageous.[32]

The unsettled times in China after the 1911 Revolution were reflected in growing lawlessness in Hong Kong and the New Territories. Armed robbery and kidnapping for ransom were prevalent, and the work of the police rendered more difficult through the plentiful availability of firearms across the border and the large numbers of men trained in their use.[33] The impact of troubled times was probably most evident at the Sino-British border and adjoining areas, where bandits, guerrillas, and warlord armies contributed to the disturbances which so often occurred there in those years, and indeed before.[34]

In a published memoir, an ex-Chief Inspector recalled how he had led a police operation against a gang of thieves intent upon the robbery, abduction and blackmail of the operator of a distillery built in a remote location on the coast at Gindrinkers Bay, though not far from Kowloon. The raid was foiled, and the chief robber was shot dead by the author, who was awarded the King's Police Medal for Gallantry on that occasion.[35]

Among the many incidents featured in annual police reports, those occurring at Cheung Chau in 1912 and Tai O in 1925 received the most detailed coverage. The Cheung Chau police station was attacked, three Indian constables shot, the safe (containing the Crown Rent collection and taxes) was ransacked, all arms and accoutrements were taken, and a pawn shop looted, before the gang of "pirates and robbers about 40 strong" escaped as they had come, by sea.[36] In the Tai O attack, a gang of "60 armed bandits" landed from a large white launch, held up and robbed the inmates of 35 houses and shops, killed a woman and wounded another, kidnapped two villagers, and left without hindrance from the police who were in entire ignorance of the raid throughout.[37]

By the 1930s, the Police Force comprised four Contingents (as they were styled), European, Indian, Chinese (Cantonese) and Chinese (Wei Hai Wei, meaning from North China). In 1935, these numbered 265, 796, 712 and 300 respectively. There was a Marine Division, with steam launches and motor boats, and Police also controlled the Anti-Piracy Guards employed and paid for by shipping companies, and registered and supervised private watchmen.[38]

Other fields of government activity included revenue protection, the special concern not of the Police but the new Preventive Service established in 1909. The production of Chinese wines in unlicensed stills, together with salt and opium smuggling into China, were common in this period. The villagers saw no reason to pay the duty introduced by the colonial government to help pay for the administration of the NT.[39] However, because (so the officials said) the villagers were hiring out equipment to "small distillers put out of business by the more stringent controls [in town]", and the greater part of the wine was being sent to Hong Kong for urban consumption or export, the unlicensed and now illegal activities soon attracted the attention of the Service. Its colourfully worded reports give vivid accounts of the repeated raids made on some villages which, it was affirmed indignantly, "regarded the distilling of illicit alcohol as their main source of income".[40]

INCOMERS

While, all along, the indigenous population had pursued the even tenor of its ways,[41] determined groups of very different kinds would enter the Colony during the 1920s and 30s. Unlike the majority of those sojourners seeking work there, or the much larger numbers who would flee from the invading Japanese, these persons were intent upon staying.

Some were farmers, like those settling in Tsuen Wan and Kwai Chung after the Communist disturbances in northeast Guangdong; others were monks and other religious personnel seeking the peace and quiet afforded by the rural NT.[42] A few were military men, warlords for whom the game was over in the areas where they had held sway. There were a number in this latter group, among them Shen Hongying of Guangxi (1874–1939). Defeated by rival forces in 1924, he had purchased ten acres of farmland at Fung Kat Heung in the upper reaches of the Shek Kong (Pat Heung) Valley, where he built a grand mansion complex which is still standing today, complete with ancestral hall and guest quarters, to which he retired with his seven wives.[43] Among lesser settlers was Yuen Wah-chiu, an East River smuggler and minor warlord, famed for his accurate, not to say deadly, pistol shooting, who built a walled farmhouse for himself at Mui Wo (Silvermine Bay) on Lantau Island in the 1930s, and served postwar as chairman of the Mui Wo Rural Committee, in which capacity I saw him frequently in his later years.

IMPROVEMENTS IN THE TOWNSHIPS

The main townships in the New Territory were at Tai Po and Yuen Long. In 1905, they were reported to have 74 shops (twenty-five of them large) and 38 (twenty-three of them large) respectively. There were some smaller townships elsewhere, plus the much larger coastal market centres at Cheung Chau and Tai O, with some others in places where there was an anchorage for boat people.[44] I shall here confine myself to the situation at Tai Po, Yuen Long and Tsuen Wan during the inter-war period.

The annual departmental reports of the District Officers, so indispensable to charting their progress, indicate an increased prosperity in the decade 1911–1920. A report for 1917 mentions how "the improved communications bring other means of money-making, and there is everywhere a gradual increase in comfort and improvement in the standard of living". Wages had also risen, and "there can be no doubt that there is more money in the Territory ...". At Tai Po Market there had been a considerable rise in the cost of living: "now 50 per cent higher than it was ten years ago".[45] It is not surprising, then, to read in the 1917 report that the township had "displayed a good deal of vitality during the year, and there was a considerable demand for building lots". From later reports, they were located on first one, then two government reclamations, with new houses and shops going up steadily.[46] By 1926, it was found necessary to level and surface open space there "to take the stalls which now on market days crowd the narrow streets".[47] In 1931, a large site had been sold to the China Light and Power Company on which it would erect its headquarters and works for the New Territory.[48] All told, development had been fairly steady, and by 1934, a Public Works Department official reported that there were already 120 houses of the first class in the township.[49] These developments were all in the Tai Po New Market. The Old Market, long declining, had suffered a further setback during the typhoon of 1937, when no fewer than 60 houses were carried away in a great tidal flood that swept up Tolo Harbour.[50]

At Yuen Long, the prewar record was somehow more exciting. Dissatisfied with the Tang lineage's centuries old control of the Old Market, the Hop Yick Company had been founded in 1916 by leaders of three of the village areas traditionally doing business there, to establish a new market. Its popularity enhanced by the financial assistance given to the local hospital and other charities, this soon eclipsed the Old Market whose profits had all gone to its private owners. Despite a bad year in 1918, when business was bad and a fire destroyed 25 old shops, the township was steadily expanding.[51] In 1931, with "large developments in progress" being reported,[52] Yuen Long would soon go from strength to strength. The 1934 report enthusiastically detailed the position:

> Most striking is the way in which the Yuen Long market town is growing. Here during the year some 40 large new shops and family houses facing wide roads have been erected to a regular lay-out plan on a large area reclaimed from the creek to the North of the town. ... The work of laying a main water supply to Yuen Long was almost completed by the Public Works department and the supply should be available in 1935.[53]

And yet the number of superior houses was less than at Tai Po.[54]

A look at Tsuen Wan during this period is instructive for comparisons with Yuen Long and Tai Po. Although included in a Government Notification of 1918 which applied special conditions of sale to the NT market towns and a few other places in which non-village development was proceeding,[55] central Tsuen Wan only showed real progress at the end of the inter-war period. A new market and a layout for two new streets seem to have been the catalyst, as shown in the District Officer's annual report for 1936:

> Since the opening of the market, plans for the erection of 29 new modern style houses, in accordance with the new layout, have been submitted and it is hoped the buildings will be completed in 1937. Prospects of a new reclamation with wharfage facilities and of a modern layout for the new town have caused a great increase in land values, from five to ten times in actual cases, in the neighbourhood of the market.[56]

Otherwise, Tsuen Wan's development in those years was mainly industrial, owing something to its proximity to Hong Kong's port and harbour, abundant hill water, and improved communications with the city by land and sea.[57]

After providing a limited mains water supply in the early 1930s, the government had decided to impose a water rate on Tsuen Wan's central area, together with the general rating charge already levied at Tai Po and Yuen Long. These proposals provoked a storm of protests from the Tsuen Wan elders. The District Officer was unsympathetic. "What they are really saying", he remarked acidly, "is that they would prefer dirty well-water to pure water for which they have to pay".[58] He was more understanding about their opposition to the intended general rating, pointing out to his superiors that the case for applying it was indubitably weaker:

> At Tai Po Market there is a whole system of streets provided and maintained by Government, but at Un Long such "streets" as exist apart from the main road have been provided by private enterprise, and at Tsun Wan no such streets have yet been provided.

He then provided a balance sheet, listing what Tsuen Wan received and did not receive from government, from which it was clear that "most of the amenities for which rates are normally charged are lacking in Tsuen Wan", one example being government-provided medical services.[59]

Asked to provide a technical report on the water supply at Tai Po and Tsuen Wan, a representative of the Director of Public Works had commented that "Taipo property is of a much higher type than that at Tsun Wan".[60] A new DO, minuting on one of the central villages, wrote that "it is old and will obviously not develop in any way. On a walk through, I saw hardly a single young man — nothing but the old, the halt, and the lame".[61]

In their petitions to government the Tsuen Wan leaders averred that Government had done little for the township, and that local people were poor and could not bear the additional burden of rates.[62] Using the exaggerated but picturesque language that so often characterized Chinese villagers' representations to their rulers, they made their objections known at all levels, from the Colonial Secretary and the Secretary for Chinese Affairs downwards.[63] They succeeded to a degree, albeit none of these officials were very pleased.[64] The amendment to the Rating Ordinance was passed and brought into law, but concessionary rating was applied for a time in Tsuen Wan.

Drawing on government reports, these accounts of inter-war developments in the main market towns of the NT can easily mask an essential truth: that the local committees, rather than the government, were the real everyday movers in the market towns. Residents owed practically everything to their own leaders, men of the kind whose abilities and assistance were, as we have seen, so freely acknowledged.

Meantime, in 1933, electric lighting had been extended to Castle Peak and Sha Tau Kok, but, wrote the District Officer, "though very popular in the market towns, electricity is not being used to any great extent in the villages, nor is it likely to be until some reduction is made in the price of current".[65] A cinema was reported to be operating at Tai Po, but "films are not very popular, and actors of flesh and blood are preferred".[66] In 1935, all postal work in the Northern District (such as it was) was taken over by the Post Office department, with branch post offices as Tai Po and Yuen Long, pillar post boxes at convenient places along the roads, and collections and deliveries by postal messengers on bicycles.[67] Another sign of change in these years was the introduction of the Registration of Births and Deaths Ordinance into the NT in 1932, to be effected through the police stations. By 1934, too optimistic by far, the DO South was stating that "Registration is rapidly becoming a habit with the villagers".[68]

RURAL EDUCATION

Since the Lease, the government had taken some steps to improve rural education and to provide modern facilities in major centres. The "Government Tai Po Vernacular Normal School" had been opened in 1925, and the "Cheung Chau Anglo-Chinese School" in 1928, while the "Un [Yuen] Long Government School" was converted from an English to a "Higher Primary Vernacular School" in 1936. Nomenclature and curricula in government schools were fluid (and in retrospect rather confusing) at this time.[69]

In keeping with the shortfalls reported during the rating saga, there was no government school in Tsuen Wan until the early postwar period, with an almost total reliance on the private initiatives that continued to provide primary schools in the old mould right up to the War. In some of the better-off families the boys, and sometimes girls, were sent elsewhere to be educated. Some provision was also being made by church bodies, and in 1913 the District Officer reported that "Tsun Wan (sic) sends fifteen boys to school in Canton at a cost of $1,000 in school fees".[70] As in some other places, the limited opportunities available locally were augmented by government scholarships to attend schools in the urban area.[71]

The "five great clans" were also contributing. The main ancestral halls of the Lius at Sheung Shui and the Tangs at Ping Shan were used for educational purposes, as had probably ever been the case, but more formal, modernized schools, registered with the Education Department and receiving a government subsidy, were now the fashion among large lineages with progressive leaders.[72]

IMPROVED COMMUNICATIONS

Until modernization of communications and services, with the appearance of franchised companies operating to government requirements and supervision, outlying places had to rely on private or local enterprise. The first mention of a motor bus service in the New Territories was made in the District Officer's report for 1919, with a service between Yuen Long and Sheung Shui.[73] In 1933, regular bus services were inaugurated by the Kowloon Motor Bus Company, a private concern which is still serving the Hong Kong public today. Its scheduled services to different parts of the New Territories are mentioned in a Chinese language guide book of 1938.[74]

Safe and reliable transportation by sea came just before the Second World War. The Hong Kong and Yaumati Ferry Company, also established in 1933 and, until recently, a public utility, had begun a regular scheduled ferry service from Hong Kong to outlying ports in the NT. Its vessels provided a more certain timetable than those of the cargo sailing junks and steam launches of local companies, whose main function had been to transport goods and livestock.[75] This too was a very good service, provided the ferry boats were reliable.[76]

Hitherto, villagers had had to walk to their destinations, near and far, often carrying heavy loads save when they traveled by boat. If they wished to take advantage of the new bus and ferry services with their advertised fixed schedules, they would have to add the cost of travel to their profit and loss calculations. Villagers took some time to adjust their thinking to the new conditions, a situation to be oft repeated in country areas in the years ahead.

Yet many New Territories' villagers travelled far on occasion, especially at the Lunar New Year, when the measure of the devotion attached to the family cult could be measured by the long journeys made to the home villages. A man born on Lamma Island in 1883, whose grandfather had settled there from the Taipo area of the mainland New Territories, told me in 1958 that he had gone back to their native village three times a year ever since he could remember. After taking a sailing junk to Kowloon, the family would walk the rest of the way, children included, there being no railway until 1910, and no bus services until the 1930s. Others travelled even further afield, to villages north of the Sino-British border.

WESTERNERS AND URBAN CHINESE IN THE NT

From before the Lease, Hong Kong's Westerners had been seduced by the charms of the adjoining mainland.[77] With the coming of the new roads and railway, and growing use of the motor car, increasing numbers of them visited the fine swimming beaches along the Castle Peak Road, and the new golf course constructed at Fanling in 1912.[78] The hills and mountains were an attraction for others who liked more strenuous exercise. There were also some who liked to hunt and shoot there.[79]

The Fanling golf course is of special interest, because its history has been enlivened with the cheerful anecdotes of Eric Hamilton, a former District Officer. Taking advantage of the NT Lease, after protracted negotiations with the government the Royal Hong Kong Golf Club (founded in 1889) laid out a course at Fanling in the same year as the Kowloon-Canton Railway (British Section) was completed, in 1910. Much of the ground at Fanling had been Crown land, scrub and heath, with few trees, and a forestry planting programme was put in hand. Relations with local villagers were reported to be good. Any fields needed for the course were all purchased by the Club, not resumed by the government, burial urns damaged by golfers had been compensated and moved elsewhere, small boys were required as caddies and earned good money, while adult villagers accompanying Westerners out shooting quail all over the plain, or snipe and wild duck in the Mai Po Marshes, got ten and twenty cent Hong Kong silver pieces for their pains, which could buy much more in nearby Sham Chun (Shenzhen) Market than the old Chinese currency then in use there. In recounting these facts, Hamilton concluded, "... to this pleasant and profitable liaison with the local villagers I put down the peaceful and easy development of the Club". The close relationship of the District Officers with the village elders was cited as another factor, as was the fact that the villagers were used to foreigners, so that, as Hamilton wrote, "the golfers did not descend upon the villagers like the crews of flying saucers".[80]

Meantime, hiking in the New Territory had also become very popular. Graham Heywood's engaging little book *Rambles in Hong Kong*, first published in 1939, describes the walking excursions of a band of friends who loved to tramp the length and breadth of the Colony. Some of their walks were scarcely rambles.[81] These visitors to the New Territories could observe the local life as well as take in the scenery, and persons like Herklots, Heywood, and the Sterickers have enriched the record with their published descriptions of things seen and done in the course of their excursions.[82]

Yet Westerners were not the only visitors. By the 1920s they were being joined by enthusiastic parties of urban Chinese. Guidebooks to the historic and scenic spots of the New Territories in Chinese language would soon appear in the bookshops of the Colony. Intended solely for young and active modern-educated Chinese, they were an indication that the pursuit of leisure activities in the NT would no longer be left exclusively to Europeans. Mr. Ng Bar-ling (1904–1976), a journalist, collector and writer, whose collection of Hong Kong memorabilia was donated to the University of Hong Kong in the late 1970s, was one of the founders of a hiking club, the Yung She, which is still operating.[83] In a less strenuous fashion, the acquiring of country houses in the NT to which friends of both races might be invited for genteel entertainment also became fashionable at this time.

Some Europeans chose to live there, happy amid rural surroundings and embedded in the community. Mrs. Gloria Baretto, recalling the 1920s and 1930s when her family lived in the Northern New Territories, wrote of how her father, a solicitor in the city, was constantly approached by villagers at his home in the evenings. The room where she did her homework was near the one in which they were conversing, and scraps of conversation drifted through. "There was, often, talk of Wuis,[84] and Chinese law, customs in marriage contracts, the kit fat (or principal) wife and her rights, of harvest tithes, farmers' servitude to money lenders, local land laws". He (Leo D'Almada) must have been a patient and courteous man, with a liking for, and a rapport with, village people, and they in turn must have appreciated his assistance and forbearance.[85]

THE OFFICIAL VIEW OF THE NT

Despite the progress recorded in this chapter, the government's view of the New Territories may be judged by the postings of "Cadets" to the New Territories Districts. By the late 1920s, in a trend still being followed much later in the century, it had become common to send younger officers there.[86] However, it had not been ever thus. As Eric Hamilton, who served for most of 1915–1923 in the Southern District, recounts:

> Sometime about 1922 [Governor Sir Edward] Stubbs sent for Tratman, Wood and myself and read the riot act, informing us that "the New Territories were no doubt very interesting and picturesque but they

were of no serious importance in the Administration of Hong Kong, and would we kindly remember it!", or words to that effect. In that year, Tratman had 18 years service, Wood 15, and I eleven!

All three had served in the District Administration for lengthy periods by then. Hamilton continues:

> It was a bomb-shell. We retired to the Hong Kong Hotel and had three big brandies and ginger ale apiece — and what we said about Stubbs was not printable. But as things were then, Stubbs was right.[87]

In short, the New Territory was a place that could be left to itself, one in which Cadet (Administrative) Officers should not be left too long, but extracted to do their fair share of more important work.

There was, in truth, some reason for taking this attitude. Stubbs had delivered his lecture soon after the 1921 Census. The total population had been found to be 625,166, an increase of 168,427 or 36.87 per cent on the figures for 1911, "the greatest relative increase ever recorded for the Colony".[88] Practically all of it was recorded in the old urban area. The NT accounted for only one-seventh of the whole, and "of the remaining six-tenths the great majority are an urban population, massed round the shores of Hongkong Harbour, the majority at present residing on the northern shore of the Island of Hong Kong".[89]

By the 1931 census, the land population had soared to 838,800.[90] Hong Kong was growing fast, and with the New Territory (the market towns excepted) still largely resting quietly in the bosom of the past, it was assuredly the least of its administrators' concerns.[91] However, by the end of the decade, all parts of the Colony were to experience the shock of war, first in China and later in Hong Kong itself.

5

New Territories People and the Japanese Occupation 1941–1945

In Hong Kong's centenary year, Japan attacked and captured the Colony after just over a fortnight's fighting. Three years and eight months of wartime occupation followed.

After over forty years of British rule in the New Territories, its still largely indigenous population was to experience the rigorous controls imposed by Japan in the former Colony, and the brutal, sometimes savage, conduct of its military and police authorities there. This jolted a population which under both Chinese and British rule had been accustomed to a slacker rein.

As it happened, the Japanese Occupation was to reveal another facet of the Hong Kong–Kowloon and New Territories relationship. This was the unexpected degree of support coming from the New Territories population. Matched by risk-taking and heroism, assistance was given to British and other Western escapees, by landsmen and boat people alike. There was also military resistance against the Japanese by Communist guerrillas in various areas of the NT, notably to the east of Kowloon, in which some native villagers took part. These phenomena must be placed in their proper context.

THE JAPANESE FEARED

Japan's undeclared war in China had begun in Shanghai and the North in August 1937.[1] Many Chinese took refuge in Hong Kong, especially after Canton was captured in 1938. The flood of refugees continued, and by 1941, almost half the Colony's population had entered since the 1931 Census.[2] This large group, even more than the rest of Hong Kong's Chinese residents, had good cause to fear the coming of the Japanese, as during air, sea and land operations in mainland China, the Japanese military forces' behaviour towards civilians had been (and continued to be) appalling. In Lord Russell of Liverpool's prophetic words, "The full extent of these crimes will never be accurately known, but in China they will never be forgotten".[3]

The resident and visiting boat people of the Colony had equally good reason for great anxiety. In September 1937, the Japanese Navy had instituted a blockade of the China coast. The fact that Hong Kong, Macau, and Kwangchouwan were under foreign rule had not deterred it from attacking the fishing fleets based on these places. The Hong Kong Chinese Fishermen's Guild reported that, by May 1938, a total of 412 junks had been burned or sunk, with a minimum estimate of 8,430 men, women and children, killed, drowned or burned to death. The monetary loss suffered by the Hong Kong fishing community was placed at 5 million Hong Kong dollars.[4] Boats operating from the major NT fishing ports with their families on board, must have suffered with the rest.

FLIGHT, AND LOCAL DISORDERS

In the New Territories, many village families sought to get out of the way of the advancing Japanese troops, and took to the hills behind their villages for a time. Some returned to China, especially those who had not been in Hong Kong for more than two generations and still had close relatives living in their native place.[5]

Meantime, bands of robbers and petty bandits took advantage of the confused and uncertain period between the British withdrawal (followed by the surrender) and the re-establishment of law and order by the Japanese army. In Tsuen Wan, a gang of robbers had attacked shops in the old market street, and meeting with armed resistance from one of the larger premises had set fire to the whole street. Sai Kung Market and many of the local villages suffered likewise. At Mui Wo, on Lantau Island, a gang from the East River area of Guangdong led by a ruffian known as "Seven-headed Lee" had been especially active just before Japanese troops arrived on the island, robbing houses where several rich men were rumoured to live.[6] On nearby Cheung Chau, however, the island's Kaifong leaders had managed to stave off similar attacks.[7] Most of these bandits were said to have come into the Colony from districts adjoining Hong Kong.

Shortly after the fighting had ceased, the victors set up a military government on Hong Kong Island, and sent troops to occupy the market towns and other main centres of population in the New Territories.[8] They then turned their minds to managing their new acquisition.

JAPANESE ADMINISTRATION: THE DISTRICT BUREAUX

In an article prepared during wartime internment in Stanley Camp, Kathleen J. Heasman, formerly lecturer in economics at the University of Hong Kong, described the system of local administration being followed during the Occupation:

> Japanese administration was exercised through the different departments of the Governor's office ... In so far as they affect the daily life of the Chinese, such matters were decentralized in the district bureau. There are three main Bureaux:- in Hong Kong, Kowloon and New Territories at Tai Po. Each of these was controlled by a Japanese with a Chinese staff. These are divided into Districts, 12 in Hong Kong, 9 in Kowloon and 4 in the New Territories. They were thus to be based on custom in Japan and should be self-supporting.[9]

Miss Heasman's account of the bodies at district level states succinctly that:

> The matters which the Bureaux dealt with were: taking of census, issue of ration tickets, removal and travel permits, birth and death certificates and other local affairs. They undertook the general supervision of persons within the district, in which at first they were aided by the Streetguards. They were responsible for carrying out the educational, cleanliness and health measures decided by the Government.[10]

One particular requirement was for householders to maintain door placards giving details of all occupants. This information was required to facilitate the census and registration work of the self-governing offices, and to keep check on house occupancy and the movements of people. Surviving documentation from the period reflects the extent to which daily life and activities were controlled during these years.[11] An account of the workings of one such bureau is provided in my book on Tsuen Wan (1993).[12]

MUTUAL RESPONSIBILITY IMPOSED

As in the city, the Japanese military authorities expected the New Territories' leaders to form, support and manage their local offices. There was no eagerness on their part to take up these duties, but as the acknowledged leaders of the people, there had been no option. All bureaux were expected to apply the doctrine of "mutual responsibility" within their areas. Heads of households and groups of households, and ultimately the leaders of each lineage, village community or town ward, were deemed responsible for the actions and good behaviour of their residents. Known as *pao-chia* in China and *hoko* (*pao-kao*) in Japan, this was the traditional method of control intermittently practiced in China, but followed far more closely in Japan and its colonial empire, and now extended to territories under its wartime occupation.[13]

This once familiar system had been seldom applied by the British administration, which generally emphasized the individual's personal responsibility under the law. Its reimposition in Occupied Hong Kong, under severe and much more stringent police controls, was assuredly one of the most feared and detested aspects of Japanese wartime rule.

The respect and obedience enjoined upon all by the Japanese military administration are perhaps best exemplified in the presence of a police headquarters in each bureau area: in effect, the seat of all local authority.[14] Sentries were posted outside it, and since in their persons they were considered to represent the Japanese imperial power, all passers-by were expected to bow towards them in the prescribed fashion. This was a universal requirement in Occupied Hong Kong.[15] Failure to bow in the manner indicated, brought cuffs and slaps, at the least.

LABOUR REQUIREMENTS FOR MILITARY WORKS

The local self-governing offices were expected to respond to Japanese demands for assistance of varied kinds. In Tsuen Wan and Sai Kung, the most notable was for labour to construct access roads to the Japanese wireless station on Tai Mo Shan and from Clear Water Bay into Sai Kung.[16] Labour was also required in places like Mui Wo (Lantau) and Lamma Island to make tunnels and caves for coastal observation and defence. Villagers who had to work on these projects said that conscription was not applied, even though many hands were required and reported gangs of over 100 workers. Men, women and children were glad to come forward, for the sake of the rice that was doled out in lieu of cash payments. "One scoop for us men, and half for women and child workers", as one of the Tsuen Wan villagers recalled. The Sai Kung experience was similar.[17]

The Japanese also recruited workers to go to Hainan Island, then also under their wartime occupation. Quite a number of male villagers went voluntarily from Tsuen Wan. Nearly fifty years later, ten elderly men from Muk Min Ha Village readily recalled the names of six or seven workers from their village — all members of their Ho lineage, and therefore cousins or brothers — who had not returned, and been reported or presumed dead.[18]

SURVEILLANCE AND SEVERITY

By using the information available through the extensive bureaucracy, and by leaning on household heads, lineage and village elders, and local leaders through the "mutual responsibility" system — aided, too, by its own network of informers — the Japanese gendarmerie, together with the Kempeitai or military police whose remit also embraced civilians,[19] maintained a strict overseeing of the population.[20] It was a surveillance which could quickly degenerate into a reign of terror if anything went wrong.

Owing to its size and difficult terrain, the Japanese authorities were especially vigilant in the New Territories, but were less able to control them. In so far as they could, their policy was to restrict movement, in order to make it easier to identify persons engaged in subversion. The Japanese forbade villagers from gathering fuel on the hills — in effect, to keep them from moving about the hillsides, as they were always wont to do. When times were already hard, this was a great deprivation indeed. As we have seen, village people used grass and firewood in their stoves, and sold them to maintain a livelihood. The restrictions also curtailed the activities and livelihood of plant-gatherers and herbal doctors from the villages, and hindered the very common gathering of plants and herbs for baths and infusions when some member of the family was unwell. The ban would explain why so many villagers have said that they did not visit their ancestral graves during the Occupation, meaning in particular those in remote upland locations. Such a break with traditional practice could only have been brought about by the unusually strong inhibitions resulting from Japanese severity. Some villagers defied the ban, but did so at their peril.[21]

Extreme sanctions were applied to offenders against public order, real or imagined.[22] Persons under suspicion were given short thrift. When the village head of Shek Pik on Lantau Island was shot dead by guerilla fighters on his way home from market at Tai O in the early part of the Occupation — he had complied with Japanese demands for food supplies — the three village men who were with him at the time were arrested and detained on suspicion of complicity. All three died during detention in the former Tai O police station, reportedly from deprivation of food, water and clothing, and general ill-treatment.[23]

GUERRILLA ACTIVITY AND THE VILLAGERS

Complicating the situation for all residents was the fact that, as now appears, not a few villagers had joined the guerrillas and were operating with them in various places.[24] It will become obvious from this chapter that the anti-Japanese groups were of different kinds, some being almost as hard on the rural population as their military occupiers. The Japanese garrisons also encountered resistance in the occupied parts of Guangdong during the war, including the area just over the Sino-British border.[25] These activities may be seen as part of a universal movement to harass Japanese units across Occupied China.[26]

Liu Shuyong's *Outline History of Hong Kong* (1997) gives a brief account of the organization for guerilla operations carried out during this period. It seems that a Hong Kong–Kowloon brigade of the Guangdong People's Anti-Japanese Guerrilla Force was established in January 1942 and commenced operations in Hong Kong territory as and when opportunities arose. In December 1943, the Guangdong Force was instructed to form the Dongjiang (East River) Column, absorbing the Hong Kong–Kowloon brigade into the larger unit.[27] Attacks on Japanese stationed in Shatin, New Kowloon and Lantau are mentioned in the same source, as well as assistance given to British and other escapees, including one American flyer, as well as liaison with the British Army Aid Group to obtain information needed for military operations. However, these activities goaded the Japanese into various "mopping up" operations on Lantau and in the eastern side of the New Territories.[28] Although useful in itself, more information is required to present a fuller picture of what really happened in the NT during the Occupation.

LANTAU ISLAND

The situation on Lantau Island is revealed in more detail (though still only in part) through press reports on War Crimes Trials held in Hong Kong in March–April 1946, and through my own enquiries there in the 1960s.[29] Evidence given at the trials shows that the Japanese military on Lantau in 1945 comprised a main detachment at Mui Wo, with a marine post at Tai O. There were, in addition, gendarmerie in various places, including Tung Chung. The immediate background to the incidents which gave rise to the prosecutions was an attack by guerrillas on the Tung Chung post in May 1945, in which a Japanese officer and five privates had been killed.

In August 1945, in the period between notification of the Japanese government's decision to accept unconditional surrender and the formal surrender ceremony, the post at Mui Wo had been attacked by a body of guerrillas, but without success. Immediately, the garrison rounded up all inhabitants of the Mui Wo villages and assembled them on the beach. The women and children and elderly men were released the next day, but around 20 younger men were tied to stakes, beaten, given the water torture, and kept without food or water for almost a week before they were released. During this period, nine persons lost their lives.

There was a so-called Peace Preservation Society at Mui Wo, comprising representatives from local villages (including Ngau Kwu Long and other hill villages of the area) and headed by the Mui Wo village leader.[30] From the evidence given, and consistent with the application of the principle of "mutual responsibility", it is clear that the Japanese held them responsible for the rest. Suspecting the villagers of complicity or participation in the attack, they had executed two of the Society's leaders. The headman of Ngau Kwu Long, whose village was attacked and burned on suspicion of involvement in the earlier attack on the police post at Tung Chung, suffered the same fate, along with two of the Mui Wo villagers. Three more men (two fishermen and another villager), ordered to row wounded soldiers to Kowloon, were never seen again, while a woman fuel-gatherer, bringing down her bundles of grass from the hill, was shot dead for no apparent reason.[31]

The form taken by reprisals was similar to those meted out elsewhere on the island, and also at Tsuen Wan and Tsing Yi.[32] The Japanese swooped on villages under suspicion for aiding guerrillas or participation in attacks on their troops and police, occasionally burning houses, and shooting or arresting villagers, detaining them under terrible conditions from which some died in custody.[33]

ROBBERS AND GUERRILLAS AT PUI O

Indicative of the times, and of the limited capability of the Japanese garrison to suppress disorders, a number of blockhouses were constructed here and at several places in the Mui Wo sub-district in the second winter of the Occupation, with stone cut or supplied by the villagers. As described to me, the structures had an upper floor for riflemen and a lower floor for miscellaneous use, including refuge in time of danger. They were reportedly not intended for use to repel Japanese troops (of whom there were too many) but to fend off robber bands coming from the Southwest.[34]

Usually, the Pui O villagers kept a look-out for Japanese, robbers, and guerrillas alike, since all spelt trouble. As at Shek Pik, they fell foul of guerrillas, who, one Lunar New Year, took away the village head of Lo Wai by boat after capturing him while playing cards around 2 or 3 a.m. in the Tin Hau Temple near the shore, the look-out men having most imprudently joined in. He had antagonized the guerrillas by refusing to allow them to stay in the village and in other small ways, and was never seen again. Another of the Pui O village heads was reportedly taken on a different occasion.

The guerrillas said to have operated on Lantau throughout the Occupation were led by an outsider and included other outsiders, as well as several men from each of many villages on the island. Their numbers rose from several tens to a claimed several hundred by 1945. Described as *yau kik tui*, they were neo-Communist, but not a regular Communist formation, such as the East River Column operating on the eastern side of the NT. They mostly avoided direct clashes with the Japanese, but operated by night to overwhelm sentries and take their weapons, or whenever favourable circumstances presented themselves.

ASSISTANCE GIVEN TO ESCAPEES AND OTHERS

Besides direct anti-Japanese activities, there must also be mentioned the assistance given by New Territories' people to escaping parties of prisoners of war and internees, and to members of the British Army Aid Group operating there during the Occupation.

A folder containing lists which provide specific information on who helped whom, where and when, signed off by John Barrow, the head of the District Administration, in 1946, gives a graphic picture of assistance rendered in hazardous times.[35] This was, he remarked, highlighted by the fact that in the months following the surrender of Hong Kong and the fall of Singapore, when it really seemed that British rule had gone for ever, there was far more reason to assist a feared and sometimes savage foe than to help persons belonging to the defeated forces of the former colonial power. Yet many villagers and boat people chose to do so. Moreover, escapees of different background all testified to the courage of the people who fed and assisted them, and were touched by what one of them called "the kindness and cheerfulness of ordinary Chinese" in difficult times.[36] Many had spontaneously offered food, shelter, guides, and even money to help them on their uncertain way. Later in the Occupation, assistance was also given to members of the British Army Aid Group, comprising escaped British and

Chinese personnel from Hong Kong who operated periodically in the NT and worked with Chinese guerilla units.

Another remarkable feature of help given over the whole period, was that in small villages, the entire community knew what was going on, but no one had alerted the Japanese. Needless to say, this was an exceedingly perilous business, for the persons caught, or even suspected of such actions, were severely punished. Imprisonment and torture followed for the latter, while instant execution was the lot of those actively involved.[37]

This heroic record surprised and gratified Barrow, who added this note to the list of "Certificates of Loyalty awarded to NT People":

> To my mind there were three reasons for the heroism displayed by New Territories people in 1942, after the fall of Singapore had become generally believed: Sheer goodness of heart and bravery; hatred of the Japanese; and traditional loyalty to us because of the links provided by our administration, by employment in firms such as shipping companies and the like, and by the tradition of emigration to such places as Jamaica, the Seychelles, etc.

The list included details of the many certificates awarded to deserving persons, and of the sums awarded to villages which had given conspicuous assistance to allied personnel. The money was usually placed in the hands of the village heads, in trust for the community. After the lists were finalized, presentations were made to those who had earned them, and a banner was presented to the Sai Kung leaders, in token of their sub-district's fine wartime record.[38] One other source of information is worth recording. After the war, a War Memorial Fund was established to pay regular allowances to widows whose husbands had been killed during the Occupation.[39]

FAMINE TOWARDS THE END OF THE OCCUPATION

For all its severity, the Japanese administration seems to have encouraged the expansion of local industries in the coastal market centres and market towns. It had also made considerable efforts to ensure a fair distribution of increasingly scarce essential commodities through a comprehensive rationing scheme for those whom it would allow to stay on in Hong Kong.[40] However, steadily deteriorating conditions undermined its efforts to ensure a basic level of subsistence. In the case of essential foodstuffs such as rice, flour, salt, sugar, and peanut oil, the rationing system broke down when steeply rising prices, the interruption of supplies, and lack of stocks, caused the rations to be suspended or decreased from time to time, and there was much adulteration. For these reasons, food rationing was virtually at an end by 1945.

Attempts to ration firewood — needed for cooking and just as essential as rice — were also ineffective in the face of severe shortages. For all commodities, most people had to rely on the black market or their own daring and ingenuity. By the closing months of the Occupation in the early summer of 1945, many people all over the territory were suffering from extreme malnutrition and were falling victim to disease.[41]

Living on its own land for the most part, one would have thought that the New Territories' population would have been better situated than urban dwellers, forever dependant upon the importation of foodstuffs. Yet it seems that in many places, the rural people were just as hard hit as the rest.[42]

One local narrative may help to explain what could have happened. At Shek Pik on Lantau Island, where the rice crop was subject to requisitioning by the Japanese soldiers who were stationed for a time in the village, stealing by fellow villagers — something strongly deprecated in normal times — had now to be guarded against. The village head recalled how an early ripening crop on fertilized fields had been stolen at harvest time; how his two sons had slept routinely in the fields before the next harvest to prevent this happening again; and how, in order to reap the crop the moment it was deemed ready, they had used their women folks' combs to ease the grains directly from the stalks, instead of cutting the rice stalks and shaking the heads into a tub as was usual. Haste had been essential.

Poor harvests (there was at least one in which worm had got into the ears of the ripening crop) had also created anxieties and dreadful uncertainties. His fellow villagers had been reduced to eating pineapple hearts, tree roots, grass, anything they could get their hands on, and a number had died of malnutrition and starvation. The temple keeper, by customary practice dependant on regulated hand-outs of rice from village families, had hung himself in one of its side rooms. Some family heads told me they had gone elsewhere to live, including the market town of Tai O, where one young couple had sold their infant son in order to buy food.[43]

Tenant rentals had been reduced during this period, for the first and only time during the elders' lifetime, owing to lack of money to buy food or fertilizers other than animal droppings, and because of diminished yields. This tallied with what I had been told during earlier conversations: that fields had sold for one-third of their former price, and that bride-price in wartime marriages was similarly reduced.

SALES OF LAND AND PROPERTY

Much land was sold during these years. Apart from the considerable number of deeds brought in for registration soon after the War,[44] cases kept coming up for the next thirty years and more. This was usually after the former registered owner of a property had died and succession was being applied for, when someone would present him or herself at the Office with proof of a still unregistered wartime transaction.[45] Drawn up in the customary form used for centuries in the region, the wording used in the text to justify these sales and mortgages of ancestral land was indicative of the general plight of many village people. These were losses for other reasons too.[46]

HIATUS

The gap between the unconditional surrender of Japan on 16 August and the arrival of a British fleet on 30 August created a hiatus of which unruly elements again took advantage. Thereafter, its commander assumed control of the Colony, and the Royal Navy became responsible for maintaining law and order in the city, until handing over to Major-General F. W. Festing and his Commando Brigade after they arrived on 11 September. Even then, there was still not an overall capability to provide support whenever and wherever needed.[47]

Cheung Chau offers an interesting example of what this extended vacuum had entailed. It appears from local leaders' correspondence with the District Officer, New Territories in 1946 that the island community had been left to its own devices from 16 August until some British troops were first sent there as late as 5 October 1945. This was only after their visit to his office in Kowloon the day before, asking him to take over control of the place. It was, in fact, their second, as they had gone to Hong Kong on 8 September on a similar mission, but reportedly (and understandably in view of the situation described above) without result, since the authorities had not then been in a position to do so.

The population had been in great fear of general disturbance after the Japanese withdrew, when members of the Hong Kong and Kowloon guerrilla force had come in to maintain order, but before long the local leaders had been obliged to do this for themselves.[48] Given the resources available to the provisional government and the military administration in this period, it seems highly likely that many (if not most) other outlying NT communities would have had to follow suit.

CONCLUSION

Though incomplete,[49] this account of the life in the New Territories during the Japanese Occupation helps to bring out the difference between the old and new parts of the Colony during this traumatic time. Most people in the old urban areas could go quietly about their business and hope for the best, but it was much more difficult to do so in the NT, where, between them, the Japanese police and military, the guerrillas, and bandits made life more fraught for all, subjecting the leadership at all levels to immense and prolonged strain, and potential or actual danger from all sides. We may infer that village and lineage heads simply could not please everybody, including their own people.

While many villagers and local boat people rendered loyal support to the British cause, others were patriotically inclined and ready to join the Communist units which were harassing the occupiers. In time, the British suspected local Communist leaders of having their own agenda.[50] By opening up new vistas, this may have led to a heightened political awareness in the territory and the questioning of old loyalties and acceptances inside the rural communities: resulting in what the anonymous author of the Hong Kong Annual Report for 1946 styled (but did not explain) the "schism" created during the Occupation between the older men and the younger men.[51] The patriotic element was surely enhanced by the fact that local young people were resisting the Japanese on their own soil.

If the events of the Occupation years truly did contribute towards the significant rift inside the indigenous community which became so evident during the 1967 Disturbances (see chapter 11), they may also be viewed as yet another element in the *yin-yang* interplay suggested in the Introduction.

EPILOGUE

Prompt action was taken by the British Military Administration to remedy the plight of the Hong Kong population after war's end. Ration cards were introduced, to enable people to buy rice and other staples as they became available, at fixed amounts and prices. Three years later, 63 per cent of the population were still receiving the rice ration, now largely restricted to those with pre-war residential qualifications.[52] In the NT, residents of Tsuen Wan, and doubtless other townships, were included in this scheme. In Tsuen Wan, as elsewhere, the ration cards continued in use into the early 1950s, and were also serving as useful items of personal and family identification for various official purposes. Overall, it is clear that rice rationing continued for at least eight years into the postwar era.

6

An End to Subsistence Farming: Opening the Way for Urban Development and Country Parks

This chapter takes the New Territories from the War's end to the mid-1970s.[1] I shall here focus attention on a most curious paradox. The essence of postwar government policy in the NT was assistance and improvement of services: spasmodic and unbalanced at first, but eventually continuous and uniform. Yet the object of these attentions, the village population, unprompted, was about to embark on a momentous change, nothing less than the abandonment of its traditional way of life, and in many cases of the countryside itself.

Briefly stated here, this involved the demise of rice farming, a sharp reduction in the economic use of the hillsides, and a continuing, self-opting, evacuation of long-established upland villages. While in no way attributable to official policies for the rural sector, their effect was to greatly facilitate the implementation of the government's development planning for the Colony by reducing the stronger opposition to development and modernization that otherwise might well have occurred; and indubitably, by making it possible to establish the Country Parks without friction in the 1970s.

A BRAVE NEW WORLD BUT NOT QUITE

At the end of the War, as in other war-ravaged colonies and captured territories, a British Military Administration governed Hong Kong until the resumption of civil government on 1 May 1946.[2] There had been little option, as it would take time to re-assemble the Colony's civil servants, many of whom had spent three years and eight months in internment or prisoner of war camps, to recruit replacements for wartime casualties and those who had retired, and to fill the additional posts created for new initiatives in government. Among the early changes was a decision to place district administration in the New Territories under one District Officer, although as prewar there continued to be two administrative districts.[3]

It had been by no means certain that, after its liberation, Hong Kong would be allowed to continue as a British Colony.[4] Also, winds of change had marked the early postwar years. The election of a Labour government at home, and the establishment of the United Nations Organization, had created a new-found concern for the condition of colonies.[5] They brought benefits to Hong Kong and other places under British rule. A Colonial Development and Welfare Act was passed in the UK in 1945, and in Hong Kong (June 1946) a committee, comprising both official members and others "representative of all communities in the Colony", was appointed, with six sub-committees to consider development and welfare planning in the fields of housing and town planning, port development, public health, natural resources, welfare and education.[6] Chaired by the District Officer, a New Territories sub-committee of the Colony's development and welfare committee was formed early in 1947. Many of its recommendations were incorporated in an important despatch to London sent later in the year.[7] In 1954, a Rural Development Committee, also chaired by the (by now) District Commissioner, with official and unofficial membership, was established, to advise the government on all matters relating to NT development, in particular to the extension of agricultural credit and the preparation of Colonial Development and Welfare schemes.[8]

Before long, a wind of a different kind would blow on the Colony, this time from the Mainland, where the prospect of the successful ousting of Chiang Kai-shek's Nationalist Government by the triumphant Communists was exercising the minds of several members of the sub-committee. Fearful of what political change across the border might entail, they (specialist government officers and a few civilian members) pointed to the uneven land situation in the NT, where the native population owned practically everything and immigrant farmers had either to rent fields or open Crown land, and pressed the case for reforms of one kind or another. The debate is too detailed to enter into here, but it was an issue at the time.[9] Suffice to say that senior administrators saw things differently and reform was not pursued.[10] However, discussion inside the sub-committee, and official correspondence outside it, had revealed that detailed knowledge on these subjects was generally lacking, and even admitted,[11] and as a result some useful surveys into land-ownership, land utilization, topography, and economic minerals were carried out, with help from the University of Hong Kong.[12] Interestingly, some democratic impulses begun in the NT after the War were not pursued, perhaps from the rising caution being bred at this time.[13]

Otherwise, a good deal of attention was paid in the immediate postwar years to providing assistance to farmers, old and new. For the first time in the Colony's history, Agricultural, Forestry and Fisheries Departments were established in 1946 to provide specialist services in these important areas of production.[14] In addition, quasi-government bodies, governed by ordinances, were set up to provide marketing services for fishermen and vegetable growers, with the objective (not totally realized) of taking them out of the clutches of the wholesalers (*laans*) who had monopolized them prewar. A Cooperative and Marketing Department (also established in 1946) originally directed these services, which were operated through a network of cooperative societies formed colony-wide through the efforts of an enthusiastic and energetic staff. In 1964, much of this work was taken into a re-titled single Department of Agriculture and Fisheries.[15]

The several departments had considerable success among boat people and vegetable growers, but less with conservative rice farmers. Their work was assisted by the substantial and sustained contribution made by the Kadoorie brothers, whose Kadoorie Agricultural Aid Association, operating through the Agricultural Department and the District Administration, did a great deal to help both the old and new population on the land.[16] Yet despite these developments, much remained to be done to ameliorate conditions in the rural areas, which still constituted the bulk of the New Territories.

In early 1955, K. M. A Barnett became District Commissioner. Imbued with the new approach, he had been shocked at the backward state of the rural population, owing largely to the lack of basic amenities in so many places.[17] In September 1955, he sent a 61-paragraph paper to the Colonial Secretary, reviewing prewar policy for the NT, and the absence of it postwar. The Government was drifting, and policy needed to be redefined. His duties should be revised to ensure more input into all government business being contemplated for the NT, with direct briefings to and by the Colonial Secretary. A District Officer post for Development, and District Assistants for each of the three administrative districts, were now urgently needed. His predecessor's scheme for local councils in the townships, with delegated responsibilities for markets and sanitation, should be approved. Postal and banking services should be provided, plus improvements to communications and water supplies.[18] The sum total in extra staff, vehicles and accommodation costs, was modest.[19]

The memorandum was a tour de force, the like of which had not been seen before in its comprehensiveness and understanding. Special attention was directed to the condition of the rural population. Both leased and so-called "empty" Crown land, were insufficient to maintain its mode of life, even under the yet existing conditions of subsistence farming.[20] The people, said Barnett, were poor – but surprisingly cheerful – and they deserved better. Besides a plea for improved management of the New Territories for the immediate future, the memorandum wanted "a new deal" for the village population.[21] This was not immediately forthcoming: save in regard to water supply and education, since the 1950s were marked by a determined drive to provide primary schools everywhere.[22]

Overall, despite some government provision for Anglo-Chinese schooling prewar, education seems to have slipped back during the first half-century of British rule. My impressions based on historical research in the villages are that more boys were being educated before than after the Lease.[23] A factor may have been that education was no longer tied to the imperial examinations and the civil service career open to the talents.[24] As before, village schools were provided by rural leaders, but student numbers seem to have dwindled. A fresh start was made after the years of war and occupation, but even by the late 1950s, my visit notebooks revealed a disturbing gap between children of school age and those attending classes, even among boys.[25] However, the initiatives taken by the Education Department, the District Administration and local leaders in that decade would pay off, resulting in some fine large primary schools in the larger villages.[26] There was, besides, much else to deplore, not all of the Administration's making.[27]

Meantime, time did not stand still. With many more people continuing to flood into Hong Kong, some of them to the NT, and the need to find more water and land there to meet urban needs, not least to support rapid industrialization, pressures on the District Administration and on rural people continued to mount. In Tsuen Wan, the situation was more or less beyond the control of the land staff of the District Office South, located in Kowloon.[28]

In the event, Barnett's successor in 1958, Ronald Holmes, soon realized the extent to which the situation had further deteriorated, and saw that the District Administration was now grossly undermanned for its job.[29] At a time when villagers had become noticeably disgruntled and less cooperative, resumptions and village removals for important public works projects had become commonplace events. More services for the rural population, and closer liaison with it, were urgently needed to maintain stability and facilitate development. This time, the Secretariat heeded the requests, and staff numbers were increased fourfold between 1959 and 1962.[30]

The great irony has already been stated. When Mr. Barnett's schemes for improvement had come belatedly to fruition, the village populations would themselves be opting out of rural poverty and be seeking a livelihood by other means. This phenomenon occurred in the 1960s and 1970s. The fall in production figures speaks for itself: from 23,400 acres under rice cultivation in 1955, to only about 280 acres in March 1979. In terms of production, there had been 19,081 tonnes in 1970 and only 351 tonnes in March 1979.[31] The spectacular decline constituted the one truly major event of the 20th century for the indigenous population, and made way for a new era.

WHY DID SUBSISTENCE RICE FARMING STOP?

In an article published in the *Hongkong Standard* in 1979, an unnamed reporter canvassed the reasons, with assistance from an agricultural scientist and a few remaining rice cultivators.[32] A multiplicity of causes were suggested, some of them mutually reinforcing, like the havoc caused by flocks of birds attracted to the few remaining patches of growing rice. The other, more weighty, factors are listed as follows: being part of a largely "hand to mouth" subsistence economy [no longer in keeping with the times]; the [also outdated] accompanying long-established need for it to be supplemented by the cash income from cutting firewood for sale in the city [where kerosene and gas had now completely replaced the old staple]; the much higher income from growing vegetables [though villagers seldom did so on a marketable scale]; a change to pond fish breeding in areas hitherto given over to brackish water paddy [one thousand acres adjoining Deep Bay];[33] water pollution in much of the low-lying plains in the northern NT; the reduced labour force now available, owing to so many men working overseas and with most children in school; plus the cancellation, ten years previously, of the Department of Agriculture's funding for rice research in view of the reduced cultivation figures.

Not mentioned specifically were the social and economic changes brought about by the growth of Hong Kong's export-led manufacturing industry from the early 1950s. Fuelling development and modernization, this had led to many more jobs, higher wages and improved standards of living which took contemporary urban life still further from the old-style farming existence, a phenomenon that did not go unnoticed in the villages. However, it is likely that another factor, not mentioned in the article, helped to bring about a situation in which large tracts of irrigated land, worked for generations, were abandoned by their former cultivators, men and women both.

Women and girls provide the key. Farm work had been nothing new for them. From the second half of the 19th century, village men and boys had been going overseas in search of work and fortune, and many had worked as sailors on ocean-going ships out of the port of Hong Kong.[34] During their often prolonged and recurrent absences, the women of the family had got on with the triple burden of rearing children, caring for parents-in-law, and doing most of the farm work. (Plate 19, 30, with another type of female labour on Plate 18)[35] Miraculously, they had somehow coped. Postwar, men began again to leave their villages. From the Hakka east, 1,200 men had gone to work in the Pacific islands in 1950–51.[36] The number of men absent from these and other villages must have been greater still by the late 1950s, when the flow of men into the Chinese restaurant business in UK had already begun,[37] but I recall how fields everywhere were in a high state of cultivation, showing that the women of the family had again filled the gap.[38]

There was an underlying reason for the long-prevailing male absence. The papers on "land reform" include statements by the District Commissioner and one of his DOs, which make clear the economic necessity which drove men to leave home. "There is little doubt," Barrow wrote in 1949, "that the average NT family cannot live uniquely from the land they own, and from the conventional side-lines of grass-cutting, domestic animals and forestry." They resorted to fishing and other rural occupations wherever feasible; and "throughout the NT, families usually welcome the chance to get a man or two permanently employed outside the village". From pilot survey returns from two demarcation districts in Yuen Long District, its DO had concluded that most of the small-holders who constituted the great majority of land owners there "did not own sufficient land from which to derive a reasonable living".[39] In this situation, all available land had to be farmed, and all economic opportunities exploited. Field work by women and girls was desperately needed.

What, then, led them to discontinue farming and leave home in their turn, and when? In 1958, when District Officer, South, I found the exodus already in train. Following a "rash" of unauthorized building on a slope above Sai Kung Market, I had gone there to enquire why this had occurred. There were women among the applicants, and their answers had been revealing:

> ... In growing numbers, daughters-in-law from the villages were no longer content to stay at home and look after their husbands' parents [and work the fields]. A growing demand for casual labour, some new factories, and burgeoning cottage industries, were providing opportunities for married (and soon, unmarried) women to break free from the village.[40]

By the mid 1960s, it was already common for unmarried girls to be living and working outside. Göran Aijmer, a Swedish anthropologist who provided a most interesting account of his research in three outlying Hakka villages in the Shatin area in 1964–1965, reported these changes when they were already well advanced:

> Most unmarried girls, from about the age of sixteen and upwards, now leave the home village and take up jobs, preferably in the industrial areas of Kowloon. Textile factories seem to attract them most. Once in town, they are captivated by the urban milieu and its possibilities, and they return to their villages only on rare occasions. [41]

Aijmer also noted that other females, who must have included married women living at home, took up casual manual labouring jobs, since owing to the absence of men, there was a strong demand for female labour in lieu.

In villages such as these and in Sai Kung, the impact upon traditional farming and the old way of life would be devastating. Without the support of wives, mothers, daughters-in-law, unmarried girls and adult daughters, neither the farm nor the old-style rural family which was dependent on it could be sustained. It can be surmised that changes of a similar nature were proceeding in other areas in this significant, because defining, decade, including the many, usually larger, Cantonese-speaking villages of the northern New Territories.[42]

Besides the new avenues for employment for women outside the home, there were now many more opportunities for the education of girls. Before the War, female illiteracy was the rule.[43] The expansion of educational provision in the 1950s, would enable girls to attend school in significant numbers for the first time.[44] These developments seem to have created a new awareness.[45] Yet there must, too, have been an underlying attitudinal shift, one which emboldened rural young women to break away in the face of disapproval from their elders, and in the case of young married women, from their surely indignant old-fashioned mothers-in-laws, that formidable Chinese institution. Perhaps, too, women had lost that capacity for infinite patience and endurance, which my late mother-in-law, born near Canton in 1907, had described as the basic requirement for all women in the old society. Or it could have been, also, a recognition by all concerned of the greater economic benefits conferred upon the family.[46]

Nonetheless, this major change in livelihood and mind-set began at a time when the government was providing considerable support for farmers and rural communities everywhere. Through self-help with government-supplied materials and by government-let contracts through the District Administration's local public works programme, all-weather footpaths, van tracks, wells, piped water from the hills, concrete dams and irrigation channels were improving the conditions of rural life and work (Plates 20 and 36).

Specialized assistance from the Agricultural Department was helping to control crop pests and protect livestock from disease, removing some of the uncertainty and loss hitherto inseparable from the farm economy. Other improvements to everyday living were due to a government-sponsored electrification programme for the villages,[47] the wider use of kerosene (long available), and then of Towngas. There was an increased number of government clinics, usually with maternity wards, and, for remoter localities) the provision of health visits (by fast jet-boat) and "flying doctor" services.[48] Decades later, while visiting two semi-ruined hill villages of the Shatin District in 1986, both abandoned in the 1960s, it was clear from the installations in the old houses that they already had piped water and electricity at that time, and had shared a two-class-roomed school, built in 1955.[49]

But by the late 1960s, the economic factor, combined with phenomenally adverse weather conditions in the middle years of the decade, was now decisive. At a Royal Asiatic Society weekend Symposium on "Change", a Senior Agricultural Officer told his audience that "the income from the quasi-subsistence pattern of paddy cultivation is [now] so low that it can hardly support a farmer and his family".[50] Using a statistical table, he showed how the position was not much improved if the rice farmer added either a vegetable or sweet potato crop.[51] He then showed how, during the period 1963–66, hardly assisting rice farmers to survive, the drought throughout 1963 and the first half of 1964 was the worst ever recorded, while the maximum intensity per hour in the rain storm of 12 June 1966 had been the highest since 1884.[52]

Notes made some years later endorse these hard facts. On a visit to South Lantau in October 1977, one of my village friends had complained about the restrictions being placed on land use other than agriculture. The catchwaters for the Shek Pik reservoir had taken some of the water needed for agriculture, but (he said) the plain fact was that rice farming was just not feasible any more. A farm of 5 *dau chung* produced 20 piculs of unhusked rice a year, which at the current value of $80 a picul, gave a notional yearly income of $1,600: that is, if none of the usual uncertainties of farming were taken into account.[53] A factory owner could earn this in two months. Consequently, no young person wanted to be a farmer. And in the same month, a check on the identity of casual workers engaged by a China Light and Power Company's contractor for excavation work near Fuk Loi Housing Estate in Tsuen Wan had revealed that they were mostly villagers from Tai Po and Yuen Long who were no longer farming because (they told my liaison staff) "the wages we earn from construction companies are much higher than what we get from cultivating our fields at home".

Yet where (whether directly, or indirectly through rice-exchange) rice-growing in the villages had been the basic item in a traditional subsistence economy, less influenced by profitability than the need to provide the family food supply, it seems more than likely that the demise of rice farming and the traditional village economy was triggered by the shift in outlook and mobility among the female members of the family, with or without the absence of many men overseas — especially taking its early timing into account.

AN END TO THE OLD COUNTRYSIDE

Subsistence farming had always involved use of the adjoining hillsides and seashore to provide home necessities and supplement income through the sale of commercial items like grass and firewood, the former needed by old-style shipyards for burning off marine growth from the hulls of wooden fishing boats, the latter a major item of home consumption in the urban areas. Grass cutting and firewood gathering had always been women's work, and the market itself was changing.[54]

The result was to remove people and animals from the landscape: at least, those engaged in traditional work. No longer would one encounter farmers toiling mutely among the hills, no more would one meet parties of grass-cutters on the hill paths, the low buzz of their conversation carrying over distance. No more, on golden December days, would one hear drumming little hooves on the hard ground, the jingle of the metal bits on their harness, and the thud of the plough as patient little beasts turned over the stubble immediately after harvesting of the second rice crop, at their owners' grunted commands.[55] Fields tended for generations would quickly become overgrown, and the once highly visible areas on hill slopes where grass-cutters had shaved off the undergrowth and removed the lower branches of stunted trees were no longer to be distinguished from the rest.

Traditional farming expertise and country lore, handed down through the generations, was now at a discount. Keith Addison, a close observer of the local scene in one of the last rice-growing villages in the 1980s, lamented the change:

> Where are the young farmers of Lantau? Ten years ago they were here. Now, a typical case works in a dyeing factory in Yuen Long, for 12 hours a day, six days a week, at HKD75 a day, sleeping on the premises, his skills and special knowledge (which is considerable) wasted, and though he hates the work, he firmly believes he is better off. Go into the mountains with this lad and he's alive with useful knowledge. He

follows wild bees to their nests and harvests wonderful honey, he knows
uses for half the plants around him: this one makes good hoe handles,
that creeper makes a tough rope, this plant's roots are a valuable
medicine, don't burn that one as the smoke is poisonous. Where will
all this knowledge go to? They have not been educated for success in
the city, and they seldom achieve it. But they do not value their own
heritage, and nor does anyone else value it.[56]

NO MORE A VILLAGE PRESERVE: THE COUNTRY PARKS

The native withdrawal from the countryside was timely. Hand in hand with
the government's newly introduced Ten Year Rolling Housing Programme,
designed to improve housing and living standards, had come its Country
Parks Scheme, intended to improve outdoor amenities for the ever-growing
urban population. It was especially aimed at those still living in Kowloon
and Hong Kong (then, the great majority) where environmental conditions
and open space provision were much less favourable than in the "New Towns"
being created in the NT.[57] A Country Parks Ordinance, Cap.208 of the Laws
of Hong Kong, was enacted on 16 August 1976 and, over the following three
years, no fewer than 21 country parks were gazetted, with two thereafter.[58]
The Country Park Authority would be the Director of Agriculture and
Forestry, whose department, provided with additional staff, would manage
the new parks. He would also be assisted by an appointed Advisory Board.[59]

There had been a lead-up. The Agriculture and Forestry Department
was already managing about one-fifth of the scenic countryside, and a New
Territories Advisory Committee for Recreational Development and Nature
Conservation had been set up in August 1970 to advise the District
Commissioner on the betterment of the recreational use of the countryside
and on the conservation of specific areas to preserve their natural state. Its
first report was presented in 1972.[60] The lengthy preparations which then
ensued for bringing in the Country Parks Ordinance had included
consultations with the District Administration and the Heung Yee Kuk.

The country parks were an immediate success, greatly welcomed by
Hong Kong people, and especially by the young. The figures speak for
themselves. An estimated "well over 2 million" persons had visited the smaller
area managed by the AFD in 1976, and in October 1978 the Governor had
told Legislative Council that "anything up to 100,000 people might be
expected on any week-end of good weather".[61] With the new country parks
and special areas long in full operation, 9.3 million visits were made in 1985,
and over 10.5 million were recorded in 1992.[62]

The new parks took in most of the upland areas of the Colony. Overall, including those located in Hong Kong and Kowloon, they would amount to no less than 40% of its land area.[63] Occupying so large a percentage of the whole, they were bound to affect villagers in various ways. Some of the higher settlements would fall within the original intended boundaries of the parks, together with all or most of their private land. Other villages located near or outside the parks might not be included, but their upland fields would be inside the parks.[64] Many village forestry lots held on annual licence from the Hong Kong government, and other areas utilized by rural communities from long before the Lease, might also be included in whole or in part.[65] While it was intended to exclude "village areas, traditional burial grounds, temples, and buildings of historic value" from any country park or special area, "no compensation would be paid to the owner of, or to any person interested in, any land merely because it is situated within or is affected by a country park", save under certain conditions.[66] The plans for each country park or special area would be drawn up by the Secretary for the New Territories and would be submitted to Governor in Council for approval before gazetting.[67]

For the reasons already given, the direct impact of opening the country parks was largely reduced, but a degree of hindrance and inconvenience for village people would be inevitable from the outset. With the countryside under management, and protective legislation in place to preserve flora and fauna of special interest, some customary usages have been restricted or curtailed. Apart from taking plants and wildlife for Chinese herbal medicine, there is more regulation of worshipping ceremonies at ancestral graves, of which there are literally thousands in upland areas of the NT. Lighting fires and the use of firecrackers are prohibited, and also littering. Permission from the Country Park Authority to repair old graves, and to bring in building materials for the purpose, became an additional bureaucratic requirement.[68] Further hassles were in store, which though not the work of the Country Park Authority, increased the pressures on native villagers.[69]

Despite the complications inherent in the creation of the country parks (perhaps not fully appreciated by the rural lobby at the time) the legislation was not opposed.[70] Yet hardly more than a decade before, expensive additional works had had to be provided to overcome major local opposition from farmers in the Yuen Long plain to construction of catchwaters for the then recently-completed Tai Lam Chung Reservoir. In determining new or extended gathering grounds, the Waterworks Ordinance of the day still allowed for "the preservation of traditional rights of any person to take water for agricultural and domestic purposes".[71] In order to safeguard the volume of water needed for cultivation, four irrigation reservoirs had been built, impounding 172 million gallons of water, and involving the surrender of 6.6 acres of private agricultural land. Completion was marked by the installation of commemorative plaques unveiled by the Director of Public Works in person, in the presence of a large gathering of notables, indicative of the importance attached to these projects.[72] Had the rural situation not changed so radically in the interim, it is doubtful that the country parks could have materialized in their present form.

ABANDONED VILLAGES

The introduction of the country parks had also been facilitated by a gradual reduction in the number of upland villages from before, during and after the Second World War. I have no reliable figures, since these removals from high ground have never been recorded.[73] However, the total number of evacuations cannot have been small, and the overall result, over many decades, was to free up large areas of hitherto inhabited and cultivated countryside. This movement from the remoter, higher areas of the territory is not only a phenomenon worthy of notice in the present context, but is also a part of New Territories history *per se*, and thus germane to this book.

Many of the communities opting for self-removal had been settled for centuries. Sheung Tong, a single lineage hill village in the Tai Mo Shan uplands above Tsuen Wan, was one such, being at least 200 years old. The survey sheet in the relevant Block Crown Lease of 1905 shows that it was a neat, rectangular type of settlement which, in the 1911 Colony census, had a population of 77, comprising 36 males and 41 females, including children.[74] A former elderly resident said that it contained thirty-six houses in good condition during his childhood in the 1920s and 1930s, and all occupied. Some families moved out a few years before the War, and by the end of the Japanese Occupation in 1945 none were left. The families had removed to many places, some to villages occupied by their Tsang cousins, others elsewhere.[75] No specific reason was given for the evacuation. Other hill villages in the former Tsuen Wan District had been similarly affected. The two nearby hamlets of Pak Shek Kiu and Ha Tong Lek, had been abandoned even before that time.[76] At the once thriving village of Tsing Fai Tong, after many years of gradual removal, the remaining families had moved down to join their relatives at coastal Sham Tseng.[77] Yet another, Yuen Tun, was resited by the Hong Kong government to the coast at Tsing Lung Tau in 1969, after its irrigation supply had been diminished by tunnels constructed for the Tai Lam Chung Water Scheme.[78] Nearer Kowloon, the hamlet of Lan

Nai Tong, in the hills near the Kowloon Reservoir, had been vacated in the later 19th century, after its inhabitants had become involved in a three-year war between the Hakkas of Shing Mun and those of Tsuen Wan.[79] Most of these former hill settlements, and their fields, are now located within or near country parks.

THE INSTITUTIONALIZATION OF RURAL LEADERSHIP AND ITS BENEFITS

I come, finally, to another element in the facilitation of large-scale development. The introduction of the Village Representative and Rural Committee systems soon after the War, and the remodelling of the Heung Yee Kuk under a special Ordinance in 1959,[80] were steps which would prove equally essential to its success. It is doubtful whether the nine New Towns could have been developed without the consultation and compromise they made possible. The resiting of old villages had always been accomplished through negotiation, and this continued postwar; but a new initiatives would have to be taken in regard to the recovery of land in agricultural status. While the draconic resumption of properties at three months' notice (or less) would continue relentlessly, alternatives to the much-disliked "cash only" compensation system operating up to the late 1950s would soon be offered. Moreover, the government would be prepared to wrangle endlessly with the Heung Yee Kuk over details of land policy, including (ultimately) the long sought-after inclusion of "development potential" in cash compensation rates. This flexibility would enable the government to match the timing of land recovery with tight land formation and civil engineering schedules in development areas.[81] It was, in retrospect, the institutionalization of rural leadership, especially of the Heung Yee Kuk in 1959, which converted the difficult and problematic into the achievable,[82] though the latter step had not been without its critics within government.[83]

The evolution of the representation system is itself of some interest. Prewar, as related in chapter 4, the District Administration had simply worked through the leaders it had found in the villages and townships, appointing some as "Advisers" and taking note, no doubt, of the Heung Yee Kuk in its initial form. The War seems to have changed official thinking. In 1946, in an intriguing early initiative, under arrangements made by the District Officer New Territories, elections were held in 21 rural districts to provide councils of elders to assist and advise him with his duties. A further set were planned for the remaining 17 districts, and a Senior Advisory Council was also intended,[84] though it seems doubtful whether either were pursued further. In lieu, other measures followed.

A Village Representative scheme was organized in 1948, and a start made with establishing Rural Committees.[85] *The village representatives* came from each of the old settlements recognized as such by the Administration.[86] A village with over fifty families was allowed a second or even a third representative, to help share the work. Elections were sometimes held, but following old custom in the matter of providing village headmen they were (by my observation) more usually secured by willingness to serve and prior nomination by the elders, endorsed by silent consensus.[87] After vetting, each representative was recognized by the District Administration and the Police and was given an identity card confirming his office. Many served for decades (Plates 21 and 22). *The rural committees* were elected every few years from among the village representatives of their sub-districts, under the supervision of the District Officer, the chairmen and vice chairmen being elected at the same time.[88] The election results were reported to the Police and the District Commissioner, New Territories.[89]

Besides performing executive duties in their own communities, the function of the village representatives (as seen by government) was to provide for two-way communication between the villages and the District Administration and to act as intermediaries who could obtain help from it when required.[90] The perceived purposes of the rural committees were similar. They, too, were accepted as being the general spokesmen of their rural communities and the advocates of their causes.[91]

Henceforth, the village populations would have established and formal links with the District Administration and other concerned departments of government, and with the armed services. In these respects, they were much better off than the much larger immigrant population. Through their ownership of much of the land that would soon be needed for large-scale development, and with the rural committees and the reformed Heung Yee Kuk in place, they constituted (as we shall see) a powerful pressure group for group and individual interests. But the importance of these institutions for the progress of development should never be doubted nor underestimated.[92]

Also, viewed another way, while the elections of Village Representatives were more observed in the breach, and though rural committee elections, and Kuk elections, were subject to a good deal of pressuring and gerrymandering by rival cliques,[93] the introduction of these Representative systems in the New Territories in the 1940s and 1950s may be said to have paved the way for the District Board and other elections in the 1980s, when voting by the whole adult population under proper safeguards and adequate arrangements was introduced for the first time.[94]

7

Village Removals for Water Schemes 1923–1974: Resitings and Compensation

In the three decades after the restoration of British rule in 1945, one new water scheme project followed another in an effort to solve the chronic problem of water supply for a swollen and ever increasing population. By 1960, despite all that was being done, supply was restricted to 3 to 4 hours daily, imposing the "grievous and constant hardship" upon "the great majority" of the urban population so graphically (and sympathetically) described in the Review chapter of the Colony Annual Report.[1] Two more large reservoirs were still needed and provided, and as was ever the case, each involved the removal, compensation and resiting of old villages.

All told, six reservoirs were constructed in the New Territories between the mid-1920s and the mid-1970s, and twenty-five villages were resited to new locations. The associated requirement for catchwaters and access roads added more to the land "take", widening the impact on the local communities. This chapter describes — for the first time — all the removals and resitings, and some of the disruptions experienced by the people in their new homes.

THE COMPENSATION PACKAGE

Reservoir removals were considered to be of a special type, since the extent and nature of these major public works required the total extinguishment of all private rights to land and property, both legal and customary, including crops. Hence an immediate and full compensation package, sufficient to induce those involved to move on time, was required. Now the norm under colonial rule, compensation was paid for all resumed land, and where villages were required to be removed, new homes were mostly built by those displaced with cash payments to the value of the old, on sites provided and formed by government. Postwar, all resite villages were built directly by government contract.

AGRICULTURAL VERSUS URBAN RESITING

The major difference between pre- and postwar resitings was that the former were intended to replicate the old rural life. This was still the age of traditional farming, and the villagers involved hoped (and were expected by the authorities) to continue as before in the new place, carrying on their agricultural pursuits as best they could, and eking out their livelihood with paid employment and any other means to hand. In the postwar removals, agricultural resiting was seldom possible, or even desired by most of the affected parties. Their future livelihood would come from financial compensation paid by the government, income from renting out surplus houses or floors, and from the employment of family members in Hong Kong or overseas.

PREWAR VILLAGE RESITING FOR WATER SCHEMES

As already noted in chapter 4, a further extension to the Kowloon Reservoir in 1923 had required the resiting of an entire village; and not long after, in 1928, the eight settlements of the Shing Mun valley had to make way for the largest water scheme to date, the Shing Mun, or Jubilee, Reservoir, completed in 1935.

Despite the authorities' good intentions, there was a down side to these early re-provisionings. By the time of the Lease, the New Territories were thickly settled. While suitable locations for the new villages could be found, finding new agricultural land for their inhabitants was a different matter. In fact, this was not attempted, and it was left to them to buy or rent whatever land was available on the market, or open ground taken on permit from the government. Either option was difficult. Most land capable of sustaining cultivation had already been opened, and even where owners were willing to sell fields to the newcomers, these would be insufficient to restore their livelihood.[2] Moreover, although under British rule regarded as Crown property, the adjoining hillsides so necessary to supplement the rural economy had for centuries been claimed, apportioned, and used by the people of existing villages.[3]

Shek Lei Pui, 1924

An account of the removal of the village of Shek Lei Pui for the reservoir of that name in 1924 has been preserved.[4] It consisted of about 26 houses, big and small, and was occupied by some 80 persons from four lineages at the time.[5] The villagers were resited to a place in the upper Shatin valley, though they had asked for Cheung Sha Wan in New Kowloon or Tsuen Wan, places where they had been accustomed to market their produce.[6]

Every house, pigsty and latrine was re-provisioned, one for one. The estimated cost to be paid for construction of each house (approximately 474 square feet in floor area, and 18 feet in height, with the usual small internal cockloft) was said to have been $1,350, but because the contractor had sub-let, it turned out that only $600 had been spent. Mud had been used instead of cement, but the villagers had been obliged to take them as the reservoir was already filling with water. The houses only lasted for a few years, and had to be rebuilt at the villagers' expense.[7]

Before removal, the villagers had been self-sufficient farmers, cultivating on sand and mud soil with plenty of water from the streams around, which gave a good production of rice, vegetables and peanuts. They were able to rear pigs and other livestock, and to collect grass and firewood from the surrounding hills. In Shatin, however, they had no fields, since the land surrounding their resite houses belonged to other villages. Even pig breeding was not easy. The villagers had to seek work away from home, and most worked for the government Waterworks Office, which made jobs available. The people suffered a lot of hardship, and the author of this report (1966) was told that about a quarter of the population died, due, they believed, to the unsuitable water and climate of the new place.[8]

The Shing Mun Eight Villages, 1928

Located at Shing Mun, an extensive upland valley and hill area above Tsuen Wan and below Tai Mo Shan, Hong Kong's highest mountain, these villages were home to 855 Hakka people settled there since the 17th century (See Plate 12). All told, the villagers owned 180 acres of agricultural land, 1180 acres of forestry rights, and 42 acres of pineapple cultivation. It was their fate to live in a place that was earmarked for the construction of the largest reservoir contemplated in the Colony to date. With a storage capacity of 3,000 million gallons, it would be equal to the total combined storage capacity of the then ten existing reservoirs of Hong Kong, and the dam wall the biggest of its kind in the Far East at the time.[9]

Separate sites were identified for each of the eight villages involved. The greater part were on Crown land, augmented by a small amount of private land recovered by government for the purpose. The largest number of villagers,

540 in all, was to be resited to Kam Tin, with the rest scattered in 7 or 8 other locations. Site formation costs for the new villages were paid for from public funds, together with the cost of sinking wells in each location. The new house lots would be provided without premium, and payments for construction of the replacement houses, by contractors privately engaged by the villagers, would be calculated at a flat rate per cubic foot according to the measured content of the old.[10] Outhouses could be re-provisioned by villagers up to the value of the compensation awarded for those left behind. Payments to enable villagers to fee geomancers for advice in siting houses and wells were provided. Graves below high water mark were to be removed (no mention was made about compensation for the cost of removal and reinstatement) but those above it could stay. The Hip Tin Kung Temple, which served the village communities at Shing Mun, was re-provisioned at Kam Tin, presumably with compensation money though there is no mention of it in published reports (see Plate 23).

Compensation for agricultural land had included an *ex gratia* amount to enable the villagers to purchase fields in their new locations, though (in what would become a recurrent theme in all such removals) it was already being frankly acknowledged by officials that "there was very little unoccupied land in their vicinity and that the new village sites were in a more populous neighbourhood than the old". Growing trees in the village forestry areas under permit would be compensated, together with pineapples under cultivation.[11]

The experience of these people, as with those removed from Shek Lei Pui, was nothing less than traumatic. There was an immense and total upheaval, with a painful transition from being confident, self-sufficient villagers in their old homes to becoming unwanted trespassers in unfamiliar places with unfriendly Cantonese neighbours.[12] Those resettled near Kam Tin and Fanling, in particular, experienced problems at the hands of the powerful local lineages. Their old people told me that the Tangs had made difficulties for the former, and that the Pangs of Fanling Wai forbade the latter to gather medicinal herbs on the hills near their new location.[13] One wonders if the older communities had been consulted before the Shing Mun people were set down in their midst (Plate 24).[14]

Such was the fate of all the villagers resited up to the War. Word must have spread about the problems to be encountered, because with the exception of the small village of Fan Pui (see pp. 90, 93–95), few of the many villagers resited for reservoir construction in the several decades after the War had ever seriously contemplated staying with a farming existence.

TWO EARLY POSTWAR REMOVALS[15]

In 1952, Hakka farmers and shopkeepers on Kau Sai, an island and boat people's anchorage in Port Shelter, off the market town and fishing centre of Sai Kung, were required to move elsewhere, because it was located in the centre of the large area of sea about to be designated as a firing range to be used for artillery and naval gun practice.[16] The villagers were resited to nearby Pak Sha Wan, off the coastal road from Clear Water Bay leading to Sai Kung Market, where "a new village of 17 houses, family temple, school hall, pigsties, grass-stores and latrine", designed by a leading Hong Kong architect, was provided for them, completed by July 1952.[17]

In this same year, long-settled Hakka farmers on Nei Kwu Chau (Nun Island) near Peng Chau (South) were affected by the Hong Kong Government's decision to create a leprosarium on the island, to be administered by the Mission to Lepers, Hong Kong Auxiliary.[18] They were the remnants of a long-settled Lam lineage, which at the time of the Lease, had already been resident there for two hundred years. Originally living in three villages, two were already abandoned and in ruins by the 1920s, and the population decline would continue thereafter.[19] My discussions with surviving elders indicated that this had been due to disease. One, born in 1895, remembered around twenty families as a boy, but by 1952, there were only a few left. Perhaps for this reason, they were not resited together in one place, but went individually to various places on the adjoining shores of Lantau, where they built houses with their compensation money, bought some fields and rented others, and tried to replicate their former way of life.[20]

POSTWAR RESERVOIR RESITINGS

Tai Lam Chung, 1956

The first of the postwar reservoir removals and resitings set a new pattern. The villagers of Tai Lam and Kwan Uk Tei, thirty-three families in all,[21] removed from a valley behind Tai Lam Chung on the Castle Peak Road to make way for construction of the reservoir of that name, would decide to move into the now rapidly developing township of Tsuen Wan, closer to Kowloon. The District Commissioner's annual report for 1955–56 describes the position as follows:

> It was at first intended that they should be resettled on the land and a search was made for suitable agricultural land. This plan was mainly

abandoned, mainly on the insistence of the villagers themselves that they would prefer an urban life. A site was found in Tsuen Wan and, in accordance with the wishes of the villagers, plans have been drawn up for a block of flats to accommodate both villages.

Thereby, they committed themselves to becoming town dwellers in a fast-developing township that would later become the first of the NT's "new towns".

The resettlement building was unique among the postwar urban resitings. Designed by a prominent Hong Kong architect, it consisted of a block of self-contained flats, with shops, a school and a temple, all contained within a rectangular enclosure, to which was given the name Tai Uk Wai, or the "Big Walled Mansion".[22] The DO involved told me that (as had happened in the 1928 removal) the waters were already being impounded before the villagers agreed to remove themselves. The decision made, the Chief Resident Engineer of the Tai Lam Chung scheme had provided labourers and lorries: "Almost everything in the village was moved, and the lorries were piled high with furniture and food stuffs and pots and pans and apparently endless loads of firewood." The move began on 8 August 1956, and in spite of intermittent rain was completed by 13 August. On 29 August the ancestral tablets of the Cheung clan were installed with due ceremony, and on 6 September, the new village was officially opened by the Officer Administering the Government, in the Governor's absence.[23]

Shek Pik, 1959–60[24]

Such was the demand for water in urban Hong Kong at that time that the Shek Pik Reservoir, with its still larger capacity, was built hot on the heels of Tai Lam Chung. The people of the two old villages (Shek Pik and Fan Pui) and one hamlet (Hang Tsai) in the Shek Pik Valley, comprising some 260 persons in all, were removed to various places, of their own choosing. All but a few of the Shek Pik residents moved into flats in five-storey apartment blocks in Tsuen Wan (Plate 25). Most of the Fan Pui villagers moved to a resite village in an adjoining bay (Tai Long Wan). Some families from both places moved to a row of shops with domestic accommodation above, built for them near the ferry pier at Mui Wo (Silvermine Bay). As at Tai Uk Wai, the Tsuen Wan apartment blocks had ground floor shop premises, with the village school and temple also reprovisioned in the buildings. The Fan Pui villagers had decided to continue farming, and by remodelling long abandoned fields in the new location, it was possible to provide them with the same acreage of rice fields. A separate school and temple reprovisioning was also carried out.[25]

In keeping with the paternal approach that characterized the old District Administration, a feature of the Tai Lam Chung removals, to be repeated for Shek Pik, was the concern evinced by its senior officers when the villagers had decided to be resited in a town. The District Officer had been asked to remind them that there would be no land to cultivate, that they would not be allowed to keep livestock (such as the pigs and chickens common to all villages), and that their new houses would be sited in conformity with the town plan, and not with the dictates of *fung-shui*. Henceforth, they would also have to buy their own fuel, instead of cutting grass and picking up firewood, as well as pay for electricity and mains water (facilities not available to them in the village). Through opting for accommodation in the town instead of the country, they would lose growing space,[26] as well as their former village identity, with all the rights and concessions accorded to indigenous villagers.[27] There was even mention of a form whereby the villagers would undertake to recognize these facts of urban resiting.[28]

The District Commissioner had also wanted to counter the expected improvidence or gullibility of some villagers. He advised that there should be a restriction on the sale of houses in the ten years following removal to Tsuen Wan, whereby the Governor's approval would be necessary and the properties should be offered first, at a fair valuation, to another villager or a lineage trust. With the best of intentions, the title deeds for the new properties in Tsuen Wan were withheld from the Tai Lam Chung villagers for a time.[29] However, this created so much suspicion among them that when the news was transmitted to the Shek Pik people, it had led them to demand the deeds for their new homes from the start.

After the Shek Pik removal, it was the town option which, despite some initial demurrals, found favour with the people removed for the Plover Cove Reservoir in the mid 1960s, who went to Tai Po Market, and also with those who moved into Sai Kung Market from the site of the High Island Reservoir in the early 1970s.

The Six Villages of Plover Cove, 1966

In December 1966, the removal of the inhabitants of six old villages and two hamlets from the site of the Plover Cove reservoir was accomplished. This would be the largest of all the resiting exercises effected during the Lease. In all, accommodation had been provided in Taipo Market for 1069 indigenous persons.[30] To quote from the District Commissioner's report, "The housing complex at Tai Po, constructed for the Plover Cove villagers, included thirteen

5-storey blocks, ground floor shop units and upper floor flats, a 3-classroom school and playground, 5 village chi tongs [ancestral halls] and 3 playgrounds".[31]

"A study in forced migration"[32]

This resiting project was the subject of an academic survey project conducted by Dr. Morris Berkovitz of Chung Chi College and others in 1968, one year after the removal to Tai Po. As the only one of its kind undertaken by a social scientist among all the communities affected by water schemes during the Lease, it is of interest not only in regard to how the Plover Cove villagers felt in their now home, but in respect of an experience shared with persons and families who had faced similar uprootings before them, and with others from the High Island villages who would share it soon after.[33]

This survey of 35 households in their new accommodation at Tai Po was clearly painstaking, and as thorough as conditions allowed. However, in retrospect, it was rather too early in the day to be more than a record of the selected villagers' initial reactions, though nonetheless valuable for that. Opinions on living in the resettlement area varied. Twelve of the households preferred the new location, 16 preferred the village, and a further seven were ambivalent. Women, considered to be "by far the more traditionally oriented" were generally less enthusiastic, though their lives were probably now physically easier.

The researchers concluded that flexibility and adaptability had not yet been acquired by the majority of these essentially rural people. Summarized, their findings comprised the following observations. "Putting all of life on a money basis has damaged confidence, even when money is not a problem" owing to the new sources of income available from renting out shops and surplus accommodation. "Current dissatisfactions stem largely from non-economic grounds", which included the inability to speak Cantonese, the language of instruction in the schools and the *lingua franca* of Taipo Market. The interviews had indicated that the behaviour of the men in the resite area was a major part of the overall problem:

> Gambling, going to the movies, and going out to eat with other unemployed men was expensive and took away household income from the household's other needs. Women became household managers and felt the strain because of their illiteracy, and because men left the family finances to their wives, a burden which left them as the most unhappy group within the resettlement area. In short, initial experiences "had distinctly dampened their enthusiasm".

The researchers noted that, thus far into their resettlement, most of the villagers had chosen "to shun the larger social scene and [to] continue living as villagers in an urban setting". They felt justified in referring to "the kind of demoralization which is beginning to appear in the Taipo Market resettlement", observing that:

It would seem legitimate to indicate that there are potentially serious problems which may arise in the resettlement area. The government (which won overwhelming approval in its handling of the resettlement) seems now to be facing a severely dislocated rural population which already shows signs of structural problems in the economic sphere, which may soon spread to other aspects of social life, such as family organization and social control over children. The primary cause seems to have been failure to recognize the human problems of environment change, as opposed to the financial and physical problems.

While reactions to resiting might differ from person to person, family to family, and from one resited community to another, these concluding remarks seem to have a general relevance for all resitings to non-rural settings undertaken postwar. The District Administration (and government in general) was primarily concerned with extending fair treatment, providing a new basis for livelihood but otherwise leaving those affected by our decisions more or less to fend for themselves in their new situations. Overall, they seemed to manage, but a lack of complaints on their problems to the District Offices in which I served may not be an appropriate criterion by which to judge the aftermath of urban resitings.[34] The fact that dislocations and readjustments were the common lot of Hong Kong people at that time of urbanization and modernization does not negate the issue of whether counselling and other specialist services should have been provided for persons subject to what the social scientists concerned with Plover Cove have termed this kind of "forced migration".

Tai Long Wan Revisited

This is not to say that postwar agricultural resiting was problem-free. Keith Addison's "Tai Long Wan, Tales from a Vanishing Village" (mid-1980s) prove otherwise.[35] Tai Long Wan, as you will recall from an earlier mention, was the new village and its reconditioned fields which had re-housed and reprovisioned those Shek Pik villagers who had opted for an agricultural resiting on Lantau.[36]

Living in a rented house and renting agricultural land in the village, and using organic techniques with integrated pest control management, Keith Addison had built up an independent on-farm research and development project there in 1983–85, while his companion Christine Thery, a professional artist and photographer, had been recording and photographing village life. During this time, they had been trying to demonstrate, both to the villagers and the government's Agricultural and Forestry Department, their project's proven viability.

By then, a generation after the resiting, the community had fallen on bad times. In 1970 there had been about 120 people living in Tai Long Wan. By 1983 there were only 22, as most of the younger villagers had moved to the city or gone overseas, leaving a village of grandparents and a few grandchildren. The whole middle generation was missing — a phenomenon repeated in many places in those years.

With declining numbers, cultivation had fallen away. Three-quarters of the village fields were fallow, three-quarters of the orchards on the hill slopes were run-down or overgrown. Only two of the families still grew rice. Half the sheds were not being used, most of the families had sold their cattle, and there were no pigs left. Only half the families kept chickens, there were only two geese, no ducks, and no ponds. The villagers fished off the rocks and gleaned the shoreline pools for a constant harvest of seafood, but they had no boats anymore (Plates 27–30).

In these gradually reducing circumstances, leadership and cooperation had been lacking — notwithstanding a long tradition of mutual self-help and the continued existence of an ancestral hall and communal property. The only remaining vestige of cooperative activity was the continuation of the daily rituals at each of the four shrines in the village area, carried out by family representative in accordance with a hand-written roster, together with gatherings to celebrate marriages in the traditional way or mark village festivals.[37]

Attempting to analyse what had gone wrong, my friends had pinpointed problems with the transportation needed to take produce to market; the failure to improve and maintain irrigation systems and even the potable supply after wash-downs of rocks and silt into the catchwater run-off had worsened some defects in the original design; labour shortages resulting from the attraction of urban work and life; together with economic and other factors listed in chapter 6.[38] But it was the absence of cooperation, leadership and public spirit which had been, and still was, most damaging, compounding all other problems.

Eventually, my friends pulled out and returned to England, despite being offered a contract by the Holiday Inn Hotel group in the city for the supply of fresh clean food. Official indifference, the conservatism and listlessness of most villagers, were partly responsible. Another adverse factor had been the anxieties created for them by urban young persons who had fastened onto this isolated off-beach community and regularly invaded the valley, swarming onto the village fields and properties, causing damage, loss, and much nuisance. The villagers were, of course, equally affected, but they had put up with it with stoical resignation in the absence of more effective help from the authorities.[39]

Could more have been done? The District Office, usually over-burdened, would have tried to help, as would related departments, but the specific tasking which might have converted spasmodic efforts into something more organized and coordinated was not established — neither in this or other reservoir resitings. And while the resitees had blamed themselves for opting to remain on Lantau and losing their families thereby — not realizing, as they said, that their children might want something different — overall, the times were against them in the decades which followed their removal to Tai Long Wan.

High Island, 1973

An account of this village removal and resiting exercise, the last in the long series of reservoir removals, is made more difficult to detail in the absence of printed reports after the annual report of the District Commissioner, NT, for 1972–73.[40] From this, we learn that by March 1973, the first three rehousing blocks for villagers on the Sai Kung eastern reclamation were nearing completion, and that a specially designed housing estate for fishermen affected by the High Island water scheme was under planning. Discussions with both groups were proceeding.[41] But no figures on the number of families and persons affected were provided.

Fortunately, a Master's thesis by a member of the District Administration's land staff submitted to the University of Hong Kong in March 1975, supplements the incomplete information available from official reports.[42] From it, we learn that some one hundred families and 500 villagers were affected, together with an undisclosed number of fishermen. The inclusion of the latter in the reprovisioning scheme was a sign of changing times, and one for the better, though no details are available.[43]

At first, the District Administration had wished to differentiate between the settlements mainly involved, namely Man Yi Wan (a village complex) and Sha Tsui, on the grounds that only the former would lose everything, whereas the latter would still have its cultivated land outside the reservoir boundary. However, after an intervention by the Heung Yee Kuk, the same terms were applied to all. The final commitment was 104 shops, 335 flats, and seven reprovisioned ancestral halls on a separate site nearby.[44] This reprovisioning was the most generous of its kind to date. The shop size was 1,035 square feet, the flat size was 700 square feet, and the ancestral halls were 600 square feet each with a separate anteroom of 400 square feet, considerably larger than the old buildings they replaced. It is a pity that more information is not available, since changing times must have resulted in new problems, requiring a flexible response.[45]

VILLAGE SCHOOLS AND RESITING

One of the interesting aspects of these removals was that the village schools were invariably included in the reprovisioning process. During a Royal Asiatic Society visit to Kam Tin in 1976, our party were given tea in the Shing Mun village school, which dated from the removals in 1928–31. At Tai Lam Chung and Shek Pik, the existing village schools were also given replacement premises in the new accommodation, as was the Plover Cove school in the Taipo Market reprovisioning in the mid 1960s.[46]

However, with population growth and "New Town" development, Hong Kong's changing education policies in time put paid to the school re-provisionings of former days. A new policy, introduced in 1981, would phase out small village schools, and wherever feasible concentrate pupils in the new standard 24-classroom schools being built in the "New Towns" or in upgraded primary schools in selected regional localities. Offering better educational opportunities, the new policy must, in the longer term, have assisted children's, and indirectly their families', integration into the wider urban community. At the same time, it must have further diluted the former village communities' identities.[47]

CONCLUSION

The removals and resitings described in this chapter are *sui generis*. In regard to compensation alone, they clearly constituted a special category for government, presenting a real dilemma to the District Commissioner New Territories when he was considering how best to deal with removals for urban development in Tsuen Wan–Kwai Chung in 1959–60. In the following chapter, I shall take up this second, even more extensive (and intensive) stage of the village removal and resiting saga.

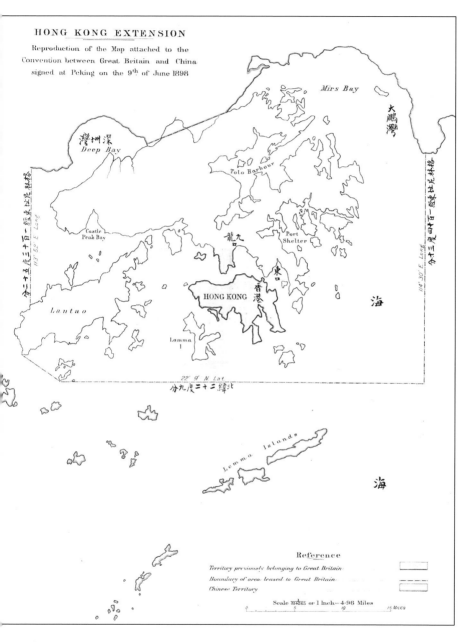

Plate 1 Map attached to the text of the Peking Convention (HMSO publication: Treaty Series No. 16, 1898).

Plate 2   Kowloon, the Kowloon Hills, and Tai Mo Shan (the highest peak in the N T) as seen from Hong Kong Island (photograph by Hedda Morrison, copyright: President and Fellows of Harvard College)

Plate 3   A walled village, Nai Wai near Castle Peak, c 1930 (courtesy Hong Kong Museum of History)

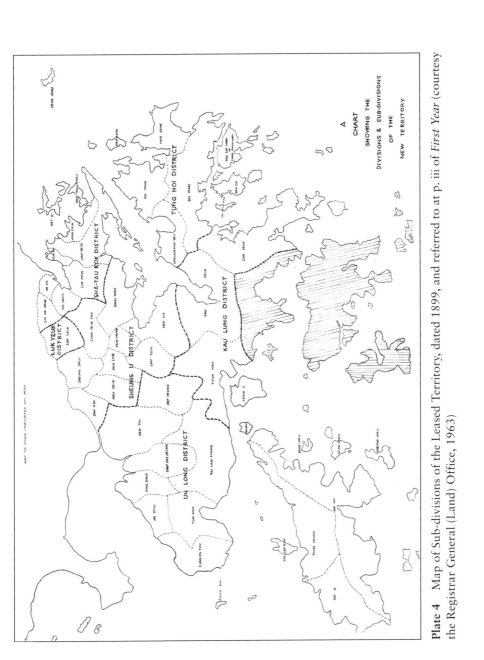

Plate 4 Map of Sub-divisions of the Leased Territory, dated 1899, and referred to at p. iii of *First Year* (courtesy the Registrar General (Land) Office, 1963)

Plate 5
A New Territories valley in winter, c. 1958 (courtesy Hong Kong government)

Plate 6 Shing Mun Tai Wai, the largest of the villages removed in 1928–1931 for the Shing Mun Water Scheme (courtesy former District Office, Tsuen Wan)

Plate 7   Stewart Lockhart, British Boundary Commissioner (*centre*), and Wang Tsun-shan, Chinese Boundary Commissioner (on Lockhart's left) with other British and Chinese officials, during meetings held in March, 1899 (courtesy Hong Kong Public Records Office)

Plate 8   The Sha Po charitable grave, commemorating men killed in the fighting during the British take-over in April 1899 (photograph by Dr. Anthony Siu)

Plate 9 Sir Henry Blake's visit to Taipo, 2 August 1899 (courtesy Hong Kong Public Records Office)

Plate 10 The eulogistic tablet presented to Sir Henry Blake at Taipo (courtesy Hong Kong Public Records Office). Another was seemingly presented at Ping Shan: *First Year*, p. xvi.

Plate 11 Sir Henry Blake and James Stewart Lockhart (both centre) meeting gentry and elders at Ping Shan, 4 August 1899 (courtesy Hong Kong Public Records Office)

Plate 12 A rugged place. The Shing Mun Reservoir, seen here, was built in former agricultural valleys within the mountains (photograph by Hedda Morrison, copyright: President and Fellows of Harvard College)

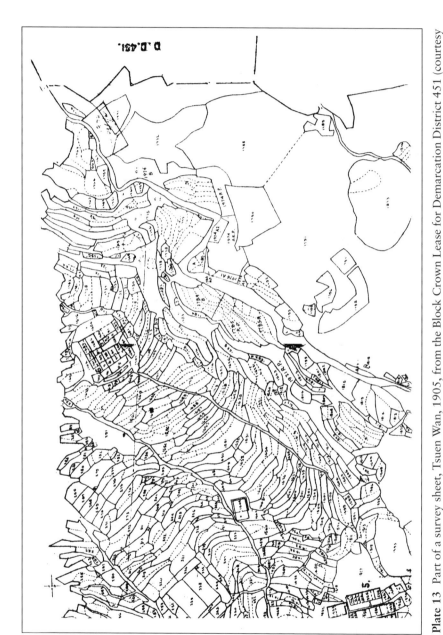

Plate 13 Part of a survey sheet, Tsuen Wan, 1905, from the Block Crown Lease for Demarcation District 451 (courtesy former District Office, Tsuen Wan)

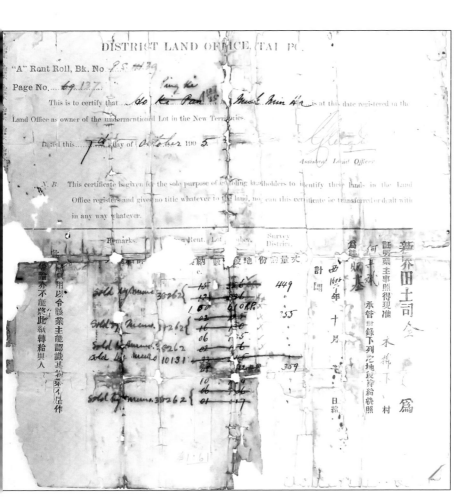

Plate 14 A *chap chiu* (certificate) showing ownership of land at Tsuen Wan, signed by Cecil Clementi, Assistant Land Officer, 1905, with later deletions upon sales (courtesy former District Office, Tsuen Wan). Clementi once wrote, "I calculate that I have signed my name half a million times in less than a year, and anything which would lessen the drudgery would be a cause for rejoicing" (C.C. to Hon C.S., 21.2.06). See n70 on p. 201.

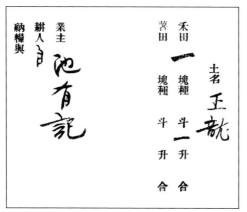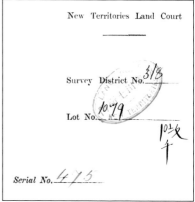

New Territories Land Court

Survey District No.

Lot No.

Serial No.

Plate 15 A *chi chai* ("little paper") issued to claimants to land at Shek Pik, Lantau Island, during the survey and demarcation of 1900–1904 (copy from original provided by the late Chi Cheung-fat of Shek Pik)

Plate 16 Walter Schofield, District Officer South, on an inspection visit to Tai O, c. 1922 (courtesy the late W. Schofield)

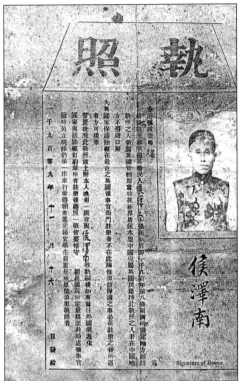

Plate 17
A naturalized British subject (1909): Hau Chak-nam of Ho Sheung Heung Village (courtesy Liu Ching-leung, JP of Sheung Shui)

Plate 18 Women's hard lot: carrying materials from the shore at Gindrinkers Bay up to the new defence works above Kwai Chung, c. 1939 (courtesy Tim Ko)

Plate 19 Women's hard lot: Hakka women on their daily journeys, along an earthen path (photograph by Hedda Morrison, copyright: President and Fellows of Harvard College)

Plate 20 Local Public Works near Sheung Shui, 1956. Denis Bray, DO Taipo with (*seated*) K. M. A. Barnett, DCNT, and their wives at a ceremony marking the renovation of an irrigation dam after storm damage (courtesy Hong Kong Museum of History)

Plate 21 Man Chi-leung, Village Representative of Tai Hang (courtesy Hong Kong Branch of the Royal Asiatic Society, reprinted from its *Journal*, vol. 16, 1976)

Plate 22
Tsui Mun-hei (*centre*), Village Representative of Shek Pik with Ho Luk-kei (Muk Min Ha) and another, unidentified, local leader, 1987 (photograph by Yeung Pak-shing)

Plate 23 Village resitings for the Shing Mun Reservoir: the Hip Tin Kung temple at Kam Tin, c. 1980 (photograph by the late Cheng Tung-on)

Plate 24
Village resitings for the Shing Mun Reservoir: New homes at Wo Hop Shek near Fanling, c. 1993. Yeung Pak-shing with an elderly Cheung (courtesy Yeung Pak-shing)

Plate 25
Village resitings for the Shek Pik Reservoir: urban accommodation in Tsuen Wan, 1960, with a party escorting an image of the Hau Wong deity to its new temple on an upper floor (courtesy Hong Kong Government)

Plate 26
Reservoir removals, Plover Cove, 1966. There is always an air of sadness when an old way of life comes to an end (courtesy Hong Kong SAR Government)

Plate 27 A village woman from Tai Long Wan, Lantau, gathering sea urchins and other items from the shore, c. 1983 (photograph by Christine Thery)

Plate 28
Happiness at the lunar new year: Mr. and Mrs. Tsui Kam-fuk and grandson, Tai Long Wan, Lantau, c. 1983 (photograph by Christine Thery)

Plate 29 Planting at Tai Long Wan, Lantau, c. 1983: Tsui Kam-pui (photograph by Christine Thery)

Plate 30 Ploughing at Tai Long Wan, Lantau, c. 1983: Mrs.Tsui (photograph by Christine Thery)

Plate 31 Development in Tsuen Wan: Sam Tung Uk Village, now a museum, amid construction work for the Mass Transit Railway 1978 (courtesy former District Office, Tsuen Wan)

Plate 32 Development: Tsuen Wan's old Tin Hau Temple being protected during site formation and construction work for the Mass Transit Railway, 1979 (courtesy former District Office Tsuen Wan)

Plate 33
The 1950s in New Kowloon: So Uk Village with Li Cheng Uk Resettlement Estate (courtesy former Resettlement Department, Hong Kong Government)

Plate 34 The Tsuen Wan District Board (now Council) Logo (*top left*), with view of modern south Kwai Chung, 1990s (courtesy Tsuen Wan Rural Committee)

Plate 35
Yeung Kwok-sui, Qing Dynasty literary graduate and early 20th-century Tsuen Wan and NT Heung Yee Kuk leader (courtesy Tsuen Wan Rural Committee)

Plate 36 Local public works on Cheung Chau: trial spin, 1962. Chow Li-ping MBE JP on the right with Fung Pak-choi on the pillion (courtesy Cheung Chau Rural Committee)

Plate 37 The 1950s: Tai O Town and Creek with salt and paddy fields (photograph by Chan Chik)

Plate 38
Old village house interior: An Injunction to Study, pasted on the cockloft, So Lo Pun village, Taipo, 1990s (photograph by Tim Ko)

Plate 39
Old village house interior: Yung Shue Au village, North Tolo, 1990s (photograph by Tim Ko)

Plate 40
Gone away: Ruined house front with Wan On and the author's wife, 1990 (courtesy Wan On's family)

Plate 41
Major public works. South Lantau Road, at Tong Fuk, Lantau Island, 1959 (courtesy former District Office South)

Plate 42 Staying Chinese: Hakka unicorn dance team from Ngau Chi Wan Village, New Kowloon (courtesy Tim Ko)

Plate 43
Village marriage mid-1950s style: Car with unicorn dance team, Ngau Tau Kok, New Kowloon (courtesy Tim Ko)

Plate 44 Staying Chinese: School-children from Sheung Shui paying respects at the main Liu (Liao) grave, 1953 (courtesy Hong Kong Museum of History)

8

Village Removals for New Town Development 1960 Onward: Resitings and New Modes of Compensation

Following on, this chapter describes the rather different compensation policies evolved for the resumptions and village removals required to bring about urban and industrial development in the New Territories. The process began in Tsuen Wan–Kwai Chung from 1959–60 onwards, and continued into the following decade during the build-up of the "New Towns" programme. Ultimately there would be no fewer than nine of these by the end of the Lease, completed or still under construction.[1] The impact of the programme on the indigenous community, and its reactions, will also be examined and assessed.

PART I: VILLAGE RESITINGS IN TSUEN WAN–KWAI CHUNG AND LATER FOR URBAN DEVELOPMENT

Making a Start

Lying close to Kowloon and facing onto the western approaches to Hong Kong Harbour, Tsuen Wan and Kwai Chung were the obvious geographical areas for initial expansion.[2] The first statutory outline plan "for a self-contained industrial township of 650,000 people to be developed over the next 15 to 20 years" was exhibited for public consultation in September 1961, and was approved under the Town Planning Ordinance in 1963.[3]

Extensive areas of seabed would be reclaimed in each place, and old villages would be removed. However, there was a most unwelcome complication in that squatter housing and squatter industry had got there first, especially in Tsuen Wan. By the mid-1950s the population had risen to around 80,000 persons, and was steadily increasing. A losing battle was being fought with often desperate newcomers who had little regard for authority. Control over land use had to be restored in order for planned development to proceed. Resulting from experience gained earlier in clearances in New Kowloon, it would also be necessary to provide alternative housing for those persons (mostly squatters on Crown and private land) who would have to be removed first. All in all, Tsuen Wan was conceivably the most difficult place to start the process.[4]

Avoiding "Reservoir Terms" in Urban Village Removals

Faced with the massive cost of what amounted to more or less a complete re-development, the reservoir-style "total compensation" package, with all replacement houses built by the Government and all village holdings resumed and compensated, presented the authorities with an awkward and unwelcome precedent. From the outset, it was considered vital to adopt different, and less expensive, policies for urban development. This might be achieved by withholding some benefits from the resiting package, and by going about resumptions in a different manner.

First, the authorities sought to *withhold government-built accommodation* in village removals for urban development. Here, the fact that the Tai Lam Chung and Shek Pik villagers had so recently removed to Tsuen Wan, into government-built accommodation, was an embarrassment. The local villagers knew what had been done for them, and not unnaturally pressed for the same treatment.

Second — and the most significant part of the difference between the two policies — was the decision to resume villagers' agricultural and other land *only as and when it was needed*, and not at the time of removing and resiting each village. This, in itself, was not difficult to arrange administratively. All resumptions for a public purpose had to be approved by the Governor in Council, with the necessary funds voted by the Legislative Council. In resumptions for urban development, care would be taken to request resumptions only for projects already in the Public Works programme and ready for implementation — as was, in fact, the usual practice.

However, as with reservoir clearances, all village removals and resitings for urban development must also be *voluntary*.[5] This would have to be achieved through negotiation, and with the villagers' agreement to build the replacement dwellings, and other structures like ancestral halls, under their own arrangements, using the compensation money paid them for their old buildings. It would also be necessary to persuade village landowners to accept that (as indicated above) their agricultural and all non-building land would only be resumed and compensated as and when it suited the government.

These were the requirements of the new policy to be implemented in Tsuen Wan in 1959–60. How to induce their acceptance was the task facing my superior, Ronald Holmes, District Commissioner New Territories at that time.

Implementing the New Policy

As with the choice of Tsuen Wan itself, the first location in which a village removal under non-reservoir terms was required was the reverse of ideal. Part of the village of Ho Pui, one of the inner coastal villages of the township, stood in the way of a box culvert whose completion was vital for completion of the new Tsuen Wan reclamation. The villagers had made strong objection, as their houses were low-lying and below the development levels. They feared flooding, and as one of their representatives wrote caustically to the District Officer:

> The villagers are now living in houses that are more like graves. It is very likely that our village will be flooded in the rainy season, and if this is the case we cannot live in the flooded area because we are human beings and not amphibians.

This sentiment, and a general malaise, dictated the course and mood of the negotiations with the people of Ho Pui, and also with the other two villages affected by the reclamation.[6]

The tortuous and at times dramatic, not to say droll, negotiations with Ho Pui have been described elsewhere. To summarize here, the salient points that arose in their course had been: the high degree of resentment and suspicion that existed among villagers at the time[7]; the amount of time and patience required on the government side; the setting aside of important public works until the opposition had been overcome by peaceful means; and the perceived necessity of arranging for the villagers to move voluntarily and build their new homes themselves on formed sites provided by the government.[8]

In the end, the owners whose houses were in the way of the triple box culvert moved willingly, and temporarily, to a public housing estate, so that work on the box culvert could resume. The basic terms for the regrant of building lots in the village resite area were also negotiated satisfactorily, and the remaining residents would move there when their building contractors had completed their new accommodation. Thereby, after considerable effort, and with the cooperation of the people, the new policy for dealing with village removals for urban development was successfully introduced and applied.

The New Compensation Scheme for Land Resumptions

Resumption was the legal process whereby agricultural and other non-building holdings were taken back by the Hong Kong Government. It had been applied quite liberally from the start of the Lease,[9] and would continue year by year through the century until its end.[10] However, the government's policy of providing compensation in cash only had never been popular, and had been a bone of contention since it was introduced during the development of New Kowloon in the 1920s.[11] The establishment of a Lands Tribunal did not remove the fundamental objection.[12]

In Tsuen Wan, like it or not, the contrast between agricultural and development values was nowhere starker. With soaring property prices, owners could hardly be expected to accept a cash compensation rate determined solely by classification. Faced with a marked reluctance to surrender agricultural land on this basis, alternative arrangements were devised. These involved what were styled "Letters of Exchange" and the provision of building lots within the development layout for granting by exchange when newly formed land was ready. A ratio of five to two was set, which meant receiving back two square feet of building land for every five surrendered, with payment of premium for the conversion to building status.[13]

This scheme was short-lived, for when this concession was demanded in other townships under development, it became impossible to meet the demand for exchanges in Tsuen Wan.[14] However, having to wait without the certainty of an exchange did not kill it. A market in exchange entitlements soon emerged. It became routine for holders to sell them direct to a company wishing to obtain land for commercial or industrial purposes or use their notional cash value to offset the premium; or otherwise to sell to a broker assembling a portfolio for trading with interested purchasers. Either way, the holder received more than had he taken cash compensation.[15]

The "New Towns" Programme

The "New Town" Programme which began in the early 1970s would benefit from the planning and construction work already undertaken in Tsuen Wan and also at Shatin and Tuen Mun (Castle Peak), these three being designated as the first "New Towns". Moreover, a separate New Territories Development Department was created within the Public Works Department to coordinate and implement the programmes in each place.[16]

The chosen three were followed by the decision to expand Taipo from a market township to a "New Town", with similar expansions at the old rural townships of Yuen Long and Fanling–Sheung Shui, and, in the eastern New Territories, by building another "New Town", largely on reclamation, at Hang Hau with Cheung Kwan O in Junk Bay. A variation was the town of Tin Shui Wai, built largely on land reclaimed from the marshes and fishponds lying in the triangle Ping Shan–Ha Tsuen–Deep Bay, in a joint venture with private capital and public funds.[17] Finally, another new town would be built at Tung Chung, adjacent to the new airport at Chek Lap Kok, Lantau, which became operational in 2000.

Generally speaking, the "New Towns" concept envisaged "balanced development". Industrial and commercial zones provided for local employment, and all the requisite services and amenities were installed. In this respect, one "new town" is much like another, varied only where the local terrain helps to dictate the layout and lend character, as at Shatin, where a river and high mountains with the sea in front make it visually one of the most attractive. Tsuen Wan–Kwai Chung, on the other hand, still bears traces of its more difficult and earlier origins.[18]

Village Resitings for New Town Development

Save for Tin Shui Wai, it was necessary to remove and resite a number of old villages in each "new town". The new villages shared certain features in common. First, before long, beginning in Tsuen Wan in the late 1960s, the government had decided that, after all, it was better for it to fund and build the new houses for the villagers. This would provide tighter control over construction time and completion dates, and thus help ensure that the families from the old villages could remove in step with the timing of public works programmes.

Secondly, resitings were from one village area to another. Unlike the postwar reservoir resitings, which were mainly to urban apartment blocks, new villages were created on the fringes of the New Town boundaries. They are clearly recognizable as such, with their rows of gleaming white houses, entrance gateways, and attractive planted-out layouts. Whereas the old settlements had mostly comprised single-storey houses with an average plot size of just over 400 square feet, each new village house had a floor area of 700 square feet on each of its three levels, built to a standard design. The shrines, ancestral halls and village offices had been reprovisioned along with the houses, and village offices, children's play areas, and limited vehicle parking were provided, all from public funds.[19]

Thirdly, as in Tsuen Wan and Kwai Chung, not all villages within a "New Town" layout had to move. Some remained in situ, but land was provided for village expansion areas, and improvements were made to sanitation and to the environment. Some redevelopment of old houses has also taken place, but this is sometimes prevented by the small size of some plots, or is complicated by disputes over boundaries, successions to property, or over *fung-shui*. It can also be difficult to provide for proper sanitation in the new houses, owing to problems with siting septic tanks in the closely built village layouts of the past.

PART II: THE PROCESSES OF RESUMPTION AND VILLAGE REMOVAL, AND THEIR IMPACT UPON VILLAGERS

At this point in the narrative, we should stand back a little, to survey the land resumption and removal scene overall.

General Aspects

The Hong Kong Government acted from necessity. It was obliged to devise means whereby a vastly increased population, mostly come to stay and continually added to by the ceaseless influx of people from mainland China, could be satisfactorily housed, protected from contagious disease, helped towards a means of livelihood, all to be provided within a modern urban infrastructure. On their side, faced with the land acquisition and development programmes resulting from these pressures upon the Administration, the villagers found themselves locked into resumption processes for years on end, sometimes prolonged for over a decade or more, and for many ending in their removal from their old homes and the total transformation of a once familiar landscape.

The resumptions, clearances and removals took place in stages within each statutorily designated development area.[20] Each stage was located as and where required, in line with the step by step planning of the overall project, or fitting in with others. They could be deferred or brought forward as the engineers required, or as dictated by the availability of public funds. The convenience of those affected was not a major consideration, though the advice of the Housing Department (which carried out the clearances) and of the District Office (which took back the land and negotiated with its village owners) was generally heeded and factored into the engineering schedules.[21] The process of land acquisition and clearance brought little but trouble to villagers, as location after location was needed, in whole or in part. Development affected all (see e.g. Plates 31–32).

Villagers' Interests and Preoccupations

The average villager was a petty landowner with his own holdings to consider (generally scattered[22]) and an undivided interest in the ownership and proceeds of other land held in his lineage and village trusts. At the *family* level, livelihood was often directly affected by the loss of produce from self-cultivated land and — increasingly as time passed — of income from rented out fields and houses. At the *lineage* level, the fate of the ancestral hall (or halls) engrossed the attention of all its members. At the *village* level, the interests of the whole community might be involved if a temple, shrine, *fung-shui* grove or other taboo spot stood in the way of a project, or was held to be adversely affected by site formation or civil engineering works. When this occurred, the village representative and all lineage heads were involved, willy-nilly, their actions watched critically by the whole body of villagers.[23]

Old graves were another source of vexation. After centuries of settlement, there were so many of them, all sited by experts to maximize good *fung-shui*, and scattered through the general area in many different locations. The family heads had to arrange for the removal of the graves of earlier generations, while the lineage and branch heads had to deal with the more important tombs of founding ancestors and their sons, arranging for their removal and reburial in, hopefully, another auspicious place that would bring good fortune to them and their descendants. Such obligations — for they were nothing less — were a real burden on those concerned, creating many anxieties and requiring the expenditure of much time and money. The cost was often more than the compensation provided by the authorities.[24]

These various preoccupations and obligations became well-known to the District Office staff engaged in development duties. On each side, patience and forbearance were needed in great measure, as people tried to explain their particular situation and needs to junior or senior officials, some experienced, others not, some sympathetic, others less so, and all generally hemmed in by regulations and government's requirements, especially in regard to the timings scheduled for works and clearance.

The villagers' underlying attitudes and outlook on life were revealed through the many visits, meetings, discussions, arguments and confrontations which took place in the course of our work, and (in a different context) as explained to us by their leaders during many useful and instructive conversations over dinners and lunches at this or that community event in the town and district. Not least among them was their reminder that the accumulated resentments of several hundred years would surface between families and branches of a lineage during village removals, complicating things still further.[25]

We learned to act with tact and circumspection, and were obliged to explain and negotiate our way through opposition and obstruction: that is, if works were to proceed on schedule or, in cases of extreme difficulty, at all. No wonder that some of my land staff, the officers who bore the brunt of villagers' annoyance and resentment, sometimes looked frazzled, especially during the major resumptions, clearances and village removals of the 1970s.[26] Not that I was exactly free from care myself![27]

So far removed from the experiences of any administrator in the city, it is small wonder that one of my senior colleagues, Denis Bray, returning to the New Territories in 1973, this time as District Commissioner, could look back on this period and state, with perfect truth, that its affairs were still, as he put it in his memoirs, "outside the knowledge of people, and officials, in the urban areas".[28]

Complications Arising from Changed Policies

"Take all our land, not just part"

Though still acceptable to village landowners as an alternative to cash compensation, the "Letters of Exchange" scheme was creating certain dissatisfactions. In 1975, during my first round of visits to villages, including some already resited, I was tackled about outstanding exchanges by villagers who had been moved from Lower, and then Middle, Hoi Pa some years before.

Hoi Pa had been the large, sprawling market village of Tsuen Wan before development began to affect the township.[29] Its older structures were on building land, but its later growth had been mainly on former agricultural lots, some converted to building status by licence and some not.[30] There had been a partial resumption of villagers' holdings in the parts already cleared, but those owners whose land was located in different parts of the whole might, as they said, have to wait for years before it was all resumed.[31] They wished us to take back all their land forthwith and issue Letters of Exchange, so that they could work out their own plans for developing urban building lots and press government to honour the exchange commitment. "We have letters of exchange for what government has already taken from us, but no exchanges of land have been given so far", they stressed, urging me strongly to do something about it.

Reasonable enough in principle, there were several snags. Firstly, the villagers had either rented out their land or seen it taken over by determined squatters. They could not give vacant possession as the tenants or occupiers would not move out without rehousing. On its part, through taking back these lots the government did not wish to become the landlord of temporary and squatter dwellings crowded with people: especially when the clearance of the rest of Hoi Pa was not yet programmed. Secondly, long before 1975 (as we have already seen) land shortages and too many village resumptions had led government to discontinue the village exchange scheme, and *in lieu* villagers were having to trade in their letters of exchange in the manner described above.[32] There was yet another reason for caution. Like the resited group, the remaining land owners reasoned that as the market village, Hoi Pa was "different" from the other villages of central Tsuen Wan, and would press strongly for *in situ* surrender and exchange terms, whereby they could erect high-rise apartment blocks with ground floor shops: but it would have been most unwise to vary the compensation terms for village removals.[33]

"But we are not allowed to do anything with it"

In other cases, vexation and frustration focused on land neutralized by a combination of earlier development and planning restraints combined. Typical of such problems was the small area of fields at Che Kwu Wan (Crow-Pheasant Bay), off Texaco Road, standing forlorn for years to one side of this, Tsuen Wan's first road for early industrial development of the headland where the Texas Oil Company (Texaco) had established itself in the 1930s.

Mostly owned by Sam Tung Uk villagers, the land had long been rented out to (or occupied by) others, and was covered with a miscellany of industrial, agricultural and domestic structures, some of them quite old. The owners could neither develop it for their own use or profit, nor could the government be persuaded to resume it. "But we are not allowed meantime to do anything with it", retorted the owners. The Village Representative of Kwan Mun Hau, a quiet and decent man, had come early to my office, more in hope than expectation, to ask whether a permitted structure on his private land could be converted to building status. Like my predecessors, I had to refuse, because lying within the town plan, Che Kwu Wan was earmarked for another kind of development.

"There have been no sales or conversions in the villages for the past twenty years"

Along with the conversion of agricultural to building land, the sale of Crown land for new village houses had also ceased. By the mid 1970s, these prohibitions had already been imposed in the undeveloped parts of the large central area for no less than twenty years. Small wonder, then, that here was another source of grievance, and a major irritant that led villagers to be more demanding when it came to negotiating the terms of their voluntary removal and resiting from the old settlements within the development area.

Under the terms of the village resiting policy, the continuing refusal to give new houses in exchange for houses still on agricultural land, even those built before such conversions were discontinued, created yet more anger. When allowed, all such conversions had been without premium, and those affected saw it as merely a matter of having a piece of paper and paying an increased Crown rent. They would cheerfully pay up the accumulated difference between agricultural and building rates upon request — a suggestion that had always to be declined. Faced with this unpalatable fact, they asserted, with some truth, that such permissions had not been needed before the territory was transferred to Britain on lease in 1898.[34]

Frustrated in these various ways, for the time being most villagers in development areas had little cash in hand until their ancestral land was resumed and their letters of exchange were sold. Also, their dwelling houses tended to remain unmodernized: there was no point in renovating or rebuilding them when it was obvious that village removal was likely sooner or later. Nor were they able to join in the "small house" development that was bringing money to many NT villagers at this time (p. 108 *seq.*). Thereby, it can be argued that village removals for "New Town" development could be, and usually were, more taxing for those concerned than the "clean sweep" within a tight time schedule so characteristic of reservoir removals.

For all the foregoing reasons, many villagers probably looked forward to village removal time: though they fully expected to have to battle for their rights with the authorities in the process. One such brave soul was in the wings, ready to come centre stage.

Accumulated Woes: A "Village Hampden"

In 1976, a clearance above the Castle Peak Road in Central Tsuen Wan involved us with a villager whose various concerns encapsulated most of the grievances listed above. They aroused strong passions in his breast, rendered more acute by the misfortunes which had overtaken his lineage after the NT Lease, with the disappearance of its two villages and its members' virtual extinction. While these could hardly be attributed to the actions of the Hong Kong Government, they had stoked the fires within.[35] It became his unshakable conviction that he and his forebears were not being fairly treated by the Hong Kong government.

Shek Wai Kok Village, and its offshoot the nearby hamlet of Ngau Kwu Tun, had vanished,[36] but some surviving members of the lineage had remained in the area, including the hero of this tale, a village schoolmaster with his two brothers, and a man from the hamlet but now living in Shatin. Others were said to be living at Sandakan in Borneo, to which three men had gone to find work before the War.

I have described the saga of our dealings with him in *Friends and Teachers*, to which interested readers are referred.[37] Suffice to say here that his complaints were repetitions and extensions of the various issues described above. They included loss of rents owing to an unexpected and two-year long delay to engineering and construction work because an economic recession had delayed government funding for the project, but only *after* the resumptions had taken effect and his tenants (and all the rest) had been resettled into a public housing estate; the low cash compensation rate for his agricultural land, which he described as being "only enough to buy a Chinese cabbage!"; a requested back-dating of Letters of Exchange (refused because he had not taken up the formal offer made before the resumption); new resite village houses for his prewar houses on agricultural land, which was not possible because his father had omitted to apply for conversion of the sites to building status (with complaints that pre-1941 outsider owners could get resite houses under the approved removal policy), and still others. At one of our meetings, the minutes record that he had "launched into his usual diatribe about having lived in the N.T. for 300 years and that the Peking Convention of 1898 precluded the Hong Kong Government from taking back people's land".[38] The government, he said, was always forcing people to give up their property. He was a deeply aggrieved and unhappy man.

However, the hand-over proceeded smoothly enough. The long debate had obscured the fact that besides the proceeds from sale of the "Letters" (when they were prepared to accept them) the brothers would be receiving three new, government-built, village houses in exchange for other houses whose sites were already registered in building status. And throughout — *mirabile dictu* — he and I became and remained good friends.[39]

Compensation in Resumptions[40]

As time went on, the cash rate described by the schoolmaster so graphically had changed, and quite dramatically. While the "Letters of Exchange" scheme had facilitated development, the volume of resumed land continued to increase and would do so for many years to come. The commitment to provide land for exchange on the basis evolved over the years had inhibited flexibility in the methods of disposing of new lots and calculating premia. As the land exchange system was under a severe strain from the sheer scale of resumptions and the extent of land required for public purposes, it became necessary to limit the commitment itself. This was achieved in 1978. Following the recommendations of Sir Y. K. Kan's "Report on Compensation for land required for development in the New Towns",[41] the cash compensation rate was raised very substantially. However, those landowners continuing to opt for Letters of Exchange would in future receive only one square foot in exchange for every five surrendered, instead of two as hitherto.[42]

Six-monthly reviews were part of the new compensation process. By June 1981, the cash entitlement per square foot had risen from the pre-Kan figure of $17 to $103, and would keep on rising. The face-value of a new "Letter of Exchange" had also risen from $10 to $52.50, and already a one-year old Letter was selling for about $160, while a three year old one currently fetched $500. No complaints had been received![43]

Meeting Legitimate Grievances: The Small House Policy

Though the benefits from having one's land resumed were by the early 1980s now very considerable, there had also been an attempt to provide for those living outside the New Towns, who were unable to share in the benefits of resumption and village resiting. The Small House Policy, introduced in 1972 was also intended to be seen as a recognition that villagers' land in many places had been, and would continue to be, affected by development and planning controls. The architect of the new Policy was the incoming District Commissioner, New Territories, Denis Bray. As he relates in *Hong Kong Metamorphosis*, just before his appointment there had been a 1,000-strong meeting of village representatives and others in Yuen Long to protest their dissatisfaction with various aspects of official policy in the NT, including the obstacles in the way of obtaining permission to build new houses in the villages.[44]

Under the new policy, all male villagers of 18 years and over would be entitled to receive a "once in a lifetime" house site on Crown land or a conversion of private agricultural land to building status. All sites were to be located within approved village environs, and would be provided at below market rates. Architects' plans were not required, nor approval by the Buildings Ordinance Office of the Public Works Department. This was naturally most welcome news; and given the catalogue of woes described above, it is not surprising that NT villagers decided to make the most of it. Fearful of losing out on their promised grants, practically all eligible adults, whether living at home or overseas, applied. It hardly seemed to matter that they might not have the funds to build their new three-storey houses. There were all the makings of a chronic situation that would last for decades, made worse by the added flow of applications from young men as soon as they reached the qualifying age of 18 years.

Neither party to the Small House Policy was satisfied. The District Administration found itself unable to cope with the demand. In many places, it was difficult to find sufficient sites within approved village environs, layouts were required, and in villages in the more populated areas it was impossible to recover sites without first removing temporary structures and rehousing their occupants. There was continuous pressure from the Heung Yee Kuk for speedier implementation, and for concessionary amendments to standard plans and building requirements. The Administration was also vexed by the frequent abuse of the policy through "under the counter" agreements with realty and construction companies to finance construction in return for title to the new properties, as well as by direct sales of new houses to outsiders following completion.

The authorities undoubtedly viewed the Small House Policy as a concession, intended to assist villagers to provide for their expanding families. On their side, the applicants and their leaders saw it as a means of capitalizing on their principal asset, land, making up for opportunities denied them by government regulations at a time of general expansion when, as they firmly believed, they should be able to use their holdings to become rich. If the government saw things differently, this was not going to change their minds or alter their behaviour. Thus many cheerfully ignored the regulations and restrictions which were devised to prevent, or at least make villagers pay heavily for, any sales to outsiders. But when all is said and done, there is no doubt that rural housing conditions were improved in many places.

Village Expansion Areas in Village Resitings

The "once in a lifetime" grants available under the Small House Policy impinged onto village removals. In Tsuen Wan, the long denial of village expansion within the development areas had led to an insistence that land for this purpose be provided in the replacement village areas when removals and resitings eventually occurred. It was a fair demand in the circumstances described earlier in this chapter, but it was also recognized by realists on the village removal committees that it would be impossible for the District Office to follow the "once in a lifetime" grant policy to the letter. In the event, only a limited number of extra house sites could be provided at the resite areas, and eligible parties (men whose names had been forwarded to the District Office) would have to be content with the grant of a single floor in the three storey houses permitted to be built thereon.[45]

Besides these demands for the inclusion of expansion areas in later village resitings, long sustained requests had come from the three Tsuen Wan villages cleared in the early 1960s and from a few others removed thereafter. Denied permission to build in their old sites, no provision had been made for expansion in their new locations either. Under policies that were less generous than those of the 1970s, some villagers had even remained houseless at removal time. They had not owned houses on building land, and been obliged to live in resettlement estates or rent from more fortunate relatives. Around a dozen of these from the three villages headed the queue for extra housing provision.[46]

In the case of the earliest resited villages (Kwan Mun Hau, Yeung Uk and Ho Pui), I was able to make available 30 house sites at Yau Kam Tau on the hillside in west Tsuen Wan.[47] Despite the difficulties involved, the village heads were able to agree on a division of the 30 sites.[48] What to me seemed even more remarkable was that a list of names for allocation was provided by each village. The 90 selected grantees would each receive one floor, with a one-third undivided share of the house site.[49] It was highly unlikely that the opportunity, or the will, to provide more land would occur in the future.

CONCLUSION

By means of the policies outlined above, the government was able to implement its development programmes.[50] It was also the case that most village landowners, whether caught up in resumptions or village removals or not, would, eventually, benefit one way or another. Some became very wealthy men in the process. By the end of the Lease, the situation of most village families in development areas had improved beyond recognition. Especially in and round the New Towns, they had become urban-villagers. With their future assured, and their links to their past preserved, they were still a readily identifiable group of persons, who were indubitably getting the best of both worlds.

But there is a wider spectrum to be considered. In his address at an Honorary Degrees Congregation at the University of Hong Kong on 3 October 1992, Professor Yu Ying-shih of Princeton University spoke of how Hong Kong had metamorphosed itself from a traditional society into a civil society without having to undergo a revolution.[51] In this context, might it not be argued that the transition would have been that much harder and more uncertain for all concerned had not the indigenous community, despite the grudges and difficulties of the time, chosen to cooperate with the authorities in the early years of major development, thereby setting the pattern for the smoother progress of later years? We should not overlook this contribution, even though, ultimately, it turned out to be to its great advantage. With the longer distance in "mind-travel" needed to make the change-over to modern times, its innate capacity to compromise and adjust, matched to a similar flexibility on the part of the authorities, is worthy of respect. Some at least of the tensions involved on each side must be seen in this broader and deeper cultural and socio-political context. This consideration becomes more cogent when we consider what happened in New Kowloon, though indubitably and legally part of the Leased territory.

New Kowloon

There, the decision taken in 1900 to incorporate it into the urban area had led to a very different outcome for the great majority of its people, and their descendants. Adjoining the older part of the Colony, it was inevitable that their fields would be resumed whenever and wherever needed, and that villages would be subject to full or partial removal. Begun early, and partly completed by 1941, the jerky process dreared on postwar by fits and starts, driven by casual or major need or expedient. Without the numbers, or powerful rural organizations like rural committees or the Heung Yee Kuk to fight on their behalf, the villages were one by one, with only a few exceptions, extinguished by 1997.[52] For as long as they lasted, their existence was precarious and uncertain, while major improvements to the remaining old settlements, for their own sake, were simply never envisaged.[53]

During the prewar period, when the central areas of New Kowloon were being redeveloped, the village fields were being compensated at agricultural rates, without enhancement as land ripe for redevelopment.[54] The old villages and hamlets were being removed, but unlike those in the NT were not being offered resiting. In lieu, besides compensation for structures, exchanges were offered to individual owners of land in building status.[55] Postwar, village situations were worsened by the huge influx of people from China, leading to the environmentally poor conditions so graphically evident from Plate 33. The continuing influx had led in 1954 to the establishment of a new department of government dedicated to squatter control and clearance operations; rendering villagers subject to more controls, and to direct action to remove old and new alike.[56] Another feature of village clearances in postwar New Kowloon was the depressing practice of part-clearance, as and when it suited government; in retrospect, made easier by the fact that squatters (who got even less consideration) had built structures in and all round the old settlements.[57]

More efforts were made in the 1960s to assist in ongoing village removals, whereby sites for constructing apartment blocks were offered to all villagers owning building land, and with interest-free loans to assist in re-provisioning their homes.[58] However, this practice seems to have been ended by an Executive Council decision in 1973 whereby, on the grounds that New Kowloon was completely urban, displaced indigenous villagers would henceforth only receive monetary compensation for their land and houses. The difference in treatment from New Territories villages was not lost on those affected, and in at least one case, a village resiting there was demanded.[59]

The outcome is not difficult to imagine. Whereas individuals might reap advantages from their proximity to the greater amenities and opportunities available in the urban area, as some surely did,[60] the village communities to which they belonged suffered greatly, in most cases being extinguished as such, no matter how long their history and significance.[61]

Though situated within New Kowloon, the Kowloon Walled City (but not its suburbs nor the inlying villages of Sai Tau and Tung Tau) had been excluded from the territory leased under the Convention. Following public protests in commercial and other expatriate circles in the Colony, it was taken over unilaterally in 1900.[62] Thereafter, up to its clearance, and conversion of the area into a splendid park (retaining some of its pre-1898 Chinese government buildings) in the late 1980s, its history constitutes a separate chapter in the Hong Kong story.

ADDENDUM

A very special organization — representing a major new initiative in government — was created for the implementation of the "New Towns" programme mentioned frequently in this book. Looking back, I do not see how we could have done without it, especially in those early years. In 1973, a multi-disciplinary team of engineers, planners and architects was assembled for each of the first three towns under the charge of a senior professional officer of the Public Works Department, styled a "Project Manager". The teams were part of the newly established New Territories Development Department (NTDD), as it was then known.

The responsibilities of each Development Office comprised planning, the coordination of all development, and the organization of civil development using Consulting Engineers and contractors. Besides cooperating with the different Offices of the Public Works Department from which its staff were drawn, and with other departments, it was necessary to liaise closely with the District Offices of the NTA, as the land authority in each "New Town", and to obtain local "feed-back".

Expenditure for each year's works programme was shown under Head 72 (New Towns and Public Housing) in the approved Annual Estimates. Each Development Office had to prepare and submit its list of projects to its headquarters for processing in October each year. This was done with the assistance of the various departments, which were made responsible for providing items for the programme but had first to ensure that they had secured policy approval from central government.

Besides the engineering projects for site formation, roads, drainage and waterworks, the development programme also contained the community facilities (schools, clinics, community centres, sports facilities and recreational open space, etc.) required to serve the existing and anticipated additional population of each "New Town".

From the start, the intention was to use civil engineering consultants for investigation and design of approved projects, and for the supervision of construction by the contractors selected by public tender. The construction of public housing within the new estates was undertaken by the Housing

Department, and of associated community facilities by the Architectural Office of the then Public Works Department.

The progress of each Development Office with its various projects was monitored and directed by an important part of the new machinery; in our case, the Tsuen Wan Works Progress Committee. This had representatives from all concerned departments, and was normally chaired by Director, NTDD, in person. Its important adjunct, the Clearance Sub-Committee, reviewed the progress of land recovery and clearance, so as to match the start of civil engineering or construction works to their intended time schedules. Like the Works Progress Committee it met every one or two months. We went carefully into the position of all land resumptions and clearances, noting problems and charting progress; or the lack of it due to difficulties of one kind or another. As and when necessary, the start programmes were revised in line with the possible. The Development Office would not let a contract unless the way was clear, since any delays to the contractors' work schedules could result in heavy claims for compensation.

Problems were of different kinds. Some were related to land recovery and the statutory or *ex-gratia* compensation payable before removal. Other difficulties could arise if completion of public housing units or temporary housing sites earmarked for clearees were delayed or not available for other reasons. At other times, the problems might lie more in the Project Manager's sphere: ranging from such factors as unfavourable reports from the Consultants on site investigation, to unexpected difficulties with site formation, or to slow or unsatisfactory work by one of the civil engineering contractors.

Through the effective administrative and operational machinery described above, the many items in the Project Manager's and the Housing Authority's approved Public Works programmes took shape and reached completion year after year.

The major contribution of the District Offices stemmed from their being the administrative and land authority in each town and district. The facilitating work of the Tsuen Wan District Office is described herein, and in chapter 6 of Hayes 1993 with chapter 6 of Hayes 1996. Those were very busy and demanding years for all involved in these programmes, but work satisfaction was immense. And in Tsuen Wan, the cordial relationships maintained by District Office personnel with the Project Manager, his principal officers and the Consulting Engineers, and with the senior staff of the Housing Department's Clearance Division, are an abiding warm memory.

9

The Rural Contribution to Community Building in the New Towns, and Its Background

One day in 1978, sitting in the front row of a large Chinese opera matshed on Tsing Yi Island, I was awaiting my call to go on stage. This was to help present banners of appreciation to representatives from the various organizations which had assisted the local Tin Hau temple committee to stage this annual event. Watching one of my rural committee friends bustling about in his customarily relaxed but efficient way, attending to his various duties, it struck me, not for the first time, how managing such events was imbibed with mother's milk, so natural did it appear. Tsing Yi was then part of Tsuen Wan New Town.[1]

During my seven years in the town and district (1975–82) there would be absolutely no doubt of the indigenous leadership's unwavering commitment to public affairs and community building, both on its own and working through the new District Advisory Board established in 1977. Based on the strong sense of local identity and long tradition of self-help nurtured in the villages of Tsuen Wan's three rural sub-districts (Tsuen Wan with Kwai Chung; Tsing Yi; and Ma Wan) the great contribution described in this chapter matched the huge extent of the need. Looking outside the district, the Tsuen Wan input was not an isolated phenomenon, but would be repeated everywhere in the NT, and especially in the other areas designated for New Town development, the degree only varying with the capabilities (in the broad sense) of persons and place. As explained earlier in this book, the leadership ethic was strong, and there was little need to encourage: for the indigenous community was already doing the job.

After recounting the initiatives taken by the Hong Kong authorities in community building and the promotion of more representative government, this chapter will examine the Tsuen Wan contribution in detail, as I experienced it, also providing information on the achievements of earlier years, there and elsewhere in the NT, which enabled the formerly rural, indigenous, organizations to give the crucial support needed in the evolutionary stages of the District Boards.

TSUEN WAN THE FORERUNNER

As in development and compensation issues, Tsuen Wan was the guinea pig selected to trial what would become the New Territories (and before long Colony-wide) District Boards. The first steps were taken there in 1976–77. The moving spirits were Governor Maclehose[2] and David Akers-Jones, the Secretary for the NT. Then in the throes of development, it was euphemistically being termed "Tsuen Wan New Town" but was, in reality, still a chaotic mixture of old, new, and the not so new.[3] With a population of around half a million, being rapidly increased through the housing-led development programme,[4] it may have seemed, despite its problems (or perhaps because of them) the obvious place to start off the experiment that would lead to more representative government, Hong Kong style. To underpin these plans, were a recently strengthened District Office, a Tsuen Wan Development Office, and local branches of service departments, all operating from premises in the town and district.[5]

With the avowed purpose of involving residents in the planning and servicing processes, a Tsuen Wan Advisory Committee for Recreation and Amenities was established in mid 1976. A start was made by making some visible and immediate improvements to parts of the existing town after soliciting suggestions from the public. The interest shown by the committee's members, and the enthusiastic response from the community, were infectious.[6] The committee's impact was immediate, not only on the Tsuen Wan public but on the Governor, who took a personal interest in its work. After only fifteen months in existence, he declared the Tsuen Wan experiment "a success" during his annual policy address to Legislative Council on 5 October 1977, in which he also announced the decision to set up District Advisory Boards in each of the New Territories' districts.[7] By 1982, the Board system had been extended to all urban districts in Hong Kong Island and Kowloon. The "Advisory" prefix was dropped from their titles, and elections by universal suffrage to one third of their membership were held for the first time in that year.[8]

In the New Territories, the wider consultation achieved after 1977 through the new District Boards represented a major departure from the existing arrangements. Up to that point, these had favoured the indigenous population, both by old practice and through the need to maintain its continuing cooperation in the development process. Some reassurances were clearly in order. In Legislative Council a few days after the Governor's announcement, Mr. Akers-Jones assured the NT leadership that the new Advisory Boards "would not interfere in the affairs of individual Rural Committees", which "would continue to safeguard the traditional rights and customs of the indigenous inhabitants". However, he explained that the doubling of the NT population expected to take place within the next decade, had made it "most important to obtain advice from a broad spectrum of the people on what is being done in the districts, and what needs to be done, and to create a sense of involvement and participation among them."[9]

By 1982, thanks to continued progress on all fronts, Tsuen Wan had made the remarkable transition described in my account of its development, published in 1993.[10] From being a depressed, mostly working class township with a population in the early 1970s of around 400,000 people, inadequately housed and provided with insufficient public amenities, it had become an increasingly balanced and confident community, well over half as numerous again owing to a large-scale building programme for public and private housing estates, and with many more facilities and municipal services.[11] This had come about despite the enormous disruptions being caused locally by the ongoing resumptions, clearances and village removals for the development programme: and, notwithstanding the extra burdens imposed, by the central government's decision (1977) to extend (forthwith) the Mass Transit Railway Extension to Tsuen Wan, completed soon after I left the District Office.[12]

Meanwhile, working primarily through the District Office and the Development Office (and with its own secretariat and committee structure to help implement its terms of reference, and with enough money from public funds, annually increased) the new District Advisory Board was able to make a real impact in community building, particularly in the sports and recreation fields.[13] Foremost among those serving the Board in those heady years of achievement were, as we shall see, the leading men of the Tsuen Wan and Tsing Yi rural committees.[14] And yet this was at a time when many of their own villages were in the process of removal and resiting, with all the extra work and worry this involved for them.

THE RURAL COMMITTEES OF TSUEN WAN DISTRICT AND THEIR HISTORY

By virtue of its larger number of member villages and location in the township centre, Tsuen Wan's Rural Committee had always been the most active of the three belonging to the newly established district (1957). As the Chuen On Kuk of the earlier period,[15] it had supplied leaders to the Heung Yee Kuk pre- and postwar, including one of the original "Advisors" to the District Officer, appointed in 1926.[16] We may also note that the two sports bodies of Tsuen Wan's inner villages, the Ching Wah Athletic Association and the Sam Luen Athletic Association, had been established as far back as 1926 and 1928, respectively.

As explained in earlier chapters, the Kaifongs and rural committees of the 1950s were still executive bodies in many places.[17] This was especially the case in Tsuen Wan. In the late 1940s and early 1950s, there had been a great influx of squatters into the township. Being then little more than a great squatter encampment, there was a great need for basic services, and for relief and assistance in time of fire, flood and disease. The District Office, South, was located in Kowloon, with a woefully inadequate staff to cope with its wide range of duties, but the Rural Committee had filled the gap nobly. Hardened in adversity by the wartime occupation of the Colony, Tsuen Wan's village leaders bore the brunt of these pressures, and can be said to have led the community through this difficult time: notably in the severe floods of 1952, when it had raised $6,000 locally for community relief.[18]

It was at this time that District Officer Coates had penned the admiring comment:

> In Tsuen Wan, these [various] duties have become overwhelming, and the same may happen elsewhere. The Chairman of Tsuen Wan Rural Committee is in effect a sort of magistrate and mayor rolled into one. All day long he has a stream of problems to attend to. He is obliged to work a full day from nine to five and maintain his own clerical staff in addition to what is paid for by the Committee.[19]

Nor had the committee let up thereafter. Its good work would span the whole thirty-two year period between the end of the Second World War and the establishment of the Tsuen Wan Recreation and Amenities Advisory Committee, and the Tsuen Wan District Advisory Board, in 1976–77. Through this long period of unceasing development and population growth, it had helped local villagers and newcomers alike with their problems and requests, which in many cases required an approach to government departments and other agencies. Through its energetic leading office bearers, and their constant readiness to cooperate with the District Office and other government departments in meeting emergency situations and joining in community projects of various kinds, it had extended its activities and consolidated its leading position in the township.

In the years before the establishment of the Tsuen Wan District Advisory Board, its personnel had been associated with various important developments in the sports and cultural fields. A Tsuen Wan Sports Association had been formed in 1960, but an umbrella organization incorporating many small groups had been registered in 1967, and with the assistance of the District Office had become a limited company in 1975.[20] And in the cultural field, several groups established earlier to promote the arts had been brought together in June 1976 to form the Tsuen Wan Culture and Recreation Coordinating Association. Much good work had also been done in these fields by the local schools, some of them with headmasters from the indigenous community,[21] and for long assisted by staff of the Education Department of the Hong Kong Government.[22]

The Tsuen Wan Rural Committee continued to work hard all through the 1970s under the leadership of Messrs Yeung Pei-tak of Yeung Uk Village, Chan Po-fong, and his cousin Chan Lau-fong, both of Sam Tung Uk Village in central Tsuen Wan. The brochures prepared in connection with the two-yearly inaugurations of new terms of office-bearers summarize the business undertaken on behalf of villagers and other long-term residents who sought assistance. For the two-year period 1976–78, besides separate mention of major matters, the list contained 131 items. For 1978–80, 178 items were listed, and 180 for 1980–82. Thereafter, with a change to a three-year term of office to accord with the District Board's terms of office, 292 items were listed in the brochure covering 1982–85. Thirteen categories of general business, mainly referrals or introductions for one bureaucratic purpose or another, were included in the reports.[23]

It was steady, ongoing work of this kind, in liaison with government departments and private agencies (and including assistance to the Heung Yee Kuk), which provided the Rural Committee's leading personnel with so much useful experience of public business, thoroughly preparing them to engage in, and further, the work of the Tsuen Wan District Board. Moreover, the Tsuen Wan Rural Committee was alive to the future, and in 1978 had established a *ching tuen* or "youth corps", designed to encourage young village people to take an interest in local affairs and bring forward "new blood".[24]

COMMUNITY EVENTS BEFORE THE DISTRICT BOARDS

A look at the major community events in the district before the advent of the District Board, helps to place the role of the Tsuen Wan and other rural committees in a wider context, showing how their own traditional activities provided the bedrock on which the newer, postwar associations in the town and later the Board, could base their new outreach in recreation and sport.

Opera Performances

Opera, and more often puppet opera, staged for the deities honoured in the local temples, were regular features of villagers' existence from the day they were born, and were among their earliest memories. With heads full of historical folklore, they were familiar with the histories and accomplishments of these gods, and with the events (sometimes viewed as "miracles") connected with them. Opera performances at the Tin Hau temples in Tsuen Wan, Kwai Chung, Tsing Yi and Ma Wan had very likely been held for as long as the temples had existed. Staged in temporary structures (matsheds) erected in public playgrounds or on vacant open spaces, they were annual events, regulated by the lunar calendar and organized by committees in each of the old local temples across the District to honour their patron deities. Public shows, and enjoyable occasions full of life and colour, they were essentially part of the village culture. Moreover, they provided an important unifying force, culture and community being indivisible.[25]

In the population at large, long working hours, in an environment in which the "work" ethic was practiced to the full, both out of necessity and out of conviction, bred conservative tastes. Large audiences flocked to opera matsheds over the weeks of the shows, and it was sometimes difficult to recover the sites. The liking of television audiences for popular dramas with heroic themes and stirring music to match, and the traditional content of the programmes provided over the Lunar New Year period, also confirmed their continued popularity. Writing in the first year of its management of the new Tsuen Wan Town Hall (1981–82), the Cultural Services Department of the Urban Services Department stated that "Cantonese operas and Chinese traditional dance programmes have remained the most popular cultural presentations".[26]

Major Festivals

Besides putting on their own opera performances, the indigenous inhabitants were still carrying out other traditional and long-established activities at other festival times. The Rural Committees always put on a special programme for the lunar new year, forming part of the larger one mounted annually by an *ad hoc* committee under the aegis of the District Office. Another wholly local occasion was the local Dragon Boat Festival on the fifth day of the fifth moon. By the late 1970s, held on Tsing Yi instead of at the now reclaimed Tsuen Wan waterfront, the celebrations were being adjusted to change through invitation to, and participation by, the ever-widening network of community bodies and government offices.[27]

Public Entertainment Programmes

There was, too, the public entertainment provided for the community at large by the local associations coming together for the purpose, old and new alike. As in other township districts, the Tsuen Wan District Office had ever been the focal point for the coordination of community-wide activities.[28]

Up to the establishment of the Boards, major community events had been financed with local contributions and donations, while their venues were usually provided by schools with assembly halls, and by using public playgrounds with the consent of the government department which managed them. Old and new alike, the major local associations could always be relied upon to participate, since this seemed to be a part of their tradition.[29] Youth organizations like the Boy Scouts and Girl Guides always participated, along with other young persons' groups, as well as the local auxiliary units of the St. John Ambulance Brigade, the Auxiliary Medical Service, and the like. In Tsuen Wan and elsewhere in the NT, leadership of these uniformed bodies was mostly held by natives.

Despite modest funding, some of these public shows had been quite impressive. In 1964, there had been a procession "to celebrate the development of the town in the space of a few years from an agricultural community and small market town into an important manufacturing centre". The Governor and approximately 250,000 people, including visitors from Hong Kong and Kowloon, had watched the procession, which had been organized jointly by all the local associations in the town, and featured decorated floats, dragon, lion and unicorn dances, a lantern parade by some 1,860 school children and a fireworks display". In 1970, "a carnival in celebration of the development of Tsuen Wan" was held, featuring, again, "a colourful procession made up of individual items contributed by various organizations, rural committees, and industries".[30]

The staging of periodic shows of this magnitude served to galvanize the organizers into ever larger-scale efforts to match the ever growing population, and to seek the help of new groups and associations as they came into being, and so into contact with the District Office.[31]

THE NATIVE CONTRIBUTION TO BOARD AND COMMITTEE MEMBERSHIP

Against this background of training and achievement, it was little wonder that when the authorities looked around for suitable persons to fill the appointed seats on the new District Board, they concluded that leading members of the indigenous and long-settled community of Tsuen Wan township were well-fitted to carry out the duties it had in mind for the Board. Besides the chairmen of the three rural committees (who had *ex officio* membership of the Board) four other persons were appointed, in recognition of their long-sustained contributions to community work in the town. Even more significant was the recognition accorded them by the other members during the elections of chairmen for the Board's sub-committees. Of the four to be chaired by Board members,[32] three were filled by indigenous members. Moreover, these three sub-committee chairmen sat on the Board's all-important finance sub-committee, chaired by a senior officer from the District Office.[33]

The sub-committees in question were those for culture and entertainment, recreation and sports, and environmental improvement. The men heading the first two sub-committees also led the town's main coordinating associations in these fields. The chairmanship of the annual arts and sports festivals also rested with them and other local people, and when the new Kwai-Tsing District was formed in 1985, the chairman of its first sports festival was another indigenous person long active in community work.

THE TSUEN WAN ARTS AND SPORTS ANNUAL FESTIVALS

Two annual festivals served to integrate the efforts being made by all concerned in sport, recreation and the arts. The Arts Festival, in particular, met these purposes very well, as from the outset it became customary for the opening programme for each year's festival to comprise a joint performance by the performing groups within the Tsuen Wan Culture and Recreation Coordinating Association. The standards aimed at by the association were high. Self-criticism led to greater achievement that heightened satisfaction and spurred all involved to further effort. The 1983 festival brochure mentions the audience-drawing effect of the joint performances upon the local population, especially among the friends and relatives of those taking part "who might [otherwise] never think of coming to a performance of this kind".[34]

In the same vein, the annual addresses of the chairmen of the Tsuen Wan Sports Festival contained exhortations for all concerned, the public and the many supporting organizations alike, to "continue to give their support in the future to promote the sports and recreation activities in Tsuen Wan, to win glory for the district, and to promote community spirit and a sense of local identity amongst local residents". This was to be described, in the following year's issue of the annual brochure, as "the community spirit of 'everybody loves Tsuen Wan'".[35] It will not come as a surprise to learn that the chairmen of the Tsuen Wan Arts and Sports festivals throughout the 1980s were all from the long-settled population of the town.

My successor in the post of Town Manager and District Officer would question the focus on recreation and sport; and the younger, largely newcomer, and certainly more politically active, elected membership of the new District Board established in 1985 for the Kwai-Tsing part of the old Tsuen Wan District would, from the start, prefer to pay more attention to social issues.[36] However, there was no doubt in my mind that, at a critical point in Tsuen Wan's development, this had been the best way to unleash energies and enthusiasms among helpers and to spearhead the drive to create an identity and sense of community in the town — and in so doing, to bring the Board's existence to the widest possible notice.[37] It was also a means to acquaint the community with the government's great expenditure on the provision of amenities to meet the needs of the new population. I have not changed these views in the intervening twenty years.

AT THE PEAK OF THEIR INFLUENCE

During that exhilarating time, by continuing their public service — something truly bred in their bones — local leaders had managed to preserve their supremacy in their own home. But inevitably, coupled to the introduction of voting by geographical constituencies for Board membership in 1982 and 1985, the huge population growth which had prompted the changes in the structure of government and local politics would soon shift the balance of power and influence in the town. The steady growth of an educated middle income group deriving from the construction of private housing estates and home ownership schemes in the town would create a new and different class of local leader. The growth of "politicking" was disliked by the old-style rural leaders and heads of the older associations, who favoured a less combative and partisan approach to local issues,[38] but the change was inevitable. Ultimately, with the abolition of appointed membership in the progression towards fully elected District Boards, only the chairmen of the 27 rural committees would retain their *ex officio* seats on the Boards, and native members were few. [39]

LOCAL LEADERSHIP ELSEWHERE IN THE NT

The Tsuen Wan record was exemplary, but it was by no means the only place in the New Territories in which such a strong lead was provided by the indigenous community, through its rural committees, chambers of commerce and other local bodies. Yuen Long and Tai Po had been more important market centres, and their leaders — in the former especially — had provided themselves with cultural and sporting venues and activities long before their townships were included in the "New Town" programme. [40] There is a stimulating account of Yuen Long in the 1960s in Sir David Akers-Jones's autobiography describing how, with some nudging from its District Officer, Yuen Long had helped itself in those days; it makes for good and interesting reading. [41] The Yuen Long Town Hall, opened by the Governor on 30 December 1970, was built through local initiative with an allocation of funds from the Lotteries Fund. It incorporated a well-equipped library, an auditorium, and other facilities. After four years' further funding, maintenance and running costs were to be met by local contributions. [42] Elsewhere in the NT at that time, to a greater or lesser extent, other old communities were doing likewise, notably Cheung Chau, with its large population and many shops and businesses. [43] Sai Kung, too, had obtained a subsidy to help build a community centre with a "civic hall and a well-equipped library". [44]

Thanks to the local practice of issuing commemorative brochures to mark major events, we can see other local initiatives at work in those years. In 1955 and 1956, two disastrous fires had struck the old market town of Shek Wu Hui in the northern NT, requiring it to be re-planned and rebuilt. On 15 March 1964, a grand celebration, attended by the Governor and the Colonial Secretary, had been organized by a Committee of All Circles of Sheung Shui District to mark the completion of the redeveloped market town, and a special illustrated brochure (in Chinese) detailing its progress had been provided to mark the occasion. [45] The District Commissioner reported:

> The main attractions were a large procession of floats, and a silver dragon over 100 feet long. The Colonial Secretary officiated at the celebrations in the afternoon, while the Governor attended a lantern procession in the evening. It was a spectacular occasion for the market town, and attracted several thousand visitors from Hong Kong. [46]

Just another of the established props which, later on, in the same area, would help to get the much larger community of the Fanling–Sheung Shui New Town off to a flying start.[47]

CONCLUSION

This enterprising public spirit, bred of local identity, did not pass unnoticed in other quarters. In the course of his Oral History Project in the early 1980s, Dr. David Faure had noted the "strong sense of community" to be found in many NT districts, remarking tartly on the fact that "one often finds a stronger sense of history among community leaders in the New Territories than among history students [in the universities]", and adding that this was "one basis for district identity, without which the district boards will not succeed".[48] How right he was!

10

Village Communities in Change

VILLAGE LIFE IN THE 1940S AND 50S

This period is the kick-off point for describing change. No better reporter can be found than John Barrow, District Officer New Territories from 1935 until his retirement in 1952, as the first District Commissioner: the war years excluded, when like the rest of the British and Allied civilian population he was an internee. With his long service, and keen interest in his charges, the early postwar situation is described in his reports and surviving papers with both humour and realism.

Save by boat, much of the NT was still inaccessible. This applied particularly to the Southern District which, under a rearrangement of boundaries soon after the War, now stretched from Lantau in the south-west to Tai Long Bay in the extreme east of the Saikung peninsula.[1] "In terms of distance to be covered (much walking is involved)", wrote Barrow, "this is a tall order, by Hong Kong standards, but containing populous centres only at Tai O, Cheung Chau, Tsun Wan [sic] and Saikung".[2] Elsewhere in the same annual report, he made the telling comment, "One striking fact has been the extent to which the New Territories remain parish-minded: Cheung Chau hardly knows of the existence of Saikung, Yuen Long is a name".[3]

Officials and country people alike continued to think in the old fashion. A widow writing (someone wrote in English on her behalf) from Sai Kung Market to the District Officer South by name in 1952, about two lots mortgaged by her husband during the Occupation, redeemed by herself but somehow still attracting a claim to ownership, had stated:

> I am an ignorant country-woman ... not fully familiar with the laws
> and regulations of the Government of Hong Kong ... As you are the

parent of the populace in this part of the New Territories, I most earnestly urge you to deeply investigate into these cases so that I may be saved from suffering further losses.

The letter was signed with her thumb-print.[4]

This was a shrewd approach. Barrow's printed reports and other papers make it clear that he was steeped in the benevolence expected of him by the widow and most indigenous residents of the NT.[5] And villagers of the day were not above taking advantage of this still prevailing approach.[6]

OLD STYLE LIVING

Little had changed in the places Land Bailiff Peplow had known so well in the 1920s. He would have had no difficulty in finding his way around, nor would he have found anything unfamiliar about the houses in the villages. In June 1950, the then District Officer, South had reported as follows on the village of Ham Tin, on South Lantau:

> The houses are all of one-room structures with the rear portion partitioned into a small dark sleeping chamber. A cockloft usually forms the upper ceiling of the sleeping chamber. Entrance to the sleeping chamber is always on your right as you go in, and the furniture in the main living-room is simple and of varied items. The family shrine (red papers with Chinese characters written on) occupies the centre of the partitioning wall, a few benches or stools would serve as seats for all occasions. Odds and ends are seen lying round all over the room — on the floor as well as on benches and stools. Very few have their floors within surfaced by lime or by cement.[7] [see Plate 39]

Time, indeed, had stood still. Exactly a century before, the German missionary Rev. Ph. Winnes, from his mission station among the Hakkas of Sha Tau Kok area, had sent home a similar description of village homes and their contents.[8]

In those days before the provision of electricity and piped water in most villages, family routine followed very old patterns. All potable water had still to be brought from a stream or well.[9] During the hours of darkness, lighting was by the feeble rays of simple lamps fed with peanut or vegetable oil, and cooking was done with firewood and grass.[10] Most people rose and went to bed early in the countryside. Life was simple, and hard.

Through their New Territories pictures and accompanying notes (1953), John and Veronica Stericker, pre- and postwar residents of Hong Kong with a great interest in the place and its people, confirmed just how old-fashioned village life still was, with pigs, chickens and children much in evidence. Change had begun, but its acceptance was yet dependent on the farmer's state of mind.[11] Some years later, I too would face many situations within this same time warp, especially on Lantau in connection with the Shek Pik Water Scheme.[12] There, in an outlying part of the Colony, never having left the island in their lives, many women had not seen a car or lorry until the investigations into the feasibility of building a reservoir had brought vehicles and mechanical equipment to the village for the first time. Fortunately, friendly elders had provided essential background for a puzzled but intrigued newcomer.

In the winter of 1957–58 (to take one last look at the 1950s) I visited some villages in the outer part of Junk Bay, opposite Shaukeiwan on Hong Kong Island, together with the small island of Fu Tau Chau between. At Tin Ha, I found a community of 150 people without a school, although one had been approved by government and the site was being prepared. The 34 persons on Fu Tau Chau were in like state. All were long-established villagers who relied on selling grass, vegetables, pigs and ducks to the Hong Kong market. Only two families at Tin Ha were rice farmers with a small area of hill paddy. Ferries did not call, and all relied on rowing sampans to take their produce to Shaukeiwan (and some children who attended school there). They were living an old-fashioned life without amenities like electricity, mains water, and convenient schooling for their children, as were many living much further from the city. In their case, one might have said, so near and yet so far![13]

It was situations such as these which so concerned K. M. A. Barnett when he was District Commissioner in those years, leading him to propose the changes in policy-making, administration, and services which he believed necessary in the interests of the native population, as described earlier.[14] Yet the people themselves were becoming catalysts of change, gradually adjusting to a new awareness of modern life and what it could offer.[15]

For those who chose to work and live in the city, the major, highly visible change there was in the height of the buildings. As K. M. A. Barnett wrote later:

> Before 1st June 1956, no building was allowed to exceed five storeys, or eighty feet in height, without a special modification authorized by the Governor, but thereafter an entirely new Buildings Ordinance and

Regulations came into force. Its effects were clearly visible by 1958 in masses of new high-rise apartments, the typical height of which, as the public got used to higher buildings, leap-frogged up from seven to eleven to fifteen storeys and higher.[16]

Thereby, Western-style apartment buildings would replace the four storey, Chinese-style, tenement blocks so common in Kowloon and outer districts of the city. It would not be very long, either, before they would extend to the townships of the New Territories, even before the New Town Programme got into its stride.

A SIGN OF PROGRESS

Electricity was essential to modernization. The China Light and Power Company, responsible for providing a supply in the NT, had begun its operations there prewar. The market towns and some of the large villages on or near roads had received a supply, but the great majority of villages were still without. The demands from government and the private sector consequent upon rapid population growth and industrial expansion, were keeping the company fully occupied, and rural electrification was proceeding very slowly.[17] But the need was great, and neither government nor company could stand still. Jointly agreed, a rural electrification scheme was begun in 1961. To a schedule agreed with the District Administration, more and more villages were to receive an electricity supply under a rolling programme that, by March 1966, only five years later, had extended supply to over 450 villages across the territory.[18]

A NEW FEATURE OF RURAL LIFE

In the decade following 1949 a large British garrison had been assembled in Hong Kong. Numbering over 40,000 troops at its peak, it had mainly to be housed in the NT. New camps were opened, requiring the resumption of farmland, mostly in the northern NT, and British soldiers and vehicles, including artillery and tanks, became a familiar part of the landscape. Traffic accidents and other mishaps were inevitable, but the District Commissioner and his officers were quick to smooth over anything unfortunate.[19] However, the military presence also brought employment and business opportunities in and near the camps, and there was no overt resentment.[20] A former DO of the time, Denis Bray, reminds us how much of the NT road system was constructed by the army in the early postwar period.[21]

As District Officer, South, my particular liaison was with the units in Gun Club Barracks, Kowloon, and Erskine Camp on the Clearwater Bay Road, and with the Command Land Agent over land matters. I had also to keep an eye on anything untoward arising from naval and artillery practice on the Port Shelter Firing Range. The range, gazetted in 1950, besides areas of sea, took in hill land, carefully marked off. Closure of the range to the public for four days a week resulted (so the people of Ngong Wo east of Sai Kung said) in villagers being able to collect firewood for storage and sale for only three days a week in the winter months instead of their customary seven. Moreover, trees had been destroyed by shell-fire from large calibre naval guns. Part of the now ever changing scene, the military presence was not always for the worse.[22]

WAN ON AND RURAL CHANGE ON LANTAU

Between 1957 and 1962, I saw much of South Lantau, owing to my responsibilities for easing progress with the Shek Pik Water Scheme, and for resiting the villagers affected by it.[23] It was then that I met my old friend, Wan On, who still lives at Lo Wai, a village of the Pui O group on South Lantau, where his family has been resident for several hundred years (Plate 40).[24] He was then the first chairman of the newly established South Lantau Rural Committee. We had a lot to do with each other in those days, and have been close friends ever since.

Wan On has spoken recently of the different periods of change during his lifetime of nearly three-quarters of a century. There had been the hazardous Japanese Wartime Occupation with foreign rulers of a different sort;[25] the gradual modernization and economic betterment that had followed construction of the South Lantau Road (1955) and its extension to Shek Pik soon after to facilitate construction of the reservoir and its catchwaters (Plate 41); and the abandonment of traditional farming in the early 1970s, with new living patterns thereafter. The last had ushered in a life no longer linked to the seasons and the natural elements, but lived in the modern style that was now available to villager and city dwellers alike. After 1982, it was also lived under the altered, but now uniform, administrative and political arrangements across the Colony which had removed the old-style District Administration. There would, in due course, be further change after the reversion to Chinese sovereignty in 1997. But in the 1950s, this was far in the future.

PUI O BEFORE CHANGE

In the late 1950s, the Pui O area was in the initial stage of its transition from an isolated rural place to one with better communications with the outside world and far greater exposure to it. The sub-district was still entirely given over to agriculture and coastal fishing. Its beauty and serenity in those early years can hardly be imagined today. Cradled within this idyllic landscape, shaped by the patient toil of man and beast for centuries, its people were steeped in traditional ways.[26] The people's character was described as being straightforward and honest, but was deeply laced with suspicion of outsiders, and anything strange or unfamiliar. Robust and combative by inclination, it was second-nature for them to combine to oppose things unpleasant or of a threatening nature, or simply not known or insufficiently understood.[27] And although normally deferential, they stood up to officials, if provoked.[28]

Construction of the first part of the South Lantau Road in 1955–56 had not been popular. The road had cut a swathe through good farming land as it crossed the Pui O valley. Many villagers lost part of their holdings and had lectured Wan On, telling him that land for farming was a basic need, more important than any road. "After all," they had reasoned, "our ancestors did without one for hundreds of years." He, in turn, had grumbled at me: and once, when having endured too much from him and others at a time when many villagers in Lantau and elsewhere in the District were unhappy with the government, I had snapped at him, he had turned on me sharply and said, "Yes, but you go home by car to your apartment, to peace and quiet, whereas I have to go by ferry, and then by lorry to Pui O; and when I get there, I have to face a hundred angry villagers!"

PUI O IN CHANGE

Later visits enlightened me on how the road was affecting the life and character of the area and its people. One day in 1970, more than a decade after its completion, Wan On and I were discussing the effects of change with other local friends over lunch. "Take transportation," they said. "Before the road, people walked to Mui Wo (Silvermine Bay) or went by sampan to Cheung Chau. It was a day's undertaking, an event. Nowadays, they can go practically anywhere in a day, provided they have the money". "Yes," said one of them, "That's it, money is everything now. Electricity, mains water, buses, all require money." Another added, "It's the same with clothing. Now we all have to have modern clothes, or be considered backward country bumpkins!"

Opening up the area to visitors from the city had caused some difficulties for local people. Initially, the franchised local bus company had given fare concessions to villagers taking produce to market, but with increasing numbers of urban families and young persons coming to the beaches at week-ends and all through the hotter months of the year, bus conductors were charging more at those times, or even refusing to allow them to board crowded buses with their baskets. "The government should licence lorries to carry half passengers, half goods," they all agreed, citing approvingly the special arrangements made by the District Office when the Fan Pui villagers had moved to Tai Long Wan for the Shek Pik Water Scheme in 1959.

The water scheme itself had caused problems by taking water from the catchment areas at Pui O and elsewhere into the reservoir, and its connecting tunnels had sometimes affected the water table, making cultivation in some places more difficult. In any event, some irrigable land was now being given up if it was too far from the road. Before long, more and more people were giving up farming, especially rice, and no young person of either sex wanted to stay on the land.[29]

The village character was also being affected. Villagers had been true rustics. All had led lives in which cooperation, freely given and as freely returned, had played an important part. In a farming community, others would help a farmer if he got sick or his wife had a baby. Those who finished their planting or harvesting first would help out. A meal was given in return. Even persons who were not on good terms with others would be assisted, since help would not be withheld on that account. It was common to loan draught animals on the same basis. Such cooperation, it was stressed, was entirely voluntary, a recognized part of village life.[30] Wan On had emphasized the importance of mutual good relations (*kam ching*) in the community. Where it existed, people would do things for you even though they really couldn't be bothered. Modernization didn't alter the need, though it affected the degree and context; but by 1977, as his alert and capable daughter had told me separately, there was less mutual aid and the *kam ching* spirit than before.

Even villagers' appearance was undergoing change. Modern clothes and an improved diet had wrought transformation in the outer man. When Shek Pik people, now become townees, returned occasionally to Lantau, as at the twice-annual grave-worshipping festivals, it was said that they were "fatter and whiter" (i.e. less tanned and weathered by the sun and wind) and decidedly "more difficult to recognize". As the Pui O villagers stopped farming and turned to other work, something of this change was also visible there. The villagers of yesteryear were no more.

THE GOVERNMENT AND THE VILLAGES

The government, too, and its changing behaviour, had come into many of the conversations I have had with Wan On and his friends over the years. During that lunchtime discussion in 1970, the local police had attracted criticism. In the past, if taken to them, quarrels between spouses or fellow-villagers were usually referred back to the Rural Committee and the elders to sort out, but there was now an increasing tendency for the police to treat them as "cases", "so as to boost their statistics" it was thought. In an incident at Mui Wo, where a village woman had become irate with a conductor who refused to let her take her basket on his bus, the police had taken her to court in Hong Kong. All present thought this unnecessary. The police did the same with gambling offences, which again, it was affirmed, were not true "crimes".[31] Youths might have little else to do for amusement and recreation, at a time when new-style local amenities were still under-provided or non-existent locally.[32]

The truth was that all parts of Hong Kong society were in the process of change, affecting government departments as well as the public. The Police Force was becoming much bigger, and more sophisticated in its training and procedures. The old-style approach and methods, serviceable and suited to rural conditions, but at times rough and ready, were now giving way to modern methods.[33] The change was bound to become more apparent and less readily accepted in country districts like Pui O, where in the past relationships had been friendly, often genuinely warm on either side, and elders' cooperation had been needed (and expected). The same change could be detected in civilian departments of the government with equally predictable results, sometimes exacerbated by ignorance, insensitivity, or by unduly bureaucratic behaviour.

With the introduction of elections to the District Board system in 1982 (to look ahead) the work of the Village Representatives and lineage elders had become more difficult. They now considered themselves less well-regarded or valued by government, while the altered political arena concurrent with profound social and economic change had weakened their standing and authority. Pondering the new situation, Wan On said that young men and women knew nothing of the old ways of life. These had gone, and were outside their experience. Nowadays, the elders had little influence. If anything untoward happened in the village, or anything displeased them, the young people thought immediately of writing a complaint letter to some authority or other, or to a District Board councillor. They did not think of the need to resolve harmony. Truly, he concluded sadly, the old and the new Pui O were now worlds apart.

CHANGE IN ANOTHER KIND OF VILLAGE COMMUNITY

Not all villages had broad acres. Coastal fishing had been common all over the territory, the methods used generally dependant on the terrain.[34] In such places, the menfolk were doubtless to be numbered among that "considerable number of the inhabitants" who were, Sir Henry Blake reported in 1903, "engaged [in fishing] for a portion of the year".[35] The Pui O villagers also fished in these various ways, but as in most places with sufficient rice fields, it was not their main means of livelihood.

Among those for whom it was more of a necessity were the members of the Ng lineage of Lo Tik Wan on North Lamma (pop. 83 in 1958). The Ngs had only an acre of rice fields, and another acre and a half of dry cultivation on which they grew sweet potatoes, so that their menfolk had had to find a principal livelihood in coastal fishing. Working as stakenet fishermen, their fishing stations had been located across the water on the south of Hong Kong Island, at Nam Wan (South Bay) and Stanley, and farther away on Cheung Chau. When I first visited Lo Tik Wan in the winter of 1957–58, only 33 persons were still living in the village, the remainder having already moved to a new settlement recently built on the shore, below the old.[36] Its beach had been covered with the coarse high rushes known as *lo so*, common to some places in the region, but these had all been cleared and planted with sweet potato, whose leaves and vines form excellent food for pigs.[37]

Pig-rearing was now their principal occupation, replacing coastal fishing, now almost at an end. This was probably the main reason for their moving from the old village, another being the inadequate water supply in the dry winter months. However, the change had involved them in a new set of hardships. The nearest outlet was the government retail market at West Point on Hong Kong Island. Mature pigs had to be taken by rowing sampan to Aberdeen, from which a wholesaler's lorry would convey them to the market. The water crossing was arduous, and even hazardous in an east wind. Like their neighbours at Luk Chau, they had asked for my help in obtaining a licence from the Marine Department for the motorized junk they hoped to buy by dint of combined savings to ease their difficulties. Pig-rearing itself was chancy, owing to fluctuating prices in competition with other suppliers, including those from the Mainland, and the ever-present risk of epidemics. One hundred pigs had died in one earlier in the year of my visit. As at Luk Chau, their pigs were not being vaccinated, and they were urged to seek the help of the Agricultural and Fisheries Department.[38]

Those Ngs living elsewhere had also been obliged to find an alternate means of livelihood. I got to know some of them quite well in the late 1960s, especially those living at Stanley and South Bay, where a man in his early 40s described their earlier history in those places, and his own problems in adjusting to changed conditions. His grandmother had been the first of his family to go there from Lo Tik Wan, probably about the time of the Lease, taking her four young sons: her husband had been a seaman, and was either dead or away for the long term. Moving later to Ma Hang at Stanley to work a stakenet there, she had built a rush hut at the site and was still living there in 1969, aged nearly 90, a woman to be respected for her fortitude. The two elder boys, one of them my Mr. Ng's father, had stayed at South Bay, and the younger ones went to Chung Hom Wan near Stanley to fish there. His father and uncle had operated three stakenets in the vicinity of South Bay, and had also set up a seine net round the bay itself. Like a few other village fishermen of my acquaintance, his father had been injured in the course of "fishing" with dynamite, losing both his hands.[39]

Steadily reducing catches obliged him to find other ways to make a living. He had been most resourceful and energetic:

> He admits, among other things that bring him an income, to looking after private bathing huts, working as a night-watchman at a beach hotel-restaurant at Repulse Bay, and doing casual work at a restaurant in Wanchai: but as he has a telephone and tap water in his house and runs a car, he must be accounted among the luckier (and more enterprising) members of a community that has otherwise suffered misfortune through the loss of its traditional occupation.[40]

His cousins at Chung Hom Kok and Stanley were still making occasional catches, but had to resort to casual employment to make ends meet; while as already mentioned, their relatives at Lo Tik Wan, also former stakenet fishermen, had all turned to pig-farming behind the beach.

MEASURING INTERNAL (COMMUNITY) CHANGE

Change can be measured in more scientific ways, and over a longer period. A study of this kind was undertaken by another of the overseas postgraduate students who studied village communities in Hong Kong during the 1960s.[41] John Brim of Stanford University assessed change by looking at activities and what he styled "goal attainment" past and present, going back to the early days of the Lease. In his words, defence, provision of economic benefits, dispute settlement, procurement of supernatural benefits, production maintenance, and representation of the villagers to outside social systems were the principal goals of the past. With its emphasis on *internal* change, Brim's work complements the descriptions provided for Pui O and Lo Tik Wan, which have more to do with external and individual manifestations.

For his investigations, Brim chose the multi-lineage village of Fui Sha Wai off the former main road between Tuen Mun and Ping Shan.[42] The village had 331 inhabitants, and was of average size for the area. There had been five lineages living and holding land there in 1905. By 1968, the amount of land owned by the villagers had scarcely altered in the intervening sixty-three years.

To attain its goals, the village had been highly integrated and tightly organized at the time of the Lease. In this regard, it was in my estimate typical of practically all other village communities of the day. There was the shared participation in protective rituals, performed on behalf of the community daily, and at certain occasions through each lunar year. With one exception they still being performed in 1968, and included the daily performance of rituals at up to seven places within the village perimeter, in the early morning and at dusk, by roster of households on behalf of the community. Each evening, the board bearing the characters for "Burn incense, every household one day" was hung on the next household's external incense holder. The materials were provided by each household, and it was usually a woman who performed the duty.[43]

Another of the old goals, defence, had been immensely important in 1905, but had become less so with the area policing and greater security provided under British rule. The last fighting with neighbouring villages had occurred in the 1930s.[44] Intriguingly, the remaining manifestation of mass action by the menfolk of the village were the attacks on anyone detected in a robbery, and the assaults made on any driver involved in an accident with a villager, irrespective of who was to blame.[45]

The provision of economic assistance to villagers from the village treasury was formerly of the utmost importance to those villagers who lost all or part of their rice crop or suffered theft of livestock (specifically, pigs). It was funded from assessments in unhusked rice collected from each family, but from the early 1960s was now collected in cash as more households gave up rice farming. A Kwan Tai Wui (association) was another source of funds, along with miscellaneous sources of income. Also organized by the village treasury, maintenance of the main irrigation system had been carried out by collective action. Although not a heavy duty, it had been important for crop production, branch maintenance being left to those households reliant on them. Neither was now required.

The representation of the community to other villages and related sub-districts was always of importance in the past. As in other places, the San Fung Wai unicorn team represented the village, and exchanged visits with those of other settlements. It still participated in the festivals held annually at the old Tin Hau temple in Tuen Mun, especially in the "rocket-snatching" competitions, in which success brought luck to the village and marked the skill of its menfolk. Representing the village to the authorities was the duty of the elders, who were also charged with the resolution of disputes, internally and at need externally.

By 1968, the only one of the six goals which was continued more or less intact was in the ritual field, though new ideas were challenging the fundamental tenets of villagers' beliefs in the old cosmology, threatening to undermine this as well. The impact of these changes had fallen not on the individual households, but on the community. In the course of change, Sun Fung Wai had lost the cohesion formerly so vital for its security and continuance in its former situation, but much less needed in the changed and changing world around them.[46]

CHANGE IN ANOTHER PART OF THE NT

Notes of visits made to other places in the NT indicate (yet again) the variety of situations to be found within the territory. Informed vignettes, rather than in-depth accounts, they are based on observation and the talks with friendly elderly persons encountered during my walks into their villages. There had been stagnation, even decline, in many places, but there was also change, past as well as present.

The Tsiu Keng Valley, near the Fanling Golf Course, is a case in point. Small, measuring only 4.650 square miles all told, it possessed eleven old villages.[47] It must have witnessed stirring events in its time, as an old cannon, cast in 1650 when a Ming royal prince was resisting the Manchu invaders of his country, was found here in 1966.[48] Tsiu Keng Lo Wai, although small, looked to have been walled and even moated, but in March 1971 was largely in ruins, with the granite fittings from its old houses lying around the enclosure. Opposite was a much newer settlement of the Pang lineage, named Pang Uk. Another village, Cheung Lek, was even newer, with an impressive collection of good quality houses, built all at one time and in the traditional style, by a branch of a lineage from the Sha Tau Kok area which had moved here in the 1920s. There were other settlements, together with an old temple completely reconstructed in 1966, said to have been built by the Tangs of Lung Yeuk Tau two hundred years before. Two old bridges, one of them (according to a tablet in Chinese and English) repaired in 1957 (after damage in a major rain storm) with the help of officers and men from the British cruiser, HMS *Newfoundland*, added to the interest. The population of the valley was mixed, with both Cantonese and Hakka, each of long standing. At the time of my visit, many of the fields were being converted into fish ponds, but not by villagers.[49]

CHANGE THROUGH IN-MIGRATION OF PEOPLE AND CAPITAL

Yet another type of change must be added to the rest. The large old settlement of Tai Po Tau had been occupied by a single lineage for around 400 years when, in 1964, the Sociology Department of Chung Chi College[50] chose it as a site for field practice by its students.[51] Located a mile outside Tai Po Market and its railway station, with its track and a highway running along its western side, and only 45 minutes by train or car from Kowloon, the village was favoured with good communications.

Formerly a tightly knit society of kinsfolk, by the end of the 1960s the indigenous residents were now greatly outnumbered by incoming migrants. By 1966, there had been 169 clan members and 388 immigrants, and in another survey three years later the figures were 156 and 440.[52] They had not opposed the postwar influx of people and capital, and as this group increased in numbers, their own declined, not only through the now common emigration to UK and Western Europe, but, in equal proportions, to Hong Kong, Kowloon, or to other parts of the NT.[53]

No longer had they to endure a subsistence livelihood. Nor were they subject to the "earthbound compulsion" (Rance Lee's phrase) which had tied them to the place for centuries.[54] With an influx of people and capital, family incomes from rents, overseas remittances, and employment other than farming had increased, and were appreciably higher than those of most newcomers in their midst.[55] These momentous changes were due to what Lee has called (in another apt description) "the impact of industrial-urbanism", which in this particular village, were more striking than in outlying places.[56] However, it may be considered quite typical of others enjoying similarly convenient communications with the city and other major centres in the NT.

THE TIMING OF CHANGE

Pondering the catalogue of change assembled in this chapter, it would appear that the alterations in life-style and outlook noted in different parts of the NT, and for a variety of reasons, appear to have taken place more or less at the same time – that is, in the 1960s – and practically everywhere.[57] This is certainly the case with younger people, as reflected in the clothing being worn by family members in old photographs left in abandoned houses in its remoter parts. After noting such mementos in the ruined villages of Yung Shue Au and So Lo Pun (Tai Po District) in the 1990s, Tim Ko told me that the Westernized marriage dress favoured by young persons of the 1950s and 1960s seemed to be as common there as in his own semi-urban village of Ngau Tau Kok in East Kowloon.

Inside the family, modern marriage meant more than favouring Western dress. In Hakka families like Tim Ko's, it brought what must, at the time, have been considered as a truly distressing change in a group otherwise so tenacious of their identity and proud tradition of being different from Cantonese (Plate 42). The widened marriage field wrought by demography, employment and urbanization was bringing non-Hakka speaking brides into very conservative families. Together with the spread of public education conducted only in Cantonese (and English), and the general use of Cantonese as the *lingua franca* of Hong Kong, this had created a situation where Hakka, formerly one of the main languages of the NT (and also of pre-1841 Hong Kong and Kowloon) was soon only in use at home, and before long would be barely understood by the grandchildren. As one of my Tsuen Wan friends told Betsy Johnson, the Hakka culture was being diluted "like a drop of ink in water".[58]

Women's lives, and marriage customs in particular, were greatly altered by modernization. How these changes came about is explained in chapter 6,[59] but if we want to focus on externals, the bridal chair is as good a symbol to consider as any. For so long the means by which a woman was conveyed to her new home in cheerful procession, along with her dowry objects and to the accompaniment of musicians and fellow villagers, it was still to be seen into the 1950s, and even into the early 1960s on Lantau, but where roads existed it became more fashionable postwar to use a motor car (Plate 43). The chairs were left to moulder away in the side rooms of ancestral halls and outhouses until they became scarce objects eagerly sought after by museum curators.[60]

HAWKERS, VILLAGE SHOPS AND BUSINESSES

Turning to a different field, the pattern of services to villages had begun to change in the postwar years. Rural people had always relied on itinerant pedlars to bring foodstuffs and many simple goods into the villages, even in places as close to the city as those of Cheung Sha Wan and the Kwai Chung area. The rest could be obtained from shops in the nearest market town, often in bartering arrangement whereby villagers got credit for purchases against the sale of produce from their farms, coastal fisheries, or hillsides.[61] Shops there carried many lines of business,[62] and a few business records have survived to show the type and scale of commercial transactions with village people in various places.[63] While there seem to have been a few small shops of the "convenience store" variety in the larger villages, selling very limited lines like groceries, kerosene, joss paper and ritual goods, cakes, sweets, fruit, and the like,[64] the hawkers had been a more significant feature of rural life, taking their wares to many remote places involving them in strenuous walking with heavy burdens, like the rough crockery used in all villages of the time.[65]

At Pui O, modernization saw the opening of shops and cafes as the new roads and bus services brought more urban people into the area to enjoy the beaches. The Europeans employed on the reservoir works had been the first to encourage novelties like Indian and Italian restaurants, which sold imported wines and spirits in addition. The roads also made it easier to bring over and distribute kerosene, and later Towngas, for home and commercial use, and for leaders like Wan On and other friends to get a franchise to run a petrol station. He himself had always shown great enterprise, opening various concerns in connection with the Shek Pik Water Scheme, including a cinema, and an eating house and transport service for workers engaged on catchwater construction; and, over many years, he had used his own and Crown permit land at Pui O for other projects, including a roadside café, a beachside restaurant with holiday accommodation, a fish farm (patronized mainly by appreciative kingfishers) and a more ambitious scheme, only now approved after years of delay, for a holiday recreation and entertainment centre. Other, equally ambitious proposals had come to nothing, since he was far ahead of government planning for the area, which was notoriously lagging for all kinds of reasons, good and bad.[66]

Like many others, Wan On had experienced a downside to progress. From 1904, the government had recognized customary village rights to what became Crown hillside by granting forestry licences, annually renewed, to cover their pre-1898 use for various purposes.[67] The licenses issued from then until around 1971 had contained a clause providing for compensation. This applied to public utility companies using such land as well as to the government itself, but by degrees this protection, "by act of grace" as the prewar licences stated, was whittled down, until in later years no compensation was either paid by, or pressed upon, the companies concerned.

THE EFFECTS OF OUT-MIGRATION

The overseas migration of so many villagers and their families is well-known.[68] Here, I shall be describing only the physical and social consequences for one of the many villages which had turned to employment abroad, though the experience was, by observation, surely general.

With its Old and New Villages, both occupied by the Ho lineage, Kei Ling Ha is located in the Shap Sze Heung in North Sai Kung. At the time of my visit in March 1990, Mr. Ho Kei-fuk, the very knowledgeable Village Representative, was kind enough to take me round the two villages. Born in 1928, the 28th generation of his particular lineage, he told me that the first ancestor to come to Kei Ling Ha was of the 12th or 13th, making the length of settlement there roughly four hundred years. The New Village had branched off from the old Wai 114 years before, with the first houses dating from about 1876. In 1960, the combined population was 135.[69]

Turning to the present, the Village Representative said that many families were in England. If all returned, together with the four families living in Sai Kung, the number of persons belonging to the two villages would be about 140. Before people went away, it had been usual at the Lunar New Year to worship at the ancestral hall in the new village and then go in procession with unicorn dancers and music to the ancestral hall in the old (Kei Ling Ha Lo Wai). Nowadays, some overseas people did still come back for New Year, staying in empty houses, but the overall numbers were much reduced. There had been only three tables at the dinner this year (1990), or around forty persons, more or less average in recent times.

We then went to the Old Village, which had its own Village Representative. However, Lo Wai was a shadow of its former self. Many old houses had fallen down, though some survived. There were a few newer structures inside the wall, with some modern village houses outside and above the old settlement. But everything considered, the Wai was far gone, with only a handful of people still in residence. One reason given for its decline was that it is too far from the present motor road, and well below it. As one woman told us, pretending to puff, it is a big effort to get in and out!

Elsewhere in those parts of the eastern NT, with a friend and former colleague, I visited many other outlying villages in those years. They were either already abandoned or well on the way to being so. We would find an apparently solid façade, with the door firmly secured in the time-honoured fashion, waiting for its occupants to return (as in Plate 40) only to find a complete ruin behind. Occasionally we got a pleasant surprise, to find old houses — in this case a whole village — being put to new use. This was the Hakka village of Shek Hang, recorded as having 30 inhabitants in 1960.

We were on a Waterworks minor road, in the mountainous and most pleasantly wooded area at the head of the Tai Mong Tsai Valley, east of Sai Kung. We heard the prolonged barking of dogs, and were passed by a van. Further up, two smart girls in overalls and pink half wellington boots appeared. Turning a corner, we came across the village, apparently intact, where the mystery was soon explained. The van and the girls belonged to private kennels, which had taken over the entire place. Other similarly attired young women were busy in the wire enclosures, which had been erected on the concreted spaces in front of the houses. Judging from all the activity, it was a flourishing concern. Of the Cheungs of that place there was no sign, though they had been resident there and lower down at Tai Po Tsai Village for two centuries.

About the same time, in Pak Lap (pop. 80 in 1960), also in East Sai Kung, after most villagers had moved out to seek a livelihood elsewhere, it seems that a contractor was running the newly restored old houses as a hostel for overnight visitors to this popular recreational area, and that the villagers' vegetable plots were being re-cultivated to supply its restaurant.[70] Clearly part of the deal, the ancestral hall of the Lau families who comprised most of the village owners had also been rebuilt.

CONCLUSION

For decades, change and modernization have affected rural life. Many villages survive, in a new dispensation, but in many places, both before and after the Second World War, others have been abandoned by their inhabitants for lives elsewhere, overseas or in Hong Kong. But even where the people have left, their ancestral villages have not been entirely forgotten by the families who once lived there, or if it was long since, by their descendants. In remote locations, the only structure still standing was — sometimes still is — an ancestral hall, without most of its roof but with a crimson carpet of firecracker fragments in front of the entrance, testifying to descendants' visits, at Lunar

New Year or one or other of the grave worshipping festivals in spring and autumn. In other places, however, nothing remains to remind us that here had been the habitations of past generations of tough, resourceful, and supremely enduring men and women.

11

Identities: Staying Chinese during the Lease

In the century of the Lease, two events stand in sharp contrast to each other: the heroic support for the Allied cause during the Japanese wartime Occupation, and the overt support for the Communist opposition to the Hong Kong Government during the Disturbances in 1967. This was, on the face of it, one more curious paradox.

What went wrong in the intervening twenty years? Or despite appearances, had there long been an undercurrent of dislike and disaffection, harking back to the armed opposition to the British take-over of the New Territory in 1899, and even reaching further back in time? And what of the effect upon local allegiances of the Chinese Revolution of 1911, which had encouraged nationalism and led to major anti-foreign incidents in the 1920s, including the Seamen's Strike and a General Strike in Hong Kong?[1] The Communist success in wresting control from Chiang Kai-shek, with its intention that China should once more "stand up" as a nation, was another and later factor; for many a source of quiet pride, but in itself of great concern for the Hong Kong authorities.

Assuredly long and complex, the background to the 1967 Disturbances in the New Territories, as in the Colony at large, will bear fuller examination; to include a scrutiny of Anglo-Chinese relationships in and through Hong Kong.[2]

CANTONESE XENOPHOBIA

The prevailing anti-foreign spirit in the Canton Delta in the 1870s and 1880s was vouchsafed by an American missionary, Rev. B. C. Henry, who by reason of his extensive travels knew the province and its people better than most:[3]

The ruling classes, the officials and the gentry ... are opposed to innovations and reforms of every kind. They are exclusive to the extremest degree, and would never have had intercourse with other nations had they not been compelled to do so ... . It is enough to say that a thing is not Chinese, especially in matters of ethics and religion, to stamp it with disapproval. ...

Intercourse with the aggressive nations of the West has developed this indifference into active hostility, and made hatred of foreigners a prominent characteristic of the influential classes, and, to a great degree, of all classes.[4]

Rev. Henry especially emphasized the bitterness of feeling against the foreigner in Canton, a view shared by a bishop of the American Methodist Church with previous service in China, after a visit to the mission field in 1878.[5] Nor was the situation much improved by the end of the dynasty in 1911.[6]

Some of this feeling must have been carried over by those Cantonese electing to go to Hong Kong in search of work before and after 1898. Although, thanks partly to Lockhart, relations with the Chinese elites in the older parts of the Colony were close and amicable, this was decidedly not the case among the labouring class. A decade later, Governor Sir Henry May (1912–1919) was decidedly frank on the subject, telling the Colonial Office in London that "the real feelings of the mass of the population towards Englishmen in this Colony", could be described in one word, "animosity"; and how the animosity against foreigners, "always existent in the Chinese mind", had been inflamed by the recent [Chinese] revolution.[7]

A BAD TIME TO BE HANDED OVER

The Lease had come at an unfortunate time in Sino-British relations. By then, the British had become accustomed to lording it over China and Chinese. The expatriates' approach had attracted Lockhart's criticism as early as 1890: "They regard themselves from first to last as teachers, not learners, and the attitude they assume with regard to China ['that old fossil'] is entirely onesided".[8] Another observer of the contemporary scene, the long-serving American missionary Bishop R. H. Graves of Canton, also complained of the "assumption of superiority and authority", which constituted the standard Western approach to most things Chinese, and of "the *overbearing manners* [his emphasis] of so many foreigners", which in his view had "created a prejudice against Western civilisation".[9]

Grounded in complacency and pride in scientific progress, these attitudes were encouraged by the failure of China to modernize, and had been reinforced by her recent ignominious defeat by Japan in 1894–95, which had increased colonial and commercial adventurism in China by the great Powers.[10] To be a Chinese diplomat in those sad days of China's weakness was a humiliation, keenly felt by those unfortunates who had to serve their country in European capitals at those times.[11]

THE CONTRIBUTION OF THE HONG KONG BRITISH

The trappings of a Crown Colony, with its governor and his officials, general and garrison, admiral and fleet, and a full array of foreign consuls, were a constant reminder to expatriate Britons of their great empire, while the presence of the world's commence in Hong Kong's fine harbour added to the prevailing hubris.[12] The sense of Western superiority and Chinese inferiority, by then so strongly entrenched, was to flourish and continue unchecked for decades to come.

There was a further element in the mix. The Colony had originated as a place where merchants could do business without the vexations and uncertainties associated with the "Canton system" imposed by the Chinese authorities on foreign trade for two centuries. This promoted the growth of the long-held view (styled by Hong Kong historian George Endacott as "the unspoken assumption") "that Asians, and in particular the Chinese, were not forced to come to Hong Kong, and if they did so that was their own affair and they must accept conditions as they found them".[13]

The Chinese residents and sojourners of Hong Kong had frequently to accept high-handed treatment from their rulers. By the nature of its duties and its street presence, the police force was a particular offender.[14] An old Chinese herbal doctor who died in the 1990s at over 90 years of age, told one of my younger friends how he detested the British because, when a boy, he had been kicked on the street simply (as he saw it) for being there.[15] Chinese in other Anglo-Saxon and European communities around the globe, from California to New South Wales, were often treated nowise differently from those in Hong Kong, and it is very likely that at least some inhabitants of the New Territory, returned from sojourns overseas, would have had similar experiences at the hands of their foreign residents.[16]

ANTI-BRITISH FEELING IN THE NEW TERRITORY

For these and other reasons, the outlook of the New Territory's people on "things foreign" must be presumed to have been similar in nature and intensity: albeit tempered for some by an awareness of the opportunities to reap economic benefits from their proximity to Hong Kong.[17] In the villages, many residents had been nervous about their transfer to foreign rule, but as Rev. Henry had remarked earlier, resentments were particularly strong among the gentry members of society. The degree holders of the powerful Tang lineage resident in the New Territory had long nursed an old grudge against the colonial government for its expropriations of their land rights in Hong Kong and Kowloon in the 1840s and 1860s, and as recounted above, they had taken a leading part in organizing the armed opposition to the British take-over in March 1899.[18] Even as late as 1966, the events of that time were still being recalled with a mixture of bitterness and satisfaction by two of their descendants, writing of past grievances in a compilation of family papers.[19]

As elsewhere in China in these years, there was a swelling nationalism, sparked by anti-Manchu feeling (and perhaps by a longing to be free of all foreign interference and domination). A few of my elderly interviewees had joined Sun Yat-sen's revolutionary movement in the years before the Revolution of 1911, and other researchers have found the same.[20] Observers like Sayer and Schofield, Cadets fresh to the Colony's Civil Service, had noted the manifestations of joy at the replacement of the Manchu dynasty with the Chinese Republic in 1911–1912. In the New Territory, this new spirit was epitomized by the heady inscription at the newly built Po Chai ("Universal Charity") Bridge at Tso Kung Tam in Tsuen Wan in 1911. Breaking with custom, it bore no reign title, only an inscription dating it in "Yellow Emperor 4609th Year", a direct reference to the legendary founder of the Chinese state.[21] As Walter Schofield recalled:

> The Revolution had excited the people, and one inscription on the earth of a road cutting read 王帝在此 implying that the writer was now as good as the Emperor! It also became fashionable to write and print 民 as 民: the implication is obvious.[22]

Queue-cutting was common everywhere, as in the British colony of Singapore with its population of predominantly Southern Chinese: perhaps even more so in Hong Kong, thought Schofield.[23] With his customary whimsicality, Sayer stated that "whereas in the spring of 1911 a Chinese discarded his queue at the risk of losing his head, in the spring of 1912 he risked his head who kept his queue".[24]

FOREIGN RESIDENTS MAINTAIN OLD ATTITUDES

While the events of the 1920s inside and outside the Colony had caused headaches for the Hong Kong and Home governments alike, there had been little or no change in the assumptions and attitudes of its foreign residents.[25] Franklin Gimson, appointed Colonial Secretary of Hong Kong shortly before the Japanese attack, but forming his opinions on his experiences in internment camp during the Occupation (and echoing Colquhoun's remarks fifty years before) considered that the Colony was:

> regarded by its European residents as [being] little different from the many "Treaty Ports" in China where they had special privileges for the pursuit of their personal and commercial activities ...

"The welfare of the local population did not come within, in any way, the sphere of concern of these foreign merchants," he continued, adding that he and the other officers of the Colonial Government were regarded as being "instruments in the pursuit of trade". He complained of the business community's narrow attitudes, explaining that "they cannot appear to consider any other world than that in which they can make money and retire".[26]

An authentic glimpse of the time is afforded by an article written by an "Old Hong Kong Hand" in a well-known 1930s periodical journal. Discussing horticulture in the Colony, he warmed to his discourse on the absorbing subject of relations with one's *fa-wong* or gardener. "Differences between master and fa-wong are not however always due to misunderstanding and are not always curable by a common language". He explained that he had once had a fa-wong who wanted to "run the show". He [the writer] asked a friend learned in Chinese to give him an equivalent Chinese expression for "is this your garden or is it mine?" The expression was duly given. "But, added the sinologue, 'You had much better give him a smack on the side of the head.'"[27]

There was, besides, the general assumption among expatriates of all ages that Britons should come first in what was, after all, their Colony. A friend born and brought up in Hong Kong in the 1920s and 30s has told me that it was normal for Europeans to go automatically to the head of any queue.[28] This may have been encouraged by the fact that, prewar, practically all professional and even supervisory grades in the Civil Service were occupied by Europeans: or in the then current officialese, "non-local officers".[29]

How much of this negativity impacted upon the NT population? It lived its own life in the villages, and was mostly left untroubled by external events.

It was administered by British officials who seem to have been thoroughly at one with them, and to have had their interests at heart. Consider Eric Hamilton, who wrote that "there was always a genial leg-pull when I spotted a bloke I had jugged [jailed] back at work in his fields":[30] The strong avuncular, almost paternal, instinct towards their rural charges was one which is very evident from their annual reports and persisted into the 1960s.[31] On their part (and I experienced it myself) there was a general bonhomie and friendliness among the people that was not forced: but this could mask a disdain and impersonal dislike among others who may have kept their own counsel, and their distance.

THE EFFECTS OF WAR AND OCCUPATION

As we have seen in chapter 5, this period had given rise to patriotic and pro-Communist sympathies in some parts of the New Territories. An unknown, but not inconsiderable number of village men (and perhaps some women also) had joined the disciplined Communist guerrillas units which operated from time to time within the territory.[32] These years of China's heroic struggle against the Japanese (from 1937 on) must undoubtedly have heightened patriotic feelings among Hong Kong's people, and some at least must have been influenced by the Communists' very considerable and emotionally charged anti-Japanese literary, artistic, and filmmaking efforts in the Colony between 1937–38 and the Japanese attack.[33]

Communists or not, not all NT persons were pleased to see the return of the British after War's end. The Kam Tin Tangs' record relates how, in the expectation that a Chinese army would soon appear in Hong Kong, the people of the various villages prepared Chinese flags, flew them from the fronts of the houses, and let off fireworks every where to express their joy at liberation from Japanese tyranny and the prospect of returning to Chinese rule. However, their joy was checked on 30 August 1945, when the British fleet entered the harbour to repossess the Colony. Nonetheless, these patriotic feelings were shared by many in the remaining urban population.[34]

THE EARLY POSTWAR YEARS

With the establishment of the People's Republic in 1949, there was now a stable and potentially powerful government in China to which appeals could be directed. A new-found patriotism, laced with self-interest, was useful to the disaffected of Hong Kong, including those living in the NT, where (as we have seen in chapters 7 and 8) many villagers had to bear the brunt of development and did not consider that either the government's land policies or compensation levels had measured up to the undertakings given at the time of the British take-over. This undercurrent meant that the colonial government's activities there had always to be viewed in a wider than local context by the Hong Kong authorities.[35]

The New China News Agency in Hong Kong, ostensibly the organization handling the Communist press in Hong Kong, was essentially a political agency, under whose aegis diverse groups carried out various and sometimes clandestine activities throughout the Colony.[36] Their main targets were those persons affected by the government's squatter control and clearance operations, workers at odds with their employers for one reason or another, and indeed any group under pressure from the colonial government. Adverse coverage of any untoward events was routinely given in the two main Communist daily newspapers, the *Ta Kung Pao* and *Wen Wei Pao*, with their overtly political and patriotic slant.

THE 1967 DISTURBANCES

The 1967 Disturbances brought out the latent antipathy of some village communities and their leaders towards the colonial British authorities. The body of New Territories leadership was divided between a minority who came out actively against the government and the majority which supported it. By and large, the higher leadership represented by the Heung Yee Kuk supported the Government and threw its weight behind the District Administration and the NT Police in the districts.[37]

Nonetheless, there was a sizeable security problem with the New Territories. In keeping with their wartime proclivities, many leaders in the Sai Kung area had been openly pro-Communist for some time, while the big village of Wang Toi Shan in the Pat Heung plain was another seed-bed of left-wing influence. The border area was apparently another such.[38] As in Hong Kong and Kowloon, the pro-Communist leadership provided active support to the organizers of the campaign to bring down the colonial government. This period has not received sufficient attention from researchers as yet, and there is little published scholarship on the subject. However, it is clear enough from printed government reports that there was a good deal of subversive activity by word and deed. As the District Commissioner reported at the close of the Disturbances:

a number of Village Representatives were known to have engaged in subversive activities ... some took part in actual riots and demonstrations, while others were involved in activities which were not in the best interests of the villages they represented.

The Tsuen Wan District, for instance, was not free from such, as revealed after police raids were made on left-wing union offices and private premises to search for incriminating evidence and to arrest persons suspected of aiding or taking part in them.[39]

In consequence, between July 1967 and the end of the year under review, the District Commissioner withdrew his approval from 41 such persons out of the total of 900 Village Representatives.[40] Again, the Tsuen Wan District had had its share of the de-registered, among them some otherwise estimable men, and from time to time I received pleas for their reinstatement. These were duly passed on to my headquarters but were never acceded to by higher authority.

It seems that neither the Heung Yee Kuk nor the government could rely on complete support and cooperation from all 27 rural committees. Besides the overtly pro-Communist, there were others which appear to have been inhibited or prevented from rendering assistance by the presence of persons on their executive committees who were sympathetic to the opposition camp. The seriousness of the situation may be gauged by the fact that no fewer than 16 entirely new bodies, styled "Public Security Advancement Associations" (PSAAs), came into being in the New Territories between 17 June and 28 July 1967, "to meet the needs of the time".

Though not providing locations and membership details, the District Commissioner's report is very specific on their functions and their usefulness to the authorities and to their communities.

> These associations, which were formed by community leaders in the towns and villages of the New Territories, concerned themselves with maintaining the confidence and loyalty of the people in the face of threats and intimidation.

> With their roots among the people they pledged themselves to the task of assisting the Government and the security forces, dispelling rumours, spreading correct information, helping to maintain adequate supplies of staple goods, and sustaining the normal life of the people.

> Since their formation they have helped to maintain the confidence of the public by innumerable public statements, broadcasts and circular letters.[41]

Were the PSAAs were formed at the urging of the District Administration, or were they formed spontaneously by local leaders who needed a new institutional outlet to be able to act in support of government and the local community?[42] It is more than likely that it was the former, because of the need for the authorities (principally the District Officers, the Police and the Army) to secure a local support organization in each rural committee area; but since alert factional leaders were available to fill the temporary vacuum, and would have also seen an opportunity to elevate themselves, there was apparently little difficulty in forming them. Taking in the leaders of postwar associations of newcomers as well as natives, their membership reflected the by now broader spectrum of local influence.

One District where this happened was Sai Kung. A glimpse of the situation there is provided by an anthropologist who carried out doctoral field-work in the township in 1971–72, close enough in time to the dramatic events which unfolded during the Disturbances. Of particular interest was the transformation of the Sai Kung Rural Committee under left-wing leadership into the Sai Kung All Circles Struggle Committee.[43] According to Blake:

> The colonial government lost political control and barely managed to keep police control of Sai Kung during the summer and autumn of 1967. The radicals' bombing campaign and the government's detention of radicals without due process completely polarized the situation in Sai Kung ... The government issued urgent requests for "responsible men" to organize support for the government and to reconstitute the Rural Committee.

The situation was saved for the government by mixed postwar settlement, and by the rivalries which had led to the creation of associations whose leaders saw personal and political advantage in responding to its call. A Public Security Advancement Association was formed under an enterprising native leader with outsider support.[44] This body was replaced the following year in nominated "elections" for a new term of the Rural Committee, in which the pro-government leader and his supporters were successful.[45] Overall, the NT situation must have varied a great deal, and more research is urgently required into the many facets of this most interesting time.[46]

A memoir by a police officer posted to command the Lok Ma Chau Police Station near the Sino-British border (1970–1972) contains interesting information on the post-Disturbances situation in that part of the NT. As he observes, the electoral system in the villages was still recovering from the problems of 1967, and many villages were still considered to be Communist enclaves and had to be treated with caution. The clearance of illegal structures in such villages always resulted in major confrontations between the police and the villagers as it was an emotive issue which provided good propaganda opportunities for the Communists.

He made a point of visiting many of the villages on his own, talking with the villagers and trying to win their support for his role as a police officer. Moreover, he organized a Christmas party, with a floor show provided free of charge through his contacts with the entertainment world for over 100 village representatives and other prominent personalities, which began at 10.00 a.m. and was claimed to be "an outstanding success, with the final stragglers leaving after dusk". By popular demand, yet another successful function was held the following Christmas.[47]

Viewed overall, it is still rather puzzling why, unprompted from Beijing, there was such a groundswell of dislike among the native population at the time, given the generally amicable relationship of prewar times, the assistance shown during the Japanese Occupation and gratitude evinced thereafter, as well as the general friendliness encountered in my first period of service in the New Territories between 1957 and 1962. Another curious aspect is that the areas most marked by left-wing sentiment and activity, especially the Sai Kung sub-district in the eastern NT, and the Pat Heung plain in the north, were not then affected by large-scale resumptions and removals for development. There remains here an enigma which is richly deserving of further investigation.[48]

Postscript to 1967

Before the Cultural Revolution spilt over into Hong Kong, farmers and fishermen on each side of the border had for long been accustomed (and allowed) to cross over into British or Chinese territory in pursuit of their daily work and livelihood. Even the change of government in 1949, while prompting many local villagers to take refuge in Hong Kong, had not altered a pattern which, for those who stayed, went back long before 1899, and would continue. This flexibility seems to have extended to ritual activities, at family graves and in temple worship, for as Lockhart had observed when wishing to incorporate Shenzhen into the leased territory, the new border was an artificial creation that interfered with traditional linkages.

A striking insight into this long-lasting continuity was provided by men from a group of villages in British Sha Tau Kok who, fearful of the destruction being wrought by Red Guards on local temples during the Cultural Revolution, went over to Chinese territory to bring back a venerated image of the Queen of Heaven (with other items) from the Man Mo Temple in Chinese Sha Tau Kok, for which they erected a new temple under the management of a newly formed association in their home area.[49]

"UNITED FRONT" ACTIVITIES

"United Front" work, a political activity for which the Communists had long been justifiably renowned, was carried on throughout the postwar period. In the New Territories, the Colony's local Communist bodies strove to influence the hearts and minds of villagers, outsider farmers, and squatters alike, wherever they saw an opening. In the 1960s, Göran Aijmer had found a credit society sponsored by Communist elements in Shatin;[50] and ten years later, in Tai Po, Judith Strauch had come across my old acquaintance from Shek Pik days, the Planters Association.[51] Styling the Association "a leftist or 'patriotic' trade union", she mentions its Farmers' Branch, then active in enlisting new members among the tenant farmers of Fung Yuen and the adjacent areas. Membership was growing in 1978, and had also included a few native villagers farming their own land. The Farmers' Branch sponsored a "six-village association" of Fung Yuen and other local villages, and organized three communal banquets each year; at the Lunar New Year, on or around 1 May (International Labour Day), and on 1 October (China's National Day).[52] It was equally active among vegetable farmers and livestock breeders in the Tsuen Wan District, where the Communist leadership was also quick to utilize fires or floods to organize relief for victims living in overcrowded urban villages and squatter areas.[53]

All such "united front" activities were intended to be in competition with the Hong Kong Government's own services, and to take advantage of any shortcoming. As Aijmer had commented of the Shatin situation, the Communists' role there was that of "political entrepreneurs in [the] political vacuum" in which the immigrant farmers found themselves.[54] They were certainly viewed in this light by the District Administration and the Police. Though mainly aimed at the non-native element, it was clear from the above that such work would continue in the villages whenever and wherever there was a receptive element among the local people.

The opening of Sino-British negotiations in 1982 for the handing back of Hong Kong in 1997 was a time for reinvigorated effort. After the signature of the Joint Agreement in 1984, the "united front" activities of NCNA were stepped up. The Agency was upgraded and expanded in 1983, and separate liaison offices established for Hong Kong, Kowloon and the New Territories. The staff of the New Territories liaison office opened and maintained contact with practically all local organizations, regardless of type or affiliation, and their leaders were invited to National Day and other celebrations.[55] From having been an event avoided by many local leaders — some told me that they had shunned "National Day" invitations from either Communists or Nationalists and had for many years remained determinedly neutral and apolitical — attendance at the First of October celebrations hosted by NCNA had now become a more or less obligatory event on their social calendar.

One can only wonder at the total number of visits paid and the "home visits" to the Mainland organized for groups from local societies with the help of its dedicated liaison staff. In this initial period of China's "Four Modernizations", local groups, especially Hong Kong's numerous fellow-countrymen's associations (*tongxiang hui*), were encouraged to take an interest in their home areas on the Mainland, and regardless of their political affiliations (if any) could be assisted to make visits and present items like electric generators and other equipment, as well as to make donations towards education and like purposes.[56]

OTHER CHINA ASPECTS

The closer connection with China resulting from its new modernization programmes affected many people in Hong Kong, not least in the NT, where (as we have seen) the artificial frontier determined in the Peking Convention of 1898 had cut across many social and economic linkages of past days. The events of 1949 and 1967 had weakened them considerably; but with the new mood and direction, and the business opportunities opening up in the Shenzhen Special Economic Zone after 1978–80, there was a revival of interest and interactions of all kinds that went two ways.

One manifestation of the change affected us in Tsuen Wan. The very numerous Guangdong branches of the Tangs had begun to take more notice of their New Territories cousins, and especially in the development programmes which were affecting their shared corporate estates, which, upon resumption, were bringing wealth to their kinsmen but not (thus far) to themselves. They learned of a negotiation in which the District Office Tsuen Wan was engaged with the NT Tangs over the planting out of their hill inside the town area on which an early common ancestor was buried.[57] Having received a misleading account of our intentions, they took out a summons in the Dongguan District Court against one of my Assistant District Officers, hoping no doubt that they could become parties to the expected compensation when this property was resumed for a public purpose, as they had surmised. We consulted the Political Adviser, who took care of the matter for us, assuring both the Court and the over-eager Dongguan Tangs that no resumption was being planned, and gently reminding the former that it had no jurisdiction.[58]

Some background is needed. The ancestral trust which owned the grave was one of the oldest in the extended lineage, and before 1949 some of the trust's managers had come *from* branches long settled in the counties adjoining Hong Kong. Their participation was practically eliminated thereafter, and the NT managers had been dealing with resumptions of trust property unaided or unhindered by Mainland interests. They were particularly fearful of any resumption of the grave lot at Tsuen Wan, in whole or in part, having explained to me on a previous occasion that it would be next to impossible to deal with such matters if the Guangdong members of the lineage trust were to take an interest, and demand consultation and their share of any proceeds. Owing to the misconception related above, this was now happening.[59]

THE KUK'S SUCCESSFUL LOBBYING WITH CHINA

To be recounted in chapter 12, the Heung Yee Kuk would always lobby tirelessly, and successfully, to preserve the rights and privilege of the indigenous population. This was especially the case during the course of the negotiations which led to the Sino-British Joint Agreement,[60] and, later, during the drafting of the Basic Law that would govern the future Hong Kong Special Administrative Region after 1997.[61]

There can be no doubt that these successes rekindled the patriotic fervour stemming from having a new protector, which notwithstanding its political complexion, had now been willing to upheld capitalist rights eradicated in the Mainland during the land reform campaigns of the early Communist years. This satisfaction was reflected by the enthusiastic welcome given to units of the People's Liberation Army when they crossed into Hong Kong territory, and by the major celebrations carried out in village communities all over the New Territories after the restoration of Chinese sovereignty brought to an end the long Lease granted in 1898.

Neither the retention of their entrenched position, nor the Heung Yee Kuk's determined lobbying or general pro-Beijing stance, were calculated to endear the indigenous community to the Hong Kong people at large. This subject is explored in chapter 12, including (indicative of changing times) the several erosions of the rights and privileges so recently reaffirmed by incorporation into the defining documents in 1984 and 1990, before and after the reversion to Chinese sovereignty in 1997.

12

Convergence and Divergence:
A Deteriorating Relationship

As early as 1980, the development programmes being implemented in the NT had progressed to the point where, opening a Royal Asiatic Society symposium on "The New Territories and Its Future", the then Secretary for the New Territories could complain, "it is strange that we should be discussing this topic at all. It is equally strange that we continue to separate the New Territories from the rest of Hong Kong".[1]

By then, less than twenty years before Hong Kong's return to Chinese sovereignty, the main features of the NT's new social, political and administrative landscape were fast becoming a reality. First was the swamping of the indigenous population on its home ground by newcomers. Second was administrative and political change. Third was the social change whereby the indigenous and newcomers alike shared the same basic lifestyles brought by modernization and increasing prosperity. There was a coming together of the old and the new, a convergence for the first time since 1898. This was the emerging situation prompting David Akers-Jones's intentionally thought-provoking remarks, one that will be developed and explained in the course of this chapter.

But first, we should recognize how far Hong Kong had traveled since the bleak days of 1945–49. The early decades of postwar Hong Kong had been marked by speedy industrialization, in which the export-led manufacturing industry, notably the textiles sector, soon developed a global stature.[2] In the 1970s, a regional services and banking industry was built up, and with the start to China's Modernization programmes at the end of the decade, this enabled Hong Kong's entrepreneurs to make a massive contribution through their well-honed skills and large capital investment.

Internally, the 1970s had been marked by a huge housing-led development programme. The construction of large "new towns" in the NT was matched by similar initiatives in public transport. A much expanded educational provision at secondary and tertiary levels, and the steadily improving standard of living resulting from the Colony's favourable economic circumstances, wider employment opportunities, and rising incomes, had gradually widened the horizons of the population, especially among the young. This encouraged a new-found interest in Hong Kong and a burgeoning sense of pride in its place in the world, marking the beginnings of a distinctive Hong Kong identity.

NUMERICAL OVERPOWERING AND A SINGLE LANGUAGE

In the postwar decades, the villagers would become outnumbered, and then swamped, by newcomers. Soon after 1945, an increasing numbers of "outsider" vegetable farmers had taken up rural land, and there was much unauthorized squatting around the NT townships, especially at Tsuen Wan. From the early 1970s, the "New Town" programmes, extending relentlessly year by year thereafter, would complete the overpowering process. By 1 July 1997, the population of Hong Kong was stated to be 6.617 millions, of which 3.05 millions were living in the NT, around 46.9% of the whole.[3] The exact number of indigenous inhabitants is not available, but it was surely no more than ten per cent of this figure. And linguistically, Cantonese had by then long displaced Hakka.

Numerically, the two sections of the NT population had been almost equal in 1898. Either one or the other language was spoken, and in mixed Cantonese-Hakka areas, both were to be heard. The language of instruction depended on the predominant group settled in the local villages, and overall the number of schools teaching in Hakka was considerable.[4] This had continued up to the Second World War, though in Hakka Tsuen Wan there was a change in the 1930s. Thereafter, all the new subsidized primary schools taught in Cantonese, and it was not long before Hakka was mostly spoken only at home. Ironically, though relative numbers of Hakka and Cantonese can no longer be traced in the Census returns, the numerical proportions of the two sections of the old population may be much the same today as in 1898.

The prolonged absence of many villagers overseas would accentuate this numerical overpowering. On a visit to the remote villages of Kuk Po with Fung Hang near Sha Tau Kok in 1987, only around 100 persons were reported as being in residence, with another hundred elsewhere in Hong Kong and about 1,000 or more overseas.[5] At the hitherto large nearby settlements of Luk Keng and Nam Chung there were many ruined houses, the major part of their active populations being overseas or elsewhere in Hong Kong.[6] At Yin Kong, close to the Shenzhen River, many persons were abroad, among them the 65-year-old Village Representative's family members, scattered in Britain, Switzerland and Australia, and all in the restaurant business.[7] Yet as was ever the case, village situations varied widely. In other places the majority of native families were still at home. At Yuen Kong, a large village with a claimed population of 1,000 people, only a hundred men were said to be overseas, mainly working in restaurants; and at Nai Wai, along the Castle Peak Road to Ping Shan, there were numbers of men and families abroad, but clearly quite a lot at home too. But overall, many people were no longer resident, though continuing their connection through ownership of property and occasional visits, especially at major festivals and when the decennial *Ta Chiu* rituals to protect the community were being performed, to whose cost they often donated generously.[8]

AN URBAN-STYLE ADMINISTRATION

After its reorganization and fourfold expansion between 1958 and 1962, the District Administration had continued to evolve.[9] Maintaining its routine land administration and registration duties and the heavy burden of land recovery and village removal for development programmes, it would soon also engage directly in community building work through the formation and servicing of Mutual Aid Committees and other bodies needed to implement the Colony-wide campaigns against crime, littering, drugs. All directed by the central government and coordinated from departmental headquarters in both the City and the NT, they had to be implemented by the district officers, with support from local organizations and their leaders.[10] There was, too, the District Administration's important role as monitor/coordinator of services for the "new towns" and the expanding erstwhile market townships, and of the work being done by the other departments involved in town management.[11]

Land and rural responsibilities excepted, these extra duties took it ever closer to the work of the Home Affairs Department in Hong Kong and Kowloon, and in March 1981 it was amalgamated with the HAD to form the City and New Territories Administration. Thereby, a single urban-focused department became responsible for district administration across the whole of Hong Kong.[12]

Soon after, other changes would further alter the old administrative and political landscapes. In 1982, the CNTA was stripped of its land authority.

This was passed to a newly established Lands Department which, henceforth, would administer land throughout the Colony.[13] In 1985, the District Officers would cease to be chairmen, or even voting members, of the recently introduced District Boards (see below);[14] and in 1985–86, a provisional (appointed) and then elected Regional Council for municipal services in the NT was established, on which the CNTA was not even represented.[15] Finally, in 1994, after a re-titling of the former CNTA to Home Affairs Department the previous year, the two Regional Secretary posts heading the Urban and New Territories areas, created at the time of the amalgamation, were abolished as such.[16] In purely administrative terms, the New Territories had ceased to exist.[17]

The transition from the immensely powerful executive department of NTA days to the essentially monitoring and coordinating — and virtually toothless — role of the combined organization was abrupt.[18] Upon being told of the transfer of the land authority, one of my Village Representative friends, used to expressing himself in picturesque language, told me, in disgust, that we had now so reduced our "clout" that in future we would have to ask for permission to go to the toilet![19] It was a far cry from the days when Peplow could write, "To the villagers of the Territory the District Officer is the Government. Whatever happens he is their particular official, and what is more, their friend."[20] I shall have more to say about administrative change, and its social and political implications, later in this chapter.

POLITICAL CHANGE

As described in chapter 9, District Advisory Boards had been established in all administrative districts of the NT in 1977. With their extension to the city districts and a change in title to District Boards in 1982, an elected element was introduced. The original all-appointed membership was reduced by one-third, and in its place, 132 members were to be returned from specially drawn constituencies. Once begun, this elective representation was extended thereafter. In 1985, the number of elected seats was increased to 237, all officials were withdrawn from membership of the Boards, and the District Officers ceased to be their Chairmen. These posts would henceforth be filled by election from within the Boards. The elected element was augmented slightly in subsequent periodic elections until, in 1994, the remaining 140 appointed members gave way to a wholly elected membership.[21]

These developments had taken place against the background of the Sino-British negotiations (1982–84) for the return of Hong Kong to Chinese sovereignty at the end of the New Territories Lease, the finalization (1985–90) of the Basic Law for the future Hong Kong Special Administrative Region, and latterly the dispute between Governor Chris Patten and Beijing over his further democratic reforms.[22]

THE HEUNG YEE KUK AND ADMINISTRATIVE AND POLITICAL CHANGE

Demographic and economic growth had prompted these major administrative and political changes, together with the rapid build up of people in the NT under the "New Towns" programme, and the perceived need to enlist wider public understanding and support for the Hong Kong government. In the process, as described in chapter 9, the indigenous community and its leadership in the erstwhile rural districts had participated willingly in the process, despite the looming indications that their position *vis-à-vis* the Administration was likely to decline as the new arrangements for consultation and management gathered momentum. It is now time to consider the reactions and proceedings of the New Territories Heung Yee Kuk, the statutory body which represented the whole body of native villagers.

Thus far, I have seldom mentioned the Heung Yee Kuk and its activities in these years. Like the District Administration itself, the Kuk had undergone a reorganization in 1959–60. Following withdrawal of official recognition owing to internal disputes and machinations in 1956–57, it had been restructured with the eventual consent of the majority of its members, and now had statutory status under its own Ordinance, Cap 1097 of the Laws of Hong Kong.[23] Truth to tell, I had had very little to do with it in the Southern District in the 1950s, or in Tsuen Wan in the 1970s.[24] Socially, I met its leaders at our or their periodically hosted receptions and dinners, but I was not present when general issues were discussed with our headquarters staff. Even when Regional Secretary, NT, in 1985–87, my meetings with the Kuk largely related to issues of the day rather than constitutional development.[25]

This being so, pending a still unwritten close study of its relations with the Government, conducted through the District Administration, and of its own internal politics and policies post 1959, it is fortunate that my former colleague in CNTA, David Man-tin Ip, has provided an interesting review of the Kuk's major negotiating and lobbying activities over these years.[26] He describes how the Kuk used its position as the recognized spokesman for the indigenous community and adviser on New Territories affairs, variously to promote goodwill with both the Hong Kong and UK governments, push for advantages, and protect or enhance its status in the face of change. He instances the strong support given by the Kuk during the 1967 Disturbances (though I believe he understates the non-cooperative or actively opposing element) and its delegation's government-assisted visit (1968) to Chinese communities in the UK.[27] The "pay-offs" included the later visits to the UK in 1973 and 1977 to push its various concerns with the British government, which gave both Kuk delegations its full attention and received them well. He describes how, on the 1973 visit, the Kuk pushed for Secretary ranking for the head of the NT District Administration to give him (and them) more "clout" following a major reorganization of the higher ranks of government in 1972–73; and it continued to lobby for improved compensation for land resumed for development, with tangible results following the 1977 visit.[28] There was another such in 1980.[29] In 1983, an approach to the New China News Agency in Hong Kong led to a sponsored visit to Beijing and a top-level meeting with a senior official which proved useful in the Sino-British negotiations for the rendition of Hong Kong in 1997.[30]

At home, the Kuk agreed to the creation of the District Boards, and to the successive increases in the number of elected seats, and later supported the establishment of a Regional Council in the NT (in return for a significant number of *ex-officio* and appointed seats on the District Boards and the new Council).[31] In his speech on the occasion marking the Kuk's 60th anniversary in 1986, its chairman claimed various successes along the way. These included "talking" [NT] people into "becoming tolerant in order to assist the Administration in accomplishing various development projects" [the New Towns and related schemes]; and, through the consultation process, in making "unceasingly constructive proposals" for achieving more representative government, as well as hailing senior Kuk members' "active participation" in the various new bodies.[32] Two years later, in a final concession, the Government acceded to the Kuk's long sought creation of a new "rural sector" functional constituency for the Legco elections in 1988, in which (of course) the Kuk's chairman was successful.[33]

Throughout, at home and abroad, the Kuk's leaders had been (as Ip puts it so aptly), "obsessed with accessibility" to higher authority, so as to maintain its status and influence in the face of change.[34] Its position was enhanced when, following the Chinese Government's disavowal of Governor Patten's unilateral political changes in 1994, leading Kuk members were appointed to its Preliminary Working Committee in Hong Kong, and subsequently to the Working Committee to prepare the interim constitutional arrangements for governing the territory in the period following the hand-over.[35]

POLITICAL OVERPOWERING

Despite the Kuk's undoubted success in obtaining adequate, even strong, representation for the indigenous community at all levels of the new political arrangements (assisted by the conciliatory approach taken, partly out of necessity, by the Hong Kong Government), the gradual shift to elected District Boards would edge out practically all but holders of *ex officio* and appointed posts from district politics. In the telling, the numerical overpowering of the indigenous population assumes a dramatic persona, but, curiously enough, there were no histrionics from the losing side. Pondering the reasons, a number of pertinent facts suggest themselves.

First, as we shall see in the Tsuen Wan case, the new arrangements initially catered to the sensitivities of the native leaders. Secondly, their strong position in the districts, their experience, and their local pride, made them enter wholeheartedly into the work of the new District Boards, with most of them realizing that self-interest dictated their participation. Thirdly, they had the money and leisure needed for full participation, derived from compensation moneys, land-holding, land-brokering, and investment.[36] Fourthly, their gradually deteriorating situation was masked by the concessions obtained by the Heung Yee Kuk for rural representation described above. But despite these initial successes, there was no mistaking the general downward trend.[37] And ironically, it was accompanied — almost aided — by the perverse behaviour of some sections of the indigenous population, which (as will be seen) drew down criticism upon the whole.

CONVERGENCE OF URBAN AND "RURAL" POPULATIONS

By the late 1980s, there was little outward difference between most parts of the Colony. Save for areas of sea and mountain unsuited to development — but with much of the latter now gazetted as Country Parks[38] — urbanization of the New Territories was well advanced. Across the face of Hong Kong, Kowloon and the NT, huge populations were living in densely packed high-rise modern buildings in all suburban areas, and in the "New Towns". A train journey from the Sino-British border to Kowloon would take the traveller smoothly through conurbations of gleaming tower-cities which, lit by innumerable lights after dusk, shone ever more brightly in the enveloping night sky.

The Hong Kong lifestyle for most, the indigenous population included, was now modern and urban, or semi-urban. For the young especially, it had coincided with the growth of a fast-emerging Cantonese–Hong Kong culture.[39] Shaped by technological advance in all fields, it placed all Hong people on a common footing. As Mr. Martin Lee observed in Legislative Council some years later, "Because of the electronic media and mass culture, any lifestyle difference between rural people and urban people is becoming indistinct".[40] This coincided with the rise in Chinese communities overseas of a new self-assurance and consciousness of their own worth as Chinese, greatly aided by the vibrant presence of many middle-income migrants from Hong Kong. In Canada at least, they had created what one local author described as "the Hong Kong Hoopla".[41] A new patriotism based on the achievements of the new China, but at a safe distance, also contributed something to the general euphoria.[42]

SEEDS OF DIVERGENCE

While the gap between urban and former rural had as good as closed, it was about to open up again, owing to their differing outlook. In the NT case, this was linked to the fundamentals noted in this book. To be on their home ground, and in sufficient numbers to maintain their own identity and to preserve, and even enhance, their privileges, had been a major factor in determining their mind set. By contrast, the urban population within which they were now embedded, was, and for long had been, overwhelmingly migrant, without much cohesion and identity. For much of the earlier period under British rule, they had been merely sojourners, while after 1949 many newcomers were people in limbo, fleeing totalitarian rule in China but living precariously without loyalty or affection for Hong Kong.[43] In the late 1970s, this was about to change. Hong Kong urban people were now constructing their own identity.[44]

Improved social conditions through the decisive housing-led programmes, educational reforms, and the greatly increased recreational amenities of the 1970s, were supplying the essential tools. Steady economic growth and the underlying confidence slowly generated by the application of Common Law and a generally efficient and well-intentioned British administration, provided the bedrock. Incomes rose, and opportunities for overseas travel with them. The recent reforms in marriage law (see below) were another liberating influence on the young. The government's strenuous campaigns in community building on a colony-wide scale, with their inculcation of self-help and civic responsibilities, provided a more positive background for individual effort. And fundamentally, in the Hong Kong case, identity came through achievement.[45]

THE CONTINUANCE OF LAND-RELATED CUSTOMARY LAW

Meantime, in the NT, title, management, and succession to landed property were still dictated by the New Territories Ordinance, unless by special exemption.[46] While law reform in the 1970s had done away with traditional and other marriage practices in the Colony,[47] the NTO remained unaltered. Within the context of a fast modernizing Hong Kong, its continued existence would soon appear increasingly anomalous and, fanned by envy at native privileges, become the underlying source of the growing discord.

However, because village society was organized along traditional lines, the New Territories Ordinance was still highly relevant in the countryside. Despite the huge amount of land taken back for development, the majority of pre-1898 land holdings outside the "New Towns" (known as Old Schedule Lots) remained largely in the hands of their indigenous proprietors. Of special import were the thousands of lineage trusts, large and small, the common property of their (male) members and in the charge of managers registered under the New Territories Ordinance.[48]

Notwithstanding practical aspects, these residual manifestations of times past, linked to the narrowly conservative attitudes of those in charge, would create difficulties for both the indigenous population and the government in the last decades of colonial rule. By the late 1980s the native population had found itself facing an increasingly critical and, before long alienated, Hong Kong society at large.[49]

SOME CAUSES OF DISHARMONY

First among the irritants was its leaders' continual lobbying to their own advantage, described above, particularly over land policies and compensation. Later, during the Sino-British negotiations for the return of Hong Kong, they lobbied both the British and Chinese governments, for the protection of their accrued interests. Further lobbying with Beijing took place when the Basic Law for the Hong Kong Special Administrative Region was being drafted by a group of Beijing-appointed persons in Hong Kong. This would be seen as yet another extension of the familiar NT pattern of advancing self-interest. No other body of Hong Kong residents was as suitably placed, or as similarly favoured.

Two concessions in regard to land and compensation attracted special public notice. The Small House Policy introduced in 1972 had resulted in the construction of a great many attractive three-storey village houses, mostly in and around old villages in what were styled "village expansion areas" approved by the authorities. Provided at concessionary premia, these "once in a lifetime" grants of land were meant to solve the problem of village expansion (so often hindered by planning restraints) and were intended only for villagers. However, many were sold to "outsiders", to the considerable profit of the grantees and developers and proportionate loss to the Treasury.[50]

The second was the highly advantageous change in compensation policy introduced after the report of a working party chaired by Sir Y. K. Kan in 1978. For the first time, and after almost sixty years of complaint and lobbying, cash compensation for agricultural land resumed for a public purpose would now reflect development potential, at valuations based on the going market price for "Letters of Exchange" of varying dates of issue, reviewed quarterly.[51] Thereby, the financial benefits accruing from resumptions and village removals had been further increased. Fortune piled on fortune indeed, as seen by envious urban onlookers![52]

The next source of urban criticism arose from actions deemed anti-social in many quarters. Owing to the chronic shortage of land available for container and other storage, many village landowners had filled their paddy fields to road level, and were renting or selling them to industrial and commercial operators. The government opposed this, but after a development company had made a successful appeal to the Privy Council in London against a decision of the Hong Kong Court of Appeal,[53] more high stacks of these unsightly but necessary items appeared in all kinds of unlikely spots. Besides creating eyesores, the careless manner in which land was filled to build temporary hard standings for storage, without making adequate drainage arrangements, had led to widespread flooding in the northern NT during storms and heavy rain.[54] Lineage trusts owned much property there.

Abuses of these two kinds were well-publicized in the media. Along with the publicity given to prosecutions of Village Representatives by the Independent Commission against Corruption for offences involving bribery, or old-fashioned "squeezing" of one kind or another, they helped turn the former good-natured contempt for "country bumpkins" into disapproval and dislike in equal measure.[55] There was, too, a growing perception, in time amounting to a conviction, that the authorities were "soft" on the indigenous population.

These negative feelings were not confined to the general public. Some civil servants were also censorious, even within the City and New Territories Administration.[56] Inside the new Lands Department, among its professional officers, there was even more criticism of the Village Removal Policy and the

Small House Policy, and the privileges which they conferred, with (it has been said) attempts on the part of some District Land Officers to have the latter abolished.[57]

RURAL CONSERVATISM AND THE NEW TERRITORIES ORDINANCE

The indigenous community had still shown no desire for changes to the New Territories Ordinance, and despite some restiveness among lawyers dealing with the complexities of NT land, who thought that some of its provisions (e.g. governing the disposal of trust properties) were hindering private investment and development, there was no significant agitation on the subject. That is, until extraneous circumstances created a novel situation, in which the rural community would find itself at a distinct disadvantage in the court of public opinion in regard to one particular matter.

When a Hong Kong Bill of Rights was brought to the Legislative Council in 1990–91, the exclusion of females from succession to landed property became an issue raised by urban women's groups (including some expatriates). In their capacities as Legislative Councillors, two leading members of the Heung Yee Kuk made impassioned pleas against their demand for amendment of the New Territories Ordinance.[58] When the bill to revise the ordinance was introduced in the Legislative Council some years later, the same two councillors again spoke against it, but without success, since the great majority of members were in favour.[59]

Whereas a spirited defence of the existing law by the two Legislative Councillors was to be expected, the boorish behaviour of some village leaders during demonstrations outside the Council Chamber and their threatening public utterances against female Councillors was not.[60] Such well-publicized misdemeanours only served to harden public prejudice.[61] Moreover, they opened the way for conflict on other matters, in which the indigenous community was forced ever onto the defensive.

In these various ways, the gap in outlook and sympathy between the now deemed to be over-privileged village population and the rest of Hong Kong's residents, was further widened. By this time, the latter now included the many times larger number of residents of the New Town communities. The prevailing strong conservatism in the NT hardly helped matters. On a visit to Hong Kong in 1992, it was no surprise to be told by friends that they did not want there to be any more elected seats on the Legislative Council, and that they were criticizing the United Democrats party for hindering the work of the government.

RURAL COMPLAINTS

On the other hand, the urban population did not always endear itself to villagers either. In 1987, during my last year as Regional Secretary NT, I paid a visit with the District Officer Tai Po to villages in the Shap Sze Heung in North Sai Kung. This was before the road connection with the Ma On Shan extension of Sha Tin New Town was completed, but already thousands of townsfolk were flocking into this area, drawn by the recreational opportunities and attractive landscape. With the calm waters of Tolo Channel on one side, and the impressive bulk of Ma On Shan on the other, the setting was very beautiful. While some villagers sought to profit from the influx by offering miscellaneous services (despite the lack of appropriate planning provision) others were less enthusiastic. At Nai Chung, a large notice had been erected stating that tourists were not allowed to enter, while the Village Representative of Ma Kwu Lam wanted to put a six foot high fence around his village to the same end.[62] And not all villages had prospered. At Tai Tung (population 45 in 1960) the old houses had been redeveloped, but by outsiders. Falling on bad times, the Village Representative and many other villagers had become Christian converts during or soon after the Japanese Occupation, possibly to help change fate, and he now lived in a squatter hut.

Such visits to rural areas showed high levels of frustration with similarly outdated planning regulations. In North Sai Kung there was no practical value in maintaining the current Agricultural Protection Area, when little or no farming was carried on, irrigation water was being taken by Water Schemes, and many villagers were working overseas or in the city. More realistic zoning was needed, to permit land usage more appropriate to the times, combined with efficient processing of applications by the Lands Department instead of refusals, stone-wallings, and occasional deterrent measures against enterprising and progressive villagers.[63]

INSUFFICIENT KNOWLEDGE OF THE NT

It can be asserted with considerable justification that the urban population had never been well-informed about the New Territories and its people. There was some history to this situation, which began, you might say, with Hong Kong's famous harbour.

Before the introduction of modern transportation, there was a real division of the urban population into those who lived on Hong Kong Island and those who lived in Kowloon. For persons of all classes, family members, acquaintances and school friends would have mostly lived on one side of the harbour or another. There had even been a snobbish prejudice among expatriates and rich Chinese against living in Kowloon: "Hong Kong looks down on Kowloon with all the well-bred contempt of Belgravia for Brixton", a visitor had observed in 1903.[64] The harbour was truly a defining barrier.

As for the NT, even to children born in the 1960s such as my Chinese nephews and nieces, it was "far away" and seldom visited, save on rare family outings or school excursions. Until the opening of the first cross-harbour tunnel in 1972, taking your car to Kowloon (if you had one) meant using the slow vehicular ferry and waiting in queue to board. For those going for sport and recreation at golf clubs and swimming beaches, the journey through Kowloon by motor or rail was merely a means to an end, and as we have seen, writing of the early 1970s, Denis Bray had noted that many important people lacked knowledge of the NT.[65] Ten or fifteen years later, the spectacular progress of development had worsened the situation, not least because, with traditional farming long defunct, the old New Territories was much less visible to the visitor, and its society even less so.

When I spoke with the law faculty of the University of Hong Kong in March 1987 about our review of the New Territories Ordinance in the context of changing times and in preparation for Hong Kong's rendition in 1997, this general deficiency seemed to underlie what were otherwise perfectly legitimate observations. In the then recently concluded Sino-British Joint Agreement, had it been wise (I was asked) to lock the indigenous population's land ownership and other privileges into the fifty-year guarantee of the maintenance of existing systems, and was this not a strait-jacket that could become irksome at some point in the future? Was it right to bolster the customary law, given that the indigenous population might continue to change in circumstances and outlook? Should not we be considering the general advantage of Hong Kong people? The fast pace of development was in everyone's minds, with less consideration of the old NT society and the direct relevance for it of the land-related customary law. Even the fact that it *existed*, and was not an inconsiderable part of the population, tended to be overlooked.

And not only in the universities. A similar view had been taken by the Registrar General a few months before, in response to my letter informing him of the formation of the working group in CNTA, the reasons for it, and its terms of reference. The paragraph in question encapsulated the general thinking on the subject within the senior ranks of government:

> My own initial view of customary law is that although it has served the New Territories well in the past it has practical application mainly to land, and the area of land now left in the New Territories to which it

could be applied in the practical sense is rapidly diminishing. Another consideration is that the reasons for distinguishing the New Territories from any other part of Hong Kong have all likewise virtually disappeared, and I think the policy is that the New Territories should be treated as far as possible on the same footing as any other part of Hong Kong.[66]

It seemed that many believed that the NT's days were over. In his reply, the Registrar General had also informed me that the Law Reform Commission of Hong Kong was then examining the matter of intestate succession (clearly impinging on an important area of the customary law as applied through the New Territories Ordinance) and that a sub-committee had already submitted its interim report, without, to his surprise, "much representation from the New Territories".[67]

In short, it was being assumed that, for all practical purposes, there were, at that point, no residual concerns standing in the way of Government's "extinction" of the NT. This would help explain how the Regional Council, in effect the municipal council for the New Territories, came to be so styled, and why my post, successor to the former District Commissioner NT's post, was entitled "Regional Secretary, NT". It was being overlooked that development itself, and a large but overall still not significant reduction in the area of private land subject to customary law, did not remove an old society, numerically important and still closely tied to and shaped by land-holding, and so vibrant and determined to survive.

In reply, I suggested that it was "somewhat misleading to relate the applicability of customary [land-related] law to the spread of concrete", and drew attention to the large number of villages and of indigenous land-owners still in continuing need of the NTO. I doubted that the reasons for marking off the NT from the rest of Hong Kong would all disappear in the foreseeable future, though many already had. Also, the Sino-British Joint Agreement had endorsed the separateness of the indigenous community, making it doubly advisable to review the existing provisions to see what might be done to improve application of the customary law through compilation or codification, and any other measures that might be suggested to and by the working group.[68]

Presented several months after my retirement, our report disappeared into bureaucratic limbo, but two years later (as related above) customary law came under the public gaze within the general context of the proposed Bill of Rights. When it seemed that debate over the exclusion of females from succession to landed property might lead to wider changes in the New

Territories Ordinance than might be wise, I wrote again, this time to the Convenor of the Legco Working Group on the Bill of Rights, reminding her colleagues:

> that the NT is a complex place, much of it still occupied by a community with a much older and different social and economic organization from the old urban areas of Hong Kong and Kowloon. This community is in course of change, but the variations are as varied as the spectrum of situations to be found in the villages. Changes will come, but it seems better to me that they should come from within, and with the consensus of its members, than from the outside.

Underlying my concern was the likelihood that the long existing self-management of the villages and lineages of the NT would be weakened thereby, leaving the government in the unwelcome position of having to provide for it by other means.[69] My perceptions of its general efficacy at that time remain, despite some views to the contrary.[70]

LATER DEVELOPMENTS INSIDE THE INDIGENOUS COMMUNITY

The change made to the New Territories Ordinance in 1994, to allow female succession, made a major inroad into customary practice, and no doubt shocked many traditionally minded persons of either sex. However, it is now clear that, from the 1960s on, some adjustments had already been made, principally owing to resumptions of lineage trust lands for development. Their large numbers across the territory, the frequency with which their holdings were being resumed, and the steadily increasing value of compensation derived from them, had elevated the question of who should benefit into a major issue in the villages. Suffice it to say here that women and girls, and even infants of both sexes, were being included in the distribution of assets, and that sometimes distribution would be split, with half or some other proportion being divided between branches of a lineage (*per stirpes*) and the rest among all descendants (*per capita*).[71] The examples coming to my notice were mostly from smaller trusts, but as Michael Palmer has pointed out, wider issues were at stake among the major lineages of the northern NT, making settlement more difficult.[72]

There had also been some change of sentiment in the wider context of how to treat daughters when, by custom, a father's landed property would pass to their brothers or in their absence to cousins. When serving in Tsuen Wan in 1975–82, I knew that no village father would by-pass his sons in favour of a daughter (this would have been against village opinion and would have been indignantly contested) but had been told that more progressive fathers would leave cash or other financial assets to their daughters, or make provision at some point while they were alive. This was likely to have been also the case in other districts.[73]

More recently, the anthropologist Selina Ching Chan has pointed to a change in how daughters, now married women, are coming to be regarded within the lineage, replacing the old perception that women no longer belonged to the natal family upon marriage. Of course, this is a logical development in modern times, when brides are no longer sent to another village and lineage, with potential for inter-village strife and loss of land and property.[74] She also makes the interesting point that in the 1990s, her respondents and informants were attributing the New Territories Ordinance with being the source of their custom, and not custom itself. Evidently, by then, custom itself needed some buttressing. How the late Maurice Freedman would have relished investigating and analysing the current, still unfolding situation![75]

In the event, the amendment of the New Territories Ordinance permitting females to succeed to family property stopped short of admitting women to the membership of lineage trusts, thereby averting the separate, and more weighty, set of problems that would have come with it; but the issue of village management would come to the fore before very long, and with it the matter of candidacy in elections to the post of Village Representative. As will be seen, the "push and shove" element came neither from the government nor the indigenous community.

VILLAGE ELECTIONS AND VILLAGE MANAGEMENT

The democratic element prominent in Hong Kong's constitutional arrangements by the 1990s was in practice largely absent from village elections.[76] Most Village Representative posts had been, and still were, filled by co-option and consensus. Where voting did take place, non-villagers, and even village women, were usually excluded, and neither could stand as candidates for election.[77] Yet by the end of the lease, many non-villagers owned or rented houses there, and in some places outnumbered the indigenous core. This element would soon demand to have a say in village affairs, especially in regard to management, but also in regard to candidature for elections. And it would include women and non-Chinese.

The lead appears to have come from the political arena. At a public meeting of the Constitutional Affairs Panel of the Legislative Council in early January 1994, Martin Lee, leader of the United Democrats political party, had pressed for the introduction of a "one man one vote" system for electing all village representatives. Since village representatives elected the members of rural committees and the Heung Yee Kuk (from 1988, a functional constituency for the Legislative Council elections) they should, he urged, themselves be subject to the electoral process. However, it appeared that the City and New Territories Administration was not about to change the system for obtaining village representatives. Its strategy (I was informed at the time) was to apply gentle pressure on the Heung Yee Kuk and the body of village representatives at large to adopt a more democratic election process, and this would continue.[78]

The Government would find it difficult to handle these matters. Like the Qing before it, the Hong Kong authorities had never managed the villages, leaving rural affairs to be handled by the village representatives and lineage elders. It had rarely intervened in village elections, and when it had done so, a satisfactory outcome had not always been attainable. Posts could be left vacant for some time, in cases of a faction's refusal to compromise, or for other internal reasons.

But in a changing world, an increasing number of non-indigenous NT residents felt aggrieved at their continued exclusion from village management. Some were prepared to contest it in court, and did so successfully.[79] A "One Village, Two Heads" scheme was proposed in 1999,[80] and has now passed into law.[81] Here, it has to be said that some — perhaps too many — of the leaders of the older communities appear not to have taken sufficient account of ongoing change.[82] Nor yet of the implications for themselves, and their fellow villagers. The tale is assuredly unfolding.[83]

EPILOGUE

There were developments in the few years leading up to the hand-over of which I have only recently become aware. These merely added to the urban/rural dissonance described above. During that period, angered by the Government's decision to amend the New Territories Ordinance in 1994 in favour of female succession to landed property, the Heung Yee Kuk mounted a campaign on behalf of the indigenous community to voice displeasure at the outcome. In an interesting paper, Selina Ching Chan has portrayed the Kuk as upholding tradition and anti-colonialism, drawing on its own version of history in and after 1898, and in the process seemingly able to obtain the polite support of Beijing's representatives in Hong Kong for its ostensibly patriotic line.[84] At the same time, by emphasizing various items in its ritual and social traditions, she suggests that the indigenous population had sought to underline its difference from the rest of Hong Kong.[85] As described by Dr. Chan:

> A conscious and increasingly systematic effort to establish and maintain a boundary between the indigenous inhabitants and more recent immigrants to Hong Kong has been made by villagers even while distinctions between lifestyles in the village and the city continue to blur. Tradition is interpreted as the sharing of a place of origin and rural customs by the villagers, and the year 1898 has assumed significance in the interpretation of shared native place (*xiangxa*) by the inhabitants.[86]

While her examples are largely drawn from one of the Five Great Clan villages — half whose residents now live abroad — there is no reason to think they are untypical of the whole, and certainly not of the older and more numerous lineages.

Basing on this account, the wisdom of the Kuk's actions and pronouncements at that time, and of the extended use of tradition (otherwise a positive contribution to community building in the New Towns[87]) are surely in question. Although essentially defensive in nature, both were guaranteed to fuel the general public's already existing antipathies. To this extent, they cannot be considered as anything but sadly misguided and out of step, adding weight to Hugh Baker's perceptive observation (1993) that it is not the indigenous population but the newcomers who may, through their efforts and identification with Hong Kong, be considered its true "belongers".[88]

Turning to the present, it is also relevant that the year by year proliferation of new homes built on former agricultural land around the villages under the Small House Policy, with the usual accompanying abuses, fuel the long-held objections to indigenous "privileges", as does the way in which some landowners still benefit from the ongoing environmental degradation caused by container and other storage on private land. Public querying on these points continues, especially on the former.[89] It must be asked whether the government itself is partly to blame for the current situation. And after the changes made in 1981–82, may not the District Administration, in its new and weakened form, be charged with gradually losing its grasp of indigenous affairs, and with it, the capability to guide the older community into more progressive channels?[90] These and other aspects of how the present situation came about, present intriguing questions for future investigation.[91]

This should also take into account a few other disruptive factors, some of very long standing, others more recent and connected with the care taken of the territory and all its residents, old and new alike. Ever seen as an appendage to the first Colony, even today Hong Kong Island and Old British Kowloon are still the core of the present SAR. Once development began in the New Territory (as it did practically from the start of the Lease) it was mostly the case that the various projects were *in*, not *for*, the NT. Seen and used as a convenient and increasingly indispensable adjunct to the City by the government, by private developers, by the urban community at large, this trend became the norm. The highways which speed the traveler across the former rural landscape mask the existence of unimproved areas: left, in effect, for the big developer to take over when the time is ripe.

Much of the still undeveloped, inhabited parts of the NT hints at official indifference, a lack or insufficiency of sustained interest, which also extends to certain aspects of otherwise thriving and still expanding villages.[92] This seeming general disengagement has led my village friends to conclude, not without reason, that the NT ceased to exist, with its own needs no longer being taken into account, upon the demise of the old District Administration in the 1980s.[93]

While not providing the answers, it is hoped that this book will help to explain much about the former New Territories and its people which may not now be readily evident to the general public: also, that with the requisite will and understanding on each side of the present divide it will encourage the resolution of ongoing problems in a more mutually accommodating spirit than has been evident in recent years. It is time for a re-think. After all, the colonial demons, if such we were, have gone for good!

Notes

Where, e.g. as at note 41 on p. 197, papers are referred to as being now or having been deposited in the HKPRO, they will be found under HKMS 178 1 1- *seq*.

Preface

1. For New Kowloon, see pp. 26–27 and 111–113. Something of the sad history of Hong Kong's own boat-people is provided in Hayes 1998.
2. *Friends and Teachers, Hong Kong and its People 1953–87* (Hong Kong University Press, 1996).
3. For a recent, most useful review of work done, see Johnson 2000. Sources included 375 books, theses, and articles in English, 35 in Chinese, and 9 in Japanese, plus others unknown to her at that time. according to Johnson 2005.
4. Atoned for in part, one hopes, by the inclusion of a chapter on the village in Hayes 1977.1, written when Tim was still a boy.
5. It is fortunate that so much work was done before major change affected the NT. Even twenty-five years ago Chan Wing-hoi could write in a research proposal that the older people who could still sing its traditional songs and ballads were disappearing rapidly, 'and that if we delay any longer, we shall never have the chance to record them'.

Introduction

1. See Shona Airlie, p. 103, with accompanying note 36 on p. 221. The ninety-nine years of the Lease began with the Convention of Peking, dated 9 June 1898, and ended on 1 July 1997 with the reversion to Chinese rule of the whole territory of Hong Kong. For the text, with map, of the Convention signed in Peking on 9 June 1898, see No. 25 in *Hertzlet's China Treaties*, Vol. I, pp. 120–122. Although the Extension was ostensibly for military defence purposes, and had been so argued since 1884 by successive generals in the Hong Kong command, the immediate reason for pressing it upon China owed

more to the diplomatic and political exigencies of the time. See Andrew Roberts's *Salisbury, Victorian Titan*, pp. 687–689. British jurisdiction was extended to the New Territory by the Royal Order in Council made on 20 October 1898, and to Kowloon City by another made on 27 December 1899.

2.   In 1902 he was appointed Commissioner of Wei Hai Wei, another leased territory, located in far off Shandong province in North China, where, to his chagrin, he remained until his retirement from public life in 1921. He was knighted in 1908. Well-versed in the Chinese language, he was a collector of Chinese art and numismatics, a scholar-author as well as administrator. His three best-known works were a Manual of Chinese Quotations (1893, with a revised edition in 1903) and a three volume work on the Currency of the Further East (1895–98) with a further volume on Chinese Copper Coins from his own collection (1915). His papers and collections are deposited in Edinburgh. See Shona Airlie's biography, 1989.

3.   Writing in 1912, Orme refers to "the so-called New Territories, more popularly known as the New Territory or simply 'the Territory'". See Orme, para. 1.

4.   A good and straightforward short account of *yin-yang* is given in Lai, Rofe and Mao, pp. 191–192.

5.   The survey and land settlement warrant a full study, not only for their own sake as major events, but also because the published reports and papers (sometimes confusing and contradictory), do not always provide answers to some of the questions which kept on intruding themselves while writing the chapter. The decisions of the NT Land Court, and colonial practice in regard to registration of titles thereafter, are thought by some scholars, especially Allen Chun in 2000, to have altered local customary law. These matters are considered in chapter 3, pp. 39–41.

6.   The wording, originally Clementi's, cited by an early British District Officer in his review of the New Territory 1899–1912. See Orme, para. 21.

7.   The ensuing dialogue was often noisy, using heady and exaggerated language, but this is a notable Chinese characteristic, adopted also by the Mainland government in e.g. its feud with Governor Patten over unwanted constitutional advance in Hong Kong in the 1990s. In its local applications, it usually masked a good deal of pragmatism and common sense.

8.   They were established in the NT in 1977, five years before their extension to urban Hong Kong and Kowloon. Retitled District Councils in 2000.

9.   The traditional rural culture is described and illustrated in Hayes 2001.1.

10.   Notably over village management and village elections, in which resident outsiders have now been given a say by the Courts, and various changes put in place by the government thereafter: see pp. 174–175.

Chapter 1   The Leased Territory in 1898

1.   Plate 1 is a reproduction of the "Map attached to the Convention signed at Pekin [*sic*]" on 9 June 1898. Excised from its parent county/district of San On

(Xinan) like Hong Kong Island and Kowloon before it, the leased territory is badly served by the county gazetteer, last revised as far back as 1819. Nonetheless, there is a useful part translation into English in Ng and Baker, with notes, and reproductions of its old-style Chinese maps.

2. HK 1960, p. 289. Lockhart had allowed 286 square miles for the mainland, and 90 square miles for the islands but greatly under-estimated their number. See LR pp. 535 and 538.

3. LR pp. 539–540. Along with Sham Chun–Sha Tau Kok, which he wished to include within the leased area (see p. 15), he estimated a round figure of 100,000. The lists of villages, population and "race" given in appendix 5 are neither comprehensive nor accurate, although the best he could provide.

4. SP 1911, p. 103 (26), Table XVIII. Exclusive of New Kowloon.

5. Faure 1986, p. 1 *seq.* See also the seminal work of the late Maurice Freedman, Professor of Social Anthropology at the University of Oxford, in this field, specifically Freedman 1966, and relevant papers in Skinner (ed.).

6. Judging from the village and hamlet populations recorded in detail at the 1911 Census, in SP 1911, pp. 103 (27–39).

7. For instance, the Liu (Liao) of Sheung Shui lived in an eight hamlet village; while the various segments of the Tangs each inhabited similarly organized "villages". Faure calls such complexes (along with other groupings) "clusters" (*op. cit.*, pp. 90–96). Freedman (who coined the term) styled the geographically extended lineage segments "higher-order lineages" (Freedman 1966, pp. 21–28).

8. Chesterton, p. 144.

9. See Lung and Friedman.

10. In 1898, five lineages were predominant among the rest, all early arrivals in the territory. These were (in Cantonese romanization) Tang, Liu, Hau, Pang and Man, though a sixth, the To of Tuen Mun, could be added. See Baker 1966, pp. 25–47.

11. The seven year coastal evacuation (longer in other coastal provinces) is described in Hayes 1983, pp. 24–26.

12. Barnett. Also, Hayes 1977.1, pp. 25–32.

13. For sub-soil rights, see chapter 3, pp. 30–31.

14. Faure 1986, pp. 6–11, extends Freedman's view of lineage and village to take in the importance of "right of settlement" and of "the territorial community" respectively; see also Chun and Faure in JHKRAS 28 (1988), pp. 240–263. The Hong Kong government recognized customary rights to the use of adjoining hillsides by issuing over 300 forestry licences in 1904, with more expected to follow; see SP 1905, p. 139. The rules governing these licences seem to have been first notified publicly in GN 276 of 1909.

15. The causes varied, but periodic epidemics were partly responsible, invariably blamed on changed or originally adverse *fung-shui*. Entire villages had moved their locations when convinced of the need; see e.g. Hayes 1983, pp. 153–155, and Hayes 2001.1, pp. 42–45.

16.   Baker 1968, chapter 7, indicates the animosities and rivalries of the major lineages of the northern NT.

17.   This fact is reflected in land registration, as ascertained during the survey and settlement of titles following the Lease. In a joint minute to the Colonial Secretary of 20 October 1904, Clementi and Messer, members of the NT Land Court, after stating that "the system of land tenancy by families or clans [was] the universal system in China", estimated that "at least 25% of all lots (in the NT) are held in clan and family names". In CSO 1902 Ext.

18.   Due in part to the character of the people. The Canton region had been notorious for its inhabitants' alleged quick temper, lack of breeding and education, and a desire for money, from early times; see the 10th-century work, *Taiping huanyu ji* (Gazetter of the World during the Taiping period, 976–983), "Customs" section of chapter 57. For 19th century statements on the same theme, see Hayes 1983, p. 129.

19.   See Murray for the years 1790–1810, and for the later period and after, Hayes 1983, pp. 26–31.

20.   There is a wonderfully funny despatch and enclosures from Governor Sir Hercules Robinson in 1864 which identifies the 18 villages of the Yuen Long/ Deep Bay area as prime culprits. A Roman Catholic clergyman had established himself in a large coastal village in the vicinity, for the purpose of promoting education. The inhabitants, it was reported, were civil and kind to him, taking a great interest in his schools, to which they sent all their children. "But he ... knows every man in the village to be a professional pirate: no disguise is made of the fact: no other occupation is even pretended: and he ... believes the neighbouring villages to be just as bad". Getting nowhere with a lugubrious Chinese brigade-general, Sir Hercules went to Canton to see the Viceroy, who observed "that the people of that District were all bad, and that we might deal with them as we pleased" (CO 129, 8810 Hong Kong, Governor's despatch of 28 July 1864 to London). As late as 1960, an urbane and distinguished-looking elder from a village on North Lamma (born 1883) told me, with a twinkle in his eye, that he had been "in all lines of business".

21.   Village wars in the Hong Kong region are listed in Table 1 on p. 279 of Hase 1990, pp. 265–281, which also provides information on recurrent hostilities over control of a landing place at Sham Chun [Shenzhen] in mid-19th century. His note on a later example is at pp. 257–265 in the same RAS Journal. See also Hayes 1993, pp. 10–11.

22.   See Hase 1992, and Baker 1968, pp. 87-88. *Fung-shui* obsessed all.

23.   A classic case, rooted in history, was reported by K. M. A. Barnett, when District Commissioner NT, in ADR DCNT 1955–56. The villages concerned, near Yuen Long, "have been at loggerheads for so long (at least 300 years) that both have forgotten how it all started". Disorders were often related to poor harvests. In this same twelvemonth period, there was "a material increase in minor civil and criminal cases, and disputes over water were numerous and often violent". *Ibid.*, para. 76.

24. See Hase 1995 for the case of the Lau Shui Heung villages in the northern NT. Watson and Watson, pp. 155–157, 161–162, 262–263, 297–298, and 445–446, describe the slow release from past domination in other parts of the northern NT long into the Lease.

25. A confrontation between the Kam Tin and Ping Shan Tangs over water supply, mediated by leaders from the Tai Po and Yuen Long branches of the lineage, was reported by DO North in HKAR 1920 and 1921, pp. J2 and J2 respectively. This was apparently nothing new.

26. For one such, convicted by entries in its own genealogy, and by local repute, see Baker 1968, pp. 182–183.

27. Hase 1995, p. 109. The memory of earlier struggles was preserved (and old grudges perpetuated) by the common practice of elevating those killed as "heroes", twice yearly honoured in commemorative rites performed at the specially provided altars in the local temples. See e.g. Faure 1986, pp. 104, 107 and index under "heroes and heroes' halls"; also Hayes 1993, pp. 10–11.

28. A propos the adjacent sub-district of Tamsui (Danshui), the *Hongkong Daily Telegraph* of 13 March 1879, quoting from the *Catholic Register*, noted "that only last year the great military Mandarin told one of our missionaries that of one village he has dozens of names in view for the next execution".

29. Told by Mr. Cheung Chi-fan, MBE, JP, Chairman of the Lam Tsuen Rural Committee, in 1970

30. Told by Mr. Yeung Ting-bun, aged 82, one of the Village Representatives, during a visit made in 1988. Two old cast-iron bells, removed to the new temple from the abandoned one, are each dated in 1749.

    The same concerns attached to buildings. In many parts of the NT, I saw how the doors of houses and ancestral halls had been slanted away from the direction of the parent structure (or row) to ensure better *fung-shui*. Sometimes this was done more than once. The doorway of a small ancestral hall on Tsing Yi island, built on the slant, had been brought back to the straight before the Second World War, and then returned to the slant as late as 1967, due to anxieties at these several times over a lack of male births.

31. The first, related to the Li Kau Yuen Tong (see p. 10) was obtained from a Lantau villager in 1960; see Hayes 1972. Nelson, p.3, heard similar stories in the Pat Heung area. The second legend, known for centuries across the NT and surely beyond, with its historical background, is recounted in Faure 1986, pp. 149–151 and note 11 on pp. 229–230, with later contributions from various pens in the JHKBRAS. On a visit to the Hakka village of Fung Chi Heung near Yuen Long in 1975, I was told by the elders (two of them in their 80s) that the ruins of the destroyed settlement were still to be seen in front of the nearby hill on which their own first ancestor and other ancestors were buried.

32. See Plate 4. This is a copy of the map found in the Registrar-General's Land Office in the early 1960s, dated "1899" on the reverse.

33. Such as *heung*, *tung*, and *yeuk* (xiang, dong, and yue, see Glossary). See Baker 1968, p. 6, n22, for other divisions variously in use at one time or another, seemingly government-inspired and for official purposes.

34. Baker 1968, p. 38. See note 10, and chapter 2, pp. 24–25.
35. The fullest description of a local market is provided in Hase 1993. He also gives the history of the immediate area from late Ming times up to 1941, and much else.
36. Hayes 1977.1, p. 36 with Faure 1986, pp. 153, 157. But at Taipo, dissatisfied small lineages in the surrounding area had set up their own market in the 1870s and continued despite an affirmation of existing rights by the county magistrate; see Groves, pp. 16–20, and Faure 1986, pp. 112–113. Also *Inscriptions*, Vol.1, No. 84.
37. Hayes 1977.1, pp. 37–38.
38. Mr Tang Hop-wan of Ha Tsuen, northern NT. For the Heung Yee Kuk (Rural Consultative Council), see pp. 83 and 175, and appendix to Hayes 1996.
39. Fully endorsed by Dyer Ball (pp. 181–182), a leading expert in the Cantonese dialects of the day.
40. Watson and Watson, pp. 12–13. Besides locality, complexity was further increased by the variants introduced through the original speech patterns of the founding families, whether Hakka or Punti-speakers, coming from different counties of Guangdong, a large province.
41. See chapter 2, pp. 30–31.
42. See *Gompertz Ts'ing I* for the Kam Tin Tangs' claim to land on Tsing Yi Island, where only a very small amount of the area for which rent was being levied, and was being claimed, was held by proper title.
43. For the holdings of the Tangs of Kam Tin and Lung Yeuk Tau, see Faure 1986, pp. 36–38, with note 24 on p. 190, together with the rest of the section on Land Rights, pp. 36–44, with extensive notes at pp. 189–192.
44. For the Liu (Liao), see Baker 1968, p. 172, and Faure 1986, pp. 37–39.
45. See Hayes 1977.1, pp. 47–50, and Hayes 1993, pp. 158–159.
46. Watson and Watson, p. 161.
47. Barnett, pp. 263–265.
48. See Hayes 1977.1, p. 30.
49. Pauline Woo, p. 15.
50. As reflected in the lists of graduates by examination and purchase contained in their genealogies, and through the formal graves of leading members still to be found on the hills of the New Territories, with inscriptions giving lineage and career details. The Tang lineage of Kam Tin contained some very wealthy men. One is supposed to have owned the whole of Hong Kong Island, and in the Wanli reign of the Ming dynasty (1573–1620) his two great-great-grandsons were credited with still owning three-quarters and one-quarter of the island respectively. See Sung, p. 182, with note 60.
51. See Hayes 1977.1, pp. 181–193, and Hayes 1984.2.
52. Faure and Lee, pp. 271–279.
53. See note 36 above. David Faure reminds us (Faure 1986, pp. 41–42) that sub-soil owners' fortunes could ebb as well as flow. Such fluctuations have been seen as representing something greater than they really were. Nelson, for

instance, p. 1, believes that the British had missed the significance of various changes taking place in the late 19th century. But even if they had, they had carried the supposed direction to its extreme in denying the claims of "rent charge owners" to wider ownership, in favour of their tenants.

54. See Hayes 1982, pp. 294–297. They could also be used in a more aggressive fashion; see the text to note 46 above.

55. The formal machinery could be used to bolster the informal. See Shuzo Shiga, pp. 50–51. There are some valuable statements on this interface in Cheng, pp. 8–9, 117–120.

56. Morse, p. 59. This being the case, it is distinctly misleading, and in fact erroneous — at any rate in the Hong Kong Region, to look no further afield — to credit the gentry with the abundant organization to be found in the countryside in late imperial times, as do Hsiao (pp. 316–317, 321) and others.

57. "For the kind of behaviour that is approved by most of the villagers, a person is everywhere honoured and praised. For misbehaviour may suffered [*sic*] the terrible punishment of social isolation. Disapproval is a powerful check". Pauline Woo, p. 16. Douglas, pp. 111–113, provides a wider spectrum, making the point that each individual in the village "is but a cog-wheel in the social machine. He must work with the rest, or the whole machine will get out of gear. Personality disappears, and ostracism of a complete and oppressive kind is the fate of those who venture to oppose themselves to the public opinion of those about them". He had served briefly in the British Consular Service in China from 1858.

58. Comprising only the magistrate, a deputy and two assistant magistrates, some skilled clerks to handle the specialized business of the office, and a crowd of police and runners to do his bidding in the countryside.

59. See the detailed studies of Qing administration by Watt and Ch'u.

60. Yet despite the preferred practice of leaving management to local leaders, the county magistrate or his seniors had intervened occasionally to settle disputes and complaints taken to him by dissatisfied groups of people, as with the interesting cases described in Faure, Luk, and Lun Ng.

61. *Inscriptions*, Vol. 1, No. 67, p. 189. The Chancellor was the *zhuangyuan* of 1871.

62. It has been necessary to use relevant material from a later period in this section.

63. HKAR 1926, J3.

64. See Siak, pp. 191–196. Also, *Rice Farming in Hong Kong*.

65. Armando da Silva describes "the traditional coastal way-of-life that had endured for so long" and its fast erosion during his field work on Lantau Island in 1962–63: a truly valuable account. See also Hayes and Tin on the village fisheries, 1987.

66. Hayes 1977.1, pp. 40–41.

67. See Hayes 1993, p. 11–12 with notes on p. 187. The economy of the territory also comprised a number of rural industries carried on where natural resources and local conditions permitted. See Hayes 1977.1, pp. 32–38.

68. See Buck, 1930 and 1937. One statement from the latter (p. 469) illustrates two kinds of obligatory major expenditure: "In every area, the cost of a wedding exceeded the total value of a labourer's yearly earnings. The cost of a funeral or a dowry exceeded it in all but two areas". The general poverty, with reasons, is affirmed in Chang, pp. 776–778.

69. Buck 1930, p. 420. One of Buck's distinguished predecessors, Professor F. H. King, had been equally appreciative. See the moving, tightly written estimate given in his book, pp. 67–68.

70. See Hayes 1993, p. 156, for a striking example from Ma Wan Island in 1897 when the inhabitants opposed high-handed actions by the Chinese Imperial Maritime Customs.

71. The necessity of both is emphasized in the Trimetrical Classic, the elementary school primer of the empire: "Gems unwrought, can form nothing useful, / So men untaught, can never know the proprieties". See also in Giles 1910, pp. 14–15. The story teller and the opera, man or puppet, provided another essential part of the cultural base. "The common people have absorbed, not read, from the master spirits of forty Centuries. Their culture thought-patterns are vertical, not horizontal, and the heroes they worship are not chosen from present day movie stars but from great men of old. ..." See Joliffe, pp. 20–21 (order of sentences reversed). Nearly forty years earlier, a well-known American missionary author had given an almost identical estimate: Smith, pp. 49–50.

72. See Hayes 2001.1. Chang's assessment (see note 68 above) that "*rural culture will remain at a very low standard unless some drastic and practical methods are adopted to change the present situation*" [my italics] is not borne out in the Hong Kong Region, where poverty certainly did not preclude culture.

73. Peninsula Jaycees, "Rescuing the New Territories' Past", 1981. Chan Wing-hoi and Patrick Hase have also contributed to our knowledge in this field, with the former emphasizing the songs' contribution to rural education and verbal arts, and to our understanding of personal relationships inside the family.

74. Entitled *The Historical Literature of the New Territories*, they amounted by 1986 (as today) to 30,000 photocopied pages: Faure 1986, p.xi, and note 7 on p. 180. Now held in local and overseas libraries. See also Hase 1984.

75. Faure and Lee.

76. See Sung.

77. Written by the late Tang Cheuk-wah, Chairman of the Ping Shan Rural Committee. These relate to his lineage and to the history (or mythology) of the northern NT. Such tales were handed down by the elders, and by travelling story-tellers, into (at latest) the mid-20th century, but have long ceased to feature in the lives of the young. For their undoubted importance, see Hayes 1977.1, p. 55.

78. Under the supervision of Mr. Patrick S. S. Lau.

79. See *Rural Architecture*.

80. It was linked to a literary capability which, though limited to a percentage of village men, was yet sufficient to facilitate self-management in the villages and

sub-districts. See the section "A Written Village Culture" in Hayes 2001.1, based, *inter alia*, on the detailed discussion in Hayes 1984. See Hase 1990.

81. Surviving commemorative tablets detail the times (often inconvenient) indicated by geomancers for important stages in the siting and re-siting of graves, and in building and reconstructing ancestral halls and temples. In an example from Tsuen Wan (1905), the (separate) graves of a founding ancestor [late Ming dynasty] and his wife had to be taken up at 4.45 pm on the second day of a certain lunar month, the joint re-burial was to begin at 7 am on the sixth day, and the grave tablet placed in position at 8.45 am on the 26th day. A series of timings for the reconstruction of the Tin Hau Temple at Sai Kung Market in 1916 is given in *Inscriptions*, Vol.2, No.130. For more on the *bazi*, see Lai, Rofe and Mao, p. 13, and Dyer Ball, p. 55, with a fuller exposition in Wells Williams, Vol.II, pp. 69, 74–75.

82. LR, p. 548.

Chapter 2   The Existing British Crown Colony and "the Great Difference"

1. Royal Princes, Vol. II, pp. 208–9.

2. She was less enthusiastic about the European society of the place.

3. Curzon, p. 428. What a profound change from the opinions of the 1840s, when certain writers were of the view that, being "an unhealthy, pestilential, and unprofitable barren rock", "a colony ... composed of raw materials, and unlicked into civilization", Hong Kong should be exchanged for Chusan: e.g. Sirr, Vol. 1, pp. ix and 179.

4. Gordon-Cumming, Vol. I, p. 5.

5. Vincent, pp. 305–310.

6. Hübner, p. 576.

7. Prominent among photographic collections on Old Hong Kong and its people are the volumes published by Frank Fischbeck's FormAsia firm, and the Asia Society Galleries' *Picturing Hong Kong*. An architectural survey of the whole, including the NT, is given in FormAsia's *Building Hong Kong*.

8. Des Voeux, p. 37. In 1885, a Land Commission had been appointed to investigate overcrowding in Victoria, and had recommended reclamation to ease congestion: *Abstract*, pp. 28–29. A report on this subject by the Surveyor-General is at SP 1887, p. 318.

9. *Hansard* 1897–98, p. 5.

10. During passage of the Water Bill through Legislative Council, in June 1902. See *Hansard*, 1901–02, p. 28.

11. "The civil population is essentially a male adult one, as no less than 72.9 per cent of the Chinese population ... are males." Report of the Sanitary Board for 1901 in HKGG, 2 May 1902, GN 265, p. 721.

12. Hübner makes it clear that Chinese coming to Hong Kong would be exposed to a much wider cross-section of humanity than was ever possible at home.

"In the lower part of the town the scene is most animated and busy: officers and soldiers in red uniforms and with swarthy complexions (sepoys), Parsees, Hindoos, Chinese, Malays, European ladies in elegant toilets, and men and women with yellowish skins, dressed like Europeans (half-caste Portuguese)". Hübner, p. 576. He also notes that "No one dreams of walking. Nothing is to be seen but chairs". [This was in late November, the best season of the year!] Another visitor, A. B. Mitford (afterwards Lord Redesdale) en route to his post in the British Legation at Peking in 1865, picturesquely observed that these "elements no more amalgamate than the oil and vinegar in a salad": Mitford, p. 5.

13. Naturalization was granted by the passage of a Bill through the Legislative Council: see, e.g., HKGG, 14 January 1888 and *Hansard* 1902, p.18. Inhabitants of the NT would become British subjects upon the cession. Also, Plate 17.

14. For Old British Kowloon, not dealt with here, see the chapter in Hayes 1983.

15. King, p. 70. Although his description was published in 1911, the regulation of the boat population went far back into the 19th century. The reason for these nightly congregations was that movement in the harbour by night was prohibited. For the Harbour Regulations of 1841 and 1862, made under ordinance, see Wells Williams, pp. 217–220.

16. See Arlington in Hayes 1983, pp. 29–30.

17. See Munn, pp. 163–169 for the decision to apply British law. However, outside the Courts and in competition with them (as recognized and condemned in some expatriate quarters: Munn, p. 377) the Tung Wah Hospital mediated disputes among the Chinese population, while the guilds and Chinese guilds and societies must have done likewise. Custom was also followed in practice in the old villages, especially in regard to ownership of land and houses, when the Village Rent Rolls kept by the Registrar General lacked names, and successions went unquestioned so long as someone in the family paid the annual fees. The *Hong Kong Land Commission* 1886–87, Report in SP 1887, provides information on the Colony's old villages.

18. Also known as "Protector of Chinese", his department was renamed the Secretariat for Chinese Affairs in 1913. The civil establishment was listed in detail in the annual *Blue Books*, and financial provision in the annual *Estimates*. For the Registrar-General's total establishment at this time, when Stewart Lockhart was both RG and Colonial Secretary, see e.g. BB 1901, pp. I 50–53.

19. As adapted to suit local circumstances. See also Bickley 2005.

20. *Hansard* 1900–1901, pp. 29 and 32–33. Dr. Ho said that lime-washing had been proved not to be a prevention against plague, and in the case of the villages "was unnecessary and harassing to the poor people who occupy them". The prohibition of hill burials and of grass-cutting and firewood gathering in government plantations on Crown land were measures which did bear heavily on villagers of Hong Kong and Old British Kowloon: see e.g., the stringently worded Police Notification in HKGG, 1 April 1876, and Hayes 1983, p. 65.

21.   Albert Smith, p. 39. The "Report of the Committee for Superintending Government Schools for the year 1858", printed in the HKGG, 12 February 1859 as GN No. 12, states that "The first rudiments of spelling and reading English are also taught in the larger schools". There were 15 schools in 1858, and the number of scholars was 675. All village schools came under the government's education scheme.

22.   Bickley 1977, pp. 88–91 and 103–113.

23.   See Carl T. Smith 1984 and 1995.

24.   CSO Ext 1903/9284, dealing with the collection of Crown Rent on Peng Chau Island (Gompertz to Hon. CS, minute of 8.12.03) "I understand that there are 90 or 100 dwelling houses on the island and that the elder sends his son to Queen's College".

25.   Verbal confirmation from Rev. Carl T. Smith. A yamen was the office-residence of a Chinese official.

26.   SP 1897, The Educational Report for 1896, para.9. See also Ng Lun 1984, pp. 139–146.

27.   Education Report for 1896, para. 7.

28.   The opening of the University of Hong Kong in 1912 (Endacott, p. 283) would be another forward step, as had been the establishment of the Hong Kong Technical Institute in 1907, with its wide range of practical subjects and evening instruction: Endacott, p. 281, and BB 1911, p. 12.

29.   Beresford, pp. 466–468.

30.   Beresford, "Summary of Trade Statistics" at pp. 480–481. Remer, p. 100, states, "At no time in the history of the foreign trade of China has British shipping been of greater importance than during the closing years of the nineteenth century". And yet, Jules Duckerts, Consul General and Chargé D'Affaires of Belgium, thought that the port was over-rated: Duckerts, pp. 115–116.

31.   Beresford, pp. 216–233. At the same time, they pointed to various frustrations owing to the lack of protection or assistance given them by British consuls in China, notwithstanding their British national status in the Colony.

32.   Beresford's interviews included some with progressive Chinese viceroys who were openly fearful for their country, and said so. The book brings home how eager some European Powers were to make the partition of China a reality through "spheres of influence" and other concessions. This situation only elevated the position of Hong Kong and the other British enclaves in China, and increased the hubris of their British and other Western residents. See also chapter 11, pp. 146–147 with 149.

33.   LR, p. 552.

34.   In 1910, Hon. Gershom Stewart reminisced in Legislative Council about the primitive condition of the NT at the time of the take-over, adding, "Where you find walled and moated villages, roads non-existent, and wheel traffic therefore unknown; commerce conducted by packman ... and the area of the market for the exchange of commodities restricted accordingly, you are sure

to find even the act of agriculture crude, and a backward and unprogressive population. Civilization is mainly dependent on means of communication and transport." *Hansard*, 1910, p. 113. He spoke, too, of the still existing "difference between the population of the New Territory and of the Colony". *Ibid.*, p. 114. Writing to me in 1958, Eric Hamilton also stressed this point in regard to the NT as it then was ("and indeed the S. Coast of Hong Kong Island as well"). Hamilton Letters, 1 August 1958.

35.   As it happened, both the Island and Old British Kowloon had old villages similar to those Lockhart had found in the New Territory. With the continuance of traditional agriculture in the settlements beyond the tightly clustered urban areas, life there might not differ greatly from the interior. However, these villages were few in number, and their several thousand residents, all told, had no effect upon how the Colony was governed. Many of the males were, in any case, working overseas or on ships.

36.   From an undated confidential memorandum from Lockhart to Blake, appended to his Report on the Extension of the Colony of Hong Kong, and cited by Airlie, p. 103. See also SP 1899, p. 179, para. 12.

37.   A *tepo* was a quasi government appointee, answerable for village security. See Ch'u, pp. 3–4 and Watt, pp. 190–191.

38.   A "Tung" was, as we have seen, one of the variously named sub-divisions of a Chinese county.

39.   CO 129 284/242. There was no tradition of district administration in the Colony. Although suggested by the Land Commission in 1886, the police stations remained the focus of local knowledge and liaison with the inhabitants in the outlying areas. See e.g. Hayes 1983, p. 53.

40.   Clyde, p. 840.

41.   See Hsiao, pp. 373–374.

42.   In 1849, Mr. Consul Alcock wrote of "the conviction under which every Chinese quails, of the terrible vengeance that may pursue them and their families, the tumult once over, if they should have been marked or recognized" in time of riot or unrest: in McNair, p. 216.

43.   Two leading viceroys advised the Throne at the end of the century that the runners were "the scourge of the people, in every province the same. It must be that the worst of the people take up this employment": No. 226 in Hirth. For the venality of the lower officers, see e.g. the case given in Hayes 2001.1, pp. 13, 17, 24 n3.

44.   "Essentially despotic", was how Herbert Giles described the form of Chinese government, after much observation of Chinese officials and their ways: Giles 1882, p. 122. Captain Denham writing bitterly of his own and his shipwrecked crew's treatment at the hands of local officials during the war of 1840–1842, said there had to be implicit obedience "not to what the laws had provided, but to what they [the Chinese officers] thought fit to order": Denham, p. 3.

45.   The Kangxi emperor in person had said as much: van der Sprenkel, pp. 76–77. See also the translations in Wade, Vol. 1, especially No. 74 on pp. 63–70.

46. See e.g., the harrowing descriptions of Chinese justice and prisons in Bird (Mrs. Bishop), part of Letter IV between pp. 67–85, during a visit to Canton in 1879: also earlier, in Wingrove Cooke, chapter XXIX.

47. The people "think it right to put up with a good deal that would not be tolerated in the extreme west," averred Herbert Giles, who considered that "the Chinese as a nation recognize the necessity of being governed". But he also attributed it to the fact that the civil service examinations by which the greater part of the mandarinate was recruited were open to all comers, whereby (as he so aptly put it) they "agree to regard successful competitors as their masters rather than their servants". He saw, too, how the strong authority of the rulers was partially offset by the "practically democratic spirit of the people" and the sanctions accorded them to resist "glaring evil in high places": Giles 1882, p. 122, with a few examples of civic action taken against oppressive or unpopular officials at pp. 224–225. See Hayes, JHKBRAS 30 (1990) pp. 6–11.

48. See chapter 3, note 45.

49. Peplow, pp.140–141. In the early 1950s, Austin Coates had noted another trait, averring that "80% of the people coming to the District Office talked in riddles. The staff were accustomed to it from their years of experience." It was, he thought, "due to their mental inability to explain anything coherently": see his novel, *The Road* (New York, Harper & Bros., 1959), pp. 298–9. This was a theme on which he enlarged in his classic account, *Myself a Mandarin* (1968).

50. Bird, p. 71, records how the prisoners of Canton were well aware of the better treatment accorded in the Hong Kong gaol.

51. They included Kowloon City, the existing Chinese customs stations in the New Territory, demarcation of its northern boundary, and whether the Shamchun Valley should be added to the Kowloon Extension. The various issues can be followed in *CO Hong Kong Correspondence*, and *Extension*. Agreement on the new frontier was reached on 11 March 1899, followed by the signing of a Memorandum on 19 March: Wesley-Smith 1980, pp. 198–199.

52. By far the best and most exhaustive account of the fighting, and of the episode as a whole, is provided in Patrick Hase's new article, "The Six Day War of 1899", which it is hoped to publish in a forthcoming issue of JHKBRAS. See also Groves 1969.

53. Despite the low estimate of casualties on the Chinese side given in the official reports, Patrick Hase has argued for severe loss of life among the insurgents on the basis of carefully analysed local evidence which seems also to me to be quite irrefutable. The large Charitable Grave at Sha Po near Kam Tin, featured in Plate 8, is associated with the fighting. In keeping with what seems to have been the strong desire to pass a veil over this unfortunate episode in government and people relations during the NT Lease, the men (and women) who died were not commemorated there or elsewhere by the bi-annual rituals long carried out for heroes killed in inter-lineage struggles. In consequence, the grave had

been overlooked by later generations, and by local historians alike. But in the years following the Hong Kong Government's 1994 amendment to the New Territories Ordinance to permit female succession to landed property, it was rediscovered, refurbished, and used in the Heung Yee Kuk's political campaign to uphold the rights and customs of the indigenous population. See Selina Ching Chan 1998, together with chapter 12, at pp. 175–176.

54. The uprising was fuelled by highly coloured accounts of likely British atrocities, interference and expropriation: see Wesley-Smith, pp. 83–85, and Groves, pp. 43–45. For general susceptibilities to rumour and panic before the days of newspapers, see e.g. the illuminating accounts in Moule, chapter V, Griffith John in Wardlaw Thompson, pp. 394–396, and Stott, pp. 45–51. For a later example from Hong Kong, see SP 1921, p. 156.

55. *Extension*, pp. 21, 26, 28. Yet in what might appear as an immediate breach of the Expropriation clause of the Peking Convention, Blake would extend the Crown Lands Resumption Ordinance of 1889 to the NT, and widen its scope to being "for any [public] purpose of whatever description" paving the way for the widespread resumptions and expropriations of the future: HKGG, 7 October 1899, and Hayes 1993, pp. 66–67.

56. "When title to land cannot be produced, occupation will be accepted as proof of ownership after due notice has been given in the village and district". Instructions "for the present administration of the Kowloon Extension" sent to Lockhart on 21 April 1899: *Ibid.*, p. 41.

57. No. 186 of 13 May 1899 to London, in CO *Hong Kong Correspondence*. Also Airlie, pp. 101–102. Patrick Hase's new article, "The Six Day War of 1899", examines the two men's very different approach to pacification, in some detail.

58. *First Year*, pp. 12–14. Treated with tea, cakes and cigars, the committeemen's replies are at CO HK Corr., No. 243. Another example of this directness was Blake's visit to a plague district in the City in 1903 to explain how he was combating the disease: Boyden and others, p. 70.

59. Not at first appreciated. "The establishment of Police Stations in the Territory was distasteful to, and opposed by, the inhabitants, who at first threw every obstacle in the way of selecting suitable sites and, after this failed, rendered no help in the construction": SP 1900, p. 241. This antagonism was surely due to the universally bad reputation of the constables and runners in the district yamens under Chinese rule. See note 43 above.

60. See the opening pages of chapter 4 for a more detailed description.

61. Hence the present day "Boundary Street". For the fence, see *Decennial Reports*, p. 203. There are photographs of it in Peter Wesley-Smith 1980, at Plate 11, and at p. 30 of the Urban Council's *Hong Kong Album* (1982).

62. Copied many years ago, but the source defies detection. See also Lockhart in *First Year*, p. 1.

63. Likewise, but there is a very similar statement in HKGG 1900, GN 201, p. ii.

64. Under the Extension of Laws Ordinance, No. 8 of 1900. "In order to provide for the proper administration and to foster the development of this area it was

found necessary to apply to it the health, rating and other laws in force in the urban districts of Hong Kong and Kowloon": see the Objects and Reasons clause 1 of the bill amending the Interpretation Ordinance of 1911. An amended plan of the area was also supplied. From HKGG 1937, p. 879.

65.　SP 1907, pp. 258, 276.

66.　SP 1911, Table XIX (a) at p. 103 (39).

67.　The important old settlements of Po Kong, Nga Tsin Wai, and Chuk Yuen, and many later ones in central New Kowloon, are merely lumped in anonymously with "Kowloon City" in what was otherwise a most detailed listing of villages and hamlets in the New Territory. The apparent decision not to appoint committeemen for New Kowloon, as was done for the NT proper (see GNs 387 and 394 in HKGG for 8 and 15 July 1899) has deprived historians of information on its sub-divisions, villages and leaders (committeemen) and diminished our knowledge of the area before 1898. It also serves to underline the authorities' different approach to the New Kowloon villages. Another instance is provided by Orme (para. 16) who tells us that none of the Crown lessees in New Kowloon would receive certificates of their holdings, "as their lands are usually well known to them, and reference to the Registers in Hongkong is for them a simple matter".

Chapter 3　Survey, Land Court, Registration and Customary Law

1.　See p. 41.

2.　By early March 1899, Blake had advised London that he wished to have a complete survey as soon as possible: see No. 93 in *CO Hong Kong Correspondence*. The reply, dated 28 April, presumed that he had satisfied himself that an immediate survey was "absolutely indispensable" and enjoined the strictest economy (*ibid*, No. 132).

3.　His instructions from the Colonial Office, dated 22 June 1898, are given in No. 2 in *CO Hong Kong Correspondence*. He was asked to specially consider "by what means revenue can in the first instance be best raised from the new territory, without exciting the suspicions or irritating the feelings and prejudices of the Chinese inhabitants. This point is very important, as the existing revenues of Hong Kong must not be unduly strained to pay for the cost of the new territory, which should be from the first, as far as possible, self-supporting. In connection with this it may be necessary to consider what taxation is at present borne by the population of the district, and how it is raised".

4.　*First Year*, Appendix VIII, paras. 8–9. For a detailed account of the confused ownership situation there, see the article on Sham Shui Po in Carl T. Smith 1995.

5.　*Orme*, para. 21. For "rent charge owners", see *Gompertz 2*, p. 8.

6.　Such land could only be transferred officially by registering the sale with the magistrate, whereupon (for a substantial fee) the name entered in the registers would be changed to that of the purchaser. He, in return, would receive a 'red' or registered deed of purchase, and thereafter be responsible for payment of the land tax. See Jamieson, pp. 97–98, and Bumbailliff.

7. According to Jamieson, p. 108, this "sort of tenant right ownership of the surface", which could be assigned or sub-let, rested solely on local custom, since "the statute law does not recognize such right". Lin Yue-hwa's classic study, *The Golden Wing*, pp. 13–14, describes a similar situation in Fujian, where "under the local laws of land tenure, the ownership of land assumes different forms". Palmer 1987 is the most detailed and reliable coverage of these complex subjects.

8. See Hayes 1977.1, pp. 52, with note 147. Also pp. 166–167, with notes 13–18.

9. "About 2 years ago in the course of the delivery of Kowloon by the Chinese authorities I was present when the principal officer (the District Magistrate I think) plainly denied the legality of the tenure of even Kowloon peninsula itself by the Chinese who were resident on it...." The context was whether compensation should be paid upon removal to families occupying Stonecutters Island in Hong Kong Harbour close to Kowloon: see CO 129/91, in No. 42 of 14 February 1863, para. 17.

10. See the examples given in Hayes 1977.1, pp. 51–52.

11. See *Gompertz Ts'ing I*, pp. 1403–1404.

12. See also *L & T*.

13. A Chinese provincial governor had attempted land tax reform on Taiwan in the 1880s, and the Japanese colonial authorities had succeeded in doing so after the island was ceded to Japan in 1895: see Myers 1972, pp. 404–407, and Hui-sun Tang, p. 25. It is not clear whether these actions were known to the Hong Kong or UK Governments at the time of the Survey and Land Court.

14. In one district of Central China, the revenue from land tax, which had amounted to 26,000 yuan, rose after the survey and registration, without an increase in the rate of tax, to a million yuan. However, time and cost precluded much being done, the latter being in many areas estimated to be more than the tax revenue. See *Problems of the Pacific, 1936*, pp. 160–162.

Yet as Dr. Ramon Myers has pointed out, while this unique form of land tenure would make it extremely difficult for the Nationalist Government to finance modernization in those large areas of China where it persisted, the under-taxation of agriculture achieved thereby had greatly facilitated the development of the old rural society and economy: Myers 1983, pp. 18–22, with the interesting longer treatment in Myers 1980, pp. 160–167, particularly in regard to the provinces of central China.

15. See, e.g., the breakdown of family holdings for two areas on Lantau Island given in Hayes 1977.1, at pp. 109 and 111, with 132 and 136, as calculated from the 1905 records by land staff of the District Office South/Islands.

16. See *Survey*, pp. 399–404.

17. However, village children had fun removing many of the wooden pickets marking the traverse stations for the survey, making it necessary for them to

be permanently marked to assist the cadastral surveyors. *First Year*, p. 35, and *Survey*, p. 397.

18.   *Survey 1900–01*. The NT was a distinctly unhealthy place in which to work. Upon conclusion of the survey, the Officer in Charge reported that "Throughout the whole period the health of the establishment was bad, and the men were constantly being sent to hospital. One Inspector, one Surveyor and 5 Indian coolies died, and 6 Surveyors and 9 Indian coolies were invalided; 4 out of 6 Surveyors died on the way home": *Survey*, Miscellaneous, para.4.

19.   *Survey*, table at p. 403. For a typical survey sheet, see Plate 13. These figures are at variance with those reported to the Legislative Council at an earlier date: see the table in *Hansard* 1901, p. 46, and note 24.

20.   The Gazette notice (Government Notification — No. 405) for "Tsing I, Ma Wan, Ping Chau, Cheung Chau", and other islands in the area, was entered in the HKGG for 4 August 1900, at p. 1242. Briefly, it stated that unless claims were presented to the [Land] Court by 1 October 1900, all persons in occupation of land in these places without authorization would be deemed trespassers against the Crown, as provided for under section 15 of the NT Land Court Ordinance 1900.

21.   *Gompertz 1*.

22.   Explained at pp. 34–35.

23.   For more details of Gompertz's experience on Ma Wan, see Hayes 1993, pp. 157–158. In the end, he recommended that all persons in occupation should be recognized as owners, upon payment of the appropriate Crown rent.

24.   *Gompertz 1*, p. 1403. It would seem, on balance, from the information available, that there had been no demarcation during the survey of Ma Wan (nor presumably of Tsing Yi). According to *Survey*, p. 400, the survey work there had been undertaken sometime in mid 1900, and surely before 1 October 1900, the last date for receiving claims. It was also stated therein that the practice of combining both survey and demarcation did not begin until November 1900, at the start of the 1900–1901 Field Season; while, overall, it appears that only 11,157.32 acres had been demarcated out of the 44,281.77 surveyed up to 30 June 1901: see *Hansard* 1901, p. 46.

         Another source states that demarcation began in June 1900 (see note 27) but, as the table shows it was initially on a smaller scale, and as Gompertz seems to infer, perhaps not undertaken together with the survey work at Ma Wan or Tsing Yi.

         There is, too, some confusion as to *when* the survey took place, since the Tsing Yi cadastral survey is stated elsewhere (*Report 1902*, p. 2) to have been carried out in 1902, and Ma Wan likewise. Perhaps this was in error? A re-survey seems most unlikely, since (as stated in *Gompertz 2*, p. 7) the first formal sitting of the Court had been held at Ma Wan on 20 February 1901, "to enquire into the local claims which were for the most part of minor importance". See also note 49.

25.   See NTLC.

26. One wonders what happened in large lineages like the Tangs, where a high percentage of the land was owned by lineage trusts. Presumably it was their managers who came out to identify the land and represent the common owners.
27. "Notes for Use in District Land Offices", p. 3.
28. Taken from the fascinating account of the work, including the detailed "Demarcation Rules" and a Schedule of "Particulars of Claim to Land ..." in *Gompertz 2*. The Schedules had to be completed for each and every lot, but unlike the "chits" or printed slips know as *chi tsai* or "little papers" — see note 29 — I do not recollect having seen a single one to date.
29. See Plate 15 with Hayes 1988.
30. All at *Gompertz 2*, p. 6.
31. See the Governor's Chinese Proclamation (in English translation) dated 12 July 1899, in which he set out what landholders had to do, and the amounts of Crown Rent to be paid on different classes of land in New Kowloon and elsewhere: in Appendix IV of *First Year*, pp. 19–20.
32. *First Year*, p. 5.
33. This number may seem small, but official Chinese deeds were far fewer in number than the unofficial customary deeds commonly in use in the NT and elsewhere in Guangdong: see pp. 30–31 above.
34. Appendix VIII to *First Year*, pp. 277–279.
35. In *Gompertz 1*.
36. At this point we may take notice of "An Ordinance to provide for the Summoning of Chinese before the Registrar General", No. 40 of 1899, enacted on 28 December 1899. This seems to have been prompted largely by the Governor's personal vexation with an initial reluctance to provide information requested by the Government. He spoke in the Legislative Council of "the great difficulty in getting the Chinese to come forward and give any information about their land or about registration", but was clearly more incensed with "their elders, their leaders", who on more than one occasion had given "no attention whatever to the invitation" to come in (*Hansard* 1899–1900, p. 41). Lockhart's remarks, recorded both in the Council (*Ibid*, p. 117) and in *First Year*, p. 11, were less indignant, and indeed purely factual: "The object of this measure is to secure the attendance of the people so that full explanations of Government measures may be given to them and so that the Government may learn from the people what their views may be regarding any proposed measure, and what objections they may have to urge when matters do not appear to be working smoothly." See also note 45.

    The Ordinance was to have a two-year term, and be renewable at need. Its first renewal was for three months only, to await the Secretary of State's reaction to a report on its operation. Since he offered no objection, it was renewed in March 1902. Further renewals in 1904 and 1906 took it well beyond the period of the survey, demarcation and land settlement.

    Curiously, those called forward had to appear before the Registrar-General, and not the administrative and legal officials working in the NT, and only after approval by the Governor. It is also rather puzzling that, not long after it became law, the Colonial Secretary was already able to provide the seemingly rather satisfactory figures for the registration of claims at the new Land Offices at Tai Po and Ping Shan and the registration of Chinese deeds at the Land Office, Hong Kong, as noted already. Was it a case of over-kill? Ultimately, power to summon, under penalty for non-compliance, was included in the New Territories Ordinance of 1910, at clauses 9–11.

37.   In regard to the first, and the major difficulties encountered along the way, see Sihombing.

Lockhart had pointed out the doubtful utility of *registering Chinese deeds* in the Land Office in his Report on the New Territory for 1900, p. 3. He referred to the fees paid for registration, and the fact that the "lot number" given upon registration "does not relate to any map, for the simple reason that there is not yet one available, and as the boundaries and the description of the land in the Chinese deed are invariably extremely vague, it is impossible to ascertain with any certainty where the land affected by the instrument is really situated".

And in regard to compiling a Crown Rent Roll from the *Claims* submitted at Tai Po and Ping Shan, both Lockhart and Gompertz had soon begun to call it the "Rough Rent Roll": see Lockhart, *Ibid*, p. 3, and *Gompertz 1*. The latter had stated that "the form in which they [the claims] were laid … was "neither sufficiently full nor sufficiently clear for them to serve as the basis for an investigation into title", and hence drawing up a reliable Crown Rent Roll. In fact, it would seem from Clementi's minute of 21 April 1904 in CSO Ext 1904 to Hon CS that four or five years after the Lease a majority had still not paid tax (Crown rent) to the British government: seemingly with specific reference to Lantau, but perhaps with wider implications. And see, also, ADR DONT 1947–48, para.29, for a truly surprising omission.

38.   The three Cadets were Cecil Clementi, C. McI. Messer and J. R. Wood: see *NTLC*.

39.   All in all, more archival work is needed to elucidate matters which are either insufficiently explained or are still obscure.

40.   The latter included the names of seller, middleman, buyer, witness to the receipt of the agreed purchase sum, writer of the deed, and sometimes of the branch or clan head and those of other lineage heads and the village headman. See also note 56.

41.   From the available evidence, it would seem that where land was, before 1898, regarded as belonging to a lineage or branch lineage, its holdings might already be divided in practice among eligible families, with consent to the divisions attested through the customary documents known as *Fan Tip*, of which copies were signed, witnessed, and given to all parties concerned. Such papers might be drawn up whenever new internal arrangements were made (as in, e.g., the Kau Wah Keng papers, now deposited in the HKPRO) or they could be oral, being known to all concerned. More work is needed on this aspect of land-holding inside lineages.

42.   See note 75 for some consequences.

43.   Crown Rents, increased several times in the early years, were claimed to be higher than amounts paid before 1898. See Hayes 1993, p. 20, for a petition from Kau Wah Keng in CSO 1906, No. 3120, with others from Sha Tau Kok and Tung Chung in 1903/9698 and 1905/6990 respectively. Besides Blake's Chinese proclamation of 18 July 1899, see Sir Mathew Nathan's proclamation of 28 June 1905, in "Notes for Use in District Land Offices", pp. 6–9. Even so, the total amount of Crown Rent (which after 1908 was never changed throughout the Lease) was reported as being only $ 398,111.57 in the financial year 1962–1963: HK 1963, p. 15.

44.   This same insouciance surfaced in my discussions with elders of Ma Tau Wai Village in New Kowloon in 1972. Their village, they said, was the biggest and richest in Kowloon and the villagers had lots of fields, but when they heard *why* they were being surveyed (in connection with ensuring a regular revenue to Government) "they weren't interested in making claims or paying Crown Rents".

45.   During the debate on the Summoning of Chinese Bill, wishing to explain why elders and people had not responded, he suggested reasons other than the presumption of non-cooperation and off-handedness on their part: " ... though many may feel inclined to appear before an official when requested to do so, they are deterred from following their own inclination either because they do not wish to seem to run counter to popular feeling or are afraid, in view of their experiences under Chinese rule, that instead of receiving any benefit they will be sufferers": *Hansard* 1899–1900, p. 117.

46.   See *Report 1900*, p. 4.

47.   Tabled in Legislative Council on 29 August 1901: see *Hansard* 1901, p. 46.

48.   I.e. from taking over the New Territory. See *Hansard* 1903, pp. 4–5.

49.   However, one aspect of the final settlement is quite perplexing. From what Gompertz has recorded, it would appear that there were earlier hearings by Members of the Land Court, including himself. As noted already with reference to Ma Wan, his second report on its work contains information on sittings in several places early in 1901, dealing with apparently ordinary claims, with a further reference to an expected "several months of regular sittings to come" to take care of disputes in the outlying districts (*Gompertz 2*, pp. 559 and 561). Why, then, was there so much work left to be done in 1904?

50.   See note 38.

51.   NTLC, pp. 150–181. It seems to have been the practice of members of the Land Court to consider each holding separately and hear each claimant personally: *Ibid.*, p. 152. See also Hayes 1993, pp. 18–19 and p. 190, notes 20–24.

52.   See *Clementi*. Some useful material on this subject is contained in Clementi's diary for the first half of 1903, but, unfortunately for present purposes, there is a gap in the diaries between July 1903 and February 1905, due to their loss when the lighter on which they were being conveyed to a P. & O. steamer was

capsized during the typhoon of 1906. The Record overlooks the work of his colleagues on the Land Court, which can be found in NTLC. See Wesley-Smith 1980, p. 97, for Clementi's consultations in Canton.

53. Each Block Crown Lease, styled an 'Indenture', is signed 'examined and found correct' by the Member Land Court responsible for its contents. In the case of (e.g.) Survey District 171, it is signed by C. McI. Messer, and countersigned by Governor Sir Mathew Nathan.

54. By good fortune, and unlike the district records, the Colonial Secretariat's land files survived the War and Occupation. They are held in HKPRO.

55. "The bill is designed to make more easy the transfer of land in the New Territory by small holders who are for the most part of the poorer class", said the Attorney General, adding that "it provides short, clear, simple forms of conveyances and other forms of documents dealing with the transfer and mortgage of landed property": *Hansard* 1905, p. 7. Henceforth, all such transactions were meant to be drawn up in this fashion, although no Chinese translations appear to have been provided. Notwithstanding their limited utility, their use was required under clause 5 of the 1910 Ordinance. See also p. 36 and n61. Leases continued to be mostly verbal: Wilson, p. 187.

56. If a deed was challenged, it would, if genuine, always be upheld by the managers of the village or sub-district — exemplifying the importance of custom and local management in safeguarding this vital area of rural life. For official support, see note 55 to chapter 1. Also Hayes 2001.1. pp. 21–22.

57. Specimen formats for these transactions were provided in printed guides to the usages of daily life, and also feature in the manuscript ones that used to be found in most, if not all, villages in Southeast China: see my article "Specialists and Written Materials in the Village World" (Hayes 1984.2). For an account of their long history, see Hansen, p. 7, who styles them "contracts". See also Cohen and others in Zelin, Ocko, and Gardella (eds.).

58. The relevance of this situation for the colonial government, and for the theme of 'the great difference', is that once again, the power of tradition in a long-settled community would unravel some of its arrangements.

59. These were printed and stamped blank forms issued by the Stamp Office of the Hong Kong Treasury, made available for sale through the district land registries or at the General Post Office. Pre-war, the Stamp Office was located in the Treasury, as shown in the *Blue Books* for the 1920s and 1930s. Revenue (as opposed to postage) stamps had to be purchased and affixed to its blank forms. Specimens may be viewed in the surviving documentary collections held by the Hong Kong Central Library and HKPRO. Their wording would remain the same as on the older formats. These papers had been in common use in Hong Kong before 1898, mainly for recording loans and agreements, presumably because their official-looking appearance appeared to afford greater security, especially if a defaulter was taken to Court. Perhaps NT people thought likewise, meeting change half-way.

60.   The evidence for this is quite categoric: see HKAR 1934, p. J 2.

61.   This was the case in New Kowloon in the early decades of the century when, in anticipation of coming development, Hong Kong entrepreneurs and their agents bought up much village land there. I purchased a large group of such documents in 1978 for the HKPRO, now held in HKMS No. 104/173–224.

62.   See the definitions of "customary land" and "customary landholder" provided in the New Territories Titles Ordinance 1902. The latter were defined as "any claimant whose claim to land has been allowed by the Land Court constituted under Ordinance No.18 of 1900, and every person to whom land is expressly granted to be held from the Crown under local customary tenure, and includes any person deriving title by transfer or transmission from such claimant or grantee from the Crown ...". With Hansard, 1902, pp. 70–71, and NTO 1910, clause 20.

63.   I have not seen any proceedings. See NTLC, para. 15, for appeals against decisions of members of the Land Court from 1901 to 1905: there were no more than eleven in all. Clementi's experience (p. 36) was therefore typical.

64.   See Hansard 1905, p. 11. Provision was also made for appeals to the Supreme Court, provoking the very pertinent question from Hon. Mr. Gershom Stewart, "How is an English judge to know Chinese law", but quickly brushed aside by the Attorney General: *Hansard* 1905, p. 12.

65.   Though required to be registered, managers were not an invention of the Hong Kong authorities: see e.g. minute of 11 June 1904 in CS0 1903/8551. For a guide to Chinese custom in land-related matters, as understood in the District Administration New Territories in the 1950s, see Wilson, Appendix A, 1–4. See also Jamieson's chapter II, The Law of Succession and Inheritance, pp. 13–31, and pp. 102–103.

66.   See chapter 12, p. 169 with notes 59–60 on p. 251.

67.   See e.g. Hayes 1996, p. 53, for the position at Shek Pik, where for two generations few had bothered to update ownership and managership. This laggard interest was, I believe, fairly common, and it shows that custom was alive and well in the countryside. Registration, besides involving travel and fees, was considered unnecessary. See also Hase 2001, p. 138.

68.   During my service from the late 1950s on, notices would have been posted in the villages and RC offices from which applications came, to ascertain (within a time limit) if there were objections, this being the practice with *all* applications involving land: see Handover Notes 1957 in HKMS 178.1. Thereby, such applications were subject to a general public scrutiny, and not simply by headmen and lineage and branch elders: also, one or other of them would have to come to the District Office with the applicants to endorse an application and witness the Memorial.

       Save where he raised a query, the DO's part in the processing of applications for succession and the like was largely routine, and it may generally be assumed that local custom was being followed. In disputed cases, the DO would usually seek advice from senior district leaders before making his own decision. There was, moreover, the well-founded belief, voiced by Austin Coates in his *Summary*

Memorandum (1955) that, as with disputes in general, they were best handled in the villages and sub-districts (rural committee areas) and not, by default, in the District Offices (see p. 205, note 20).

69. It was probably for this reason that many persons kept the slips ("Chi Tsai") issued for each lot claimed during the survey and demarcation, of which many survived until comparatively recently: see p. 33 with note 29.

70. *Orme*, para. 16, and HKAR 1910, I, p. 10. Unlike the six formats, these were bilingual documents, as indeed were most of the other permits and licences from the time that I have seen. A small collection of these, mostly Xerox copies, has been placed in the HKPRO. Clementi and Wood were engaged on this burdensome task in 1906. Responding to criticisms over expenditure, Clementi reminded his superiors tartly of the facts. "I do not think you realize that that at the present time my office is about the largest (if not the very largest) purely clerical office in the Government. I have 49 clerks whose business it is to write as fast and as much as they can during office hours daily. The consumption of pens, ink, blotting papers, etc. is therefore necessarily very considerable." His long minute to the Colonial Secretary of 6 July 1906 in CSO 807/06 gave a graphic description of his tireless work, and the appalling conditions in his temporary office (a matshed), beset by rats, white ants, rain and damp, all playing havoc with the land records. A similar exercise was carried out in the Southern District in 1908: see CSO 1908/5246 with its many pages of minuting on the subject. See also note 67 to chapter 2.

71. The plots for sale were identified by their local place names — there were many such within each village area — or by describing the boundaries in the several (often four) directions, more usually done with larger plots, as for a "pine hill" on upland slopes.

72. Though not at the start: see HKAR 1912, I, p. 11. See also note 67.

73. See the statement in *Orme*, para. 16.

74. Clementi, in particular, fulminated against errors due to this cause: "... specimens of almost every error of which the intellectual turbidity of the rural Chinese rustic is capable have found their way into the Crown Lease schedules ...": CSO 5646 of 1908, minute of 4 May 1909. See also in his caustic remarks when commenting on minutes from the Crown Solicitor and Land Officer regarding a time limit for reporting errors and omissions, in CSO 9812 of 1904.

75. In one case of the kind from the Tsuen Wan District that came to light in the 1970s owing to an internal dispute, nothing had been done to rectify an error already known at the time of the land settlement by taking their own documents to the District Land Office and obtaining consent to a Memorial rectifying the situation. See the Kau Wah Keng papers in HKPRO. See also Nelson, pp. 13–14. We have therefore to be careful about constructing lineage organization solely on the basis of what was entered in the registers.

76. In 1978, I wrote to my headquarters as follows: "I have now much experience in village removals and in unravelling difficult land situations where the various records in our [Land] Registry are missing, inadequate, confusing, or even

contradictory. No one village is like another, and the only way through the complications of the documentary, ground, and human factors involved is by trusting the senior officers in the District to act in a responsible way ... Therefore the approved policy should be regarded as providing guidelines; a framework, not an 'iron clad'." From my (78) in [TW] 12/20C II of 29 June 1978 to SNT, now in HKPRO.

77. Allen Chun, *Unstructuring Chinese Society, the Fictions of Colonial Practice and the Changing Realities of "Land" in the New Territories of Hong Kong*, published in 2000.

78. Notably in regard to building houses on leased agricultural land without let or hindrance, and without payment of premium; and in regard to other rights deemed to be adversely affected by planning and development. Clementi had conceded the first as early as 1906: The villagers "certainly consider themselves entitled — and I think that they are entitled — to build houses on their own padi land ...". Minute of 11 January 1906 to Hon. Col. Sec. In CSO 1906/807. See also Wesley-Smith 1980, pp. 101–103; and n41 on p. 231.

79. Chun, p. 45, note 15, with e.g. pp. 9, 24–25, 39–40.

80. Nelson, p. 33. One of Freedman's postgraduate students, Nelson observed custom closely in regard to holding and occupying land, and provided interesting information on theory and practice in changing times, especially after the transfer of the District Officers' legal powers to the Judiciary in 1961: ADR DCNT 1961–62, para.57/Supp.1 to HKGG 14 April 1961. Unfortunately, he was unable to ground his findings more widely by further research, in any case rendered more difficult by the loss or destruction of records during the Japanese Occupation and since: such as the "major burning" in the Yuen Long District Office (his p. 22 with n70), and repeated in other Districts in that time of rapid expansion and removals to new offices.

81. By means of "Letters of Exchange", the ensuing market in such documents, and the government's differentiated monetary weighting of them by age, location, etc., for use in granting land exchanges to those companies and individuals amassing portfolios of exchange entitlements. These new policies, for the various reasons discussed in chapter 8 of this book, had become a political necessity if large scale urbanization and modernization programmes were to be implemented, to take account of population growth from the 1960s on.

82. Here (his p. 39), Chun takes further the earlier views expressed by Howard Nelson in 1969 (p. 33) and by Peter Wesley-Smith in 1982, pp. 12–13.

83. Take mediation, still quite widely practised in the Hong Kong of the 1950s to the 1970s (see Hayes 1984.3). In the New Territories, this meant the rural committees: see ADR DCNT 1954–55, para. 44, for their arbitration in "local clan and family disputes"; para. 72 also. Even in Tsuen Wan (as observed in 1975–1982), there was no doubt of the capacity and willingness of senior leaders to mediate, nor of the existence of the community views which provided the necessary support for their decisions.

84. See the cases reported in the annexes to Hayes 1988 and 1989, and relevant text.

85. An account of the specific and overall situations as I saw them around 1990 is provided in Sections Eleven and Twelve in Hayes 1991, pp. 124–132.

86. In which process, the reprovisioning of ancestral halls was a *sine qua non*, many of them still tied to land-owning customary trusts dating from before 1898.

87. See also chapter 12, p. 169 with pp. 173–174.

88. I am excluding here the many cases taken to the law courts, in which the large financial considerations involved made the parties concerned unwilling to reach agreement within the framework of customary law and practice — sometimes itself in dispute, in vastly changed times.

89. The reasons are given in ADR DCNT, 1964–65, para. 55, among them to find "the best means of legally rectifying the many discrepancies discovered in the records". A professional commentary on the shortcomings of the original survey, and of later additions to the records through the sale of "New Grant Lots" by the District Administration, was provided in Seach, 1962.

90. See HK 1963, p. 25. For examples of the air photography and survey plans produced from it, see the spread in ADR DPW 1965–1966.

91. At a seminar organized in 1986 by the Hong Kong Institute of Land Surveyors and the Hong Kong Institute of Surveyors, the accumulated difficulties were frankly recognized. The Secretary for Housing read a paper on "Land Administration and the Boundary Problems"; while a senior government Land Surveyor spoke on "the ill-effects of these [NT] records, the background to the system, and the crucial areas needing improvement". The Proceedings were published. The problems and deliberations, and doubtless further remedial action, have continued beyond 1997. In 2004, Dr. Patrick Hase provided a paper, "The Origins of the New Territories Land Registration System" as yet unpublished, for another seminar in the series.

92. *Survey*, pp. 401–402.

Chapter 4 "Give and Take" in the New Territory up to 1941

1. District Office, New Territories, was the term in use up to the early postwar years. However, since there were two District Officers from early on, who reported separately in the annually published Hong Kong Administrative Reports (HKAR), it seems better to use this umbrella term, in use until about 1960, when it was replaced by the term "New Territories Administration" (NTA). The title of the officials and their offices was "Lee Man Fu" in Chinese, in use from the very start: see Hayes 1988, p. 230. Its background and implications (as being "father and mother officials") are explained in Hayes 1996, pp. xiii, and 195–196. See also pp. 127–128 herein.

2. For the less satisfactory arrangements up to this time, see HKAR 1909, p. J 1.

3. See *Orme*, paras. 10–14.

4. For the two ordinances, see HKGG under GN 425 in the issue of 7 July 1905, and GN 338 in that for 28 October 1910. See *Hansard* for the debates during passage of the bills, at the meetings held on 1 and 22 June 1905, and on 13, 20, and 27 October 1910. The debates on the first bill were unusually acerbic.

5. *Hansard* 1910, p. 116.

6. See chapter 1, p. 8, with pp. 25–26.

7. Welsh, p. 330. For an exceedingly good account of the Irish scene during Blake's service in Ireland, see Trench 1869.

8. All at *Hansard* 1903, p. 52. For the last sentence, see also Wesley-Smith 1998, pp. 112–114.

9. See chapter 2, p. 26.

10. For the appointees, see GNs 387 and 394 in HKGG of 8 and 15 July 1899, respectively. The lists are very comprehensive. Local knowledge and enquiries lead me to believe that these men were indeed the recognized leaders of the day in the villages and sub-districts.

11. "This Ordinance is useless and was never actually put in force. The districts and sub-districts and local tribunals have never had any real existence": Memorandum to the 1910 Bill, in HKGG, 1910, p.593. See also the Attorney General's remarks at p. 115 of *Hansard* 1910. *Orme*, para. 15, said it was due to "the waning influence of the elders throughout the Territories ... their authority of no account with the stronger authority of the [British] magistrates so easily accessible". Nelson's view (his p. 26) was that the committees and tribunals were a "total failure ... an alien creation, a structure imposed from outside". But, despite Blake's conciliatory approach, might the Hong Kong authorities' decision not to proceed also be ascribable to the fact of the elders of major lineages' participation in the 1899 uprising? And the leaders across the territory were in any case continuing to provide local management, which had always included dispute settlement. This whole topic warrants detailed archival research.

12. See Peplow, pp. 146–150. The gift was made for preserving the *fung-shui* of the grave (which dates from the year 1100) when part of its purlieus was taken for construction of the road from Sham Shui Po to Castle Peak. The District Officer also received a scroll: see Schofield 1977, p. 156.

13. HKAR 1926, J3. They were "appointed by H.E. the Governor to assist the District Officer with advice on matters of local interest or dispute": The death of two of the older Advisers was recorded in ADR DONT 1946–47, at para. 46.

14. See HKAR 1935, p. J 4. This followed after a similarly appreciative statement in the 1934 Report (para.17). A few years later, when 50,000 refugees had entered the New Territories, the Heung Yee Kuk's leaders had been described by D.O. North as being "very steady, and their common sense remarkable": in HKAR 1938, p. J 5.

15. As noted in Hayes 1977.1, pp. 83–84.

16. Schofield wrote, "I was never given any list of them, nor, so far as I know, was any formal election held … Anyway, I'm afraid we never went closely into details of how or why so-and-so acquired the status of village elder; we just accepted the natural leaders we found": *Schofield Letters*, 27 July 1962. Substantiated in D.O. North's annual report for 1934: "There are no heads of villages appointed by and responsible to Government for the conduct of village affairs": HKAR 1934, p. M 106.

17. Peplow, pp. 87–89.

18. "He calls his sedan chair — it is not the proper thing for a magistrate to walk on foot — to go out and see what is the matter": Cockburn, p. 105.

19. At Kiaochow (Tsingtao), the German administrators for the Chinese community claimed that they sought the advice and cooperation of the "most distinguished members of the local population". Schrecker 1971, pp. 62–63.

20. Austin Coates wrote in 1955 that they included carrying out small local public works with materials supplied by the district offices, the provision of certain sports facilities, organizing the annual theatre shows, maintaining simple cemeteries and mass [charitable] graves, running markets and renting out hawker sites, assisting education, organizing fund-raising. The settlement of disputes, in family cases, between neighbours, tenancy problems, inheritance and property cases, disputes between clans or villages, over grass-cutting and breaming rights, etc., was another important part of their work. This was carried out with thoroughness and fairness, Coates stated, even in the worse committees: "A hard case should in the ordinary way only come to the [District] Office when the committee has failed to solve it". From *Summary Memorandum*, pp. 42–45. A copy is now in the HKPRO. See also the descriptions of what the Cheung Chau Kaifong and the Tsuen Wan Rural Committee were still doing in the early 1950s, at note 17 in chapter 6, and pp. 117–118 of chapter 9, respectively.

     The executive duties of village heads mirrored the above, and could be similarly arduous, especially in large and multi-lineage villages. See Hayes 1977.1, pp. 119–122, for a review of what they had comprised under Chinese rule, continuing (defence apart, now largely provided for) into the colonial period. By report, they included a good deal of petty dispute settlement, especially where lineage elders were unable to compose differences.

21. *Hansard* 1901, p. 2, and *Abstract*, p. 63.

22. SP 1904, para. 25, p. 171. Information on compensation practices for land and houses in Qing times (if any) is hard to find, and contemporary statements point to its total absence in the Warlord and Republican periods.

23. See chapter 7.

24. Roads built before 1941 fell far short of what the Director of Public Works (one of Lockhart's inspection party) had proposed in Appendix No. 4 to LR. Among the suggested routes, some were built for military purposes early postwar, Tai Mo Shan and Lam Tsuen in 1950: then the Sai Kung Road in 1960 (a Japanese wartime military road, further improved) with extensions to Tai Mong Tsai and North Sai Kung in the following decade.

25.   See the entries in *Abstract* from 1900 to 1930.

26.   HKAR 1936, p. J3, para. 13 with Table IX (882 lots resumed).

27.   HK 1947, p. 56.

28.   MacIntosh, p. 2. For a later account of the frontier see Griffiths, pp. 92–93.

29.   The police districts, on land and sea, were used as census districts: see the Census Reports in SP 1907, 1911, and 1921.

30.   It was, as Stewart Lockhart had remarked, within the extensive plain in which the largest market town in the region was located, i.e. Sham Chun. See chapter 1, p. 15. For traffic on the principal roads of the New Territory in 1905, see Hayes 1977.1, p. 209, n73.

31.   *Abstract*, entries under 1900–1902 and 1911. An early statement of police in the Districts, including patrolling launches, is given in the Report for the Northern District in HKAR 1909.

32.   Eric Hamilton wrote, "I want to stress the great need for smooth cooperation of Police and DO/S [South] which was so essential to the prosperous running of the Southern District in those days — no doubt, Northern District too". *Hamilton Letters*, 1 August 1958. This, indeed, would be the case for as long as the old system lasted.

33.   HKAR 1920, p. J 3.

34.   A considerable increase in serious crime in the Northern District was "... largely due to the unsettled conditions prevailing over the border, where the Sun and Chan armies indulged in a continual war for the control of the Po On district". HKAR 1924, p. J 2. [The District had been renamed Po On shortly after the Revolution]. See also "Calendar of Disturbances in the Border Area, 1899–1940" at Appendix 1 to Hase 1993.

35.   Andrew, pp. 19 and 25.

36.   In HKAR 1912, annual report, pp. 28–29. The gang's other activities were noted, and its base stated to be an island near Macau.

37.   HKAR 1925, p. K 16. The police station was not in the town.

38.   HKAR 1935, annual report, at pp. 43–44.

39.   Revenue from the production of liquor is not included n the statement of annual revenue derived from the San On district provided for Lockhart by its magistrate, and included as Appendix No. 6 to LR.

40.   High levels of production were seemingly quite common. See Welsby, pp. 3–7, 21–23, 29–30 and 47. See also HKAR 1914, pp. I 8–9, and Hayes 1996, pp. 139–140.

41.   The detailed analysis of the Census Reports of 1911 and 1921 given in Hase 1996, provides us with much valuable information on conditions in the early decades. This is complemented by the oral history reports from the Sai Kung and Tsuen Wan Districts in Faure 1982 and 1984.

42.   For some of these, see Hayes 1993, pp. 28–29.

43.   His grandson, Mr. Shen Qingju, kindly allowed me to inspect the premises and gave me written accounts of his grandfather's career. Another major Southern warlord, General Long Xiguang (1860–1921), a native of distant

Yunnan province, is reported to have built "his tall terrace in front of [Wong Nei Chung Village on Hong Kong Island] overlooking the racecourse". *Schofield Letters*, 8 June 1967. Biographies of these two men are given in Boorman, Vols. 2 and 3, pp. 455b–457b and 101b–103b respectively.

44. See Hayes 1977.1, pp. 36–38.
45. See variously HKAR 1916 and 1917, pp. J 5 and J 2 respectively.
46. HKAR 1918, J 2 and 1920, p. J 2. But "contrary to expectation", demand fluctuated: HKAR 1921, p. J 2.
47. HKAR 1926, p. J 3. This shows that the old regular schedule of spaced market days was still being followed there.
48. HKAR 1931, p. J 2.
49. See note 60.
50. HKAR 1937, p. J 7.
51. HKAR 1918, p. J 2. See Young pp. 20–29 for the Hop Yick Company.
52. HKAR 1931 p. J 2.
53. HKAR 1934, P. J 2.
54. Note 60.
55. Seen, but not yet located.
56. HKAR 1936, p. J 5.
57. See Hayes 1993, pp. 24–25.
58. *Rating*, Minute to Hon. CS, dated 27 February 1934.
59. *Rating*, D.O.S. minute to Hon. CS dated 16 April 1934. "The Government travelling dispensary will stop at Tsuen Wan by the road side, if requested when passing, but it is not a regular place of call".
60. *Rating*, report of 12 May 1934, with an undated comparison of houses and metering at Taipo [*sic*] Market, Un Long Market (New Market) and Tsuen Wan. There were 120 houses in the first class at Taipo, 67 at Un Long New Market, and only 22 at Tsuen Wan.
61. *Rating*, minute of 15 October 1937.
62. As claimed in the petitioners' written representations to Government dated March 1937.
63. "If the payment of rates is enforced, surely petitioners will have to live in caves and the remote wilds in order to remain alive ... It will mean the scooping out of the inhabitants' flesh to cure the sores of the Government": petition in March 1937. In another, dated 5 August 1938, after the authorities had issued demand notes, it was stated that "Some of them were unable to pay, and so the European Policeman acting upon orders from his superior, had their household articles and cattle taken away. ... The scene was indeed such that immediately on the arrival of the Policeman, who might be compared to [a] wolf, [even] chickens and dogs would feel uneasy". From the English translations in the folder, as no Chinese texts are available.
64. Among expressions of official vexation in the folder are the SCA's descriptions of them to the CS as "a difficult lot of people [who] have made no effort to meet Govt. half-way"; and again, as having "always been a stiff-necked

generation": *Rating*, minutes dated 21.6.37 and 11.8.38. A senior Secretariat officer took exception to the later petitioners' comparison of the police to the wolf, calling it "reprehensible" and "typical of Tsun Wan insolence", and that it "should not be tolerated": minute of 15.8.38. The District Officer had advised that "the Tsun Wan [*sic*] people, though very sensible, are not easy to deal with": minute of 5.2.37.

65.   HKAR 1933, p. J 3 with 1931 and 1932, also J 3.

66.   HKAR 1937, p. J 6.

67.   HKAR 1935, p. J 3, para. 14. The streets at Yuen Long were named during the year, and name plates fixed in connection with the assessment and rating scheme: *Ibid.*, para. 15.

68.   HKAR 1934, p. J 21, para.20. In 1957, the then DCNT had perplexed me, a new incumbent, by asking me why the Clear Water Bay part of the Southern District was "teeming with children, none of whom had ever been born".

69.   Sweeting 1990, pp. 351, 356–357. Also *Abstract*, p. 19.

70.   HKAR 1913, p. I 11.

71.   Hayes 1993, pp. 27, 31. However, the government had made some attempt to improve the situation. Teaching standards and curricula were scrutinized in what were considered to be the better schools through a subsidy scheme that operated from 1913, while a degree of supervision over all was sought, and perhaps maintained, through the application of the 1913 Education Ordinance to the New Territories in 1921, under which schools with 9 or more pupils were required to register with government. From my enquiries, some attempt was being made to bring in newer text books and broaden the curriculum in even the smaller village schools.

72.   Changes in rural education over the period are indicated in Ng Lun Ngai-ha 1982, with Baker 1968, pp. 72, 74. At Ping Shan an elegant red and gold name board dated in 1931 still hangs in the Tangs' main ancestral hall, commemorating the new-look Tat Tak Primary School.

73.   HKAR 1919, p. J 4.

74.   *Guide to Hong Kong 1938* (in Chinese), pp. 118–119. It was not until 1953 that the Kowloon Motor Bus Co. began to run later buses on most of its NT routes: ADR DCNT 1953–54, para. 49.

75.   Cargo junks of the type still known as *kai to* or "local ferry" had long plied between NT ports, Hong Kong, and places in the Canton Delta: see e.g. the list of ports in the papers at GN 170 in HKGG, 17 November 1866. They were sometimes operated in the public interest, and paid for from public funds.

76.   It seems that this was likely: see HKAR 1934, p. J 21. For destinations, schedules and fares, see *Guide to Hong Kong* (in Chinese), pp. 128–130. Also HKAR 1938, annual report p. 45.

77.   Hong Kong Guide 1893, pp. 114–117 for Tai Mo Shan and Tsuen Wan.

78.   DO South reported 189 permits for bathing sheds, as of 1935, adding "Practically no good sites are now left unoccupied along the Castle Peak Road": HKAR 1935, p. J 2, para. 16.

79. These drew down the ire of Hon. Mr. Osborne who asked the government to "take steps to prevent the destruction of birds by sham sportsmen, who by means of the railway are enabled to invade the New Territory and threaten extinction to every form of bird life, game and otherwise". *Hansard* 1910, p. 134.

80. In Waters, pp. 19–20. He drew heavily upon an [unpublished?] "Short History of the Golf Club" [*sic*] which Eric Hamilton had written around 1933: see *Hamilton Letters*, 1 August 1958.

81. Heywood, p. 15.

82. See Bibliography.

83. This was indeed a novelty, since Confucian teaching had no place for physical exercise for the scholar class: see, e.g. Ross, pp. 337–340. The club is referred to by Mr. Chan Chik in his preface to Wong Wai King's book on Tai O.

84. In this context, money loan associations, in which disputes were "distressingly frequent": HKAR 1919, p. J 1.

85. Letter dated 15 November 1979. Mrs. Baretto was personal secretary to DO Tai Po when I first served in the District Administration.

86. As usual, S. H. Peplow has something useful to contribute on the subject. "They [these posts] are given to them for two reasons. The first being to enable them to get a good idea of the habits and customs of the people, and the other, to get a thorough knowledge of the Territory in general". Peplow, p. 87.

87. *Hamilton Letters*, 1 August 1958.

88. 1921 Census Report, para. 2.

89. *Ibid*, Section I, paras. 2–3. The figures quoted here include the NT.

90. Endacott, p. 289.

91. "The population of the Northern District is almost entirely agricultural and is more stable than any other section of the community. There is practically no immigration and the net increase is, therefore, the net increase less the loss by emigration". SP 1931, in Census report, p. 105.

Chapter 5   New Territories People and the Japanese Occupation 1941–1945

1. Japan's massive encroachments on China during the 1930s are conveniently and succinctly described in Gathorne-Hardy, chapter XIX.

2. A census by air-raid wardens on 14–15 March 1941 gave a total of 1,444,337 persons, to which was added 200,000 for the New Territories, making about 1,650,000 in all. Endacott and Birch, p.11. For the influx, its several stages, and the extent of urban overcrowding, see HKAR 1938, pp. 5–6, 14–16.

3. Russell, p. 52. See also Chang's *The Rape of Nanking*.

4. *Chinese Year Book 1940–1941*, pp. 403–404. The whole section IV between pp. 401–405 deals with the sinkings of fishing and local trading junks, mostly in the vicinity of Hong Kong. At this time, Japan was not at war with Great Britain.

5.   See Hayes 1993, pp. 34–35. The Occupation pushed some NT villages that were already few in numbers towards extinction as communities. The two hamlets of Tai Wong Wu and Fung Shue Wo, on Tsing Yi island, lost their identities at this time when, as survivors recounted later, "through persecution and hunger, their inhabitants scattered and went to live elsewhere".

6.   Local information, corroborated by papers seen in the former District Office South, indicates that Lantau people had suffered periodic banditry in the few years before the Japanese Occupation. The headman of Shek Pik had fled the village when one such band, said to be in league with a bad character in Tai O, was robbing and kidnapping people for ransom. A senior police officer (Mr. N. B. Fraser) had recalled (1949) having investigated a homicide case in 1941 in which the villagers of Fan Pui (in the Shek Pik valley) had killed the leader of an armed band that had been terrorizing the area for some time.

7.   See Faure 1982, pp. 186–188. For Cheung Chau see Felix Cheng's *History*, pp. 167–168. Both these accounts were taken from the personal memories of persons, including local leaders, who lived through the Occupation.

8.   In the opening months, according to the historical record kept by two members of the Tang lineage at Kam Tin, Japanese troops occupied some of the larger buildings there, including the ancestral halls and the various colleges, demanded poultry and cattle for slaughter, looted every useful article, and forced villagers to do their carrying and other manual work. See also Lee and Distefano, p. 75.

9.   Heasman: the mixture of tenses reflects the fact that it was first circulated privately in July 1945, before the War and Occupation had ended.

10.   *Ibid.*, p. 66. The "self governing offices" were styled *kui yik so* in Cantonese, as shown on the seals used to authenticate official papers.

11.   See the documentation cited in Hayes 1993, pp. 38–39. The Hong Kong Museum of History has a collection.

12.   The information from Tsuen Wan was collected twenty-five years ago, and would be difficult to replicate today. Strictly speaking, the Tsuen Wan Bureau came under the Kowloon Main Bureau, and not the NT Main Bureau at Taipo (probably because of its proximity to, and ease of communication with, Kowloon), but Tsuen Wan was otherwise, in all respects, an NT community.

13.   "Applied for police purposes, it is well suited to repression and terror": Linebarger, p. 107, adding that the Japanese used it in occupied China "as a device for despotism and exploitation". In Japan itself, the civil government had long exerted strong surveillance over its own population: "a system of espionage", as Dr. Philipp Franz von Siebold had described it: 1973 reprint, pp. 153–154, and was separately reported as having required an "absolute and almost abject submission" from the common people: Brinkley, Vol. IV, p. 99. See also the first chapter of Lamont-Brown's book on the Kempeitai.

14.   In Formosa, we are told, "the policeman's box at the village corner and the police office at district headquarters were looked on as 'tiger's dens' into which no Formosan entered willingly". Kerr, p. 60.

15.   Endacott and Birch, p. 119.

16. Japanese troops were reportedly stationed at Chuen Lung, on the slopes of Tai Mo Shan for about a year, probably in connection with supervising construction of the road up from Tsuen Wan. On a visit made in 1978, I was told by the VR and a 70-year-old man, that Japanese troops requisitioned the 18 to 20 houses in a detached part of the village for accommodation, and grazed their horses on fields beside the stream. The occupants did not wish to return, and the houses became ruins.

17. See Faure 1982, pp. 190, 192 and 195.

18. HK 1946, p. 59, mentions the repatriation of 2,343 persons from Hainan Island by hospital ship (two trips) in May 1946, but these men were reported to have been "cajoled or conscripted" to work in the Hainan iron mines, and to have been stranded at the end of the war in various labour camps, in urgent need of food, clothing and medical attention.

19. Russell, pp. 274–281. See also Lamont-Brown.

20. Locally recruited Indians and Chinese assisted the gendarmerie: Endacott and Birch, pp. 122, 134–136. In Tsuen Wan, such men were viewed as being collaborators; unlike members of the self-governing offices, who were obliged to carry out their duties because of their position in, and responsibilities for, their own communities. Faure 1982, p. 190, reports the same from Sai Kung.

21. In one village in Northwest Kowloon, I was told that men and women had disappeared while fuel-gathering, and how word had got back that they had been caught by Japanese police or soldiers.

22. The Cheung Chau people were left more to their own devices, to the extent noted by Felix Cheng, pp. 169–170, 178. However, "the death penalty was applied to all sorts of crime which was, of course, an effectual deterrent to all would-be offenders" (p.173), with public executions of offenders (p. 170). See also Hayes 1993, p. 41.

23. Japanese police were stationed in the village (a barrack had to be constructed for them from salvaged materials from the old village, by then long abandoned) and the new headman, elected to this unenviable post some months later, told me that he had been required to walk over the hills to Tai O early each morning, usually with a junior officer and two policemen, to report to the Japanese captain there.

24. It is next to impossible to know how many native villagers joined guerrilla groups, Communist or otherwise. Faure 1982, pp. 199–202, provides useful information from Sai Kung District. For Lantau, Wong Wai King, p. 92, making enquiries in her native Tai O, stated that some twenty people from the island joined the guerrillas, seven of them from Tai O. However, indications would suggest that, on Lantau alone, there could have been many more, including others who had left their villages earlier. There and elsewhere in the NT, numbers probably rose towards the end, when it was clear the Japanese would lose the war.

25. *The Chinese Year Book 1940–1941* mentions the activities of Chinese guerrillas in Kwangtung (Guangdong) in the earlier part of the Sino-Japanese War at e.g. pp. 184–185. See generally p. 812.

26. The *China Handbook 1937–1945* includes 13,977 guerrilla engagements in its "Table of Campaigns Fought" at p. 301.

27. Liu Shuyong, pp. 111–113. Liu (p. 112) mentions an "annihilating battle" at Tai O, in which 30 Japanese officers and men were allegedly captured by guerrilla forces, but my enquiries in the 1960s did not extend to Tai O.

28. The East River Column appears to have won the sympathy and support of the local villages. Elderly New Kowloon people told me in the 1970s that its local base was at Hang Hau, on the Clear Water Bay peninsula, which personnel used to visit once or twice a week, to check on village security, get foodstuffs, and obtain information on Japanese movements.

29. The trials were reported in the SCMP, between 27 March and 26 April 1946. See also Hayes 1967, which recorded events in the old Southern District of the NT and in New Kowloon.

30. In the proceedings reported on 3 April 1946, it was described [by a Japanese?] as being "for the relief of villagers who became sick". However, its various names and membership, together with a mention that the villagers, for payment in cash and kind, were ordered to carry materials for construction of defence works at Mui Wo, leave little doubt of its real nature and purpose.

31. One of the witnesses (SCMP 3 April 1946) described an earlier execution which had taken place two years previously, in the fourth lunar month (May–June 1944).

32. All villagers of Leung Uk, Tai O, were twice paraded en masse by Japanese troops, but were lucky to escape death: see Wong Wai King, p. 92. For a similar parade on Tsing Yi, see Hayes 1993, p. 42.

33. More instances provided in Hayes 1967.

34. From an early postwar District Office ms report on Mui Wo by a former D.O. South (Paul C. K. Tsui) now kept with his other reports in HKPRO. At Pui O, the stone blocks were not cut specially, but obtained by borrowing from fellow-villagers. They were marked by their owners, and reclaimed in 1958 when the fort was demolished to make way for a petrol station. The credit for these initiatives has been given to the late Mr. Yuen Wah-chiu of Mui Wo: see chapter 4, p. 50. Where Yuen was during the Japanese atrocities at Mui Wo in August 1945 remains a mystery.

35. Barrow. There were two versions, one more detailed, both seemingly compiled, by him.

36. Gwen Priestwood, see e.g. pp. 108, 118.

37. Barrow's lists included one harrowing tale from Kau Sai in Port Shelter, Sai Kung: "The escaping party signed five chits of appreciation and gave them to the five persons [who had fed and helped them]. One of the chits was discovered by a Jap searching party about a year later and the holder ... was arrested and executed by the Japs." Imprisonments and executions of helpers are also mentioned in the lists.

38. For the presentation of the banner by the Commander in Chief, Far East Land Forces in April 1947, see ADR DONT, 1947–48, para.43: also para. 44, in regard to rewards to villages "for good work during the war".

39. In 1966, twenty-one years on, I requested the Director of Social Welfare, who administered the Fund, to send details of payments still being made to persons living in the New Territories. Of the thirty cases listed, twelve were from villages in the Sai Kung sub-district, and three from Lantau. The remaining 15 came from other areas, including at least one from Tsing Yi Island. See Hayes 1993, p. 42.

40. Snow provides wide-ranging coverage of Japanese measures and behaviour during the period of their rule, especially in chapter 4, "The Japanese Miss Their Chance", between pp. 149–205. Besides additional evidence for atrocities, such as shooting villagers out of hand when suspected of subversion (p. 163) and the savage treatment of female grass-cutters (p. 167), Snow describes the action taken in regard to reviving industries, encouraging fisheries, maintaining food rationing, and actively promoting public health., albeit such measures were intended, in part, to safeguard their own garrison.

    The Administration's periodic economic journal, the *Azhou Shangbu*, contains items on the sea fisheries of Cheung Chau and Tai O, and on rural businesses in the market towns of Yuen Long and Tai Po: as contained in numbers 54, 61, 73 and 39, 47 and 77 respectively. There is an incomplete set in the Hong Kong University Main Library, Hong Kong Collection. On Cheung Chau, the Japanese established a fish wholesale market and a fishermen's society which offered loans and other facilities, whereby the fishing industry is said to have prospered greatly: see Felix Cheng, pp. 174–175. It is also worth noting that, in mid-1942, the Japanese authorities provided a free train service to Taipo for those persons willing to return to China and made free rice available under this arrangement. I owe this information to Tim Ko. Wong Wai King, p. 92, indicates that rice rationing and supply had been organized for Tai O people during the Occupation.

41. Endacott and Birch, pp. 142–144.

42. "On the whole, New Territories people had suffered less during the Occupation than the urban population. There were however … places where August 1945 found the inhabitants in a pitiable condition". ADR DONT 1946–47, para. 1.

43. Yet one must beware of generalizations, too. From what I have been told, it would appear that not all NT people suffered extreme want and hardship by the end of the Occupation, nor were all villages harassed.

44. See ADR DCNT 1948–49, para. 38 and 1949–50, para. 31.

45. See Hayes 1986, pp. 581–582 with notes 29–33 for a description of cases from the Sai Kung district.

46. After the War, the Hong Kong government compensated the many village and other landowners in New Kowloon who had lost land and houses when the Japanese extended the airfield. See the Airfield (Kai Tak) Extension and Reversion Ordinance, No. 33 of 1948, and Hayes 2000.

47. Donnison, pp. 197–213. The Chief Civil Affairs Officer under the military government, a senior Hong Kong civil servant, had arrived in early September,

with nine of his assistants, but of course there would be no functioning district administration for some time.

48.   Letter to DONT dated 26 April 1946, reporting the election of office bearers for the second term of the Cheung Chau Residents' Association (in effect, the successors to the prewar Kaifong), with an information paper enclosed, on which this paragraph is based: Salkeld papers 1996. Also Faure 1982, p. 202, for Sai Kung.

49.   Some materials on the War and Occupation (in English translation) are provided in the relevant chapter in (ed.) Faure 1997. Even at that late date, he could write (p. 209) that the events of the Japanese Occupation were "still a largely unwritten chapter of Hong Kong history. At present, the documents appear as snippets". Yet his account of the Sai Kung District, published in 1982, provides much first-hand information on the period (pp. 184–202). In contrast, the Northern NT, especially the market towns of Tai Po and Yuen Long, is poorly covered in English, or it seems even in Chinese, but intelligence reports by members of the British Army Aid Group may assist. There are a number among the Ride Papers at the National Library of Australia, Canberra: Intelligence Summaries, Series 12 in AWM PR82/068. I owe this reference to Sir Lindsay's daughter, Ms. Elizabeth Ride. These should include the reports from Captain D. R. Holmes's two-month long reconnaissance of the NT in late 1942 mentioned in Endacott and Birch, p. 224. I am unable to access Japanese language materials — another task for those researchers with the necessary skills. For a useful comparative account of another Chinese-populated territory under wartime Japanese military occupation, see Paul H. Kratoska, *The Japanese Occupation of Malaya 1941–45* (London, C. Hurst & Co., 1998).

50.   Snow, p. 236, states that the BAAG broke off its ties with the East River Column in August 1943, and mentions Holmes's report of July 1944, in which he "expressed his opinion that their prime aim was, and always had been, to expand their military and political presence in the Hong Kong region".

51.   HK 1946, p. 2.

52.   The remainder subsisted on local rice and substitute foods: HK 1948, p. 80. For background information, see *Hansard* 1946, pp.48–51. Also HK 1946, p. 53, and *ibid*, p. 26 for price controls. By 1948, flour rationing had been discontinued: see HK 1948, p. 80. The later period is not so well documented.

Chapter 6   An End to Subsistence Farming

1.   For the general progress of Hong Kong, together with related events in the NT, see the opening paragraphs of chapter 12.

2.   A brief, but inspiring, account of the period of military administration is given in HK 1946, and specifically at pp. 1–2: "The keynote of the Military Administration was hasty improvisation, desperate overwork, a sense of close community of interest between the people, the civil officials and the Fighting Services and progress which, though appreciable in retrospect, was barely perceptible at the time."

3.   His title was "District Officer New Territories", and his department the "District Office New Territories". See HK 1946, p. 104.

4.   See Steve Tsang, pp. 125, 130–132 for the debate from 1942 on, in regard to the retention of Hong Kong after war's end, involving the Colonial Office, the Foreign Office, the American and Chinese governments, and Mr. Churchill's famous "over my dead body" pronouncement.

5.   Chapter XI of the Charter of the UN, the "Declaration Regarding Non-Self-Governing Territories", together with chapter XII the "International Trustee System" and chapter XIII, "The Trusteeship Council", set standards for the Member Nations' administrators of colonial and trust territories. Head "A" of the Declaration reads: "to ensure, with due respect for the culture of the peoples concerned, their political, economic, social, and educational advancement, their just treatment, and their protection against abuses". See Schlesinger, 2003), pp. 312–317, and also at pp. 98–100 and pp. 235–6. In the UK, the "Devonshire Declaration" of 1922 had sought to define modern — post-Victorian — British colonial policy, affirming that "The fundamental principle ... is that the interests of the local people are paramount" (Haddon-Cave 1995) but for Hong Kong at least, the material benefits had been less tangible than in the early postwar period.

6.   HK 1946, p. 4.

7.   ADR DONT 1947–48, para. 12. Some of these recommendations bore fruit later: for example, ferry piers in the islands (ADR DONT 1947–48, para. 37, with the report for 1951–52, para. 10) and an irrigation engineer for the NT (ADR DONT 1947–48, para. 35, with the same for 1951–52, paras 4 and 9). A list of locally administered grants and loans was contained in the Hong Kong Annual Reports: see, e.g. Appendix I to HK 1958. Works projects were being jointly funded. All sums were shown in pounds sterling.

8.   HK 1956, p. 88. See also note 16 of this chapter.

9.   Those advocating land reform, of one kind or another, were concerned for the immigrant vegetable and livestock farmers. A body called the Hong Kong and Kowloon Chinese Farming and Agricultural Association seems to have made much of the running. Rather grudgingly, the District Commissioner conceded that "there was some substance in the complaints made", but was otherwise equally biased on the side of his beloved native farmers. Nonetheless, the Association's complaints bore fruit, in a series of discussions between the concerned heads of departments and its representatives, and in action by the DOs to clear up outstanding disputed rent cases in their Districts. See ADR DCNT 1950–51, para. 29, and ADR DCNT 1951–52, at para. 37.

10.   Para. 20 of ADR DCNT 1949–50 gives the flavour of official thinking: The District Commissioner wrote that "Press reports about large scale rack renting and eviction of New Territories' farmers proved to be greatly exaggerated". Also, the results of some pilot surveys into land ownership showed to others what he already knew, namely that "the big non-farming landowner is not a common feature of the New Territories (though some do exist), whereas the

owner-farmer is": *Ibid.*, para. 30. Of course, this did not of itself preclude rack-renting.

11. A striking, and candid, confession of ignorance had been made by a senior Cadet (W. J. Carrie): "I should, perhaps, preface this Minute by stating that during the whole of my 30 years service in Hong Kong, I have never been stationed in the New Territories, and I have, therefore, a very superficial knowledge of them, of the system of land tenure in force and of the general conditions of life of the inhabitants. *But at the same time I cannot help feeling that there are not many Government officers with very much deeper knowledge than my own"* (my italics). His memo to the CS in 1949 is in Land Tenure in the New Territories, HKRS N. 156, D&S N. 1/1003(1).

12. I am most grateful to Professors Chris Airriess and Alan Smart for sharing relevant archival information with me. For the land utilization surveys, and later publications, see HK 1958, pp. 81–82.

13. See pp. 83–84. Nonetheless, as there described, institutional changes of a different sort were soon put in place, contributing much to government and people liaison, and achieving development goals thereby:

14. The work was carried out by expatriate and local staff, although the first officers from the Colonial Agricultural Service (replacing temporary holders of senior posts) did not arrive in the Colony until May 1949 — "at long last", as the DCNT wrote in ADR DCNT 1949–50 (para. 27). In the 1950s, the voluminous and illustrated annual departmental reports, running from 84 pages in 1951–52 to 127 in 1957–58, testify to the good work being done in its various divisions. The reports of the District Administration are thin by comparison, until the late 1950s. See also the Director of Agriculture, Fisheries and Forestry's 93-page Report on *Agriculture in Hong Kong with Policy Recommendations* (Hong Kong, Government Printer, n.d. but likely to have been in 1954–55).

15. The establishment and development of these various departments, and the bewildering series of changes in titling between 1946 and 1964, with a further reorganization in 1966, are detailed at pp. 199–202 of Ho Pui-yin's *Administrative History*, 2004).

16. For the work of the Kadoorie brothers, see Blackie 1972. Loans for agricultural improvement were channeled through the Rural Development Committee (see note 8 above). In 1957–58, it met 23 times, usually twice a month: see ADR DCNT 1957–58, para. 36.

17. Those places with good Kaifong bodies, like Cheung Chau, were still carrying out many duties which would soon be taken over by government. The Cheung Chau Residents Association report for 1950 states that its funds came mainly from the market stalls, "upon which our public services, such as the Fong Bin Hospital, the Public Free School, street lighting, public latrines, playground, fire-fighting service, street repairs, etc., are maintained". The reports for 1952 and 1953 are similarly detailed. See Salkeld, 1996. The account of Peng Chau given in *Notebooks* is another good example of the kind.

18. Even in early 1958, the large village of Mang Kung Uk, with around 600 inhabitants, had no mail deliveries, nor even a letter box in which outgoing letters could be placed. All letters had to be collected under local arrangements from Tai Po Tsai Village on the Clear Water Bay Road: *Notebooks*.

19. Barnett was a legendary character. See Hayes 1996, pp. 25 and 30n75, also Wilson, pp. 87–88, Clark, p. 167, and the obituaries in JHKBRAS 27 (1987). See, too, his own record at pp. 24–26 of Rola Luzatto and Joseph Walker's *Hong Kong Who's Who* (Hong Kong, 1973). Wilson's interesting and insightful book is a good introduction to a District Officer's life of that day and age. Austin Coates's classic *Myself a Mandarin, Memoirs of a Special Magistrate* (London, Frederick Muller, 1968) is also of interest, as reflecting the characteristics and personalities of those we were expected to look after.

20. See chapter 10, pp. 127–129 below.

21. Confidential memorandum N.T. Z/20 dated 27 September 1955 to Hon. C. S.: without its enclosures (courtesy John Walden). About the same time, Barnett had given an interesting talk entitled "Politics in the New Territories" to officers of 48 and 21 Brigades (text available in the HKPRO) which adds further to our understanding of those times.

22. The review chapter of HK 1960, pp. 15–18, details the start made with irrigation and potable supplies.

23. It had been surprising to discover, from detailed questioning, how all but a very few of my rural informants, males born 1875–1898, had received at least some years of schooling in their village schools: see Appendix 9 to Hayes 1983. None of my female informants from the same period had been educated.

24. Abolished in 1905. See Franke, pp. 69–71.

25. By the end of the decade, despite a strenuous building programme which saw many new primary schools provided across the NT, there was still much to do, particularly in villages that had existing old, and now inadequate, school buildings, privately financed prewar. At Mang Kung Uk, in the Clear Water Bay peninsula, only 85 children aged between 6–16 were reportedly at school out of a claimed total of 275. The old school was too small, and not even operating bi-sessionally, but construction of new, much larger, premises was being delayed by a necessary revision to the building plans. Another large village, Tseng Lan Shue, along the road from Kowloon, was in a similar plight, with 90 children attending the old school, but in morning and afternoon sessions, out of 132 aged between 6–16, pending construction of the new building approved by the Education Department on a site allocated by the District Office: *Notebooks*. Perturbed at the Mang Kung Uk situation, I had made a note to push through the revised plans for the new school as fast as possible.

26. Sadly, with urbanization of the NT, new educational policies to suit the times would bring about the demise of a number of these larger, hitherto flourishing schools. See Hayes 1996, pp. 256–258.

27. The contents of my notebooks indicate that many villages in the old Southern District were in a sad way in the late 1950s; and also seen on visits elsewhere in the NT. Close inspection would reveal many derelict houses, ancestral halls in ruins or being used for storage or as cow-byres, or even as shops and (in places with road access) workshops and factories. See my long note on depopulation over a sixty year cycle in Hayes 1977.1, pp. 213–214.

28. See p. 118 below, with Hayes 1993, pp. 48–52.

29. (Sir) Ronald Holmes was, to my mind, the most gifted Administrative Grade officer of his day. Fluent in Chinese, intelligent, quick-witted, an excellent judge of persons and situations, compassionate and very practical, he was widely respected. He later became Acting Colonial Secretary and Chairman of the Public Services Commission. See also Clark, pp. 167–168.

30. See the ADRs DCNT for these years, especially 1959–60, chapters V and XVI.

31. Figures taken from the article noted below, most likely obtained from Dr. C. T. Wong, then Deputy Director, Department of Agriculture, Forestry and Fisheries, mentioned in the text.

32. HKS, 3 November 1979.

33. Up to 1964, there had been 1000 acres of brackish [not "blackish"] water paddy, but this had all been turned into fish ponds in the intervening fifteen years, according to Dr. Wong.

34. This was an old tradition in some places. Even in 1957–58, all the 50 men reported to be abroad in the large village of Sha Lo Wan on North Lantau were working as sailors (and curiously, all as firemen, not deck hands): *Notebooks*.

35. The Hong Kong and New Territories Evangelization Society's Report for 1917 touches on this point: "A noteworthy feature of the conditions here [Lam Tsuen Valley] is that the men of the countryside leave their homes, and seek, in distant places, means of livelihood, and over considerable areas the women and girls do, practically, all the field work, heavy and light, including the ploughing of the soil" (courtesy Rev. Carl T. Smith). See also the extract from a 1939 report by H. R. Butters, Labour Officer, included in Faure 1997, p. 190. The second wife of a farmer in the northern NT, found turning over earth under water before rice planting, had said that the wives of her husband's three sons also worked in the fields, and the cooking for the combined household was done by a step-daughter aged 12.

36. Reporting this, the District Commissioner had added, a trifle sententiously, "I had of course given careful consideration to the possibility that too many men might go, leaving villages undermanned. So far there has been no indication of this": ADR DCNT 1950–51, paras. 56–57, with the comment at para. 58.

37. By 1967, there were already over 1100 restaurants and take-aways in UK, rising to about 3,500 by 1980. Cited in Baker 1997, p. 35.

38. Male assumptions that they would always do so — had always done so — were revealed by a remark made a decade later by a shopkeeper friend from

Tai O, met on a ferry when I was on my way to visit some elderly village women on Lantau: "Why do you bother to interview women? They are illiterate, always stayed in the village, and knew little about what went on outside the home".

39. Minutes of 8.12.49 and 19.5.49 respectively, in Secretariat file L/M B & L, 6/ 47, in HKPRO.

40. Hayes 1996, pp. 21–23.

41. Aijmer 1967, at p. 70.

42. Jack M. Potter, another anthropologist, who conducted field research in the Ping Shan villages of the Tang lineage in 1961–63, describes the changing situation there in two chapters dealing with "Family Finances and the Rising Standard of Living", and "The Social and Cultural Effects of Economic Change", in his book, commenting on "the rising status of women" (Potter, p. 162) and the new interest in education, including, by implication, for girls (p. 143). We need more information about outcomes in education and agriculture as between Cantonese and Hakka villages, and between different areas. See e.g. note 51.

43. See Hayes 2001.1, pp. 55–66.

44. But even so, my visit notebooks from 1957–58 show that many were still not in school, and not a few boys also.

45. On a visit to four hamlets near Sai Kung Market in late 1957, during which the villagers had asked for a school of their own instead of having to send their children to the township, I noted as unusual the fact that "the village women all came in and joined in the discussion about schooling". They had been interested in the prospect of education for their daughters as well as for their sons. Yet there was nothing special about these women, nor their hamlet, which I described as "a poor little place". *Notebooks*: visit to Ta Ho Tun.

46. I owe this suggestion to Dr. Colin Day. My friends the Johnsons concur.

47. See chapter 10, p. 130.

48. See Hayes 1996, pp. 20–21 with p. 29 n65.

49. Visit note, Shan Mei and Au Pui Wan, 1986.

50. Wong 1971. His Figures 1–2, with Table 1, cover variously the years 1954–68.

51. *Ibid*, Table 1 and p. 25. Wong also reminds us of the diversity always to be found in the NT: "Many [indigenous] Punti farmers living in the market gardening zones have gradually changed from traditional rice cultivation in recent years. But most of the Hakka villagers still stick to their traditional farming. This could perhaps be explained by the hilly nature of their farm land and the inaccessability of their farms" (p. 33).

52. *Ibid*, p. 27.

53. For the *dau chung* and other measures, see Hayes 1977.1, pp. 202–203, with notes. A vegetable farmer's income was roughly double: see Lin Bin's article in HKS 8 December 1985. A picul is a Chinese weight of 133.333 pounds.

54.   See Hürlimann's evocative photograph at his p. 117. In 1969, the Director of Commerce and Industry stated that "coal and firewood have lost their significance", adding that "steps are being taken to delete them from the [reserved commodities] list": see ADRs DC&I, 1955–56, para. 106, and 1968–69, para 295 with 282.

55.   "The local cattle [*sic*] is a small, compact and hardy beast, highly suitable for work [ploughing and harrowing] in the small terraced fields of the Colony": ADR DAFF 1951–52, para. 33. See Plate 30.

56.   From p. 9 of his letter to me of 1 May 1985, now in the HKPRO; and also at chapter 7, pp. 93–95.

57.   The Governor specifically mentioned the "noisy, densely packed and exceptionally busy" nature of the urban area in his opening address to the Legislative Council in October 1976: *Hansard*, 1976–77, p. 21. At the 1976 By-Census, the population of Hong Kong Island, Kowloon and New Kowloon totalled 3,411,220, by comparison with the 951,120 then resident in the NT: HK 1977, p. 202.

58.   The Governor reported to Legislative Council on 18 October 1979, with obvious satisfaction, that the programme had been completed eighteen months ahead of schedule: *Hansard*, 1979–80, p.19.

59.   See *Hansard* 1976, pp. 383–386 and 637–648 for the Bill's passage through the Legislative Council. Detailed descriptions of the parks, their topography and ecology are provided in Thrower, who also describes the administrative background to the Country Park Ordinance. See also Stokes, pp. 36–39.

60.   See HK 1977, p. 184, and ADRDCNT, 1972–73, para. 56, for more information.

61.   *Hansard* 1978–79, p. 16.

62.   HK 1977, p. 184, HK 1986, p. 236, and HK 1993, p. 356.

63.   Governor in Legislative Council, 18 October 1979, cited in note 57 above, also in Stokes, p. 37.

64.   Answering a Legislative Council question on cleanliness in the country parks, the Secretary for the NT had referred in the course of his reply to the "large areas of private land, much of it abandoned paddy, which is extensively used for picnicking and camping": *Hansard* 1976–77, p. 304–305.

65.   These were all on Crown land. See Hayes 1983, chapter 14, "The Use of Hill Land".

66.   *Hansard* 1976, p. 385.

67.   The boundaries for the 21 parks and for special areas were gazetted under Designation Orders during this period: e.g. LN 148 of 1977 for the Shing Mun, Kam Shan and Lion Rock Country Parks, LN 204 of 1977 for the Shing Mun Fung Shui Woodland Special Area, and LN 54 of 1979 for the Tai Lam, Tai Mo Shan and Lam Tsuen Country Parks. All had passed through the Country Park Advisory Board, which had a Legal and Boundary Committee. Any objections from rural interests would have been sorted out there, with the help of the Authority, and the New Territories Administration.

68. The minor roads constructed inside the parks to facilitate development and management of the new amenities were (like those already constructed inside water catchment areas by the Water Supplies Department) mostly closed to public access. While appearing to improve access to villages inside the parks, in fact they usually did nothing of the kind.

69. More upsetting still, following the introduction of new public health regulations in 1980, was the posting of notices at all graves located inside the parks, prohibiting further hill burials, and advising that existing graves were in breach of the regulations. Villagers had long accepted that new burials would have to take place in specially designated village cemeteries, but they were not prepared for being advised that *all* existing graves, no matter how old, were technically illegal! Referring to the notices, one letter received in the District Office Tsuen Wan began with the statement, "Descendants of our clan called an urgent meeting at which it was resolved to make strong objections ...". See Hayes 1992, at p. 14.

70. The published proceedings of Legislative Council sessions 1976–77 to 1979–80 are silent on rural concerns over this period, although a senior member of the Heung Yee Kuk, Mr. Charles Yeung, was sitting *ad personam* in the later sessions.

71. At section 23 (2) of Part V of the Waterworks Ordinance, Cap.102; also at sections 19 and 20 of an earlier Ordinance, No.16 of 1903, at p.1659 of the Alabaster (1913) edition of the *Laws of Hong Kong*. Many of the areas set aside for country parks were already gazetted as catchment areas, owing to the water schemes implemented over the years.

72. See ADR DCNT 1959–60, paras. 145 and 147, and ADR DCNT 1961–62, para. 102, with the text and photograph opposite p. 30. See also HK 1960, pp. 18–19, and Bray 2001.1, pp. 31–32.

73. The compilation of such a record would require a knowledge of local families and local history, together with a close acquaintance with the schedules and survey sheets of the Block Crown Leases, such as made possible the information provided herein of instances from the Tsuen Wan District.

74. SP 1911, p. 103 (29).

75. Thirty years on, lineage members were still close. I was given a list of twelve men who were living in various places, besides two others whose personal names could not be recalled. Nine of the twelve were aged from 53 to 80. It was reported that five other persons were in Singapore, and no less than 48 in England, presumably all younger members of the lineage.

76. The former, inhabited by Lai families, with seven houses, one an ancestral hall, had been vacated (said elderly descendants) because its adverse *fung-shui* "did not permit them to raise people". The Tsui lineage of the latter place, with nine houses, had sold their agricultural land in 1911–1914, and had surrendered most of their house lots before 1910, or allowed them to be re-entered by the Crown for non-payment of Crown rent. Information from DOTW land records and elderly family members.

77.   Population 90 at the 1911 census, and still around 100 at the 1961 census. At Sham Tseng, in the late 1970s, they were all reunited in a new village. See Hayes 1996, pp. 143–146.

78.   Population 87 at the 1911 Census. See Hayes, pp. 139–140.

79.   Concluding that its remote location exposed them to undue danger, they had moved down to Kwai Chung. See Hayes 1977.2, p. 189.

80.   Cap. 1097 of the Laws of Hong Kong. ADR DCNT 1959–60, paras. 98–109.

81.   The new compensation policies are described in chapter 8, pp. 100, 108.

82.   Even in the years before the deluge, in routine rural administration between 1957–62, I had found the village representatives and rural committee network invaluable, enabling me to ascertain facts and better understand and address problems with the help of knowledgeable and experienced men.

83.   I recall how the reordering of the Heung Yee Kuk by statute in 1959 had been described by the senior police officer in the NT at the time, as "making a rod for our own backs": and so it might appear, if one does not take into account the successful transition to modernity achieved through ceaseless talk rather than endless confrontation with its dangerous volatility.

84.   HKAR 1946, pp. 7–8 provides details. Eligibility to vote was to be through possession of a rice ration card, for which seven years' residence was required. The 38 "electoral districts" were not specified, and were larger in number than the 27 which elected rural committees after 1948. The ADRs for these few years are not helpful, save for 1946–47, para. 9, and also 1947–48, para. 15 which states that "Elections were held experimentally over the areas Saikung, Lamma, Cheung Chau, and Lantau. Varying degrees of interest were shown, but a start was made in this important experiment". Archival research is needed to explain why the early move towards elections in this form was not pursued.

85.   The village representative and rural committee schemes are described in ADR 1947–48, paras. 9–11. Most ADRs thereafter provide information on their further development, those for 1956–57 (paras. 62–68), 1957–58 (paras. 58–63) and 1959–60 (paras. 110–114) being the most useful. Whereas the village representatives appear to have been organized quickly (doubtless because they were in many cases the same men who had functioned as village heads up to that time) the rural committee system took longer to emerge, with the last (South Lantau and Cheung Chau) not until 1958 and 1961 respectively.

86.   In effect, all those villages accepted as having been established before the start of the Lease in 1898. See also para. 2 of Annex II to the Sino-British Joint Declaration on the Question of Hong Kong.

87.   In handover notes to his successor, one of my contemporaries summed up the selection process as follows: "They are 'elected' in many and devious ways. *Sometimes* it is a genuine secret ballot, more often a question of a couple of chaps getting together and saying Joe Soap's the man" (The notes are now in HKPRO). It was an apt rendering of what usually happened inside the villages. But underlying the choice was the fact that the men filling these posts at that time and for long after, were persons who, generally speaking, had, and would retain, the confidence of their communities.

88.   Each operated under a constitution approved by the government and all were exempted from registration under the Societies Ordinance so long as they followed its provisions.

89.   Two District Commissioners commented on the new arrangements. Barrow wrote at the outset, "The idea of unselfish public service is new and strange. And office-holders show a tendency to look for the perquisites of office, rather than opportunities for service. Nor do the exploited take this amiss, rather taking it for granted, and we have a long way to go before we reach a satisfactory standard in this field": ADR 1947–48, para. 11. Barnett wrote in 1956–57, "The gradual development of representative institutions, which may in the future ease the District Officer's burden, at present adds greatly to its weight, since however carefully the new machinery is handled it always needs a ready oil-can and an eye on the pressure gauge, and sometimes has to be dug out of a hole": ADR DCNT 1956–57, para. 14.

90.   See the chapter on the New Territories Administration by the then District Commissioner in *Government and People*, Second Series (Hong Kong, Government Printer, 1964), p. 7. He added: "They are not 'headmen' as the term is understood in other Colonies [he had served prewar in Ceylon] in that they have no direct responsibility to the Government and they have no statutory powers or duties".

91.   *Ibid.* The VRR were never paid, but the rural committees received a monthly subvention from government of $450 from 1960–61, to assist with the basic expenses of providing a service to the rural community.

92.   Archival research will establish whether the motivation was benevolent (in line with the spirit of the time) or was more calculating. Meantime, Allen Chun's categorization of such moves "mechanisms of indirect control" seems to me unwarranted: see Chun, p. 146. He lumps vegetable and other marketing societies together with village representatives and rural committees under this rubric, which for the former, is, I believe, even less appropriate. I also dissent from the view expressed by Kuan Hsin-chi and Lau Siu-kai in their article on Development and the Resuscitation of Rural Leadership in the New Territories, published in the June 1981 issue of the *Hong Kong Journal of Public Administration*, in which it was suggested that rural leadership was in decline, and would have decayed completely without development and the government's manipulation of leadership to achieve its desired programmes. As with Allen Chun's similar projection of state manipulation and control, I have to reserve judgment.

93.   See e.g. Brian Wilson, pp. 84–85. I had a similar experience with the North Lamma Rural Committee elections of 1960, when a fearful row broke out after the outcome of the count (by secret ballot) had indicated that someone must have reneged on his promised vote, quelled only by a dignified 80-year-old elder who suddenly shouted "Shut up", which surprisingly they all did! Also ADR DCNT 1961–62, para. 68, which recounts how the election of the Shap Pat Heung Rural Committee (Yuen Long District) in March 1961 had to

be postponed *sine die* because of clashes between members of the two opposing parties on election day. It was not reconvened until 23 December, with a few minor disturbances during electioneering but none on election day. Such continue to this day, with many alleged offences against the legislation for the new-style VR elections in July–August 2003 — see Kevin Sinclair and Stella Lee in SCMP 7 May and 30 July 2003 respectively — and others connected with the ensuing rural committee elections, with two postponements: Peter Michael, SCMP 16 September 2003.

94.   I owe this observation to Mariann Ford.

Chapter 7   Village Removals for Water Schemes 1923–1974

1.   HK 1960, pp. 4–5.

2.   One prewar DO (Walter Schofield) wrote "I always considered [resumptions] the most distasteful and unpleasant task a D.O. can be expected to perform: … I never felt that money could in any way make up to a peasant for the loss of his land. Nearly always they wanted land in exchange, which it was rarely possible to find". See Schofield 1977, p. 145.

3.   See chapter 14 and appendix 7 of Hayes 1983: Richard Webb, "The Use of Hill Land for Village Forestry and Fuel gathering in the New Territories of Hong Kong" in JHKBRAS 35 (1995), pp. 143–154: with note 14 on p. 181.

4.   It was written by Mak Kai-yim, Senior Demarcator, District Office Tsuen Wan, in 1966, after he had been to the resite village and discussed the village removal and resiting with surviving participants. These included the Village Representative, who had been 26 years old at the time.

5.   The village was shown as Lots 1675 and 1699 in Kowloon Survey District IV.

6.   From the wording of the report on expenditure on "the reservoir and contingent works", which states that "a sum of $57,200 was spent in constructing a new village …", it might appear that the houses were built by government contract. (HKAR 1924, p. Q146). If so, this practice was not followed for Shing Mun. The village name is here rendered "Shek Lai Pui". The removal date given in HK 1960 p. 19 is wrongly stated as being between 1902–1910, when an earlier extension had taken fields not houses.

7.   In New Kowloon village removals, it was government's practice to provide cash compensation for houses on building land, assessed at the value at the time they were resumed. Individual owners might obtain exchanges of land elsewhere, but it seems that sites were not offered for *village* resiting, as was done for the Shek Lei Pui and Shing Mun villagers. See, e.g., HKAR 1924, pp. Q22–29, which lists exchanges for the Kowloon Tong redevelopment.

8.   This was a common belief among rural folk, but by the time of Mr. Mak's enquiries, the population had increased to 250. Descendants were still in government employment: see HK1960, p. 19.

9.   Facts as stated in Traveller's Handbook 1951, p. 48. It was inaugurated for use on 30 January 1937. The granite facing of the dam, which comprised of

large lozenge-shaped pieces of carefully quarried stone, all interlocking to form an impressive surface, is a tribute to its designer and to the stone-masons who created it.

10. During my visit to Wo Hop Shek, a Cheung resited there from Shing Mun, recalled how his father and three uncles with five sons had received $900 compensation for their old houses, with which they could only build two new ones in the resite village; which seems low compared with the payments recalled for Shek Lei Pui noted above. The masons had come from Ping Long in the Lam Tsuen Valley, and were fellow Hakkas. See Plate 24.

11. "The new villages have where possible been sited with reference to their suitability for pineapple growing, and their proximity to land suitable for forestry and grass-cutting". See the report "Move of the Shing Mun Villages" in SP 1928 together with HKARs 1930 and 1931, at p. J 3 in each. Walter Schofield stated that the negotiation for the removals was "long and difficult" (Schofield, p. 152), as confirmed in the reports. The villages were far from being "settled down comfortably in their new homes" (1931 p. J 3).

12. DO North's report for 1935 would note the strong opposition which met any application from strangers wishing to buy hill land on which to establish orchards, because of their own needs for fuel, grazing and interment: HKAR 1935, p. J 2, para. 8.

13. At Wo Hop Shek resite village near Fanling, a man whose forbears had been Chinese herbalists for three generations said that the Pangs levied fines on anyone caught collecting. But as another old man had said it had been his profession also, I think they had carried on regardless. The herbs were sold to well-known Chinese medicine shops in Kowloon and Hong Kong, save during the Japanese Occupation when, too frightened to travel and unable to make a living, they had gone to live with a married sister in present day Shenzhen. The resitees had not rented fields from local villagers, but did take Crown land on permit from government.

14. It was usual, postwar, to post notices on site of government's intention to sell land or issue permits. But we shall probably never know if this was done in the prospective village resite areas, since the department's files were destroyed during the War.

15. Not removals for water schemes, but inserted here for chronological reasons, and for comparison.

16. The range was to replace that located near Castle Peak, affected by the intended Tai Lam Chung Water Scheme. ADRDONT 1947–48, para. 33.

17. ADR DCNT 1952–53, para. 20. "Disturbance compensation was paid to villagers and boat-people, and new land granted on permit to the villagers". The architect was Mr. G. A. V. Hall.

18. ADR DCNT 1951–52, para. 13. Called Pak Pai in the report. Inexplicably, nothing was added about the dispossession of the Lams, nor the arrangements made to compensate them.

19.   Schofield, pp. 149–150, contains interesting information on schooling on the
island in the 1920s. Also in JHKBRAS 23 (1983), at p. 106.

20.   I had been able to find three families, re-established variously at Ngau Kwu
Wan (Shap Long) and at Tai Pak and Yee Pak, below the present Discovery
Bay residential area. Pop. 78 in 1911: SP 1911, p. 103 (38).

21.   In the Yuen Long District Office file, PS 1/1001/55, which I had borrowed to
make comparisons of the cubic area of the accommodation provided at Tai
Uk Wai with the area being made available to the Shek Pik people at Tsuen
Wan, the number of families was stated to be 36, rather than 33, comprising
91 adults and 84 children, 175 in all. These must be the final figures.

22.   Hayes 1993, p. 57 and Plate 7. The village owners sold this unique building
to a development consortium a few years ago. A forty storey block is now
on the site.

23.   ADRDCNT 1955–56, para. 21, and ADRDCNT 1956–57, para. 29. The files
relating to the Tai Lam Chung removals are not in the HKPRO. The Shek Pik
files cannot be found either: to my lasting regret, as they included a complete
photographic record of all the villagers, by family groups, with women and
girls in traditional garb, taken during the preliminary engineering investigations.

24.   As the official responsible for all dealings with the villagers between 1957 and
1960, I have provided an account in Hayes 1996, pp. 30–56, which fills out
this summary. Please note that, as emphasized in note 19 therein, events at the
reservoir site bore no resemblance whatsoever to those depicted in Austin
Coates's novel, *The Road* (1959). Shek Pik was also my introduction to the
traditional Chinese village world, and I like to think that my keen interest in
them and in their past, and how it impinged on the present, assisted the work
in hand. Through the general friendliness and assistance given me by the elders
engendered thereby, and the dedicated work of my small staff, I was able to
negotiate land recovery and resettlement within the desired time-frame. And
though there was much that, as an ignorant newcomer, I overlooked, what I
learned during that strenuous and sometimes harrowing time provided the
basis for my ongoing studies into rural society and local history.

25.   ADR DCNT 1959–60, para. 9, with ADR DAFF 1958–59, para. 110, on the
plan for developing the new fields. Fifty-five families from the larger village
chose urban resettlement and three had opted for accommodation at Mui Wo.
Eleven families had preferred a rural relocation. As stated above, the village
temple was accommodated in the specially designed resettlement building,
but in the Shek Pik case, resettled to normal town apartment blocks, I think
the villagers selected the most favourably located one for their Hau Wong
Temple, on a geomancer's advice. See Plate 25.

26.   The new accommodation would be offered in accordance with the size and
composition of each family at the time of the removal, and the space it occupied
in the village, with no provision for expansion later on.

27.   In the event, with the consent of the Tsuen Wan Rural Committee, the DO
recognized their status as indigenous villagers and allowed village burials in a
rural cemetery at Heung Shek, on the slopes of Tai Mo Shan.

28. The same points were made to the Shek Pik villagers; but of course, the more worldly members of the two settlements were quite aware of the facts, or these essentially communal decisions to move to a town would not have been made.

29. Information in these paragraphs taken from the Yuen Long District Office file mentioned at note 21 above.

30. The removal and reprovisioning are described in detail in ADR DCNT 1966–67, paras. 75–78. The transfer of people and their belongings, organized by the District Office, Tai Po, with the help of the Army and the Marine department, took twelve days from 28 November to 9 December 1966.

31. ADR DCNT 1966–67, para. 78, with photo spread in HK 1967.

32. The subtitle of Berkowitz's article in 1968. For a fuller study of the Six Villages, with a different focus, see Berkovitz, Brandauer and Reed, 1969.

33. Berkowitz, pp. 96–108, at p. 107. See the poignant photo at Plate 26.

34. Though I was in amiable discourse with the elders of both the Tai Lam Chung and Shek Pik new villages during my seven years in Tsuen Wan, 1975–82.

35. Contained in his website www.journeytoforever.org/about.html, "Tai Long Wan, Tales from a Vanishing Village".

36. See p. 90.

37. A phenomenon also noted by John Brim at Fui Sha Wai, at p. 137 of chapter 10.

38. At pp. 75–79.

39. A detailed statement of their experiences at Tai Long Wan can be found in letters and enclosures to me, written mostly in 1985–86, copies of which have been placed in HKPRO. There is other material on Keith Addison's website (note 35) to which interested readers are referred. I here gratefully acknowledge the insights and assistance provided by my two friends.

40. This was the last in this series, and the published Colony annual reports for the following years do not provide any further details.

41. ADR DCNT 1972–73, para. 132.

42. Lo Hsien-hau, "Public Administration and Public Opinion in the New Territories". Thesis presented for the Degree of M.Phil. at the University of Hong Kong.

43. For background, see Hayes 1998. No re-housing provision was made at Shek Pik for the small group of fishermen who had used the anchorage as their home base, and there is no mention of this for boat people from Plover Cove either. They were simply expected to move on.

44. Lo, pp. 223–226.

45. Not that everything had changed. Villagers' belligerence was still a factor. A former police officer (Griffiths 1997, p. 131) recounts how he defused a threatening situation on the approach road to the High Island Dam site, where a group of villagers, "exasperated by the problems and inconvenience caused by the work", and armed with poles, had erected a barricade to block access. A police riot company was en route to the scene, but before its arrival, he had

dismantled the barrier himself, using bad language laced with humorous asides in Cantonese — both calculated to amuse and divert country Chinese.

46.   I am not clear whether this was also the case with High Island.

47.   See Hayes 1996, pp. 256–258. The Shek Pik school closed in 1985, but the Tai Uk Wai school was still operating a year or two later. Remaining village schools were still losing out in 2002: see Klaudia Lee's article in SCMP 19 September 2002.

Chapter 8   Village Removals for New Town Development 1960 Onward

1.   See pp. 100–101 for a listing of the nine new towns.

2.   Together with Tsing Yi and NE Lantau, they were excised from the old Southern District to become the new administrative District of Tsuen Wan in 1957. Its staff were not moved from Kowloon to premises in the town until 1959. See Hayes 1993, p. 183, n4.

3.   HK 1961. P. 169, and ADR DCNT 1964–65, para. 64. An outline plan for the Shatin Valley was also under consideration in 1961, but development began in Tsuen Wan.

4.   See Hayes 1993, pp. 46–52, for the early postwar situation.

5.   I am not sure when this principle was laid down, but it was obviously early. (See note 11 to chapter 7). It was one followed throughout the Lease, save in New Kowloon (see pp. 111–112).

6.   See Hayes 1993, pp. 64–74.

7.   "We hope that you will be kind enough not to exert any pressure. The grievances of the inhabitants of the New Territories living under the dictatorial government of Hong Kong are beyond description" wrote the same VR to the DO.

8.   As Mr. Holmes had explained to a fellow departmental head: "The whole trick in Tsuen Wan in my view is to arrange for the voluntary removal of the old villages without getting ourselves in the position of being forced to remove them, in which case treatment on the lines of Tai Uk Wai and Shek Pik would be inevitable. Such treatment is far too expensive to be envisaged": confidential memorandum NT 1223/59c dated 19 April 1961, District Commissioner, NT to Commissioner for Resettlement. The DO's confidential memo to DCNT ref. T.W.2A/155/60 of 13 April 1961 also refers. Tai Uk Wai was the name given to the building constructed for the villagers removed from Tai Lam Chung.

9.   The annual reports of the two District Officers, North and South, up to 1939, the last published before the Japanese attack on the Colony, contain regular statements on land recovered and for what purposes.

10.   Even during the Occupation, land and houses were taken for development by the Japanese military authorities, notably for the extension to the Kai Tak airfield in New Kowloon. See Hayes 2000.

11.   See Wesley-Smith, pp. 101–103, leading to the formation of the HYK.

12.   For the Lands Tribunal see Wilkinson in Wacks (ed.) 1989.

13. A DO of the time has emphasized that this was a policy "conceived *in* Tsuen Wan *for* Tsuen Wan". This may well have been so in regard to "Letters of Exchange", but the 5: 2 ratio for the exchange of building land for agricultural land was seemingly a practice that had been adopted in the urban area. When land policies for and in the NT were being threshed out from 1949 onwards, the eventual decision to apply urban rules in layout (development) areas was agreed by 1957, and a blunt refusal sent to the Heung Yee Kuk, which had been pressing its own, unacceptable, views upon the government. After further amendment, a revised land administration policy for the NT was approved by Executive Council in mid 1960: see Allen Chun, pp. 129–141.

14. A few fortunate Tsuen Wan villagers had benefited, as ascertained by Dr. Betsy Johnson during her research in Kwan Mun Hau New Village in the late 1960s.

15. The exchange documents were bilingual, and specimen copies are included in a small collection of land documents placed in the HKPRO. The policies and practices evolved at the start of Tsuen Wan's urbanization were to serve as the blueprint for development schemes elsewhere in the NT. It is not too much to say that Tsuen Wan was the guinea pig for the massive urbanization of the next four decades, which is still proceeding today.

16. See Ho Pui-yin, *Administrative History*, p. 122.

17. For the New Towns and Rural Townships as at 1987, see e.g. HK 1988, pp. 177–181. By the time the then existing programmes were completed, the NT population would rise to an estimated 3.5 millions.

18. See Hayes 1993, p. vii.

19. As described by the Secretary for the NT in Legislative Council on 11 April 1978: Hansard 1977–78, p. 717, ending, "The new villages are built to modern standards, to a proper layout, and with modern services."

20. For further information see Hayes 1993, p. 200 n4.

21. Principally through the inter-departmental District Operations Committees chaired by the Project Managers of the NTDD.

22. It was the general rule for villagers' fields to be scattered, partly through the vagaries of what was available for purchase, and partly through prudence, so as to avoid losses in case of crop failure or natural disaster.

23. In matters affecting all, like new housing, villagers (and Village Representatives) found it was expedient to insist on having village removal committees on which all lineages in the village would be represented, and to press their requirements through negotiation with the authorities. We found them useful too: indeed, indispensable.

24. Compensation paid for old graves was graduated in accordance with age, condition, materials used in their construction, and the importance of those buried there to the lineage, such as the graves of a founding ancestor and his wife, or of branch heads and their wives. Only in the latter cases would resiting outside the new designated village cemeteries be permitted.

25.   Past events which had shaped current dispositions inside local lineages in regard to membership of trusts and rights to their once common property were revealed.

26.   It was up to senior staff, and especially the District Officers, to perceive where circumstances required that policies or compensation levels be modified or replaced, and make the necessary case for alterations or additions, ultimately for consideration by the Government Secretariat and Governor-in-Council.

27.   Copies of instructions to senior staff on the subject, together with other papers on village removals and resitings which help to convey the concerns of the day, are now held by HKPRO. See *Instructions to the Land Staff.*

28.   Bray 2001.2, p. 161. See the candid admission made by a senior Cadet Officer in the late 1940s as to his own, and other colleagues' ignorance of the NT, recorded in note 11 on p. 216.

29.   See Hayes 1993, pp. 3–4.

30.   Up to the mid 1950s, this had been possible without payment of premium, provided that the DO approved of the site. It was then decided not to issue any more licences of this kind, since Tsuen Wan was clearly going to be developed, and to a town plan, making it advisable not to permit haphazard conversions to building status.

31.   And did. Though none of us could have foreseen it then, the Hoi Pa landowners were going to have to wait another eight years before their *choi tei* (vegetable fields) as they called their agricultural holdings, were resumed for the redevelopment of the Upper Village in the early 1980s.

32.   See p. 100. The Hoi Pa people were aware of all this, but no doubt thought they would have another "go" with a new District Officer.

33.   See Kevin Sinclair in SMP, 25 April 1992 for another such attempt of many.

34.   See also p. 40 with note 78 on p. 202.

35.   The lineage was a very old one. Its founding ancestor had settled in Tsuen Wan during the Wan Li reign of the Ming dynasty (1572–1620), which made it the oldest still represented in Tsuen Wan.

36.   Shown as a rectangular enclosure on the 1900 survey sheet, Shek Wai Kok had been included in the list of villages attached to Lockhart's Report in 1898 and was among those having a member on the "Committee" gazetted for Tsuen Wan under the Local Communities Ordinance, No. 11 of 1899; in short, an influential village head. See Appendix No.5 to LR, and HKGG, 8 July 1899, p. 1070.

37.   Hayes 1996, pp. 148–150.

38.   It was not uncommon for villagers to identify with their ancestors in regard to length of stay. For parallels in north China, see Johnston 1910, pp. 139–140. "The Weihaiwei farmer has indeed so limited a conception of his own existence as a separate and distinct personality that in ordinary speech he continually confuses himself with his ancestors or with living members of his family. Examples of this are of repeated occurrence in the law-courts." With instances.

39. In the course of his visits, I began to learn more about him, and to appreciate his personal qualities. He spoke animatedly of the village and his early education prewar, from a teacher hired to instruct children in his clan's ancestral hall. Well-versed in the Chinese classics, he (Mr. Tang On-tong) helped me to prepare a paper on the popular culture of old China, by writing an interesting account of Chinese couplets, tracing their history back to the great poets of Tang and Song, and greatly assisting my understanding thereby.

40. A useful reminder of other aspects of compensation in resumptions and clearances, affecting owners and all tenant and crown land permit farmers, is provided in Lin Bin's article on farming in HKS 8 December 1985. See also Hayes 1993, pp. 77–78, and Hayes 1996, pp. 146–147, 293–294.

41. Announcing the appointment of the Committee, the Secretary for the NT told the Legislative Council on 10 November 1977 that it would comprise "four Heung Yee Kuk representatives, three Members of this Council, one other member, and two Government officers with particular knowledge of the New Territories and land resumption problems and procedures". The method and rates of compensation for resumption of agricultural land had, he said, "been the subject of an almost continuous dialogue between my predecessors, myself and the Heung Yee Kuk for a great many years". In that year alone, resumptions would "amount to something of the order of 16 million square feet". *Hansard* 1977–78, p. 215.

42. Thenceforth, the rates for cash compensation, varying according to location, were to be on a sliding scale, calculated in line with market rates as revised at regular intervals. A copy of the Report has been placed in the HKPRO. Though surely not prompted by this thought, the measure would answer the deep-rooted feeling among many village landowners — sometimes voiced directly to me and other officials — that government's cash compensation should reflect the strenuous effort required of their forbears over the generations.

43. Taken from para. 2 of "Note of a Meeting to discuss Outstanding Points on Hoi Pa Village Removal, 15 June 1981", District Office Tsuen Wan, now in the HKPRO. See HK 1982, p. 121 for sites being made available for exchange entitlements.

44. Bray 2001.1, pp. 39–41, with Bray 2001.2, p. 163 *seq.*

45. The situation described here must have been repeated to an equal or lesser extent in other "New Towns". This note is intended as a pointer for readers wishing to take this further.

46. At the time of its removal in 1963, the native population of Kwan Mun Hau had numbered 562. By 1982, it had risen to 716, of whom 204 were younger males over 18. Yeung Uk's population had risen from 160 to 240, with over 50 males of eligible age. At Ho Pui, there were now around 400 villagers, with those over 18 in proportion.

47. The site had become available through the need for a Water Supplies Department installation at Yau Kom Tau. Preparation of a formed site for 60

village houses, half of them for the resiting of the village of that name, had been part of the arrangement made with the Public Works Department.

48. Fourteen would go to the largest village (Kwan Mun Hau) with eight each to the other two. It must be realized that agreement from the village side did not come easy. It was the result of many difficult meetings which members of village removal committees held with the body of villagers, with the likelihood that comparatively few of them understood the constraints imposed upon their leaders and the District Office staff.

49. The breakdown showed that only 42 of the 204 claimants from Kwan Mun Hau, and 24 of the 50 odd in Yeung Uk would benefit, with probably a higher proportion from Ho Pui.

50. I had done my best to achieve results within the policies framed for village removal, suggesting (and requesting) changes where these seemed necessary, and exercising as much flexibility as I could, including use of the Small House Policy in regard to village resitings. In all things I worked closely with the Project Manager, Tsuen Wan. But towards the end of my stay, surprised indeed, I received a written request from my headquarters to provide justifications for my various actions. This was not difficult. The episode enabled me to give a full account of my stewardship, and nothing further came of it. A copy of my memorandum is in HKPRO. Besides what I have written in *Tsuen Wan* and *Friends and Teachers*, some readers may still find useful the longer discussion of village concerns during development provided in Hayes 1991.

51. He had discussed the enduring importance of Chinese learning in maintaining Chinese identity and cultural tradition during such transitions: *University of Hong Kong Gazette*, Vol. XXXIX, No. 3, August 23, 1993.

52. Patrick Hase (Hase 1999–2000) has described the long history of the last remaining major village of central New Kowloon and its people, and much else about the area. In East Kowloon, Cha Kwo Ling remains the only other still recognizable village entity. Though truly epic, the story of the Kowloon villages has never been written, and together with the history of urban development in Kowloon is a fitting subject for a book-length study.

53. The two departments concerned were the Secretariat for Chinese Affairs and the Crown Lands and Survey Office of the Public Works Department, but in truth their main interests and preoccupations lay elsewhere. Prewar, lacking expertise, the latter seems to have called in NT District Officers and former DOs to undertake work on its behalf, such as major resumptions for development and surveys on updating records of village properties, both in Hong Kong and Kowloon: see the *Schofield and Hamilton Letters* dated 12 April 1962 and 1 August 1958 respectively.

54. As stated, this had created concern among New Territories' leaders in the 1920s, since New Kowloon was part of the Leased Territory: see p. 100.

55. If they wished to continue as communities, villagers removed for development had to make what arrangements they could, as happened in the case of the Ma Tau Wai clearance in the 1920s, when a number of families built new

homes together in Shek Lung Street, Kowloon City. However, such an outcome depended upon total clearance at the one time and all owners of building land being of like mind. Total clearances were rarer in the postwar decades: see note 57.

56. A terse account of what this involved is contained in a letter dated 22 March 1962 to the Secretary for Chinese Affairs: "On 19 March 1962, at 8 a.m., a group of Resettlement Department officers came to register all the houses and people of our [Sha Po] village. The villagers were notified that their houses were due to be demolished and they themselves were to be resettled [in public housing rental estates]. All the villagers have been greatly startled and perturbed by this in the past few days." The rest of the letter is equally compelling. There was no fairy godmother at hand to assist, as in the NT, and the mere fact that the RD took direct action without apparently consulting the SCA was indicative of the situation. It took a succession of former NT DOs in the post of Chief Assistant SCA to provide more support for long-settled village communities like Sha Po, leading to the issue of a government General Order requiring all departments to advise and consult in matters affecting old villages. Under GO 2532, re-numbered as GR 523 at the revision and reissue of 1964. "... Heads of Departments should consult the Secretary for Chinese Affairs when considering schemes which would have an important bearing on the livelihood or social structure of the residents of these [old village] areas [on Hong Kong Island and in New Kowloon] and should clear in advance with the Secretary for Chinese Affairs their proposed timetable for the carrying out of any such project. This also applies to any major new survey or field work."

57. The fate of So Uk, the largest village of the Cheung Sha Wan area in northwest Kowloon was a typical example of the kind. A one-lineage village established in 1739, its houses and fields were taken by degrees over a long period, and the affected families were dispersed and lost contact. See chapter 5 in Hayes 1983. There was a Court appeal to a final resumption in 1877: SCMP, 2 July 1977. Chuk Yuen and Ngau Chi Wan in central and east New Kowloon suffered similarly. See, generally, Smart 2002.

58. ADRSCA 1966–67, paras. 23–24, ADRSCA 1968–69, para. 13, regarding the Ngau Tau Kok clearance of 1966, with information on other cases. See also Hayes 1996, pp. 92–95.

59. See Smart 1992, pp. 81–82, for the clearance of old settlements at Diamond Hill in 1989. Periodic appeals for help were made by New Kowloon villagers to the NT Heung Yee Kuk, but these were generally disregarded, since (as we have seen) there was insufficient land available for village housing in the NT.

60. In discussion with old persons from the former New Kowloon villages, it would seem that some men had become wealthy contractors from even before 1898. Ng Pak-wan, a building contractor in urban Kowloon and the father of one of my female informants, is shown in BCL entries for Kowloon Tsai Village as owning over 40 building lots there in 1904–1905. For an instance of the opportunities for social advancement deriving from self-created wealth in Kowloon, see Hayes 1983, pp. 58–59.

61.   Tim Ko has written recently: "Now, 40 years after the village was demolished, the old Ngau Tau Kok community has disintegrated. The last *Da Jiu* for Tai Wong Yeh was held in the mid-1980s, of which my uncle Ko Kei-fat was still one of the organizers. Since then, there has been nothing to keep the villagers together". A telling, and sad, commentary.

62.   By the Hong Kong Volunteer Corps: see the reference in *Hansard 1899–1900*, p. 39. For Kowloon City, see Wesley-Smith 1998, especially chapter 7, and (with its suburb, Kowloon Street) my chapter 7 in Hayes 1977.1.

Chapter 9   The Rural Contribution to Community Building in the New Towns, and Its Background

1.   Some years after, in 1985, together with Kwai Chung, it was hived off to become Kwai-Tsing District.

2.   Sir Murray Maclehose, later Lord Maclehose of Beoch.

3.   When notice boards were proposed at the entrances to the town, my friend and colleague Eddy Short, the Project Manager, wrote to say they ought to read, "You are now entering Tsuen Wan New Town. Would passengers please close their eyes." See Hayes 1993, p. 90.

4.   It was reported in HK 1978, p. 114, that 70% of its population lived in public housing, in one form or another.

5.   The effective start to the "New Towns" Programme had been signalled by the establishment in 1973 of the New Territories Development Department and its New Town Development Offices, one of them located in and responsible for Tsuen Wan. For the work of the two offices, and the close liaison between them, see Hayes 1993, p. 206 n5, with pp. 113–114 above.

6.   Not the least of its achievements was to obtain a logo for the town through public competition. It was adopted by the District Board after its formation, and appears on the Board's notepaper, and on all its printed reports and brochures. It is the breast pocket badge on the blazers worn by members of the Board and its committees, and of the many teams formed among its various promotion groups. See Plate 34.

7.   *Hansard*, 1977–78, p. 21. See also Hayes 1993, pp. 136–137.

8.   Sir David Akers-Jones's memoir, *Feeling the Stones* (Hong Kong University Press, 2004) describes at p. 114 his part in creating the Tsuen Wan Advisory Committee (he says "Board", but the context indicates the Committee), in response to the Governor's queries as to what might be done about increasing non-indigenous representation in public affairs. The memoir also sheds light on how the transition to elected Boards came about. Sir David continues: "A small group of officials, myself included, had met privately with the Chief Secretary, Sir Jack Cater, and recommended adding elected representatives to the boards. This recommendation, too, was accepted by the Governor and Executive Council": Akers-Jones, pp. 114–115.

9.   *Hansard* 1977–78, pp. 214–215.

10. Hayes 1993.
11. One truly novel feature was the provision of private sector housing for middle income families. By early 1982, the 50,000 residents of around 10,000 new apartments, mostly thought to be owners, were among the 700,000 inhabitants of the new town. Government's 'home ownership' schemes accounted for another 2,000 flats housing 10,000 persons, to which would soon be added the commercial-residential developments above the Mass Transit Railway stations at Tsuen Wan, Kwai Hing and Kwai Fong, providing new apartments for yet another 30,000 persons upon completion.
12. Hayes 1993, chapter V. See the resumption, clearance and village removal figures at p. 81 and notes 12 and 13. The decision to extend the Mass Transit Railway had meant bringing forward the North Tsuen Wan development, thereby compressing seven years work into two (see *Ibid.*, pp. 80–81).
13. Described in Hayes 1993, chapter IX. Its efforts were greatly assisted by the availability of the several major sports complexes provided in the previous five years and the new Tsuen Wan Town Hall opened in 1980, and with the enthusiastic assistance of a newly-formed Recreation and Sports Service.
14. Development came much later on Ma Wan.
15. See Hayes 1993, pp. 13–15 for the traditional organization.
16. This was Yeung Kwok-sui of Yeung Uk Village, a literary graduate of the Qing Dynasty by examination, whose photograph is at Plate 35.
17. See e.g. chapter 4, note 20, chapter 6, note 17, and note 43 below.
18. ADR DCNT 1952–53, para. 44, and also 1955–56, para. 81.
19. Coates 1955, p. 45.
20. By 1980, it had 28 member associations. In 1979–80, North and West Kwai Chung formed their own Sports Associations. Meantime, the Tsing Yi Athletic Association, under indigenous leadership, had been registered in 1968.
21. Notably, the Tsuen Wan Public School and Ho Chuen-yiu Memorial College, established to commemorate the former rural committee leader and erstwhile chairman of the Heung Yee Kuk. Using traditional historical and cultural material, the Tsuen Wan schools were trainers in speech, song and drama performances and competitions, owing much to their dedicated and competent staffs.
22. Through the Education Department, a branch of the NT School Sports Association had been established in 1954, with new branches in North and South Kwai Chung in 1970. By early 1982, 114 schools were members of the three branch associations. Funding was by government subvention, subscriptions, and donations.
23. Copies of these brochures have been placed in the Hong Kong Collection at the University of Hong Kong's Main Library. See also HKPRO.
24. See the brochure prepared by TWRC for the inauguration of the Committee's 18th term of office bearers.
25. Besides the indigenous villagers, persons from various ethnic groups, congregated in Tsuen Wan Town and District since the War, had struggled to

build temples and arrange their own operas, sometimes in intense competition for vacant space. See Hayes 1996, chapter 7, which provides details on temple festivals and community rituals among indigenous villagers and newcomers alike.

26.   There was the same broad emphasis in the 110 outdoor presentations provided by the Cultural Services Department across the town and district that year, the first in which a regional office had been established for the NT.

Yet there had been some casualties. In the city, trying to locate the professional story-tellers who were once so popular, Bertha Hensman found that by the autumn of 1968, it seemed they had disappeared from the night markets and seasonal fairs of Hong Kong and Kowloon: see her *More Hong Kong Tale-Spinners*, pp. xxxi–xxxii. Nor, a little earlier, could she find one "in village after village in the New Territories". See Hensman and Mack, p. vii. Traditional entertainment in the old-style teahouses would go the same way in the next decade. See JHKBRAS 14 (1974), pp. 218–220.

27.   See Hayes 1996, pp. 169–170.

28.   In every part of the NT, the District Office was the place to which local leaders could take their public schemes and personal aspirations: the two being often closely connected. The District Office and the headquarters office of the District Administration were also the conduit through which honours flowed twice yearly in the Honours Lists issued on New Year's Day and on the Queen's Birthday.

29.   Entertainment was provided for children, the elderly, the handicapped and so on, at such times as the lunar new year and other major Chinese festivals, on the Queen's Birthday (a public holiday in colonial Hong Kong), during the month-long government-promoted Summer Youth Programmes, and for events promoting the various other government-led community campaigns introduced everywhere in the 1970s. See Hayes 1993, pp. 130–135.

30.   See Hayes 1993, p. 128, for these two major events.

31.   Here, the political role of the District Office as the principal liaison and political information link with the community provided it with the reason for making contacts across the spectrum.

32.   The other three were chaired by officials, including the Finance sub-committee.

33.   The factors behind this whole-hearted support are listed in chapter 12, pp. 164–165. An organization chart of the Board and Committee structure, and of the District Office, is given in Hayes 1980.

34.   See Hayes 1993, pp. 139–140, and the 1983 Tsuen Wan Arts Festival brochure, pp. 60 and 66.

35.   Fifth and Sixth Tsuen Wan Sports Festival brochures, 1984 and 1985. Copies in Special Collections, Main Library, University of Hong Kong.

36.   Indeed, the Board decided to combine sports and arts in a "Kwai Tsing Festival", in order to apply money and manpower to these other purposes, which included surveys and services. Information kindly provided by Paul Tang, a later District Officer, Kwai Tsing. Nonetheless, the Tsing Yi Rural

Committee maintained its long-established initiatives in the sporting and recreational fields.

37. The Chief Secretary, Sir Jack Cater, who with Lady Cater had attended the opening performance (by local groups) of the Third Tsuen Wan Arts Festival in January 1982, wrote afterwards to say how "very professional and enthusiastic" it had been, and how we all "must be (properly) very proud of what has happened in Tsuen Wan these past few years", adding that he knew it had been "far from easy". From a personal letter dated 31 January 1982.

38. They did not care to stand for election, especially when numerical odds rendered their success unlikely. The difference was remarked by a younger colleague who, after serving as an Assistant District Officer in Yuen Long, was posted to a City District as City District Officer. There, he told me, "It was them and us. It was not possible for us to be friends, as was the case with rural leaders in the NT".

39. When Secretary for the New Territories in 1974–1985, Sir David Akers-Jones frequently pointed out this growing problem to leading NT persons, and asked his District Officers to encourage the younger generation to spare time from their professional and commercial careers in order to continue in their fathers' footsteps. Some did.

40. As in Tsuen Wan, successful community-building in each place was largely owing to the strong local identity and ingrained sense of public service shown by the indigenous community, providing the indispensable platform on which others could build.

41. Akers-Jones, p. 35 *seq*, especially at pp. 43–46.

42. See ADR DCNT 1969–70, and ADR DCNT 1970–71, paras. 44 and 54 respectively.

43. Its Kaifong had long earned golden opinions for its civic enterprise, even as far back as the 1910s: see HKAR 1911, p. I 15, "a notable centre of progress"; 1913, p. I 11; and 1914, p. I 9. It was certainly a lively place when I was District Officer 1957–62, under the genial and capable leadership of the late Chow Li-ping, MBE, JP (Plate 36), with his flair for attracting outside help with his various community projects. These included building several fishermen's villages on land, initially for re-housing families who had lost their house-boats in Typhoon Mary in 1960.

44. ADR DCNT 1970–71, para. 55.

45. Brochures of this kind constitute an invaluable record, as well as providing eloquent testimony to the vibrant local spirit and capable leadership. A copy has been placed in the HKPRO.

46. ADR DCNT 1963–64, para. 190. A carnival 'in celebration of the development of Tsuen Wan' was held in December 1970: see ADR DCNT 1970–71, para. 159.

47. See the detailed account of the township of Shek Wu Hui given by Michael Palmer in his article at pp. 70–106 in Baker and Feuchtwang (eds.) 1991. Palmer notes how the leadership was taken by a technical outsider instead of

by the major Liao lineage of nearby Sheung Shui, but this person, Hon. Cheung Yan-lung, CBE, JP, was from a nearby cross-border lineage with many links to the NT, and in this wider sense was to be regarded as an indigenous inhabitant of the region.

48. From a talk given on 27 June 1981. See Peninsula Jaycees. On the same occasion, I had stressed that "the worth of the old society lay in two things: in being self-reliant and self-supporting; and in carrying on and transmitting its own cultural tradition", within the great cultural heritage of the Chinese people.

Chapter 10   Village Communities in Change

1. It took in the present Islands, Tsuen Wan, Kwai-Tsing and Sai Kung districts.
2. ADR DONT 1947–1948, para. 2. Sequence inverted.
3. *Ibid*, para.11. This would have been so among their ordinary residents, but their leaders were probably more conscious of the unity of the NT, at least as expressed in terms of their common material interests.
4. Lots 365 and 510 in DD 215. The redemption reference cited by the widow was to "Reg. Vol 207, Fol. 35 and 36". See, too, Barrow in HKAR 1937, p. J 5.
5. A paragraph in a postwar report is fairly typical. A new Stamp (Amendment) Ordinance 1948 required the extension of stamp duty to various transactions in the NT. Changes were made in the NT regulations on the subject, but "Care was, of course, taken to exclude transactions to which the humble countrymen would normally be the parties." ADR DCNT 1948–49, para. 39.
6. In my own case, to utilize the DO's name to lend authority to their own decisions. See the example from the Shek Pik village removal cited in Hayes 1996, pp. 53–54.
7. Paul K. C. Tsui's hand-written reports on villages on Lantau and Lamma islands are now deposited with the HKPRO. They may have been connected with the surveys mentioned in chapter 6, p. 72.
8. Basel Mission Archives, Document A — 1.2 Nr. 44, Half-yearly Report of the Missionary Rev. Winnes, from 1 January to 1 July 1850. I am indebted to Dr. Patrick Hase for this paper, in translation.
9. At the hamlet of Tai Lam Wu, near the large village of Ho Chung, I found in late 1957 that the 49 persons in residence had sufficient drinking water but walked 20 minutes to the source to fetch it. In one of the Sai Kung hill villages (Ping Tun) they were carrying water from the nearest stream, 400 feet away; and in another (Sheung Yeung) had to fetch water from a nearby settlement (same lineage) when their well was dry. There was no use deepening it or digging another, and 1,500 feet of piping would be needed to bring a supply from the nearest stream. *Notebooks.*
10. At the same time, we must not overlook the utility of the equipment in use in village homes for boiling water, cooking pig food, or (say) preparing and cooking the delicacies associated with the new year and other festivals. It was economical, and well suited to the tasks in hand.

11. Sterickers, text for Photographs 66, 67 and 89, at pp. 147, 149 and 156. The conservatism they describe was a common condition among rural Chinese of that time, nation-wide. See Cochran and Hsieh, Part III, "Superstitions" and Popular Religion, in pp.139–183. In this connection, at Pui O on Lantau, the elders told me that before the Second World War, no one would have dreamed of carrying out any important activity without first consulting that year's almanac; or, when erecting any building or opening land for cultivation, without engaging a Taoist priest to perform the old rituals deemed essential for the protection of individuals and of the community at large. The lay persons who carried out these rituals and also wrote protective charms, were known generally as *nam mo lo*. Usually ordinary villagers, they were in possession of manuscript books, handed on by a teacher, which enabled them to provide these services and make a good living thereby. There was one such at Ham Tin, Pui O in the 1950s, but when he died the family promptly burned all his books!

12. See e.g. Hayes 1983, chapters 10–13, and appendices 1, 4 and 5; and also Hayes 1996, chapter 2.

13. For a vignette of other parts of the Southern District at that time, see my chapter in Hase and Sinn 1995, pp. 19–25, also taken from my Notebooks.

14. See chapter 7, pp. 90–91.

15. Within a few years, Barnett's successor would write (ADR DCNT 1959–60, para. 4) that "with more contacts with the urban ways of life" the villagers had suddenly become aware of the various facilities being offered through and by the District Offices. "Throughout the year requests came forward in great numbers for these services and, in general, the better the service given, the greater became the demand". It "was still not always possible to keep pace with the volume of public business".

16. Introduction to Maunder 1969. See also Pryor, p. 111.

17. Factors of which I was unaware were also responsible, as I found when I visited Cyril Wood, the then general manager, at the company's head office at Argyle Street, Kowloon in 1958 or 1959 to press for a speedier supply to the mainland parts of the Southern District. After I had explained how my visit had been prompted by the recurring grumbles of the rural committees of Sai Kung and Clearwater Bay peninsula, Mr. Wood leaned over his desk and said, with a twinkle in his eye, "Well, you can help, and so can they!" I was asked to tell the leaders of the larger villages near Sai Kung Market (in particular) that, for as long as the company's newly laid copper cables were being stolen, by person or persons unknown, the company would be unable to continue with its plans to extend supply. In those days, when the traditional social organization still worked, they would know where to look and what to do — and, as an "old China hand", Mr. Wood knew this.

18. ADR DCNT 1965–66, para. 20. By the time of the last published departmental report for 1972–73, this figure had increased to 650 (para.33). All areas of the NT save Lamma (served by Hong Kong Electric) and Cheung Chau (which

had its own electric company) were included in this scheme. The District Officers were involved in determining priorities in line with the Company's own proposals. These, naturally, took various technical and practical considerations into account, and our land staff had to assist, also sorting out any difficulties with villagers that might occur in the course of laying cables and providing installations.

19.   See, e.g., ADR DCNT 1955–56, para. 87, for conciliatory action taken when soldiers "unwittingly dug up an ancestral grave at Pat Heung". See also Brian Wilson, pp. 39–41, 47–48, and 72–74 for interface with the military. A copy of one of Commissioner Barnett's periodic talks to assembled officers of the NT units has been placed in HKPRO. For one of the rare accounts of military life in Hong Kong in those years, see Crook, in this case a good one.

20.   No fewer than 14 men were employed from Mang Kung Uk village in the Army's ammunition depot at Clearwater Bay Road, but lost their jobs when it closed: *Notebooks.*

21.   Bray 2001.2, pp. 170–171.

22.   Crook describes one of the regular Village Penetration Patrols carried out for years by military units in liaison with the District Offices, pp. 146–158. Similar to police patrols of the same kind, in both, medical assistance was provided and other needs reported. For the firing range, see Ordinance No. 7 of 1950.

23.   See Hayes 1996, chapter 2.

24.   For a detailed account of the Pui O sub-district, see Hayes 1977.1, pp. 129–150.

25.   See chapter 5.

26.   Elaborated in note 11.

27.   Like the villagers of Shek Pik described in Hayes 2001.2, pp. 42–45, 47–53, their recent history had been disastrous. The drastic steps taken to end epidemics and secure what they hoped would be safer lives, were still fresh in their minds. See Hayes 1983, pp. 153–155.

28.   During those years, I had had plenty of experience in handling old-fashioned people, including their leaders. Pondering on whether my Chinese colleagues found them any different from me, a Westerner, I told some of them that I had either experienced a bland, uncomplaining, invariably polite response or — at the other extreme — an angry, rude and, at least for a time, completely unreasonable approach. I was advised that this was the common experience. They expected government officials to show respect and sincerity in their dealings with them. Once they had become aggrieved and taken up a resentful, stubborn attitude, it took a great deal of time and trouble to bring them back to normal.

29.   Wan On's family along with the rest. The bags of delicious homegrown rice which his daughter had brought to our home from time to time became, alas, a thing of the past. See chapter 6, p. 78.

30.   There was generally very little hiring of labour in the Pui O villages up to the 1950s, save for the stakenet fisheries which needed men for the long hours of watching and operating the nets, and as food and lodging was supplied on

site, wages had been low. For the stakenet, positioned on a high place overlooking the sea, see Hayes 1986–87.

31. The Tsuen Wan elders particularly objected to police action over the lunar new year period, which they considered as being a "closed season" for raids. In Yuen Long, police raids over this period could lead to scuffles between villagers and police, as reported now and then in the media.

32. A playing field had been constructed with help from the British Army, and playgrounds had been provided with materials supplied by the District Office. The final ADRs DCNT in 1960–73 provide other instances of this cooperation in rural areas like Pui O. See also Akers-Jones, p. 42.

33. It would no longer be possible for a senior European officer to box the ears of young constables, as I saw being done at Shek Pik in 1957–58, however richly deserved. They had allowed an opium divan to be operated in the labourers' lines.

34. See Hayes 1986–87.

35. SP 1903, p. 348a.

36. *Notebooks*. In 1969, on another visit to the old village, a mere handful were left, with only one house occupied. Many of the other houses were locked, indicative of some lingering connection with families living elsewhere, but the doors of the remainder were open to the elements and their interiors in decay. Beyond the village, there were some abandoned rice fields.

37. See da Silva, p. 45.

38. *Notebooks*.

39. Hayes 1977.1, p. 39.

40. From a note made at the time.

41. John A. Brim, *The Modernization of Local Systems in the New Territories of Hong Kong*, Unpublished doctoral thesis, Stanford University, 1970. An anthropologist, Brim lived in his village for sixteen months. My copy was given to me by the author before he left Hong Kong.

42. However, he took care to place them in the wider context of a survey of 38 other villages in the Yuen Long sub-district, including five in a remote valley which at that time had no motor access.

43. This account is the fullest I have yet seen. Of particular interest is the detailed information given on the rosters — dating in their then form from 1944, but reorganized in 1946 and 1954 — which were drawn up by the person managing the village treasury. At Pui O (to provide additional information) all villages of the sub-district used to join together to perform rituals of supplication and thanksgiving (*tso san* and *waan san*) at the beginning and end of each lunar year, as described in Hayes 1977.1, pp. 148–9. Participation was already diminished by the 1970s, and the series had ended there by the late 1980s.

44. Affrays were still occurring postwar. See K. M. A. Barnett's graphic and illuminating tale in ADR DCNT 1955–56, paras. 77–79, with other cases of the kind mentioned at paras. 97 and 43 in the reports for 1957–58 and 1958–59 respectively.

45.   This reaction was not unusual. It was commonly said, in the 1950s and 1960s, that if you knocked over one of the Chiu Chau coolies employed at the waterfront godowns in the Western District of Hong Kong Island, you had better abandon your car and quickly exit, lest you be attacked by the man's fellow-workers.

46.   However, it should be noted here that care was still being taken to ensure that ritual protection was available for all the ancestral halls being re-provisioned as part of the village removals and resitings described in chapter 8. When (e.g.) the Fu ancestral hall at Sham Tseng New Village was being built in 1976, the geomancer whose advice had been sought advised that the ground should be opened (site formation) at 5 a.m. on 2nd January, that the foundation wall line-up should take place at a specified time on the 9th, and likewise the doorway on the 18th. These, he said, were the last lucky days for undertaking these important stages of the work until sometime in the following lunar year. Later, I recall, the ancestral tablets had to be brought down from the old building in the abandoned Tsing Fai Tong village in the hills above at or around midnight, in order to install them with due ceremony on the altar in the new. Such consultations were paid for from public funds, being accepted as necessary elements in the village resitings.

47.   *Gazetteer*, p. 202.

48.   See Goodrich in JHKBRAS 1966, pp. 152–157.

49.   Note: visit made in late March 1971.

50.   The college became part of The Chinese University of Hong Kong in 1967.

51.   It is the subject of the chapter by Rance P. L. Lee, in King and Lee (eds.) 1981.

52.   *Ibid.*, p. 108. Immigration is discussed in pp. 110–114.

53.   But, most significantly, despite the numbers leaving the village, "there were very few cases where entire family [*sic*] moved away from the village. Most often, some members of a family emigrated while others remained". "Outmigration" is discussed at Lee, pp. 114–116.

54.   "According to our major informants, relatively self-sufficient farming and population immobility were two of the marked characteristics of the village about twenty-odd years ago". *Ibid.*, p. 107.

55.   See pp. 116–119 for economic aspects, particularly for clan members and their families; stated to be Tangs, *Gazetteer*, p. 174.

56.   Prompted also by the availability of industrial sites and labour, it had led some of the outsiders to bring in capital and establish small factories, increasing to "nearly 20 in recent years" (p. 118).

57.   Professor Maurice Freedman's report on Social Research in the New Territories, prepared for the District Administration in 1963 (Freedman 1976) seems to confirm this. See his paras. 8, 72–101, and especially after para. 84.

58.   In Yau Yuk-kuen's apt analogy from a Hakka expression.

59.   See chapter 6, pp. 75–77.

60.   Out with the bridal chair went some long-practised associated rituals, like the instructions given by a geomancer on the timings for the bride's entering and

leaving her chair, and for the different places in the her new home, especially the kitchen, where she was required to perform worshipping rituals.

61. See Hayes 1984.1, p. 51.

62. The signboard of an old shop in Sai Kung Market, copied in 1957, indicates the range and type of goods provided there in prewar times: "Chinese rice wine, rice, [dried] grass, marriage items from Suzhou and Hangzhou, cloth, preserved fruits, paper goods, nets and dyes [used in fishing] oil, firewood, bamboo goods, salt: sole agent".

63. See Hayes 1984.1, also at p. 51.

64. They were operated part-time by local persons, usually men, as I was told, "the women were illiterate, and couldn't count or keep simple accounts".

65. Besides individual family crockery, there were (and are, to this day in the villages) communal stocks of bowls, plates and other basic items used at festivals, weddings, or any other occasion on which large gatherings were usual.

66. E.g. Hayes 1996, p. 254.

67. Chapter 1, note 14. Copies of forestry licenses now in HKPRO.

68. The classic study is Watson 1975.

69. *Gazetteer*, p. 183.

70. All agricultural land had been sold to a developer on (the reported) condition that the village houses would be rebuilt for the sellers. However, due to adverse financial circumstances, the original agreement between the two parties was altered by mutual consent. The houses were restored instead of being re-built, and the right to use them was passed to the contractor since the developer could not pay the cost in full. See pp. 9–10 of Sydney Cheung, 2005.

Chapter 11 Identities

1. The strikes of the 1920s, and their economic impact on the Colony, are well-documented between pp. 160–174 of Faure 1997.

2. It should also take in the Opium War and the later War with Britain (and France), especially in Guangdong, where much of the fighting had taken place, including the Hong Kong area. Canton itself had been under foreign occupation from 1858 to 1861: see e.g. Fisher, 1863.

3. In 1881 alone, Rev. Henry traveled on mission work by boat 2540 miles, by chair 80 miles, and on foot 670 miles, and visited 280 different towns and villages: Bird (Mrs. Bishop), p. 73n.

4. Henry, pp. 32–33. The celebrated Welsh missionary-scholar, Griffith John (1831–1912) of the London Missionary Society stated that Western attempts to teach and innovate were regarded by most officials and literati as an insult to China and its most cherished tenets, and while the people at large were peaceable at heart, they could be easily stirred up from above. See pp. 254–257 of the excellent biography by R. Wardlaw Thompson (London, Religious Tract Society, 1906). John's assessment was made in 1870, but his biographer

commented (p. 251) that "despite great and remarkable changes of late, yet the bulk of the Chinese people, literati and commoners, still answer to Mr. John's description of them". See also chapter VI, "Work amongst Officials and Scholars, 1881–4", of the eminent Protestant scholar-missionary educator, Dr. Timothy Richard's *Forty-Five Years in China* (London, T. Fisher Unwin, 1916) with its most illuminating insights into the mind and outlook of the Chinese government of the day.

5. "Here have been developed the greatest prejudices against the foreigner," wrote Rev. I. W. Wiley in 1879: Wiley, pp. 320–421.

6. See chapter IV, "Wesleyan Methodist Missions in South China" by Rev. S. G. Tope, then with twenty-eight years' service in Guangdong, in Cornaby.

7. Jung-fang Tsai has drawn attention to the gap between the Chinese elites of Hong Kong and the labouring class at this time: Tsai, pp. 152–153 and 266–268. There was major unrest and street violence in the city between November 1911 and March 1912, with emergency powers under the Peace Preservation Ordinance invoked by proclamation, and an increase in the garrison. See Miners 1982, pp. 280–281.

8. Airlie, p. 58.

9. Graves, p. 304. Dr. Bard's *Voices from the Past* (HKUP, 2002) is useful.

10. Morse 1918, chapters IV and V. See also Asakawa, pp. 102–103, 108–109, 125–129, 145–146. for illuminating glimpses of the highly aggressive words and actions of the time.

11. Dom Pierre-Celestin Lou Tseng-Tsiang, p. 9.

12. A well-informed British traveller and publicist of the day had observed acidly of the foreign concessions in the Treaty Ports that there, "the foreigner is on his own ground; it is, if any one, the native who appears ridiculous and out of place: Colquhoun 1900, pp. 162–164. The same might have been said, with even more force, of contemporary Hong Kong.

13. Endacott and Birch, p. 320. Sent to the NT to deal with the 1899 disturbances, Captain Berger of the Hong Kong Regiment criticized the "basely material life one continuously sees in Hong Kong", and indirectly the insular attitudes common among its European male population, stating that it was "a treat to find oneself among purely natural people where … a man would not actually die if he had forgotten to put a flower in his coat, or to curl the ends of his moustache". Cited in Welsh, p. 327.

14. Norman, pp. 21–22. Also McMillan, p. 105.

15. From Dr. Po-king Choi, The Chinese University of Hong Kong.

16. E.g., Cronin, chapter 4. That large numbers had gone from Tsuen Wan and Sha Tau Kok (for instance) is attested by the long lists of names of native overseas subscribers to temple repairs: see *Inscriptions*, Vol. 1, items 92 and 104, dated in 1894 and 1900 respectively.

17. Exploited from its earliest days as a port: see Hayes 1993, p. 7.

18. See chapter 1, p. 8, together with chapter 2, p. 25, and chapter 4, p. 45.

19. Copy of relevant portion, in English translation only, passed to the HKPRO.

20. An anti-Manchu pamphlet of 1908, and a poem composed by a local girl in her bridal chair after finding that her elder brother, who had been away, had already cut his queue, are narrated in Hase 1989, pp. 382–384. See generally Ng Lun Ngai-ha and others (editors) 1988.

21. *Inscriptions*, Vol. 2, pp. 431–434. Another example is given in Headland, pp. 41–42, citing a revolutionary proclamation dated in "the 8th moon of the 4609th year of the Hwang Dynasty". I have also seen land deeds from Guangdong dated in the same way, the latest acquisition bearing the equivalent dating of 21 November 1911. For the Yellow Emperor, see Dun J. Li, p. 34.

22. *Schofield Letters*, 14 June 1962.

23. For Singapore, see Turnbull, p. 112. In 1913, the Chinese National Assembly passed a bill to abolish the queue: E. T. Williams, pp. 564–565.

24. Sayer, p. 112. See also HKAR 1911, p. I 5. The turbulence in urban Hong Kong in late 1911, after the Revolution spread to Canton, is part of the essential background to excitement and heightened national feeling in the New Territory. See note 7. This period in New Territories' history is badly under-researched at present, for which Hase 1996 provides the base.

25. Somehow, "the passionate hatred which the Chinese openly showed at this time" of tumult in China, although closely, and interestingly, analysed by a perceptive contemporary American career diplomat (see Lensen, pp. 164–165) does not seem to have altered the outlook of most Hong Kong expatriates.

26. See Gimson's unpublished manuscript quoted in Endacott and Birch, pp. 348, 360–361.

27. L. Gibbs, at pp. 123–124. For a less striking example, but evocative of the superior position and attitudes of Britons blessed with a cook or "market-boy", sent to buy your fish for the table in prewar days, see Herklots, *Common Marine Food-Fishes*, published in the late 1930s, pp. 5–6.

    "Sinologues" (*sic*) must have been rare birds in Hong Kong in those years. N. L. Smith, later Colonial Secretary, author of *Elementary Cantonese* (1920) asked in his preface, "Why are about nine-tenths of the British population of Hong Kong content to live without even a working knowledge of the language of their adopted country, and to remain in a world bounded by 'boys', compradores, and pidgin English?" Exemplified in Bella Sidney Woolf's otherwise charming book, *Chips from China* (1930). She was Lady Southorn, wife of the Colonial Secretary. See also my paper "East and West in Hong Kong...", in Sinn (Ed.) 1990.

28. Information from the late George Maitland Scott of Sydney, born in Kowloon in 1926. It was still to be found among some expatriates after the War: see Hayes, *op.cit.*, Addendum, pp. 18–20.

29. See the revealing passage in HK 1946, p. 6, "Greater Responsibilities for Local Staff".

30. *Hamilton Letters*, 1 August 1958.

31. It is worth noting that benevolence would be appreciated, regardless of its foreign source, because it met the age-old Chinese expectation that rulers would

show benevolence or ultimately lose the "Mandate of Heaven". See Dillon, p. 209.

32. Chapter 5, p. 64 *seq.*

33. Liu Shuyong provides an interesting account of the considerable fund-raising activities by Communist organizations in Hong Kong between 1937–1941 (pp. 99–107) together with the extensive cultural activities carried out from there by literary figures, artists, and film-makers who had escaped from the Mainland and were subsequently rescued after the Japanese capture of the Colony (pp.147–149, and 107–108, respectively).

34. These patriotic feelings seem to have been shared by the remaining urban population. Upon the fleet's arrival, "Immediately the life of the harbour and the town began to revive. Chinese firecrackers were heard instead of rifle shots. Union Jacks were displayed that had been concealed throughout the Occupation. But on every junk and on nearly every house there flew the flag of China": Donnison, p. 202.

35. It was probably for this and other reasons that, from the 1950s, the British government sent a succession of "Political Advisors" from its foreign and diplomatic service to assist the Hong Kong governors in handling local matters liable to cause difficulties with China. The land and sea borders of the Colony were always politically sensitive areas, as was the so-called Kowloon Walled City, retained in Chinese sovereignty under the Convention but occupied by the British soon after: Liu Shuyong, pp. 69–74, with p. 112 above.

36. There had been the fear, after 1949, that Communist propaganda, conveyed through such organizations, might unsettle rural communities, as expressed by some contributors to the debate on whether some kind of land reform was needed in the NT: see chapter 6, p. 72. See also pp. 155–156.

37. The Kuk had reacted quickly to the emergency and on 25 May 1967 addressed a firm declaration to the Governor pledging its loyal support for the maintenance of law and order, among the first of over 600 local community organizations in the Colony to do so. See also HK 1967, p. 11.

38. See pp. 153–154.

39. Cooper, at pp. 135, 139, 143–144 and 145. In the course of reporting on the lack of progress with effecting a village removal at Kau Wa Keng in the late 1970s, owing to furious internal disputes over lineage trust properties, the senior land officer concerned wrote, under the sub-head, "Political Factors": "As if the above were not enough, reliable information shows that about 80% of the villagers are pro-leftist, including the Village Representative, and their customary behaviour and attitude has and will make things more difficult". From a copy made at the time.

40. ADR DCNT 1967–68, para. 8.

41. ADR DCNT 1967–68, para. 7.

42. It was indicative of the situation that one of these Associations was established in Tsuen Wan, where the divided loyalties brought about by business and kinship ties (or in some cases from personal inclination) was inhibiting the

work of the Tsuen Wan Rural Committee — and perhaps equally indicative of the Committee's regained position of authority and influence that this was the only PSAA in the NT to have been disbanded thereafter.

43. The local leader responsible was an able, likeable, charismatic man, and well-known to me. His family background and personal history (under the disguised name of Chan Yat-Kuan) is given by Fred Blake at pp. 121–126, within chapter 6. As Blake says, he gave "balanced and competent leadership" to Sai Kung. Unlike some of his supporters, he evaded arrest and detention in 1967: see Hayes 1996, pp. 113–114.

44. Blake gives an account of the Sai Kung PSAA at pp. 70–75 of a later article in Aijmer 1984. It is clear that, as in Sai Kung, local political rivalries and affiliations would determine the composition of PSAAs, and whether they were necessary.

45. Blake, pp. 129–130. In 1974, when open elections were resumed, opposition to him, partly owing to his support for the government line in two contentious local issues led to his replacement by a rival faction leader: *Ibid.*, pp. 130–131. The names used in Blake's study for local leaders are fictitious, but the facts are not. Background events during the Japanese Occupation and after, contributing to, and explaining the local situation are described elsewhere in this most enlightening and useful account of a rural community and market town in change. Blake later provided a more detailed account of the 1967 situation in Sai Kung in the article listed in note 44.

46. There is revealing "ground level" material on this period in another part of the NT in the last chapter of Aijmer 1986, between pp. 264–278. Nor should the attitudes of the young be overlooked in any future study of the period. At the Ting Kok Ming Tak Public School in Tai Po District, students came to class wearing Mao badges, and the school principal, who tried to stop this was severely "criticized": see Sweeting 2004, pp. 254–255.

47. Griffiths, pp. 107–108.

48. It is pertinent here to note that, perturbed by the Disturbances, the authorities set out to improve government and people communication, especially in the city. Chinese was to have parity with English in official correspondence, and city district offices in the NT style were established across the urban area. See Hayes 1996, pp. 197–198, 114–119 respectively.

49. See my note in JHKBRAS 10 (1970), pp. 196–197. Also HK 1967, p. 11.

50. From notes taken during a talk given in 1967.

51. It represented the covert political side of the NCNA's activities.

52. Strauch, p. 198.

53. Communist aid in emergencies could be prompt and efficient. See the example from Tsuen Wan in 1976 described in Hayes 1996, p. 212.

54. Aijmer, notes from, 1967

55. The head of the NT Office, located in Shatin, paid a courtesy call when I was RSNT between 1985–87; senior staff of CNTA all received invitations to attend either the NT liaison office's or the NCNA's celebration of the National Day;

and when I retired, the NT office hosted a farewell lunch. For NCNA in Hong Kong, see Ching Cheong's essay in Ngaw Mee-kau and Li Si-ming (eds.), *The Other Hong Kong Report 1996* (Chinese University Press, 1996), specifically at pp. 115–119.

56.   As earlier among trade unions: see Eugene Cooper's article in JHKBRAS 13 (1973), pp. 83–100.

57.   The property was largely surrounded by high rise residential estates. In order to enhance their environment, I had tried to get the managers either to plant out the hill (one of the conditions required under the 1927 sale agreement, but only partially carried out) or agree to let us do it for them.

58.   See Hayes 1996, pp. 184–186 for the grave and its hill.

59.   For the historical facts which gave rise to this incident, see Faure 1984b, pp. 24–42, and particularly at pp. 24 and 28 for the To Hing Tong which took out the court summons. I have no information about later developments elsewhere in the NT with regard to the extensive properties held by this particular trust, but am sure the Hong Kong managers' worst fears were being realized.

60.   Signed in Beijing on 19 December 1984. The documents which include the clauses protecting its rights are conveniently included as appendices in Liu Shuyong, pp. 205–268, including related papers.

61.   Adopted by the National People's Congress on 4 April 1990.

Chapter 12 Convergence and Divergence

1.   Birch 1982.

2.   Comparing the Hong Kong and Singapore economies with other regional transformations, David Reynolds states that the two former were characterized by "catch-up" industrial growth, distinctive from the rest of Asia. "Because of their miniscule agricultural sectors, growth resulted from a shift of labor and capital from commerce to manufacturing, not from farming to industry. Second, growth was based unequivocally on free trade, with none of the barriers against imports of goods and capital apparent elsewhere in East Asia". By the 1980s, both had become major financial centers. Their success — measured by high growth rates and income levels at least double those of [South] Korea and Taiwan — was noted the world over. *Ibid.*, pp. 424–425. Hong Kong was also "an administrative state par excellence, in which officials ruled with minimal political interference." Reynolds, pp. 426–427.

3.   *Hong Kong: The Facts* as at 1 July 1997.

4.   Appendix G to Orme lists 105 $^1/_2$ (*sic*) Hakka to 117 Punti.

5.   This case is perhaps abnormal, in that farming had stopped, there was no road into the area, and entry was from the Closed Border Area — though these places were still quite lively.

6.   Visit Note for 19 October 1987.

7.   Visit to the Hau Villages, 16 October 1987.

8.   See Baker 1997, pp. 35–36 for Chinese restaurants and NT men and their families in the UK.

9. The reorganization is described in ADR DCNT 1959–60, chapters V and XVI, and later ADRs for the gradual undertaking of these extra duties. With increased numbers and proliferation of grades and ranks, internal sensitivities developed between them. See David Ip, pp. 39–42, with charts which aptly cover this situation.

10. See Hayes 1993, pp. 136–137.

11. See Hase 1980 and Hayes 1996, pp. 245–248.

12. The change was reported tersely, and without explanation, in HK 1982, p. 248: "In November [1981] the administration was restructured to become the City and New Territories Administration with a regional secretary appointed for New Territories affairs [the post I held 1985–1987]." Its head was retitled "Secretary for District Administration".

13. HK 1983, pp. 118–119.

14. HK 1986, p. 21.

15. HK 1986 and HK 1987 pp. 19–20 and 22–23 respectively.

16. HK 1994, p. 30.

17. A few years later, they did not even receive an index listing in e.g. HK 1996, nor in *The Other Hong Kong Report 1996*, nor *Colony to SAR*, two solid academic publications from The Chinese University of Hong Kong Press.

18. In a submission entitled "Note for the District Officers" Meeting on Saturday, 14 November 1981, I had expressed strong misgivings to the complete change-over, giving reasons and suggesting various possible alternatives to mitigate what I felt were its likely adverse impacts. The fact that the meeting was to be held on a Saturday, and that my submission was stated at the foot to be "in haste", indicates that the change was sprung upon us at short notice. The decision had, of course, been taken in high places, as a matter of major policy change, and we were simply being "advised". A copy of my paper has been placed in the HKPRO, together with other documents from the time

19. Ip, p. 45, describes the general concern felt in the Kuk at the "downfall" of the Administration. Meantime, battles over resumptions and compensation would continue, and since political responsibility still rested with the CNTA, those DOs serving in development areas had to do their best. In 1985, there were problems with three major projects: at Sai Kung in connection with a large new waterworks installation; at Lok Ma Chau in the frontier area for new cross-border facilities ; and for the Light Rail Transit between Tuen Mun and Tuen Mun. See Hayes 1996, pp. 259–269 for these and other problems.

20. Peplow, p. 88.

21. With the exception of the *ex officio* seats for rural committee chairmen: HK 1993, p. 18. The District Boards were retitled "District Councils" in 2000 (HK 2001, p. 10).

22. See Steve Tsang, pp. 255–267.

23. How this came about is described, from the government side, in Bray 2001.2, pp. 97–98, 99–101.

24. In Tsuen Wan, by and large, we were working so closely and amicably with the rural committees that there was no need for appeals to or intervention by the Kuk.

25. See Hayes 1996, pp. 269–270.

26. Unpublished M.Soc.Sc dissertation, 1988.

27. *Ibid*, pp. 69–71.

28. *Ibid*, pp. 71–83.

29. *Ibid*, pp. 84–67.

30. *Ibid*, pp. 118–122.

31. *Ibid*, pp. 108, with 122–129. The new Regional Council would elect one of its Members to the Legislative Council. Thereby, the Kuk's chairman, one of its number, would obtain a seat, but not as the Kuk's own elected representative, which was then the goal.

32. Published separately, but included with the main volume marking the event, as at the following note.

33. There is a good deal of information on the contents of this paragraph in the periodic bulletins published by the Kuk in Chinese during this period. A few issues from the 1980s have been placed in the HKPRO, together with some of the notices placed in the English and Chinese language press on the occasion of "New Territories Day": e.g. the illuminating "Messages on The New Territories Day 1982", in the *Hongkong Standard*, 22 October 1982. This event, originated in 1961, had lapsed until revived in 1981, presumably with the intention of bringing the Kuk and its policies and aspirations to wider public notice. There is also the substantial commemorative volume, in Chinese only, issued on the 60th anniversary celebrations held on 28 October 1986, of which a copy is now also with the HKPRO.

34. In p. 86. He has also provided some interesting speculation on the future, as of 1988, at pp. 145–148.

35. Allen, p. 132.

36. As early as the 1960s, Baker 1968, p. 117, could point to a village councillor from Sheung Shui "who was away on a world cruise for most of my time in the village, and another is to do likewise in 1967". The majority of the Village Council members were practising businessmen. "Wealth has become the dominant factor, its possession at once enabling a man to make his way in a highly materialistic society and proving to others his ability to do so."

37. Whereas there had been 95 candidates for the first District Board elections in 1982, there were only 49 in 1988: see Ip, p. 113. Also indicative of the general decline was the gradual reduction in the invitations sent to Village Representatives to attend District Administration functions, consequent upon the larger numbers of invitees required after the introduction of district boards and the like. See Hayes 2001.2, p. 38 with notes 35–38 on p. 99.

38. See chapter 6, p. 80 *seq.*

39. As explained by Dr. Po-king Choi in 1990, instead of being part of the Chinese mainstream cultural tradition as hitherto, Hong Kong had developed, and

exported, its own distinctive genre. Hong Kong had become "the largest centre of Chinese popular music world-wide", and also "the creative and production centre for popular songs, films, and TV programmes for Chinese communities worldwide". See Hayes 1993, p. 181: also Baker 1983 and 1993.

40. *Hansard* 1993–94, p. 240.

41. Cannon, p. 206.

42. Wang Gungwu 1980, p. 652. Also Wang 1991, p. 7.

43. Elizabeth L. Johnson, in Hayes 1993, p. 206, n43.

44. See Hayes 1993, pp. 179–182, and Baker 1983.

45. As explained in Hayes 1993, chapter IX, and Hayes 1996, chapter 11.

46. Clause 7 (2), 1984 edition, originally 13(1)–(3) of 1910.

47. What the Hong Kong Annual Report had been pleased to describe as "Chinese customary marriages, so-called Chinese modern marriages, and the ancient Chinese custom of concubinage". See HK 1966, p. 246, HK 1969, p. 217, and HK 1970, pp. 14 and 221. Also at note 67 below.

48. See note 17 on p. 182, and p. 133 of Hayes 1977.1

49. Ip, chapter 1, reflects the attitudes already prevalent by 1987–88, when it was written.

50. See chapter 8, pp. 108–110.

51. This change is described in chapter 8, p. 108, and came about mainly through the increasing shortage of land for exchange which dictated an immediate reduction in the exchange commitment.

52. In 1993, one legislative councillor (Hon. Martin Lee) recalled that "when I was small, people were still talking about 'country people' with 'feet covered with cow dung' and 'illiterate'. But today we see that the members of the Heung Yee Kuk are all tycoons in smart suits and travelling in Rolls Royces." I owe this quotation from *Hansard* 1993, p. 240, to Sally Engel Merry.

53. In the Privy Council. Record of Proceedings Winfat Enterprise (HK) Company Limited and the Attorney General, Appeal No. 76 of 1983. The issue at law was the use to which Old Schedule lots in agricultural status might be put.

54. See Patricia Tse in *SCMP*, 1 September 1990, and Victoria Finlay in *SCMP*, 13 October 1993. The curbing legislation mentioned by Tse became the Town Planning (Amendment Ordinance, 1991.

55. See e.g. the report of the prosecution of a village representative for taking "tea money" (actually $10,000) from a film company: *SCMP*, 25 April 1990. Fairly representative of urban attitudes was the comment made by a female friend who, after recounting how her husband had paid exorbitantly for a favoured piece of Crown hillside for his father's grave — yet another type of money-grubbing practised by some villagers and village representatives — had concluded with the observation, "Village people are like that!" Periodic ICAC arrests for alleged corruption continue, e.g. SCMP 23 November 2003.

56. Cf. the tone and wording of the preface to Ip.

57. On the authority of a former colleague and friend, a Chief Land Executive, who served in the Lands Department for many years after the change-over.

58. See Hayes 2001.2. p. 89.

59. NT (Land) Amendment Ordinance 1994. Hon. Martin Lee, who regarded the exclusion of females from succession as belonging only to the past, had advised that "outdated customs are a cultural burden. We must discard them without the slightest hesitation", and asked what reasons the members from the Heung Yee Kuk had for insisting on keeping them. *Hansard* 1993, p. 239–240.

60. For citations and references to media and other coverage of this and later issues, see Lee and Distefano's useful listing at pp. 83–96, 110–112.

61. The outcome was notable in other ways. First, the Administration's willingness to go along with legislators' wishes suggests that it now felt less constrained to support NT attitudes than in the past, and especially when public opinion inside and outside Legco was so overwhelmingly in favour of a change. Secondly, even the Chinese Government's Working Committee on the interim arrangements for governing Hong Kong after the hand-over (on which the Kuk was well represented) had decided to exclude it from its list of 25 new unacceptable laws to be repealed in 1997 — to the vexation of its leader, Lau Wong-fat, who had walked out of the meeting: Jamie Allen, pp. 132–133.

62. See also chapter 7, at p. 95 for the havoc caused by city youths at Tai Long Wan New Village on Lantau.

63. Visit Note, 29 September 1987. At Pui O, as mentioned in chapter 10, p. 141, Wan On and others were similarly frustrated.

64. For illuminating asides on European society, see chapters VII and VIII of Lethbridge, and especially at p. 200. Even today, a 70-year-old Chinese herbalist, living and working always in Kowloon, has told me that Kowloon people (*sc*, Chinese) were rougher and not so law-abiding as Hong Kong folk.

65. Chapter 8, p. 104.

66. Ref. LO 4/1951/82 dated 15 December 1986.

67. Presumably a review of the operation of the Intestates' Estates Ordinance, Cap. 73 of 1971 which had followed the important Marriage Reform Ordinance, Cap.78, enacted in 1970. For the impact of these changes on the customary law within the Hong Kong legal system, see D. J. Lewis, "A Requiem for Chinese Customary Law in Hong Kong", *International and Comparative Law Quarterly*, Vol. 32 (1983) pp. 347–379. The article focused more on the urban area than the New Territories, and did not address the continuing role of customary law there in regard to succession and title in land-related matters.

68. My reply to the Registrar General in CNTA/L/CON/26/16, dated 30 December 1986. Copies of this exchange of correspondence are now with HKPRO.

69. Letter dated 25 June 1990, with copy to the two Hon. Members from the New Territories, now in HKPRO. There was no response as far as I can recall. In this connection, see pp. 76–79 of Hayes 2001.2, in which I described the increasing difficulties besetting village representatives and other managers, after the transfer of the land authority to the new Lands Department and the establishment and development of the District Boards.

70. Kuan Hsin-chi and Lau Siu-kai 1981 suggested that rural leadership was in decline, and would have decayed completely without development and the government's manipulation of leadership to achieve its desired programmes. However, my field experience of leadership during development and in routine administration (plus my observation of the social, economic, religious and political aspects of their work inside the villages) is that it was generally effective, until the changing times and conditions of the later 1980s rendered their duties much more difficult to carry out. As with Allen Chun's projection of state manipulation and control through the village representative and reordered Heung Yee Kuk system of rural representation and liaison (see n92 on p. 223), I have to reserve my agreement until archival material becomes available and is closely scrutinized.

71. See the Annex to Hayes 1991. Also, Hayes 1989, pp. 461–462, for the part played by village leaders in customary law case work.

72. Disputes of this kind were less easy to resolve in major lineages, whose trust holdings were much larger, and therefore more valuable. See Palmer's illuminating summary of an important case in Sheung Shui, long drawn out, which (as he notes) brought up the more fundamental question of the place and organization of the trust itself in modern times, and of the many others like it in the northern NT, as discussed in an article in Baker and Feuchtwang, notably between pp. 93–103.

73. Custom apart, it must not be forgotten that the Chinese tradition was to esteem sons over daughters: as the old saying had it, *chung nam heng nui* (Cantonese), by no means dead even at present.

74. Selina Chan 1997. This interesting study is diminished to a degree by not being sufficiently clear on land details (family or trust property, sale to government, through resumption, or to other parties) but is otherwise useful and stimulating. It should be read in combination with the companion paper by Eliza Chan on Female Inheritance and Affection in the same publication, pp. 174–199.

75. See Skinner (ed.), Introduction, and the reference to Freedman's work in note 5 on p. 181.

76. See chapter 6, pp. 83–84 for background.

77. This was the general situation. There may have been some variations, as in the old market towns and coastal market centres, as on Cheung Chau where the franchise was wider.

78. Information received through my colleague John Telford in January 1994.

79. For a convenient account, with citations and references to media and other coverage, see Lee and Distefano, pp. 83–96, 110–112.

80. For the Kuk's initial objection, see their p. 95, and for its formal approval, see Ambrose Leung, SCMP 9 October 2002.

81. The Village Representative Election Ordinance (Cap. 576) of 2003. The first elections for the two sets of VRs were held in late 2004. As with the electoral changes of the 1980s, they have favoured the indigenous population initially.

In Tsuen Wan District, I am informed, many of the non-indigenous VR positions are filled by villagers (they are eligible to stand). In South Lantau, the same is generally the case, but there a Westerner has been elected to the non-indigenous post at Shan Shek Wan village, and an "outsider" at Cheung Sha Lower Village.

82. When Lee and Distefano were enquiring into the population of Shui Tau Tsuen at Kam Tin, "the village elder who quoted us the men-only figure grinned apologetically as he explained that it was customary only to consider men as village members while women born or married into the village were not counted": *Ibid.*, p. 110. Kam Tin, of course, has always been conservative.

83. At the first elections, there were 693 recognized villages, with 1,291 posts for the two types of VR. Of these, 930 seats were uncontested, and 189 lacked nominations, of which 100 had insufficient registered voters to make any: Klaudia Lee, SCMP 12 July 2003.

84. As mentioned in chapter 2, note 53, the grave of (or to) those killed in the 1898 uprising has been reported as an important element in the patriotic ("Chinese") and anti-colonial scenario projected by the Heung Yee Kuk in those years, though ignored previously.

85. Through the increasingly lavish ten yearly protective *jiao* rituals, emphasizing the male elements in ancestral worship in the ancestral halls and at the graves, and through perpetuating the "basin feast" culinary tradition: see Chan 1998.

86. *Ibid*, pp. 90–91.

87. Chapter 9, especially at pp. 119–123.

88. Baker 1993, pp. 873–874. The flowering of a large middle class and the growth of a new breed of local entrepreneur between 1976–82 are the subject of chapter 5 of Felix Patrikeeff's *Mouldering Pearl: Hong Kong at the Crossroads* (London, Hodder and Stoughton, Coronet Books, 1988), a book whose lasting worth is belied by its title. Jan Morris in *Hong Kong* (London, Viking, 1985), p. 331, drew particular attention to the coming into being "only in the previous few years, [of] that well-educated young middle class which was the true pride of the Crown Colony, and which would be a credit to any country". Such persons could hardly be expected to empathize with the indigenous population at large, though it provided its quota to the new group.

89. According to a private property consultant cited in SCMP 11 December 2002, "At present, more than 80 per cent of the small houses were constructed for sale rather than for villagers to use": and officials had estimated that 240,000 villagers were eligible, but that the government had handled only 27,957 cases, with at least 13,493 more awaiting processing: Jimmy Cheung, SCMP 8 February 2003.

90. See e.g. Hase 2001, 137–138. Indubitably, this weakening owed something to the transfer of the numerous land staff (land executives and land inspectors) to the new Lands Department: for, in performing their specialist duties, they had become well known to, and well informed about, rural leaders and their fellow villagers, providing the District Officers with reliable information and valuable contacts thereby. Yet more crucial, in the remodelled District

Administration, rural affairs would now take a poor second or third place to the intense preoccupation with the District Boards and with providing and monitoring services for the populations of the fast-developing New Towns. Intended or not, the 1982 changes had represented a turning away from the indigenous population in favour of establishing much closer links with the new population and a full-time engagement with the new political forces unleashed in the staged moves towards more representative government, especially in the districts.

Pondering the changes at the time they were announced, and seeking ways to maintain the Administration's status and authority, and the influence that went with them, I had thought it timely to extend the Town Manager concept to all the new towns, and to remodel its staffing at both the district and headquarters levels by the inclusion of officers from the "service" departments to work more directly with, and to a degree under, the town managers and the regional secretary, the better to accommodate the new political arrangements and the anticipated greater pressure for improved services of all kinds, and to maintain the balance between old and new. However, this simply could not be, since the usual and time-honoured Hong Kong bureaucratic path was, as on this occasion, the issue of Secretariat directives enjoining branch secretaries and heads of department to give the new arrangements "their fullest cooperation and support": see Hayes 1996, pp. 288–289, with n27 on p. 303. Stripped of much of their authority, and with lessened "clout" and status, the work of the DOs was rendered much more difficult. More recently, a general weakening of the Government's executive authority emanating from the various levels of more representative (but not yet responsible) government has not helped the situation.

91.　Taking into account the view from each side, and including an investigative history of the Heung Yee Kuk is part of this requirement.

92.　Such as the lack of proper layouts and ancillary services in those villages with road access in which many new homes have been constructed in the past twenty years, with many more to come. After a recent visit, Denis Bray deplored the situation he found in so many villages, and advocated a new initiative. A copy of his paper has now been placed in HKPRO.

　　Lisa Hopkinson presented a paper entitled "Problems with the Small House Policy" to the Land Policy and People's Lives Forum at the Centre of Asian Studies, University of Hong Kong, on 21 February 2003. For ease of reference, the background to the accumulated clutch of dilemmas attaching to the Small House Policy today is provided herein at pages 109–110, together with pp. 168–169 with note 55 on p. 251, and notes 89–90 to this chapter at pp. 254–255 above.

93.　A view shared by two of my long-serving Chief Land Executive friends. As they saw it, the hallmark of the NTA had been its concern for people, especially those affected by development projects, whereas the new Lands Department was headed in the districts by professionals who invariably took little interest in the indigenous population and its concerns; resulting, they said, in a deteriorating relationship between government and NT people. This confirms what was surely predictable, and to be expected: though from my wider perspective, I would prefer to say that it had *contributed* to the present situation rather than created it, the root cause being (as they themselves have said) the administrative decisions taken in 1981–82. See also Hayes 1996, p. 294.

Bibliography

Abstract, *Historical and Statistical Abstract of Hong Kong 1841–1930* (Hong Kong, Noronha & Ccompany, Third Edition, 1932).

_____. Subject Index to the foregoing: a Typescript, probably prepared in the Colonial Secretariat, to provide a handy reference, the Abstract itself lacking an index.

Aijmer, Göran, "Expansion and Extension in Hakka Society", in JHKBRAS, 7 (1967), pp. 42–79.

_____, *Atomistic Society in Shatin, Immigrants in a Hong Kong Valley* (Goteborg, Acta Universitatis Gothoburgensis, 1986).

Airlie, Shona, *Thistle and Bamboo, The Life and Times of Sir James Stewart Lockhart* (Hong Kong, Oxford University Press, 1989).

Akers-Jones, [Sir] David, *Feeling the Stones* (Hong Kong University Press, 2004).

Allen, Jamie, *Seeing Red: The Uncompromising Takeover of Hong Kong* (Singapore, Butterworth-Heinemann Asia, 1997).

Andrew, Ex Chief Inspector Kenneth, *Hong Kong Detective* (London, John Long, 1962).

Asakawa, K., *The Russo-Japanese Conflict* (Westminster, Archibald Constable & Co., 1904).

Asia Society Galleries, *Picturing Hong Kong: Photography 1855–1910* (New York, 1997).

Baker, H. D. R., "The Five Great Clans of the New Territories", JHKBRAS 6 (1966), pp. 25–47.

_____, *Sheung Shui, A Chinese Lineage Village* (London, Frank Cass & Co. Ltd., 1968).

_____, "Life in the Cities: The Emergence of Hong Kong Man", *The China Quarterly*, No.95, September, 1983, pp. 469–479.

_____, "Social Change in Hong Kong: Hong Kong Man in Search of Majority", in *The China Quarterly*, No. 136 (December 1993), pp. 865–877.

_____, "The Myth of the Travelling Wok: The Overseas Chinese", in *Asian Affairs*, Vol. XXVIII, pt.1, February 1997. pp. 28–37.

Barnett, K. M. A., "The Peoples of the New Territories", in J. M. Braga (comp.), *The Hong Kong Business Symposium* (Hong Kong, South China Morning Post, 1957), pp. 262–265.

Barnett Letters and Papers sent to the author. Now deposited in the HKPRO.

Barrow, John, Unreferenced lists of postwar awards to local Chinese for assistance to escaping prisoners of war and other Allied personnel during the Japanese Occupation, 1941–45. Copies found in my office drawer upon becoming DO Tsuen Wan in early 1975. Two versions, one more detailed, and now deposited in HKPRO.

Basel Mission Archives, Document A — 1.2 Nr. 44, Half-yearly Report of the Missionary Rev. Winnes, from 1 January to 1 July 1850.

Beach, Harlan P., *Dawn on the Hills of T'ang, Or Missions in China* (New York, Student Volunteer Movement for Foreign Missions, revised edition, 1905).

Beresford, Lord Charles, *The Break-Up of China* (London and New York, Harper & Brothers, 1899).

Berkowitz, Morris I., "Plover Cove Village to Taipo Market: A Study of Forced Migration", JHKBRAS, Vol.8 (1968), pp. 96–108.

Berkowitz, Morris I., Brandauer, Frederick P., and Reed, John H., *Folk Religion in an Urban Setting, Hakka Villagers in Transition* (Hong Kong, Christian Study Centre on Chinese Religion and Society, Tao Fong Shan New Territories, 1969).

Bickley, Gillian, *The Golden Needle, The Biography of Frederick Stewart (1836–1889)* (Hong Kong, David C. Lam Institute for East/West Studies, Hong Kong Baptist University, 1997).

———, (ed.), *A Magistrate's Court in Nineteenth Century Hong Kong: Court in Time* (Hong Kong, Proverse Press, 2005).

Birch, Alan, (ed.), *The New Territories and Its Future*, Proceedings of a Symposium of the Royal Asiatic Society, Hong Kong Branch, 13 December 1980, published in 1982.

Blackie, W. J., (a former Director of Agriculture, Fisheries and Forestry), "Agriculture and Forestry in Hong Kong" in J. M. Braga (comp.), *The Hong Kong Business Symposium* (Hong Kong, South China Morning Post, 1957), pp. 207–220.

———, *The Kadoorie Agricultural Aid Association* (Hong Kong, K.A.A.A., 1972).

Blake, C. Fred, *Ethnic Groups and Social Change in a Chinese Market Town* (The University Press of Hawaii, 1981).

———, "Leaders, Factions and Ethnicity in Sai Kung: Village autonomy in a traditional setting" in Göran Aijmer, *Leadership on the China Coast* (London, Curzon Press, 1984), pp. 54–89.

Boorman, Howard L., and Howard, Richard C. (eds., with index by Krompart, Janet), *Biographical Dictionary of Republican China* (New York, Columbia University Press, 5 vols., 1967–79).

Boyden, S., Millar, S., Newcombe K., and O'Neill, B., *The ecology of a city and its people, The case of Hong Kong* (Canberra, Australian National University, 1981).

Bray, Denis, "Recollections of a Cadet Officer Class II" in Elizabeth Sinn (ed.), *Hong Kong, British Crown Colony, Revisited* (Hong Kong, Centre of Asian Studies, University of Hong Kong, 2001). Cited as Bray 2001.1.

_____, *Hong Kong Metamorphosis* (Hong Kong University Press, 2001). Cited as Bray 2001.2.

Brim, John A., *The Modernization of Local Systems in the New Territories of Hong Kong*, Unpublished doctoral thesis, Stanford University, 1970.

Brinkley, Captain F., *Japan, Its History, Arts and Literature* (London, T.C. & E.C. Jack, 1904).

Buck, John Lossing, *Chinese Farm Economy, A study of 2866 farms in seventeen localities and seven provinces in China* (University of Nanking and Institute of Pacific Relations, 1930).

_____, *Land Utilization in China, A study of 16,786 farms in 168 localities, and 38,256 farm families in twenty-two provinces in China 1927–1933* (University of Nanking, 1937).

Building Hong Kong (Hong Kong, FormAsia, 1989).

Bumbailliff, "Land Tenure in China", *China Review*, Vol. IX, 1890/91, p. 58.

Campbell, Charles Walter, *China* (London, Historical Section of the Foreign Office, HMSO, 1920).

Cannon, Margaret, *China Tide, The Revealing Story of the Hong Kong Exodus to Canada* (Toronto, Harper & Collins, 1989).

Census Reports, Hong Kong, with dates, as published in Hong Kong Sessional Papers or HKGG.

Chan, Selina Ching, "Negotiating Tradition, Customary Succession in the New Territories of Hong Kong" in Grant Evans and Maria Tam (eds.), *Hong Kong, The Anthropology of a Chinese Metropolis* (Honolulu, University of Hawaii Press, 1997), pp. 151–173.

_____, "Politicizing Tradition: The Identity of Indigenous Inhabitants of Hong Kong", in *Ethnology*, Vol. 37, No. 1 (Winter 1998, pp. 39–54. Reprinted in Pun Ngai and Yee Lai-man (eds.) *Narrating Hong Kong Culture and Identity* (Hong Kong, Oxford University Press, 2003), pp. 73–94.

Chan, Wai Kwan, *The Making of Hong Kong Society: Three Studies of Class Formation in Early Hong Kong* (Oxford, Clarendon Press, 1991).

Chan, Wing-hoi, *Traditional Folksongs in the Rural Life of Hong Kong*, unpublished M.A. Thesis, The Queen's University of Belfast, 1985. Also, his typescript Research Proposal, circa 1982.

Chang, C. C., in *The Chinese Year Book, 1937 Issue* (Shanghai, Commercial Press, 1937), pp. 776–778.

Chang, Iris, *The Rape of Nanking* (London, Penguin Books, 1999).

Cheng Kai Tai, Felix, Hong Kong University, Department of History, B.A. Hons Thesis, *A History of Cheung Chau from Prehistory Times to the End of World War II* [1970s].

Cheng, Sih-Gung, *Modern China, A Political Study* (Oxford, Clarendon Press, 1919).

Chesterton, Mrs., *Old China and Young Japan* (London, Harrap, 1933).

Cheung, Sydney, "Traditional Dwellings, Conservation and Land Use: A Study of Three Villages in Sai Kung, Hong Kong", in JHKBRAS, Vol. 43 (2005), pp. 1–14.

Chinese Year Book 1940–1941 (China, The Commercial Press Ltd.), pp. 403–404.

China Handbook 1937–1945, A Comprehensive Survey of Major Development in China in Eight Years of War (New York, The Macmillan Company, 1947).

Choi Chi-cheung, in *Proceedings of the Tenth International Symposium on Asian Studies, 1988*, Volume 1: China (Hong Kong, Asian Research Service, GPO Box 2232, Hong Kong, 1989), pp. 489–497.

Choi, Po-king, "Popular Culture", in Richard Y. C. Wong and Joseph Y. S. Cheng (eds.), *The Other Hong Kong Report 1990* (Hong Kong, The Chinese University Press, 1990), pp. 537–563.

Ch'u, T'ung-Tsu, *Local Government in China under the Ch'ing*, (Stanford University Press, paperback edition, 1969).

Chun, Allen, *Unstructuring Chinese Society, The Fictions of Colonial Practice and the Changing Realities of "Land" in the New Territories of Hong Kong* (Amsterdam, Harwood Academic Publishers, 2000).

Clark, Trevor, *Good Second Class, Memories of a Generalist Overseas Administrator* (Stanhope Old Hall, The Memoir Club, 2004).

Clementi, "A Record of the Public Services of Cecil Clementi, M.A. (Oxon), Assistant Colonial Secretary, Hong Kong", being a typescript paper prepared by his father, according to Lady Clementi who very kindly gave me a copy when I visited her at Holmer Court, Bucks., in 1965, and now placed in HKPRO. Sir Cecil's *diaries* run from 1899 until 15 months before his death, but there is a vexing gap between July 1903 to February 1905, due to their loss when the lighter on which they were being conveyed to a P. & O. steamer was capsized during the Hong Kong typhoon of 1906. Sir Cecil's papers are believed to be deposited in the Rhodes House Library, University of Oxford, as part of the Oxford Colonial Records Project begun in 1963. **Cited as Clementi.**

Clyde, Paul Hibbert, "Confucianism and the Government of China", Supplement I to his *The Far East, A History of the Impact of the West on Eastern Asia* (New York, Prentice-Hall Inc., Second edition, 1952).

Coates, Austin, *A Summary Memorandum on the Southern District of the New Territories*, Spring 1955, at pp. 42–45. A copy is now in the HKPRO.

_____, *Myself a Mandarin, Memoirs of a Special Magistrate* (London, Frederick Muller, 1968), with numerous reprint editions by other publishers).

Cockburn, Rev. J., *John Chinaman, His Ways and Notions* (Edinburgh, J. Gardiner Hitt, 1896).

Cochran, Sherman Hsieh, Andrew C. K., with Cochran, Janis (translators, editors and introducers), *One Day in China, May 21, 1936* (New Haven, Yale University Press, 1983).

CO Hong Kong Correspondence. *Hong Kong. Correspondence (June 20, 1898, to August 20, 1900) Respecting The Extension of the Boundaries of the Colony.* Printed for the use of the Colonial Office, November 1900.

Colquhoun, Archibald R., *The "Overland" to China* (London and New York, Harper & Brothers, 1900).

Cooper, John, *Colony in Conflict, The Hong Kong Disturbances May 1967–January 1968* (Hong Kong, Swindon Book Company, 1970).

Cornaby, W. A., *The Call of Cathay* (London, The Wesleyan Methodist Missionary Society, 1910).

Cronin, Katherine, *Colonial Casualties, Chinese in Early Victoria* (Melbourne, Melbourne University Press, 1982).

Crook, John, *Hilltops of the Hong Kong Moon* (London, Minerva Press, 1997).

CSO/CSO Extension, being Colonial Secretariat files 1898–1908 on land matters, either for the older part of the Colony (CSO) or the newly leased territory (CSO Extension). Partly indexed, they contain internal minutes and correspondence with, e.g., the president and members of the NT Land Court, the Crown's legal officers, some departmental heads, and the governors of the day, on the many administrative and legal matters which arose in the course of taking over the New Territory, especially during the survey and land settlement, and after. Beginning with 1906, apart from a few residual problems from the land settlement, they relate more to routine land administration in the New Territory. They were still held in the Registrar General's Department when I made notes on their contents, before the establishment of the Hong Kong Public Records Office in 1973, to which they were later transferred. As I wrote at the time, "the great days of the Land Court and of minuting and writing on the various Bills, and on grand principles and exciting cases, are over". While I have not consulted them since, these volumes are an indispensable source for detailed research. Cited as CSO/CSO Extension.

Curzon, Hon. George N., *Problems of the Far East* (London, Longmans, Green & Co., 1894).

da Silva, Armando, *Tai Yu Shan, Traditional Ecological Adaptation in a South Chinese Island* (Taipei, Orient Cultural Service, 1972).

Decennial Report. Chinese Imperial Maritime Customs, *Decennial Report 1892–1901* (Shanghai, Inspectorate General of Customs, 1906).

[Denham, Capt.] Journals kept by Mr. Gully and Capt. Denham during a Captivity in China in the Year 1842, Edited by a Barrister, (London, Chapman and Hall, 1844). In Elibron reprint, 2003.

Des Voeux , Sir G. W., *Report on the Condition and Prospects of Hongkong* [in SP, 1888].

Dillon, Michael (ed.), *China, A Cultural and Historical Dictionary* (London, Curzon Press, 1998).

Donnison, F. S. V., *British Military Administration in the Far East 1943–46* (London, HMSO, 1956).

Douglas, [Sir] Robert K., *Society in China* (London, A.D. Innes & Co., 1895).

Duckerts, Jules, *La Chine en 1899, Rapport de la Mission Commerciale* (Verviers, Ch.Vince, Imprimeur-Éditeur, 1900).

Dyer Ball, J., *Things Chinese: or Notes Connected with China* (Shanghai, Hongkong and Singapore, Kelly & Walsh Limited, Fifth edition, revised by Werner, E. Chalmers, 1925). First edition, 1892.

Endacott, G. B., *A History of Hong Kong* (Hong Kong, Oxford, 1958).

_____, *Hong Kong Eclipse*. Edited with additional material by Birch, Alan (Hong Kong, Oxford University Press, 1978).

Faure, David, "Saikung, The Making of the District and its Experience during World War II" in JHKBRAS, Vol.22 (1982), pp. 161–216.

_____, "Notes on the History of Tsuen Wan" in JHKBRAS, Vol. 24 (1984), pp. 46–104. **Cited as Faure 1984.1.**

_____, "The Tangs of Kam Tin — A Hypothesis on the Rise of a Gentry Family", in Faure, David, Hayes, James, and Birch, Alan (eds), *From Village to City, Studies in the Traditional Roots of Hong Kong Society* (Hong Kong, Centre of Asian Studies, University of Hong Kong, 1984) pp. 24–42. **Cited as Faure 1984.2.**

_____, *The Structure of Chinese Rural Society, Lineage and Village in the Eastern New Territories, Hong Kong* (Hong Kong, Oxford University Press, 1986).

_____, *A Documentary History of Hong Kong, Society* (Hong Kong University Press, 1997).

_____, *Colonialism and the Hong Kong Mentality* (Hong Kong, Centre of Asian Studies, University of Hong Kong, 2003).

Faure, David, and Lee Lai-mui, "The Po Tak Temple in Sheung Shui Market", in JHKBRAS 22 (1982), pp. 271–279.

Faure, David, Luk, Bernard H. K., and Lun Ng, Alice Ngai-ha, in "The Hong Kong Region According to Historical Inscriptions" at pp. 43–54 in Faure, Hayes, and Birch (eds,) *From Village to City, op.cit.,* 1984).

Fisher, Lt-Colonel Fisher, C. B., *Personal Narrative of Three Years' Service in China* (London, Richard Bentley, 1863).

Franke, Wolfgang, *The Reform and Abolition of the Traditional Chinese Examination System*, Harvard East Asian Monographs 10 (Harvard University Press, 1968).

Freedman, Maurice, *Chinese Lineage and Society: Fukien and Kwangtung* (University of London, The Athlone Press, 1966).

_____, "A Report on Social Research in the New Territories of Hong Kong, 1963", in JHKBRAS, Vol. 16 (1976), pp. 191–261.

Gathorne-Hardy, G. M., *A Short History of International Affairs 1920–1939* (London, Oxford University Press, Fourth Edition, 1950).

Gazetteer of Place Names in Hong Kong, Kowloon and the New Territories (Hong Kong, Government Printer, Foreword November 1960). **Cited as Gazetteer.**

Gibbs, L., "The Hongkong Horticultural Society" at pp. 123–4 of *The Hong Kong Naturalist*, Vol. 1, No. 3, August 1930.

Giles, Herbert A., *Historic China and Other Sketches* (London, Thomas de la Rue, 1882).

_____, *A History of Chinese Literature,* (London, William Heinemann, MCMI), p. 54.

_____, *Elementary Chinese, San Tzu Ching* (Shanghai, Kelly & Walsh, second edition, revised, nd but 1910).

Gimson, Sir Franklin, *Unofficial History of Hong Kong, 1941–5,* an unpublished manuscript quoted in Endacott and Birch, *op.cit.,* pp. 348, 360–1.

Goodrich, L. Carrington (with Lo, Hsiang-lin), "A Cannon from the End of the Ming Period", in JHKBRAS, Vol. 6 (1966), 1966, pp. 152–157.

Gordon-Cumming, C. F., *Wanderings in China* (Edinburgh, William Blackwood and Sons, 2 vols, 1886).

Graves, Rev. R. H., *Forty Years in China, or China in Transition* (Baltimore, R. H. Woodward Company, 1895).

Griffiths, John Tudor, *Reminiscences and Observations of a Hong Kong Chai Lo* (London, Ratcliffe Press, 1997).

Groves, Robert. G., "The Origins of Two Market Towns in the New Territories", in Marjorie Topley (ed.) *Aspects of Social Organization in the New Territories* (Hong Kong, Royal Asiatic Society, Hong Kong Branch, 1964) pp. 16–20.

_____, "Militia, Market and Lineage: Chinese Resistance to the Occupation of Hong Kong's New Territories in 1899", JHKBRAS, Vol. 9 (1969), pp. 31–64.

Guide to Hong Kong (香港指南) (Changsha, Commercial Press, 1938).

Haddon-Cave, Sir Philip, former Chief Secretary and Financial Secretary, Hong Kong. Talk to the Hong Kong Society, UK: Annex A to the Society's Autumn Bulletin, 1995.

Hamilton Letters to the Author in HKPRO HKMS 83.

Hansen, Valerie, *Negotiating Daily Life in Traditional China* (New Haven and London, Yale University Press, 1995).

Hase, P. H., "The Work of the District Officer and his Role in New Town Development", in Birch, Alan, (ed.), *The New Territories and Its Future,* Proceedings of a Symposium of the Royal Asiatic Society, Hong Hong Branch, 13 December 1980, published in 1982, pp. 51–60.

_____, "Research Materials for Village Studies", in Birch, Jao and Sinn (eds), *Research Materials for Hong Kong Studies* (Centre of Asian Studies, University of Hong Kong, 1984), pp. 31–36.

_____, "A Song from Sha Tau Kok on the 1911 Revolution" in JHKBRAS, Vol. 29 (1989), pp. 382–384.

_____, "New Territories Poetry and Song", in *Collected Essays on Various Historical Materials for Hong Kong Studies* (Hong Kong, Urban Council, 1990), at pp. 24–27.

_____, "Sheung Wo Hang Village, Hong Kong: A Village Shaped by *Fengshui*", in Ronald G. Knapp (ed.), *Chinese Landscapes, The Village as Place* (Honululu, University of Hawaii Press, 1992), pp. 79–94. With Lee Man-yip.

_____, "Eastern Peace: Sha Tau Kok Market in 1925", in JHKBRAS, Vol. 33 (1993), pp. 147–202.

_____, "Traditional Village Politics, Lau Shui Heung", in Hase and Sinn (eds.), *Beyond the Metropolis: Villages in Hong Kong* (Hong Kong, Joint Publishing (H.K.) Limited, 1995), pp. 103–109.

———, "Traditional Life in the New Territories: The Evidence of the 1911 and 1921 Censuses", in JHKBRAS, Vol. 36 (1996), pp. 1–92.

———, "Beside the Yamen: Nga Tsin Wai Village", in JHKBRAS, Vol. 39 (1999–2000), pp. 1–82.

———, "Customary Law in the New Territories, Hong Kong: A Century of Change", and "The Clan and the Customary Law: Tso and Tong in the New Territories", at pp. 155–204 and 211–268 respectively, in *Nagoya University, Journal of Law and Politics*, No. 82, June 2000, an issue devoted to The Impact of the Handover of Hong Kong.

———, "The District Office", in Elizabeth Sinn (ed.), *Hong Kong, British Crown Colony, Revisited* (Hong Kong, Centre of Asian Studies, University of Hong Kong, 2001).

———, "The Origins of the New Territories Land Registration System", unpublished paper, 2005.

———, "The Six Day War of 1899", unpublished paper, 2006.

Hayes, James, "The Japanese Occupation and the New Territories", in *SCMP*, 15 December 1967.

———, "Letting Go the Wooden Goose", in JHKBRAS, Vol. 12 (1972), p. 207.

———, *The Hong Kong Region 1850–1911: Institutions and Leadership in Town and Countryside* (Hamden, Archon Books, 1977): **Cited as Hayes 1977.1.**

———, "Royal Asiatic Society — Visit to Tsuen Wan, Saturday, 10th Dec., 1977", in JHKBRAS vol. 17, 1977, pp. 189, 197–8. Cited **as Hayes 1977.2.**

———, "Building a Community in a New Town: A Management Relationship with the New Population" in Leung, Chi-keung, Cushman, J. W., and Wang, Gungwu (eds.) *Hong Kong, Dilemmas of Growth* (Hong Kong, Centre of Asian Studies, University of Hong Kong), 1980, pp. 309–340.

———, "The Village Watch in the Hong Kong Region", in JHKBRAS Vol. 22 (1982), pp. 294–297.

———, *The Rural Communities of Hong Kong, Studies and Themes* (Hong Kong, Oxford University Press, 1983).

———, "Collecting business papers of Chinese enterprises in Hong Kong", in Birch, Alan, Jao, Y. C., and Sinn, Elizabeth (eds.) *Research Materials for Hong Kong Studies* (Hong Kong, Centre of Asian Studies, University of Hong Kong, 1984). **Cited as Hayes 1984.1.**

———, "Rural leadership in the Hong Kong Region: Village autonomy in a traditional setting", in Aijmer, Göran, *Leadership on the China Coast* (London, Curzon Press, 1984), pp. 32–52. **Cited as Hayes 1984.2.**

———, Review of Michael Moser's *Law and Social Change in a Chinese Community*, in *HKLJ*, Vol. 14, No. 1 (1984), pp. **Cited as Hayes 1984.3.**

———, "Specialists and Written Materials in the Village World", in Johnson, David, Nathan, Andrew J., and Rawski, Evelyn (eds.), *Popular Culture in Late Imperial China* (Berkeley, University of California Press, paperback, 1985), pp. 75–111.

———, "Education and Management in Rural South China in the late Ch'ing", in *Proceedings of the Sixth International Symposium on Asian Studies, 1984*

(Hong Kong, Asian Research Service, GPO Box 2232, 1986), Vol. 1, China, pp. 575–592. **Cited as Hayes 1986.1.**

———, "Stakenet and Fishing Canoe: Hong Kong and Adjacent Islands in the 19th and Early 20th century. The Sea and the Shore in Social, Economic and Political Organization" in *Proceedings of the Eighth International Symposium on Asian Studies, 1986* (Hong Kong, Asian Research Service, GPO Box 2232, 1986), Vol.1, China, pp. 573–598. **Cited as Hayes 1986.2.** Also, its sequel (with Jack Tin), "Some Aspects of Traditional Life in Hong Kong: The Village Fisheries", in *Proceedings of the Ninth International Symposium on Asian Studies, 1987*, Vol. 1, China, pp. 53–63.

———, "A Glimpse of the Land Settlement at Shek Pik Village, Lantau Island, Hong Kong", in JHKBRAS Vol.28 (1988), pp. 228–233.

———, "Chinese Customary Law in the New Territories of Hong Kong", in *Proceedings of the Tenth International Symposium on Asian Studies, 1988*, Volume 1, China (Hong Kong, Asian Research Service, GPO Box 2232, Hong Kong, 1989) pp. 455–476.

———, "East and West in Hong Kong: Vignettes from History and Personal Experience", in Elizabeth Sinn (ed.), *Between East and West, Aspects of Social and Political Development in Hong Kong* (Hong Kong, Centre of Asian Studies, University of Hong Kong, 1990), pp. 7–24. **Cited as Hayes 1990.1.**

———, "Chinese Customary Law in the New Territories of Hong Kong, Part II", in *Proceedings of the Eleventh International Symposium on Asian Studies, 1990*, Volume 1, China (Hong Kong, Asian Research Service, GPO Box 2232, Hong Kong, 1990) pp. **Cited as Hayes 1990.2.**

———, "Government and Village: Reactions to Modern Development in Long-Settled Communities in the New Territories of Hong Kong", in Baker, Hugh D. R., and Feuchtwang, Stephan (eds.), *An Old State in New Settings, Studies in the Social Anthropology of China in Memory of Maurice Freedman* (Oxford, JASO, 1991), pp. 107–136. **Cited as Hayes 1991.1.**

———, "Chinese Customary Law in the New Territories of Hong Kong: The Background to the Operation of the New Territories Ordinance, 1899–1987", in *Asian Profile*, Vol. 19, No. 2, April 1991. pp. 97–136. **Cited as Hayes 1991.2.**

———, "Ancestral Graves and the Popular Culture of China, Some Examples from Hong Kong's New Territories", in *International Association of Orientalist Librarians*, Bulletin 39, 1992, pp. 10–21.

———, *Tsuen Wan: Growth of a New Town and its People* (Hong Kong Oxford University Press, 1993). A Chinese version entitled 滄海桑田話荃灣 was published in 1999 by the three rural committees of Tsuen Wan, Tsing Yi and Ma Wan, together with the Yuen Yuen Institute, Lo Wai, Tsuen Wan.

———, "The Traditional Background: Hong Kong Villages in the 1950s", in P. H. Hase and Elizabeth Sinn (eds), *Beyond the Metropolis: Villages in Hong Kong* (Hong Kong, Joint Publishing (HK) Company Limited, 1995), pp. 19–25.

————, *Friends and Teachers: Hong Kong and Its People 1953–87* (Hong Kong University Press, 1996).

————, "Hong Kong's Own Boat People, Vignettes from Life and History", in *The Hong Kong Anthropologist*, the annual Journal of the Hong Kong Anthropological Society, Number Eleven (1998), pp. 2–12.

————, "Model Village, Kowloon Tsai, Hong Kong," in JHKBRAS, Vol. 40 (2000), pp. 269–274.

————, *South China Village Culture* (Hong Kong, Oxford University Press, 2001), a volume in the Oxford series, "Images of Asia". **Cited as Hayes 2001.1.**

————, "Colonial Administration in British Hong Kong and Chinese Customary Law", in Elizabeth Sinn (ed.), *Hong Kong, British Crown Colony, Revisited* (Hong Kong, Centre of Asian Studies, University of Hong Kong, 2001). **Cited as Hayes 2001.2.**

————, Instructions to the Land Staff, District Office, Tsuen Wan, along with other papers relating to Village Removals and Resitings. Now in HKPRO.

Headland, Isaac Taylor, *China's New Day, A Study of Events that have led to its Coming* (West Medford, Central Committee on the United Study of Missions, 1912).

Heasman, Kathleen J., "Japanese Financial and Economic Measures in Hongkong", in *Hong Kong University, Journal of the Economics Society*, 1957 (Hong Kong, The H. K. U. Economics Society, 1957), pp. 65–92.

Henry, Rev. B. C., *The Cross and the Dragon, Or Light in the Broad East* (New York, Anson D. F. Randolph and Company, 1882).

Hensman, Bertha, *More Hong Kong Tale-Spinners*, (Hong Kong, The Chinese University of Hong Kong, 1971).

Hensman, Bertha, and Mack, Kwok Ping, *Hong Kong Tale-Spinners* (Hong Kong, The Chinese University of Hong Kong, 1968).

Herklots, G. A. C., *Common Marine Food-Fishes of Hong Kong*, published by the author at The University, Hong Kong, n.d. but late 1930s.

Herklots contributed to the prewar *Hong Kong Naturalist* (which he edited), and his several books on the Hong Kong Countryside were published postwar by the SCMP, Hong Kong.

Hertzlet, Godfrey E. P., *Treaties, Etc. Between Great Britain and China; and between China and Foreign Powers ...*, Third edition, Vol. I, London, HMSO, 1908). **Cited as *Hertzlet's China Treaties*.**

Heywood, Graham, *Rambles in Hong Kong* (Hong Kong, Kelly and Walsh, Second edition, 1951). Reprinted with a new Introduction and Commentary by Gee, Richard, Oxford University Press, Hong Kong, 1992.

Hirth, F., *Text Book of Documentary Chinese for the Special Use of the Chinese Customs Service* (Shanghai, Inspectorate-General of Customs, Second Edition, 1909).

Ho, Pui-yin, *The Administrative History of the Hong Kong Government Agencies 1841–2002* (Hong Kong University Press, 2004).

Hong Kong Guide 1893 (Hong Kong, Oxford University Press, reprint of 1982).

Hsiao, Kung-Chuan, *Rural China, Imperial Control in the Nineteenth Century* (Seattle, University of Washington Press, 1960).

Hübner, Baron de, *A Ramble Round the World 1871* (London, Macmillan & Co., single volume edition,1878).

Hürlimann, Martin, *Hong Kong* (London, Thames and Hudson, n.d. but 1962).

Inscriptions: Text of Chinese historical inscriptions from Hong Kong and the New Territories, principal compiler David Faure, published in three volumes by the Urban Council of Hong Kong, 1986, entitled 香港碑銘彙編.

Ip, David Man-tin, *An Assessment of the Influence of Access and Bargaining in the Formulation of Policy on the New Territories*, University of Hong Kong, unpublished M.Soc.Sc. dissertation, 1988.

Jamieson, G., *Chinese Family and Commercial Law* (Shanghai, Kelly and Walsh, Limited, 1920).

Japanese War Crimes Tribunal. The trials were reported in the SCMP, between 27 March and 26 April 1946. Copies of the coverage, and of related papers, are contained in HKPRO (HKRS 256-4-1).

Johnson, Elizabeth L. *Recording a Rich Heritage: Research in Hong Kong's "New Territories"* (Hong Kong, Leisure and Cultural Services Department, 2000).

_____, "Recording a Rich Heritage: Research in Hong Kong's "New Territories", in Lee Pui-tak (ed.), *Colonial Hong Kong and Modern China, Interaction and Reintegration* (Hong Kong, Hong Kong University Press, 2005), pp. 103–114. Although this article is named for the book listed above, the content is different.

Johnston, R. F., *Lion and Dragon in Northern China* (London, John Murray, 1910).

_____, *Confucianism and Modern China* (London, Gollancz, 1934).

Joliffe, R. O., in Wu, Yi-fang and Price, Frank W., *China Rediscovers Her West, A Symposium* (London, George Allen and Unwin, 1942)

Kamm, J. T., "Two Essays on the Ch'ing Economy of Hsin-an, Kwangtung", JHKBRAS, Vol. 17 (1977).

Kerr, George H., *Formosa, Licensed Revolution and the Home Rule Movement 1895–1945* (Honolulu, the University Press of Hawaii, 1974).

King, Professor F. H., *Farmers of Forty Centuries*, published by his widow, Winsconsin, 1911.

Kuan, Hsin-chi and Lau, Siu-kai, "Development and the Resuscitation of Rural Leadership in the New Territories", *Hong Kong Journal of Public Administration* (June 1981).

Lai, T. C, Rofe, Husein and Mao, Philip, *Things Chinese* (Hong Kong, Swindon Book Company, 4th edition, 1983).

Lamont-Brown, Raymond, *Kempeitai, Japan's Dreaded Military Police* (Stroud, Gloucestershire, Budding Books, 2000).

Lau, Yun-wo [劉潤和], formerly Government Archivist, *Short History of the New Territories*. [新界簡史] (Joint Publishing (HK) Co. Ltd., 1999).

Lee, Belinda Wong Sheung-yu, "Chinese Customary Law — An Examination of *Tsos* and Family *Tongs*", in Hong Kong Law Journal, 13 (1990).

Lee, Ho Yin and Distefano, Lynne D., *A Tale of Two Villages, The Story of Changing Village Life in the New Territories* (Hong Kong, Oxford University Press, 2002), p. 75.

Lee, Rance P. L., "The Fading of Earthbound Compulsion in a Chinese Village: Population Mobility and its Economic Implication", in King, Ambrose Y. C., and Lee, Rance P. L. (eds.), *Social Life and Development in Hong Kong* (Hong Kong, The Chinese University Press, 1981), pp. 105–126.

Lensen, G. A., *The Asian World, A Brief History* (Tokyo, Charles E. Tuttle Co., second edition, 1968).

Lethbridge, Henry, *Hong Kong: Stability and Change* (Hong Kong, Oxford University Press, 1978.

Li, Dun J., *The Ageless Chinese, A History* (New York, Charles Scribner's Sons, third edition, 1978).

Lin, Yue-hwa, *The Golden Wing, A Sociological Study of Chinese Familism* (London, Kegan Paul, Trench, Trubner & Co, Ltd., 1947).

Linebarger, Paul M. A., *The China of Chiang K'ai-Shek, A Political Study*, (Boston, World Peace Foundation, 1941).

Liu, Shuyong, *An Outline History of Hong Kong* (Beijing, Foreign Languages Press, 1997).

Lo, Hsien-hau, *Public Administration and Public Opinion in the New Territories*, unpublished M. Phil. thesis, University of Hong Kong.

Lou, Dom Pierre-Celestin Tseng-Tsiang, *Ways of Confucius and of Christ* (London, Burns Oates, 1948).

Lung, David , with Friedman, Anne, "Hong Kong's Wai: Defensive Architecture of the New Territories", in Hase and Sinn (eds.), *Beyond the Metropolis: Villages in Hong Kong* (Hong Kong, Joint Publishing (H.K.) Limited, 1995), pp. 66–75.

MacIntosh, D. W., *Policing Hong Kong* [booklet] (Hong Kong, Government Printer, 1952).

McMillan, R., ("Gossip") *The Voyage of the Monsoon, or The Adventures of a Stowaway* (Sydney and Brisbane, William Brooks & Co., 1900).

McNair, H. F. (comp.), *Readings in Modern Chinese History* (Shanghai, Commercial Press, second edition, 1928).

Maunder, W. F., *Hong Kong Urban Rents and Housing* (Hong Kong, Hong Kong University Press, 1969).

Miners, N. J., "The Attempt to Assassinate the Governor in 1912", in JHKBRAS, Vol. 22 (1982), pp. 279–285.

Mitford, A. B., *The Attaché at Peking* (London, Macmillan and Co., 1900).

Morse, Hosea Ballou, *The International Relations of the Chinese Empire, The Period of Subjection, 1894–1911* (Shanghai, Kelly and Walsh, 1918).

———, *The Trade and Administration of China* (London, Longmans, Green & Co., 1908). Citation from the third edition, 1921, p.59, text unchanged.

Moule, Arthur Evans, *Half a Century in China, Recollections and Observations* (London, Hodder and Stoughton, n.d. but 1911).

Munn, Christopher, *Anglo-China, Chinese People and British Rule in Hong Kong 1841–1880* (Richmond, Surrey, Curzon, 2001).

Murray, Dian H., *Pirates of the South China Coast 1790–1810* (Stanford University Press, 1987).

Myers, Ramon H., "Taiwan under Ch'ing Imperial Rule, 1684–1895: The Traditional Economy", in *Journal of the Institute of Chinese Studies of The Chinese University of Hong Kong*, Vol. V, No.2 (1972), pp. 404–407.

_____, *The Chinese Economy Past and Present* (Belmont, California, Wadsworth Inc, 1980)

_____, "Dysfunction of Chinese Rural Society", with the discussion that followed the talk, in JHKBRAS, Vol. 23 (1983), pp. 18–22.

Nelson, Howard, unpublished paper, "British Land Administration in the New Territories of Hong Kong, and its Effects on Chinese Social Organization", prepared for a Conference organized by the London-Cornell Project for East and Southeast Asian Studies, 24–30 August 1969 (copy now placed in HKPRO).

Ng Lun Ngai-ha, "Village Education in Transition: The Case of Sheung Shui", in JHKBRAS, Vol. 22 (1982), pp. 252–270.

_____, *Interactions of East and West, Development of Public Education in Early Hong Kong* (The Chinese University Press, Hong Kong, 1984).

Ng Lun Ngai-ha and Others (editors), *Historical Traces of Sun Yat-sen's Activities in Hong Kong, Macao and Overseas* (Hong Kong, United College, The Chinese University of Hong Kong, The Zhongshan University, Sun Yat-sen Research Institute, c. 1988).

Norman, Sir Henry, *The People and Politics of the Far East* (London, T. Fisher Unwin, 1895).

Notebooks. Two manuscript notebooks on my visits to 180 villages in the Southern District, New Territories, Winter 1957–58. They record facts provided by village representatives and elders. A typescript of part is now in the HKPRO, with rest to follow. **Cited as Notebooks.**

Notes on various visits to villages and areas of the NT made at different times thereafter. **Cited as Notes, with dates.**

Palmer, Michael, "The Surface-subsoil Form of Divided ownership in Late Imperial China: Some Examples from the New Territories of Hong Kong", in *Modern Asian Studies*, Vol. 21, No. 1, (1987), pp. 1–119.

_____, "Lineage and Urban Development in a New Territories Market Town", at pp. 70–106, in Baker, Hugh D. R., and Feuchtwang, Stephan (eds.), *An Old State in New Settings, Studies in the Social Anthropology of China in Memory of Maurice Freedman* (Oxford, JASO, 1991).

Peninsula Jaycees, Seminar and Photo Exhibition, "Rescuing the New Territories' Past", 27 June 1981.

Peplow, S. H., *Hong Kong, About and Around* (Hong Kong, Ye Olde Printerie, Ltd., 1930).

Potter, Jack M., *Capitalism and the Chinese Peasant, Social and Economic Change in a Hong Kong Village* (Berkeley, University of California Press, 1968).

Priestwood, Gwen, *Through Japanese Barbed Wire, a Thousand Mile Trek from a Japanese Prison Camp* (London, Harrap and Co., 1944).

Problems of the Pacific, 1936 (Chicago, University of Chicago Press, nd).

Pryor, E. G., "A Historical Review of Housing Conditions in Hong Kong", in JHKBRAS, Vol. 12 (1972), pp. 88–129.

Rating , a folder from the former District Office Tsuen Wan, compiled early postwar from prewar files in the CSO, now placed in the HKPRO.

Remer, C. F, *The Foreign Trade of China* (Shanghai, Commercial Press, 1926).

Reynolds, David, *One World Divisible, A Global History since 1945* (London, Penguin Books, 2000).

Rice Farming in Hong Kong [illustrated booklet] (Hong Kong, the Regional Council, 1990).

Ride Papers: Papers of Sir Lindsay Tasman Ride, wartime commander of the British Army Aid Group, China, 1942–1945, at the National Library of Australia, Canberra: Intelligence Summaries, Series 12 in AWM PR82/068. I owe this reference to Ms. Elizabeth Ride.

Roberts, Andrew, *Salisbury, Victorian Titan* (London, Phoenix Books, 1999).

Ross, Edward Alsworth, *The Changing Chinese, The Conflict of Oriental and Western Cultures in China* (New York, The Century Company, 1911).

Royal Princes. Prince Albert Victor and Prince George of Wales, with Additions by John L. Dalton, *The Cruise of Her Majesty's Ship "Bacchante", 1879–1882* (London, Macmillan & Co., 2 vols., 1886).

Rural Architecture in Hong Kong (Information Services Department, Hong Kong, 1979, reprinted with a new preface, 1989).

Russell of Liverpool, Lord, *The Knights of Bushido: A Short History of Japanese War Crimes* (London, Corgi Edition, 1960).

Salkeld. Papers in the District Office Islands, kindly made available by Kim Salkeld, the then DO, at my request in 1996, and now deposited in the HKPRO.

Sayer, G. R., *Hong Kong 1862–1919* (Hong Kong University Press, 1975).

Schlesinger, Stephen C., *Act of Creation, The Founding of the United Nations* (Boulder, Colorado, Westview Press, 2003).

Schofield, Walter, "Memories of the District Office South, New Territories of Hong Kong", in JHKBRAS, Vol. 17 (1977), pp. 144–156.

Schofield Letters to the Author in HKPRO HKMS 83.

Schrecker, John E., *Imperialism and Chinese Nationalism, Germany in Shantung* (Cambridge, Mass., Harvard University Press, 1971)

Seach, T., Crown Lands and Surveys Office, Hong Kong. Unpublished thesis, the Royal Institute of Chartered Surveyors, 1962, "The Survey and Administration of Land in the New Territories". A copy is now in the HKPRO.

Selby, Stephen, "Everything You Wanted to Know About Chinese Customary Law (But Were Afraid to Ask)", in *Hong Kong Law Journal*, 45 (1991), pp. 45–77.

Shiga, Shuzo, "Some Remarks on the Judicial System in China: Historical Development and Characteristics", in Buxbaum, David C (ed.), *Traditional and Modern Legal Institutions in Asia and Africa* (Leiden, E. J. Brill, 1967).

Siak, P. L. (Department of Agriculture, Forestry and Fisheries), "Traditional Farming Techniques and their Survival in Hong Kong", in JHKBRAS, Vol. 14 (1974), pp. 191–196.

Siebold, Dr. Philipp Franz von, *Manners and Customs of the Japanese in the Nineteenth Century* (Rutland, Charles E. Tuttle Company, 1973 reprint).

Sihombing, Judith, "The Torrens System in the New Territories", in *Hong Kong Law Journal* (1984), at pp. 291–297.

Sinn, Elizabeth, "Sin Xi Guxiang: A Study of Regional Associations as a Bonding Mechanism in the Chinese Diaspora. The Hong Kong Experience," *Modern Asian Studies*, May 1997, v. 31, no. 2, pp. 375–397 [a sequel to "A History of Regional Associations in Pre-War Hong Kong", in Elizabeth Sinn (ed.), *Between East and West* ... (Hong Kong, Centre of Asian Studies, 1990) pp. 159–186].

Sirr, Henry Charles, *China and the Chinese* ... (London, 2 vols, 1849, reprinted by Southern Materials Center, Inc., Taipei, 1977).

Skinner, G. William (ed.), *The Study of Chinese Society, Essays by Maurice Freedman* (Stanford University Press, 1979).

Smart, Alan, *Making Room: Squatter Clearance in Hong Kong* (University of Hong Kong, Centre of Asian Studies, 1992).

_____, "Agents of Eviction: The Squatter Control and Clearance Division of Hong Kong's Housing Department", in *Singapore Journal of Tropical Geography*, Vol. 23 (3), 2002, pp. 333–347.

Smith, Albert, *To China and Back* (Hong Kong, Oxford University Press reprint, 1982).

Smith, Arthur H., *The Uplift of China* (London, Church Missionary Society, 1908).

Smith, Carl T., *Chinese Christians*, (Hong Kong, Oxford University Press, 1984).

_____, *A Sense of History, Studies in the Social and Urban History of Hong Kong* (Hong Kong Educational Publishing Co., 1995).

_____, "Sham Shui Po: From Proprietory Village to Industrial Urban Complex", in his *A Sense of History, op. cit.*, pp. 162–202.

Smith, N. L., *Elementary Cantonese* (Hong Kong, Kelly & Walsh, Ltd, 1920).

Snow, Philip, *The Fall of Hong Kong: Britain, China and the Japanese Occupation* (New Haven, Yale University Press, 2003).

Stericker, J. and V., *Hong Kong in Picture and Story* (Hong Kong, Tai Wah Press, 1953)

Stokes, Edward, *Exploring Hong Kong's Countryside* (Hong Kong Tourist Association and Agriculture and Fisheries Department, 1999).

Stott, Grace, *Twenty-Six Years of Missionary Work in China* (London, Hodder and Stoughton, 1898).

Strauch, Judith, "Middle Peasants and Market Gardeners, The Social Context of the 'Vegetable Revolution' in a Small Agricultural Community in the New Territories, Hong Kong" in Faure, David, Hayes, James, and Birch, Alan (eds.),

From Village to City, Studies in the Traditional Roots of Hong Kong Society (Hong Kong, Centre of Asian Studies, University of Hong Kong, 1984), pp. 191–205.

Sung, Hok-pang, "Legends and Stories of the NT", first printed in *The Hong Kong Naturalist* in 1935–38, and reprinted in the JHKBRAS, Vols. 13 (1973) and 14 (1974), pp. 111–129 and 160–185 respectively.

Sweeting, Anthony, *Education in Hong Kong Pre-1841 to 1941: Fact and Opinion, Materials for a History of Education in Hong Kong* (Hong Kong University Press, 1990)

_____, *Education in Hong Kong 1941–2001, Visions and Revisions* (Hong Kong University Press, 2004).

Tang of Kam Tin. Copy of a typescript translation of an account written by two members of the lineage in 1966, Chinese text not available. Now in HKPRO.

Tang Cheuk-wah, "Ping Shan Stories". Copies of the longer Chinese texts, with some summary translations into English by R. Hamet, are now in the HKPRO, along with a letter to me from Mr. Tang.

Tang, Hui-sun, *Land Reform in Free China* (Taipei, Free China Review, 1957).

Teichman, Sir Eric, *Affairs of China, A Survey of the Recent History and Present Circumstances of the Republic of China* (London, Methuen Publishers, 1938).

Thrower, Stella L., *Hong Kong Country Parks* (Hong Kong, Government Printer, 1984).

Traveller's Handbook 1951 (香港、九龍、新界旅行手冊) (Hong Kong, Wah Kiu Yat Po).

Trench, W. Steuart, *Realities of Irish Life* (London, Longmans, Green and Co., 1869).

Tsai, Jung-fang, *Hong Kong in Chinese History, Community and Social Unrest in the British Colony 1841–1913* (New York, Columbia University Press, 1993).

Tsang, Steve, *A Modern History of Hong Kong, Hong* Kong, Hong Kong University Press, 2004).

Turnbull, C. M., *A History of Singapore 1819–1975* (Kuala Lumpur, Oxford University Press, 1977).

van der Sprenkel, Sybille, *Legal Institutions in Manchu China* (University of London, The Athlone Press, revised paperback edition, 1966).

Vincent, Mrs. Howard, *Newfoundland to Cochin China, By the Golden Wave, New Nippon, and the Forbidden City* (London, Sampson Low, Marston & Company, 1892).

Wade, T. F., Translations of official documents in Governor Han Wen Ch'i's papers in *Key to the Tzu Erh Chi, Documentary Series*, Vol. I (London, Trubner & Co., MDCCCLXVII [1867].

Wang, Gungwu, "Some Reflections on Hong Kong's Regional Role and Cultural Identity", in Leung, Chi-keung, Cushman, J. W., and Wang, Gungwu (eds.) *Hong Kong, Dilemmas of Growth* (Hong Kong, Centre of Asian Studies, University of Hong Kong), 1980, pp. 649–653.

_____, *The Chineseness of China, Selected Essays* (Hong Kong, Oxford University Press, 1991).

Waters, T. R. F., *A History of the Royal Hong Kong Golf Club* (Hong Kong, 1960) pp. 19–20. Incorporates material from an unpublished history of the Club by Eric Hamilton.

Watson, James L., *Emigration and the Chinese Lineage, The Mans in Hong Kong and London* (Berkeley, University of California Press, 1975).

Watson, James L., and Watson, Rubie S., *Village Life in Hong Kong: Politics, Gender and Ritual* (Hong Kong, The Chinese University Press, 2004, pp. 12–13.

Watt, John R., *The District Magistrate in Late Imperial China* (New York, Columbia University Press, 1972).

Webb, Richard, "The Use of Hill Land for Village Forestry and Fuel Gathering in the New Territories of Hong Kong", in JHKBRAS 35 (1995), pp. 143–154.

Welsby, G. E., *A History of the Preventive Service, 1909–1939* (mimeographed copy in HKPRO).

Welsh, Frank, *A History of Hong Kong* (London, Harper Collins Publishers, revised edition, 1997)

Wesley-Smith, Peter, *Unequal Treaty 1898–1997, China, Great Britain and Hong Kong's New Territories* (Hong Kong, Oxford University Press: first edition 1980, revised edition [without plates] 1998).

———, "Some Legal Problems Relating to Land in the New Territories", in Birch, A., *The New Territories and its Future, Proceedings of a Symposium of the Royal Asiatic Society, Hong Kong Branch* (published Hong Kong, 1982).

Wiley, Rev. I. W., *China and Japan, A Record of Observations* ... (Cincinnati and New York, n.d. but Preface dated 1879).

Wilkinson, R. M., in Wacks, Raymond (ed.), *The Law in Hong Kong 1969–1989* (Hong Kong, Oxford University Press, 1989).

Williams, Edward Thomas, *China Yesterday and Today* (London, George G. Harrap, fifth edition, 1933).

Williams, S. Wells, *The Chinese Commercial Guide* (Hongkong, A. Shortrede & Co., fifth edition, 1863).

———, *The Middle Kingdom, A Survey of the Geography, Government, Literature, Social Life, Arts and History of the Chinese Empire and Its Inhabitants* (New York, Charles Scribner's Sons, 2 vols., revised edition, 1883).

Wilson, Brian, *Hong Kong Then* (Edinburgh, The Pentland Press, 2000).

Wong, C. T., "Uses of Agricultural Land: Some Changes in New Territories Farming Patterns", at pp. 17–35, in D. J. Dwyer (ed.), *The Changing Face of Hong Kong*, (published by the RAS in May 1971).

Wong Wai King, *Tai O, Love Stories of the Fishing Village*, bi-lingual publication in English and Chinese (Hong Kong, the Author, 2000).

Woo, Pauline, *A Brief Study of the Villages and Agriculture of Kam Tin*, BA (Hons) Thesis, University of Hong Kong, 1956. In Hong Kong Special Collection, University of Hong Kong Libraries.

Woolf, Bella Sidney (Lady Southorn), *Chips of China* (Hong Kong, Kelly & Walsh, Ltd., 1930).

Young, John Aubrey, *Business and Sentiment in a Chinese Market Town* (Taipei, The Chinese Association for Folklore, The Orient Cultural Service, 1974).

Zelin, Madeleine, Ocko, Jonathan K., and Gardella, Robert, *Contract and Property in Early Modern China* (Stanford University Press, 2004).

Official Reports: New Territory/New Territories

[*Extracts from a*] *Report by Mr Stewart Lockhart on the Extension of the Colony of Hong Kong.* In HKGG, 8 April 1899, pp. 535–552. Also in SP 1899, within No. 9 of 1899, pp. 181 seq. **Cited as LR.**

Despatches and Other Papers relating to the Extension of the Colony of Hong Kong. Hong Kong: Noronha & Co., Government Printers, 1899, pp. 1–69. Also in SP 1899, No. 32, p. 511 seq. **Cited as *Extension.***

> *Note:* The two sets of papers above were compiled and printed in Hong Kong. Another, printed in London by the Colonial Ofice, is listed under *C.O. Hong Kong Correspondence* in the Bibliography. Dr.Patrick Hase, who has used all three for his article, "The Six Day War of 1899", advises that "neither collection is complete: both contain documents not transcribed in the other, although the Colonial Office collection is the fuller. Both edit documents, sometimes without indicating this: the Colonial Office collection includes a number of documents which have been paraphrased, whereas the full original documents survived in the Sessional Papers collection. In some documents in the Legislative Council [SP] Collection (which was a quasi-public document) some sentences of a personal character, and others of a confidential character have been omitted, with the Colonial Office collection including them." Etc. from his Note 1 to the cited paper.

Report on the New Territory during the First Year of British Administration. Hong Kong: Noronha & Co., Government Printers, 1900, pp. 1–41. Also HKGG, 28 April 1900, GN 201, pp. i seq. **Cited as *First Year.***

Report on the New Territory for the Year 1900. In HKGG, 17 August 1901, GN 446. Also in SP 1901, No. 38, pp. 565 seq. **Cited as *Report 1900.***

Report on the New Territory for the Year 1901. In HKGG, 2 May 1902, GN 264. Also in SP 1902, No. 22, pp. 663 seq. **Cited as *Report 1901.***

Report on the New Territory for the Year 1902. In HKGG, 7 August 1903, GN 498. Also in SP 1903, No. 27, pp. 337 seq. **Cited as *Report 1902.***

Some Notes on Land Tenure in the New Territory. Appendix No. 1 to *First Year*, prepared by Messrs. Lockhart, Messer and T'soi. **Cited as L & T.**

Memorandum of Work done in the Land Office, Hong Kong, in respect of the New Territories for the year 1899. Appendix No. 8 to *First Year*, pp. 26–28. **Cited as *Land Office HK.***

A General Report on the Survey of the New Territory from November, 1899, to April, 1904. In SP 1904, pp. 399–404. **Cited as *Survey.***

Report on the Survey of the New Territory at the Close of the Field Season 1900–01.
In SP 1901, p. 565. **Cited as *Survey 1900–01.***

*Report on the Work of the Land Court for the Seven Months ending December 31st
1900.* Being Appendix No. 1a to **Report 1900**. **Cited as *Gompertz 1.***

Report upon the ownership of Ts'ing I (Chung Hue) Island, dated 27 June 1901, as
Appendix 2 to **Report 1900**. **Cited as *Gompertz Ts'ing I.***

Report on the Work of the Land Court up to the 31st December, 1901. Being Appendix
No. 1 to **Report 1901**. Has an Appendix on Demarcation Rules, and a useful
Schedule. **Cited as *Gompertz 2.***

New Territories: Land Court, Report on Work from 1900 to 1905. By J. R. Wood,
with reports by C. McI. Messer, Cecil Clementi, and J. R. Wood. See SP 1905,
No. 10 of 1905, pp. 143–52. **Cited as NTLC.**

Notes for Use in The District Land Offices, New Territories, 1908. Printed, 39 pp.,
retyped in HKPRO in 52 pp. An abbreviated and mimeographed copy (35
pp.) was prepared by the Senior Land Bailiff, NTA HQ, about 1958, and was
circulated to District Officers. Copies held in the HKPRO. **Cited as *Notes for
Use.***

Report on the New Territories, 1899–1912, by G. N. Orme, District Officer.
Published separately by Noronha & Co., Government Printers, 1912, pp. 1–
21. Also as No. 11 in SP 1912. **Cited as *Orme.***

Other Printed Official Materials

Blue Books. These contain miscellaneous official papers including annual reports,
published in Hong Kong from *1871* onwards. **Cited as BB.**

Colonial Estimates. The Hong Kong annual estimates were published annually by
the Government Printer. **Cited here as *Estimates.***

Hong Kong Hansard. The proceedings of the Legislative Council of Hong Kong
were published in yearly volumes under this title from the early 1890s by the
Government Printer. **Cited here as *Hansard.***

Hong Kong [or earlier Hongkong] Government Gazette. The repository for all official
matters intended for public notice. **Cited here as HKGG.**

Hong Kong Administrative Reports 1908-1939, containing annual Colony and
departmental reports. **Cited as HKAR.**

Hong Kong Annual Reports. See "HK" in Abbreviations.

Sessional Papers. Reports and other papers tabled before the Legislative Council of
Hong Kong, and printed in annual series. **Cited as SP.**

Hong Kong: The Facts (by subject/date). A series of periodically updated fact sheets
on a wide variety of subjects connected with government. **Cited as HK Facts.**

Gazetteer. *A Gazetteer of Place Names in Hong Kong, Kowloon and the New
Territories* (Hong Kong, Government Printer, Foreword, November 1960).
Cited as Gazetteer.

Glossary

Mainly in Cantonese, for personal names of local people and local terms, with pinyin equivalents where appropriate.*

Term	Pinyin equivalent	Chinese
Azhou Shangpu		亞洲商報
bazi		八字
Chan Chik		陳迹
Chan Lau-fong		陳流芳
Chan Po-fong		陳浦芳
chap chiu (certificate)		執照
Cheng Tung-on		鄭同安
Cheung Chi-fan		張枝繁
Chi lineage of Shek Pik		池族
Chi Cheung-fat		池長發
chi tong	citang	祠堂
ching tuen	qingtuan	青團
Chiu Chau (aka Teochiu)		潮州
Choi Chi-cheung		蔡志祥
choi tei		菜地
Chow Li-ping		周理炳
Chuen On Kuk		全安局
chung nam heng nui	zhongnan qingnü	重男輕女
Chung Wah Athletic Association		中華體育館

* With apologies, several persons mentioned in the text and notes are not included here, owing to the want of the Chinese characters for their names.

Term	Pinyin equivalent	Chinese
dau-chung (local measure/area)		斗種
fa wong (gardener)		花王
Fong Pin Hospital		方便所
Fu lineage	Fu	傅族
fung-shui	fengshui	風水
Guan Yin (Goddess of Mercy)		觀音
Guangdong		廣東
guotai minan		國泰民安
Hakka	Kejia	客家
Hau Chak-nam		侯擇南
Hau lineage	Hau	侯族
He Zhen (Earl of Dongguan)		何真 (東莞伯)
heung (local sub-division)	xiang	鄉
Heung Cheung (village head)		鄉長
heung sz wai yuen wui		鄉事委員會
Heung Yee Kuk		鄉議局
Hip Tin Kung (temple)		協天宮
Ho Chuen-yiu		何傳耀
Ho Kei-fuk		何麒福
Hoklo (Fuklo)		學佬 (福佬)
Hui Wing-hing		許永慶
kaifong (neighbourhood association in a town)	jiefang	街坊
kai-to (local ferry)		街渡
kam-ching	ganqing	感情
Ko Kei-fat		高己發
Ko Tim-keung		高添強
kui cheng so (local office, Japanese Occupation)		區政所
kui yik so (alternative name for above)		區役所
Kwan Tai Wui		關帝會
Kwangtung	Guangdong	廣東
laan (wholesaler in fish or vegetables)		欄
Lai lineage	Li	黎族
Lau Wong-fat		劉皇發
Lee Man Fu Kwun (district officer)		理民府官
Li Kau Yuen Tong		李久遠堂
liangmin		良民
Liu Ching-leung		廖正亮

Term	Pinyin equivalent	Chinese
Liu Fo-yan		廖伙隱
Liu lineage	Liao	廖族
Lo Sheung-fu		盧湘父
lo so (coarse rushes)		蘆鬚
Long Xiguang		龍濟光
Mak Kai-yim		麥啟炎
Man lineage	Wen	文族
Man Mo Temple		文武廟
Mo lineage	Mao	毛族
nam mo lo (Daoist ritual specialists)		喃嘸佬
Nam Tau	Nantou	南頭
Ng lineage	Wu	吳族
Ng Bar-ling		吳灞零
nuen fu (protective charm/ritual)		暖符
nung-muk chek-kung wui (loosely, Planters' Association)		農牧職公會
pai lau (formal arch)		牌樓
Pang lineage	Peng	彭族
pao-chia	baojia	保甲
pin nga**	biane	匾額
Po On County (San On County after 1914)	Baoan	寶安縣
Punti (the Cantonese)		本地
Sam Luen Athletic Association		三聯體育會
San On (Xinan) County (to 1914)		新安縣
Sham Chun	Shenzhen	深圳
Shen Hongying		沈鴻英
Shen Qingju		沈慶駒
Siu Kwok-kin		蕭國建
ta chiu (protective ritnal)	dajiao	打醮
Taiping huanyu ji		太平環宇記
Tai Wong Yeh (village shrine)		大王爺
Tam Shui	Danshui	淡水
Tang lineage	Deng	鄧族
Tang Cheuk-wah		鄧灼華

---

* "Honorary tablets consist of names of buildings, brief congratulatory statements, pleas for spiritual blessings, or records of examination successes, mostly on horizontal wooden boards" (David Faure).

Term	Pinyin equivalent	Chinese
Tang On-tong		鄧安堂
Tang To Hing Tong		鄧都興堂
Tat Tak Kung So (office)		達德公所
tepo (village official, where appointed)	dibao	地保
Tin Hau deity	Tianhou	天后
To lineage	Tau	杜族
To Hing Tong (Tangs' major lineage trust)		都興堂
Tsang lineage of Kau Wah Keng	Zheng	曾族
Tsui lineage of Shek Pik	Xu	徐族
Tsui Mun-hei		徐滿喜
tsz yi (honorary advisers)		諮議
tso san ritual	tsoshen	作神
tso/tong (customary landed lineage trusts)	zu/tang	祖堂
tsuen (village)		村
tun fu (protective charm/ritual)		蘆符
tung (local county division)	dong	洞
Tung Kwun county (local county division)	Dongguan	東莞縣
tung heung wui	tongxianghui	同鄉會
Wai Chau (local county division)	Huizhou	惠州
Wai Yeung (local county division)	Huiyang	惠陽
Wan On		溫安
waan san ritual	huanshen	還神
Wong Man-cheuk		王文卓
xiangxa		鄉下
xiucai		秀才
yamen (official's office and residence)		衙門
yau kik tui (guerrilla band, sometimes Communist)		遊擊隊
yeuk (local division)	yue	約
Yeung Kwok-sui		楊國瑞
Yeung Pak-shing		楊百勝
Yeung Pei-tak		楊彼得
Yuen Wah-chiu		袁華照
zhuangyuan (the top scholar in the old civil service examination system)		狀元

Index

Entries from the main text make no reference to their linked and numbered notes. Entries from the Notes section itself, e.g. 182n21, are given separate mention when they provide other information.

Barrow, John, 66–7, 127–8, 215nn9–10, 223n89
Basic Law of the Hong Kong SAR, and the HYK, 157, 164, 167
Beresford, Lord Charles, 21–2
Berkowitz, Morris, 92
Births and deaths, registration of, 53
Blake, Fred, 153
Blake, Sir Henry, disapproval of Lockhart's actions in 1899, 25–6; on co-option, 44, 153; and resumptions, 192n55
Block Crown Leases, with schedule of Crown Lessees and Survey Sheets by Demarcation Districts, 36–7
Boat people of the NT region, xiv, 179n1; but not "rehoused" during coastal reservoir development until High Island, 95
Border area, 15, 153–5
Bray, Denis, 104, 109, 131, 171, 255n92, Plate 20
Brim, John, 136–7
British Army in the NT, 130–1
British Kowloon (Old British Kowloon), 188n14
British Military Administration 1945–46, 71
Bus services in the NT, prewar, 54

C
Cadet Officers and the NT, 56–7, 209n86
Cantonese (Punti), 6, 8; historic characterizations, 182n18
"Cantonization" of Hong Kong population, linguistically and through popular culture, 140, 160, 166
Carrie, W. J., 216n11
Cater, Sir Jack, 234n8, 236n37
Certificates of land ownership (*chap chiu*), 39, Plate 14

Chan, Selina, 174, 175–6, 191n53
Change in NT rural life: end to traditional farming, 73–6; measuring change 1898–1968, 136–8; postwar at Pui O, Lantau Island, in regard to livelihood, young persons' attitudes, police behaviour, protective rituals, mutual assistance and rela-tionships, etc., 132–4; at Tai Po Tau, 139; at Lo Tik Wan, Lamma Island, 135–6; in the Tsiu Keng valley, 138–9; elsewhere, 160–1; dilution of Hakka culture postwar, 140, 160; as regards women and girls, 75–7, 140; timing of change, 140; through emigration and outside em-ployment, 75–6, 139, 142, 160–1; in retail and marketing services, 141. *See also* Livelihood in the villages
Cheung Chau Island, 9; its community and Kaifong committee, 45–6, 124; attack on its police station in 1912, 48–9
Cheung Sha Wan (Kowloon), confused land ownership, 30
Chinese Customary Law in land-related matters: applied throughout the Lease, 37–9; documentation, 37–8; believed warped by the land settlement and by registration and colonial practice thereafter, 40–1; this view queried, 38–40
Chinese local government system, pre-1898, 8, 9–11
Chun, Allen, 40–1, 180n5, 223n92, 229n13, 253n70
Claims to land during the survey and demarcation of 1900–1904, 32–3, 34–5; slowness in making claims, and reasons for this, 32–6